THE SOUTHERN COUNTRY EDITOR

Southern Classics Series

John G. Sproat, General Editor

King Cotton and His Retainers: Financing and Marketing the Cotton Crop of the South, 1800–1925
By Harold D. Woodman

The South as a Conscious Minority, 1789–1861: A Study in Political Thought
By Jesse T. Carpenter

Red Hills and Cotton: An Upcountry Memory
By Ben Robertson

John C. Calhoun: American Portrait
By Margaret L. Coit

The Southern Country Editor
By Thomas D. Clark

The Southern Country Editor

by Thomas D. Clark

with a new introduction
by Gilbert C. Fite

University of South Carolina Press

Published in Columbia, South Carolina by the
University of South Carolina Press in cooperation
with the Institute for Southern Studies and the
South Caroliniana Society

Manufactured in the United States of America

Library of Congress Cataloging-in-Publication Data

Clark, Thomas Dionysius, 1903–
The southern country editor / by Thomas D. Clark ; with a new introduction by Gilbert C. Fite.
p. cm. — (Southern Classics series)
Reprint. Originally published: Indianapolis : Bobb-Merrill Co., 1948.
Includes bibliographical references and index.
ISBN 0–87249–766–6. — ISBN 0–87249–767–4 (pbk.)
1. American newspapers—Southern States—History. 2. Journalism, Rural—Southern States—History. 3. Southern States—History—1865–1951. 4. Country life—Southern States—History. I. Title. II. Series.
PN4893.C5 1991
071'.5—dc20 91-10189
CIP

General Editor's Preface

THE Southern Classics Series returns to general circulation books of importance dealing with the history and culture of the American South. Under the sponsorship of the Institute for Southern Studies and the South Caroliniana Society of the University of South Carolina, the series is advised by a board of distinguished scholars, whose members suggest titles and editors of individual volumes to the general editor and help to establish priorities in publication.

Chronological age alone does not determine a title's designation as a Southern Classic. The criteria include, as well, significance in contributing to a broad understanding of the region, timeliness in relation to events and moments of peculiar interest to the American South, usefulness in the classroom, and suitability for inclusion in personal and institutional collections on the region.

* * *

Editors of southern country newspapers in the late nineteenth and early twentieth centuries have as much to tell us about life in the rural South as any source. Integral members of their communities, they reflected the hopes, fears, prejudices, and everyday concerns of their readers. In his perceptive examination of the role and influence of the southern country editor, Thomas D. Clark made a significant contribution to the institutional history of the South. As Gilbert Fite notes in his essay introducing this edition of the work, Clark also gave his readers an engaging look at a distinctive way of American life that has long since receded.

JOHN G. SPROAT
General Editor, *Southern Classics Series*

Introduction to the Southern Classics Edition

HISTORIES on many subjects are written, published, and soon forgotten. Library shelves are full of historical studies of minimal importance because they fail to explain anything significant about the human condition. Many writers have burrowed around in the wormholes of history without ever coming to grips with matters that make a major impact on a society. Fortunately, this is not the case with *The Southern Country Editor* by Thomas Dionysius Clark, first published in 1948. Looking through the writings of country editors, Clark's book provides many keen insights into southern life and society in the years between the end of the Civil War and the 1930s. It is a volume that richly deserves to be kept in print.

By the 1940s, Tom Clark had emerged as one of the preeminent historians of the pre-Civil War southern frontier and the changing postwar South. By the time he published *The Southern Country Editor,* he had written seven books that dealt with the frontier, southern railroads, and aspects of the history of Kentucky. His most widely acclaimed book up to that time was *Pills, Petticoats and Plows,* which was a delightfully written history of the southern country store. Clark had not only become a thorough researcher, but he was also a graceful and entertaining writer. Perhaps most important of all was the fact that Clark had a special firsthand acquaintance with the South. He had a particular feel for the region, for its people and its culture. In this regard, Clark had no peer among southern historians of his time.

Born on July 14, 1903, Tom Clark was raised on a farm in north central Mississippi. Hundreds of small farms dotted this part of the state, along with numerous villages and hamlets. Clark's home community around Louisville was predominantly rural, having been untouched by the nation's growing industrialization and urbanization. As a boy, he did all of the chores and field work expected of youth growing up on a farm. He received his early education in a country school. In brief, he came to know firsthand the life experienced by the great majority of southerners in the late nineteenth and early twentieth centuries. To fully understand the South one had to understand agriculture and rural life which were the backbone of southern experience up to the 1930s. Before Clark began to research the records, he knew and understood the rural South from the viewpoint of a participant. By combining life experience with research in a vast array of primary and secondary records, Clark's writings brought an unusual degree of authenticity and understanding to his readers.

After finishing the seventh grade in a country school at age twelve, Clark dropped out and worked full-time for two years on his father's farm. He grew cotton, corn, and other crops and deepened his agricultural experience. Too young for service in World War I, he found a variety of jobs until 1921 when he entered the Choctaw Country Agricultural High School at Weir, Mississippi. Graduating in 1925 at age 22, he next enrolled at the University of Mississippi at Oxford. During his college days at Ole Miss, he worked on the school newspaper, the *Mississippian.* Both his class essays and his reports for the school newspaper demonstrated a strong writing ability that he honed and polished throughout his career. History and literature were his favorite subjects.

Graduating from Ole Miss in 1928, he moved on to the University of Kentucky to pursue a master's degree in history. He completed the degree in one year and wrote a thesis entitled "Trade in Livestock, Slaves, and Hemp Between Kentucky and the Lower South." This study provided an early pillar in the broad foundation of research in southern history that Clark began to build upon, and continued to work at, for more than sixty years. Receiving his doctorate from Duke University in 1932, Clark wrote as his dissertation "The Development of Railways in the Southwestern and Adjacent States before 1860." This study, plus much additional research, resulted in two books on southern railroads.

In 1935 Clark joined the history department at the University of Kentucky as an assistant professor. There he earned a reputation as an interesting and sparkling teacher and at the same time pursued his research interests. His books appeared at frequent intervals. In 1937 he published *History of Kentucky,* and in 1939 *The Rampaging Frontier,* a volume that dealt largely with pioneer social history. As if teaching, research, and writing were not enough, Clark was appointed chairman of the history department at the University of Kentucky in 1942, a position he held until 1965.

By the 1940s, when Clark was researching and writing *The Southern Country Editor,* southern society was undergoing a great economic and social transition. The South that Clark had been raised in was rapidly losing its farm and rural character as industrialization and urbanization advanced rapidly throughout the region. World War II also played a major part in bringing social and economic change to the South. The number of farmers and farms was beginning to decline noticeably, a trend that greatly accelerated in the second half of the twentieth century. Indeed, those southerners reaching adulthood at mid-century would be the last generation to experience the South as Tom Clark knew it. Even though people might live on farms, mechanization, chemicals, changing crop patterns, electricity, and advances in crop and livestock breeding were beginning to make drastic changes in the rural South. Farms got fewer and larger, sharecropping nearly disappeared, small towns withered away, 7-Elevens and malls replaced the country store, and school consolidation obliterated the once popular country schools. Where would a reader living in the modern era turn for an understanding of and true feel for the earlier rural South?

Having already written about the country store and the role it played in the economic and social life of the rural South, Clark turned next to the country editor and the small-town weekly newspaper as a way to reveal other aspects of the southern farm and small-town life that was rapidly vanishing from all but memory. He believed that much could be learned about southern rural society by examining the columns of scores of these small-town weeklies published throughout the region. His bibliography includes 183 newspapers, published in towns that stretched from North Carolina to Texas.

The small-town newspaper was a national, not just a southern or regional, institution. But the South did have special problems that country editors had to deal with that were not common elsewhere. These included sharecropping, the racial issue, and a predominantly one-party political system. These were matters of great importance that related uniquely to the South. The editorials and news stories in small-town weeklies reflected attitudes and recorded actions that revealed a great deal about southern rural society, both how it was changing and how it remained so much the same. Clark placed the rural press in the larger social, economic, and political context of a changing and developing region.

After providing a general introduction to *The Southern Country Editor* which he calls "Beyond Appomattox," Clark first examines the place of the country editor as a publisher and a member of the community he served. To a large extent, a rural newspaper reflected the personality of its editor and publisher. Some editors spoke out on controversial issues, while others avoided controversy and conflict. Most of them, however, dealt with a wide range of topics and questions of general interest to their rural readers. Editors wrote about agricultural practices, health conditions, strange and unusual happenings, economic development, and a host of other topics.

They concentrated most, however, on writing about people and events that occurred in their communities. People liked to see their own names in the newspaper and were much more interested in weddings, funerals, neighborhood visits, school programs, and organizational meetings than they were in some national or international event. The editors of country weeklies dealt with local community life, and through the columns of these newspapers people could see a reflection of themselves and their community. Local news was supplemented by ready-print material purchased from compilers in Chicago or elsewhere. By the 1880s most editors were using ready-print news and advertising, which reduced the amount of local news but also provided readers with some national and international coverage. It was never the function of the country editor to inform people about national and international affairs, however. His task was to let people in the community know about local events and happenings. Surely the small-town newspaper was one of the most important community institutions and the editor one of the most admired citizens.

While Clark writes about the period between Appomattox and the 1930s, the heart of his study, and most of the illustrative material, covers the years from the 1870s to about 1910. He includes chapters on the place and role of women in southern society, humor, folklore, entertainment, the place of the postwar South in national politics, race relations, violence and law enforcement, lynching, feature stories, agricultural improvement, and the image of Theodore Roosevelt in the South. By looking at some of Clark's chapters in detail it is possible to see how country editors approached and handled matters that seemed of vital interest to their readers.

Violence was one of the issues to which southern editors devoted a great deal of attention. Country newspaper columns were filled with accounts of shootings, hangings, and other violent acts. Few of the gory details of a public hanging, for instance, were left unrecorded. Although the South was a violent section, country editors called for a kind of law and order. They urged people to cease carrying guns which were responsible for so much of the violence. Also most country editors opposed lynching, although they did not make a determined effort to abolish the vile act. They denounced mob rule, but since most lynchings were of blacks, editors could not speak too forcefully without appearing to be weak and unreliable on the question of racial segregation and white superiority.

Indeed, violence and race relations were closely connected. Southern country editors were in the vanguard of southerners who demanded two societies in the South, one white and the other black, separate and unequal. If blacks got out of line, they must pay the price. While these editors professed no ill will toward blacks, and many of them favored some education and economic advancement for blacks, whatever progress blacks made must be within their own segregated society, and at a level well below that of whites. Editors wrote much about blacks, but it was usually in the unfavorable context of riots, rebellions, or rapes. Southern country editors confirmed the worst stereotypes of blacks in the post-Civil War era, portraying them as lazy, unreliable, sensual, and without morals.

Clark's book clearly shows that the country editors failed to provide any leadership in reducing or solving racial problems. Rather, these community leaders actually strengthened the idea that blacks must be segregated and subservient. However much the editors of small-town newspapers opposed racial equality, they did not generally support the idea of returning blacks to Africa or favor them leaving the region for other economic opportunities. They believed that the cheap labor blacks provided was necessary to foster the South's growing economic development.

Southern country editors presented all of the arguments against integration and civil rights for blacks that opponents of civil rights legislation advanced in the 1940s and 1950s. Unless blacks were strictly segregated, they said, white civilization would be endangered. Editors argued that integration and social equality would lead to that worst condition of all—interracial marriage. Southern country editors reacted viciously against Theodore Roosevelt after it was learned that the president had had lunch with Booker T. Washington in the White House. They insisted that Roosevelt's action was an insult to the South and implied a social equality that southerners could never accept.

Country editors in the South expressed the opinion on blacks and their place in society held by the vast majority of white southerners. Whether they made or influenced public opinion, or just reflected it, cannot be accurately determined. However, there is no doubt but that southerners were strengthened and supported in their racism by the writings of these editors. When newspapers printed stories and articles that endorsed prejudices already held, readers seemed more justified in their attitudes. By examining the attitudes toward blacks expressed by country editors, Clark explains a good deal about racism and the hold it had on the thinking and actions of southern whites. The country editors played an important role in resisting changes in race relations in the two generations between Appomattox and World War II. They were a strong voice for white supremacy.

Farm life, and agricultural change and reform, were other issues that country editors wrote a great deal about. This is not surprising in light of the fact that in the final analysis the small towns, and the country newspaper itself, depended on the surrounding farms. As Clark points out so well, most editors of small-town newspapers were confirmed and committed agrarians. They believed that farm people were superior to urban dwellers and that country life was to be preferred over city life. Living close to the soil and working in harness with the Almighty built strong character and provided the basis for a happy life, or so they claimed. Editors tended to be very sentimental about living on a farm. It made people more independent, democratic, and neighborly. Southern country editors urged young people not to abandon the farm for the sins and bright lights of the cities. Moreover, they believed that farmers and the family farm had been great stabilizing influences throughout the nation's political history. Thus the welfare of farmers, and the nation, went hand in hand.

Some of these editors even seemed to outdo Thomas Jefferson, the patron saint of agrarianism, in their devotion to the values of farm life.

Most country editors were critical of southern farming practices. They argued that farmers relied too heavily on cotton and advised farmers to grow more food and feed crops. They wanted farmers to become more self-sufficient. This was the same message that was going out from the newly formed agricultural colleges and the United States Department of Agriculture. None of the advocates of diversification, including the country editors, had much influence on changing southern agricultural practices.

The ineffectiveness of those calling for changes in southern farming was partially due to the farm credit system in the South. Those who advanced agricultural credit under the lien laws usually required that the farmer grow cotton. Thus country editors attacked the laws that gave merchants and landowners a lien on the crop. They argued that southern agriculture needed a different method of providing operating capital. The lien laws, they said, forced farmers into debt and to engage in single crop farming, instead of producing vegetables, grain, and livestock which would provide a better living.

Since there seemed to be no way to change the credit system, editors fell back on the idea that farmers should produce their own food and stay out of debt. Their columns were filled with editorials and articles on this subject. It was not so much that the farmers rejected the editor's advice as it was their inability to implement it. There was simply no other source of credit available except that provided by merchants and landowners. Editors actually had a good view of southern farm problems—high interest rates, discriminatory transportation costs, marketing problems, and the one-crop system. They also gave wide publicity to other problems such as the spread of the boll weevil and the dangers of cattle ticks. Editors wrote, too, about the need for conservation of land and timber resources. However, they paid little attention to the need for better farming practices and treated the whole matter of tenancy rather casually.

By looking at the writings of southern country editors, the main problems connected with farming in the South after the Civil War emerge clearly enough. The editors, however, had little influence in producing changes. The structure of southern agriculture—millions of small, poor farmers without adequate land or capital resources—was so encrusted on the region that it took the federal programs of the 1930s and World War II to begin to break the grip of tenantry and poverty.

But country editors did play an important role in keeping alive the agrarian tradition in American thinking at a time when the nation was becoming a predominantly urban society. Their agricultural fundamentalism helped perpetuate the belief that farmers and farm life were superior to urban living long after farmers became a small minority of the South's and the nation's population. Anyone searching for the roots of agrarianism would, as Clark points out, find them in southern country newspapers.

Throughout the late nineteenth and early twentieth centuries, southern country editors spoke about a New South. Although they held to the Old South's position on race, they favored better schools, improved roads, economic growth and development, and a better system of agriculture. They opposed lynching and other forms of violence. While initially southern country editors emphasized local events and happenings, over time ready-print and boilerplate provided more stories of national and even international importance.

Clark's *The Southern Country Editor* provides many insights into life and society in the rural South after the Civil War. Accounts on the place of women in southern society tell the reader much about rural social life. The editors' writings on race relations emphasize the unbending attitude of white racial superiority. The editorials and articles on farming show not only the need for change, but also how difficult it was to modify the agricultural system. The articles on unusual happenings, humor, folklore, violence, law and order, religious faith and ideals, and politics combine to reveal the mind and thinking of the rural South. Clark presented what one reviewer called "a fairly complete social-intellectual history of the day."

Country editors were strong defenders of the South and its institutions. They had a great influence in establishing and perpetuating the idea that the South was a special place and a superior section of the nation. They were quick to defend the region against criticism and attacks by outsiders. A common theme in their writings was how northerners had abused and mistreated the South and its people. This was also a common theme among southern politicians before World War II.

The Southern Country Editor was widely reviewed when it first appeared in 1948. Hodding Carter, famed publisher of the Greenville, Mississippi, *Delta Democrat-Times* and Pulitzer-prize winner, wrote a highly favorable review for the *New York Times.* A keen and knowledgeable observer of life and society in the South, Carter declared that Clark had added much to a fuller understanding of the region. He noted that country editors had "an enviable community status and a cultural importance whose extent is still largely underestimated." Clark, Carter wrote, had made a valuable contribution "to an understanding of how far the South has come in eighty years." Carter declared that no previous study dealing with the South had "given proper recognition to these forgotten editors of a South in transition." According to Carter, the book was important to understanding the South and had national significance as well.

The reviews in scholarly journals were written by some of the nation's most distinguished authorities on southern history. Avery Craven of the University of Chicago reviewed *The Southern Country Editor* for the *Mississippi Valley Historical Review,* the leading journal in American history. Frank Luther Mott of the University of Missouri, the country's foremost scholar on the history of American journalism, wrote a review for the *Journal of Southern History.* Fletcher M. Green of the University of North Carolina provided reviews for the *American Historical Review* and the *Georgia Historical Quarterly.*

These and other contemporary scholarly assessments of Clark's work were generally favorable. To Craven, reading this book was "like sitting down to a meal of turnip greens, black-eyed peas and corn bread, with a glass of butter milk on the side." In other words, it was a delight for readers. Clark had a familiarity and feel for his subject that readers recognized and appreciated. Craven concluded that Clark had made "a real contribution to the history of the South because he has sensed the significance of the local and the personal in a section that is still [1948] essentially rural and which still bears something of the frontier about its ways and values."

Fletcher Green's review was less favorable. His assessment, however, never quite came to grips with what Clark was trying to convey, namely that editors and their country weeklies mirrored rural life and thought in the South. Frank Luther Mott had some criticism of Clark's discussion of technical matters relating to publishing country newspapers, but, as a journalism professor, he was more concerned over Clark's inability to determine whether the country press "was an actual molder of public opinion" or "a mere reflector of attitudes." He admitted, though, that Clark was right in concluding that "no accurate device has been discovered to gauge its precise influence." What was certain, Mott wrote, was that the country editor had cultivated the idea of a southern tradition.

More important than the contemporary reviews is the question of how the book stands the test of time. The answer to this question is clear. *The Southern Country Editor* still holds the central place in scholarship dealing with country newspapers in the South. Since Clark published his book in 1948, hundreds of volumes have been written on subjects that he dealt with by looking at the columns of the rural press. None of them replaces *The Southern Country Editor* or even reduces its value. It is one of those books that has enduring importance.

Besides having chosen a significant subject and done thorough research, Tom Clark wrote with style and grace. A distinguishing characteristic of all his books is their literary quality. Clark did not write about the southern country editor to have his book rest on dusty shelves and remain unread. He believes that history should be interesting, even entertaining, as well as informative. In *The Southern Country Editor* Clark combines his own deft touch with words and phrases with interesting quotations from the editors he writes about. He has given us a book of strong literary interest. He is a master at description and his well-chosen words give the reader a feel for the event or activity he is describing.

About a particular patent medicine, for example, Clark wrote: "Here was a tonic which would restore romance, cheer childless marriages, lead perennial bachelors to marriage altars and straighten the kink in Grandpa's back." Clark quotes the editor who was seeking subscriptions to his newspaper by writing that there were "two things in life which will make a man happy if he will attend to them, one is to marry for love and the other is to subscribe to this paper." The idea expressed after World War II that too much written history was tedious and clumsy could not be said of Clark's books. It would be a dull reader whose interest would lag while reading *The Southern Country Editor.*

It is unfortunate that Clark could not provide more material on the personal lives of country editors. This lack resulted mainly from the fact that his publisher, Bobbs-Merrill Company, insisted that he reduce the manuscript in order to save on publishing costs. At that time the company was under some financial strain. Had it not been for this circumstance, the book would have included biographical sketches of the important editors, as well as additional material on folklore and other matters. In that case, the book would have been even richer.

More than a long generation has passed since this book was first published. More than a century has elapsed since many of the events and activities were recorded by country editors that Clark wrote about. Despite the passage of time, in some ways the study is more valuable now than when it first appeared. Today's reader may profit even more from reading the volume than those who read it at mid-century.

At that time there were many Americans, including Clark himself, who could remember rural life in the South and who had the experience of living on a farm and reading the local weekly newspaper. Many people had some familiarity with southern farm and small-town society. That is no longer the case. The only way for modern, urban Americans to understand and get a feel for that aspect of the nation's history is to read about it. *The Southern Country Editor* provides one of the clearest windows through which modern readers can catch a realistic glimpse of the interests, excitements, hopes, and attitudes of southern farm and small-town people in the days before modernization of the South. College students studying journalism, history, economics, sociology, political science, and other subjects will find much in this book to increase their insights into a section of the country which defies easy understanding in its premodern period. The University of South Carolina Press is making an outstanding contribution to the intellectual and social history of the South by republishing *The Southern Country Editor.*

GILBERT C. FITE

THE SOUTHERN COUNTRY EDITOR

TO THE MEMORY OF

RUTH DORMAN TURNER

PREFACE

THE country press has been one of the most vigorous institutions in the New South. It has functioned alongside the country store, the rural and small-town church and school as a common man's institution. So-called common people of the South have left few private personal records to tell their story. Instead their history is preserved in those records of institutions which have served their economic and cultural needs. The most literate chronicle of rural progress is to be found in the weekly newspaper. Ambitious editors, country reporters, ready-print publishers, local poets and public letter writers have all been in the business of creating the literary record of their communities.

There was a wholesome informality about country news reporting and a genuine neighborliness in its popular reception. Libel suits were few, and never too successful for the plaintiffs. Editors assumed popular responsibility as community spokesmen, and their moods varied from stern Jovelike sanctimony to droll humor. They generally felt a keen responsibility for the welfare of their communities, and they devoted an enormous amount of energy toward an improvement of both public decorum and economic welfare. Few public-spirited men have exhibited so much courage and determination as these Southern country editors who helped build a new South.

I am thoroughly aware that the country newspaper is an American institution that is not contained by sectional lines. It is much the same North, South and West. My only justification for considering the Southern rural paper separately is the fact that there were some peculiarly sectional problems which were given much prominence in both news and editorializing. The race problem, a one-party political system, one-crop agriculture, the Southern frontier, Reconstruction and industrialization of the region were distinctly regional problems. Likewise, I am conscious of the fact that there are many papers in the South which would have given an equally good picture of country journalism as the ones which I used. It would take at least two lifetimes to turn the pages of all these country papers. In many cases the files are lost or badly broken. Every county seat has had its own colorful editor and its beloved local paper; at least this is the view of a considerable number of patrons. I am sorry that I had neither time nor gasoline to reach the dusty files of all these fascinating local scribes. Fortunately the newspaper directories and guides give a fairly good picture of the nature of the papers in every community since the Civil War.

In presenting the views of the editors and the materials of their correspondents and exchanges, I have tried to preserve the spirit of their written words. Most of my text is based upon a safe number of comparable cases, and conclusions rest on the same foundation. I did not undertake a statistical study of the country paper. There is a place for such a study, but it is of questionable value in a study which undertakes to retain the rich humanity of so informal an institution as this one. Where it has been possible I have endeavored to allow editors to speak for themselves, instead of using an inanimate meter rule on the amount of space they gave to various subjects. In the same manner I have attempted to go somewhat behind the paper itself and become acquainted with its reading constituency in order to appraise its susceptibility to the weekly's influence as an organ of public opinion.

Southern institutions are fairly well publicized in the country paper. Since historically the region's population has been rural and small town, it has come predominantly under the influence of the weekly press. I have made no effort to draw a line of distinction between the rural and small-town subscribers. Except for a few superficial interests in social affairs it is doubtful that there was a fundamental difference between the two.

In a more rugged age when the public generally was less sensitive to the effects of the printed word, a refreshingly full and frank report was made of news as publishers believed it happened. Reporters wrote both the good and the bad. Since editors saw only one issue of their papers at a time they perhaps never were conscious of the type of record they were recording in composite form. There is no evidence that any considerable glossing over of the news occurred. Papers were keenly aware of the personal element of the news, and the nearness of the editor to his patron frequently led to the publication of news from a more immediately personal and emotional standpoint than was true of the daily paper. Personal responsibility and propinquity were perhaps the most significant press controls. No other publisher had to be so well acquainted with his readers as did the country editor. The informal way in which he received a constant flow of local news forced him to be a master of the probability of news rather than of technical truth.

No effort has been made in any case to write the history of any special topic discussed nor has any effort been made to correct editorial errors in the use of factual material. The object has always been to present the point of view of the editor as it was found in the material which was read by Southerners.

A statistical study of a country paper would be at best a rough approximation. Precise information was not always a part of the country editor's philosophy of his obligations to his patron. In the field of politics, for instance, no effort has been made to cover any considerable amount of specific matter. Essentially every country paper was a political organ, and from the standpoint of space, political news often ran away with the paper, but the basic news and editorial patterns were seldom varied from one election to the next.

More sophisticated scholars in the history of journalism have dismissed the country paper in the shortest possible space. Unfortunately this plain little journal often has been damned for its prostitution to proprietary medicine companies and for using stereotyped patent sides. Although much of this adverse criticism is deserved, the country journal has been far more virtuous than such an attitude would indicate. Its pages tell a rich human story which can be duplicated nowhere else.

Research on a project such as this one of necessity obligates an author to many people. I would first like to thank those patient Southern country editors who were tolerant in answering my foolish questions when I seemed to be checking the obvious. Editors working desperately to meet a belated press time always were willing to stop long enough at least to nod to their dusty files in a corner cabinet, and to show me to a table and chair which I could use. Many of them were generous enough to permit me to borrow precious files to be taken to Lexington for more leisurely study amidst more familiar surroundings. Among these were Mrs. Mildred L. Brantly, Ordinary, and the County Commissioners of Hancock County, Georgia; Mr. Billoat Brown of McMinnville, Tennessee; Mr. Shelby Woodward, Chancery Clerk of Winston County, Mississippi; Messrs. Ed and Claiborne Walton of Stanford, Kentucky; Mr. Percy Haley Landrum of Hartford, Kentucky; Mrs. B. A. Evans of Russellville, Kentucky; Messrs. B. C. and Edwin Knapp of Fayette, Mississippi; Mr. G. M. Ketchin of Winnsboro, South Carolina; Mr. Fred Hughes of Leitchfield, Kentucky; Mr. George Joplin of Somerset, Kentucky; Mr. Sageser Kash of Carlisle, Kentucky; Dr. Jesse Van Meter of Jackson, Kentucky, and Mr. W. S. Winston of Ackerman, Mississippi.

Especially do I wish to thank Mrs. Will C. Hight and Mr. William H. Hight of the Winston County (Mississippi) *Journal* who allowed me to use Will C. Hight's file of that interesting Mississippi paper.

Dr. William D. McCain of the Mississippi Department of Archives and History and Miss Frances Hails and Mr. Peter A. Brannon of the Alabama Archives and History were generous with their assistance, as was Mrs. John Trotwood Moore of the Tennessee State Library. Mr. Wymberly DeRenne of the University of Georgia, Miss Allene Ramage of Duke University, and the staff of the University of North Carolina Library were most helpful. Dr. Robert Meriwether of the South Carolina Collection at the University of South Carolina supplied many volumes of useful material. Mr. and Mrs. E. A. Resch of Siler City, North Carolina; Mr. G. B. Moore of Sparta, Georgia, and Mr. Fred West of Abbeville, South Carolina assisted me in collecting a large sampling of modern country papers. Because of the nature of this sampling of more recent material I have not seen fit to pad my bibliography with it. Mr. West made available his excellent file of the Abbeville *Press and Banner*.

That most genial of all historians, Professor E. M. Coulter of the University of Georgia, not only permitted me to rummage at will through his fine collection of country papers, but also supplied comfortable working surroundings for me. Dan A. Bowmar, Jr. of Lexington, Kentucky, read most of the manuscript, as did my colleagues Dr. Albert D. Kirwan, Dr. William Clement Eaton and Dr. James Merton England. Colonel J. Winston Coleman, Jr., Earl Senff and Dr. William Haag were patient in preparing the photographic material for me. My neighbor A. B. Guthrie, Jr., a country newspaper shop apprentice, has given generously of his wisdom and encouragement. Dr. Neil Plummer of the University of Kentucky read much of the manuscript. Mr. Wright A. Patterson gave me much useful information on the ready-print services. Mrs. Elizabeth L. Arnold gave me timely assistance.

Dr. William B. Hamilton and Dr. Charles S. Sydnor of Duke University read one chapter and gave me sage advice. Dr. Robert Kincaid of Lincoln Memorial University helped me locate valuable material and gave me an insight into the working of a country print shop. Dr. Jacqueline Bull of the University of Kentucky Archives helped arrange the index.

Dr. D. L. Chambers, Mrs. Rosemary York and Mr. Harry Platt of the editorial department of the Bobbs-Merrill Company assisted me materially in a good job of editing. Dr. H. L. Donovan, President of the University of Kentucky, and the General Education Board made it possible for me to be relieved of some of my teaching responsibilities to do the research for this study.

Finally I wish to acknowledge the capable and long suffering assistance of Miss Dorothy Curtis and Miss Elsie Hurt. My wife, Elizabeth Turner Clark, has, as always, been generous in reading my manuscript and making helpful suggestions.

THOMAS D. CLARK
June 1, 1948

TABLE OF CONTENTS

Book One

LET THE PEOPLE READ

Book Two

THOSE WERE THE DAYS

Book Three

LOOK TO THE FUTURE

TABLE OF CONTENTS—*Continued*

Book Four

THE NEW SOUTH

LIST OF ILLUSTRATIONS

Book One

LET THE PEOPLE READ

Chapter 1

Beyond Appomattox

On a cold January day in 1887 Henry Jenkins shouldered his ax and crossed over the river from Louisiana to Vicksburg. He was going to perform an act of social service on the streets of the Mississippi town by indulging in "dude killing." Henry proposed to chop down the foppish citizens across the river as though they were so many spindling cottonwood sprouts growing along the river bank. With uplifted ax he stood on a corner awaiting his first victim. Impetuous policemen, however, arrested him before he could cleave a single head with his trusty blade.

The Vicksburg *Herald* said that some people felt the officers had exceeded their authority. Nevertheless the sober *Herald* was of the opinion that, if the case were considered objectively, the police were right. Perhaps it was not a crime against society and good morals to kill a dude, but there was an enormous amount of responsibility attached to the selection of victims. It was doubted that Henry Jenkins could exercise enough "nice judgment and discrimination" to avoid making horrible mistakes. There was great danger that he might strike down an innocent man on his way to a wedding, a waiter on his way to a restaurant, a footman or just a plain idiot dressed like a dude. Dude killing, in the South at least, was no job for a rank stranger. As the editor said, each town should have a regular "fool killer" but he should be a man of much discretion and skill. It would not do to trust this delicate business to strangers.

Just as in the case of dude killers, the position of country editor demanded a man of competent judgment. It was his responsibility to know what was happening in his community and to report the news with reason, humanity and intimate understanding of local background. The editing of a country paper was an extremely important function, and an editor had to be able to use "nice judgment and discrimination" so as not to strike down innocent people who appeared to be something they were not. He had to develop with care the delicate instruments of public opinion and community pride. After 1865 the country paper was to herald, in its own inimitable way, the rise of a new South.

When the Confederate troops straggled home from Appomattox, only 182 tattered weeklies had survived the conflict to greet them. Even the appearance of these impoverished papers dramatically documented the ravages of war. Greasy homemade ink spread a dark, discoloring film from one impression to the next. But these little journals boldly assumed the task of welcoming a new age in the South. Among the many institutions that contributed to the rebuilding of an exhausted land, one of the most important was the rural weekly newspaper.

The local editor helped to give his region a sense of direction and a hopefulness that enabled the Southern people to endure the rigors of Reconstruction. That the country newspaper met a genuine need is shown by the rapid increase in the number of papers. The original 182 formed a nucleus. Three years after the end of the war there were 499, and twenty years later there were 1,827 weeklies in twelve states. By 1869 it was evident that the country editors were giving the common man a vital part in the rebirth of the region.

Prior to the war, most weekly papers existed as the kept handmaidens of politics and they reflected the views of the party putting up the money. In New South journalism, although the subject of politics was not neglected, it was given somewhat less prominence. The field of the weekly expanded to include the whole gamut of human relationships. The scope of the newspaper became as broad as Southern life itself. True, a vast majority of the papers established after 1865 boldly asserted their intention of upholding the principles of the Democratic Party. Occasionally this vigorous declaration was challenged by papers sailing under opposition banners and proclaiming the virtues of Republicanism. These were usually operating safely in solid Republican districts, or were seeking favors from the hands of radical state officials, and their number was never great. Among the partisan papers the whole confused process of Reconstruction was bitterly contested. Democrats spoke of Republicans with contempt, and the badgered Republicans snarled back like frightened animals. Political rivalry was not new. Whigs and Democrats had battled before the war, and Republicans inherited some of the Whiggish fight.

It was important, however, that the new-type country journal reduced its emphasis on politics and extended its coverage of social and economic affairs. In an age when transportation and communication facilities were being improved and expanded news took on a more vital importance. The demand for human-interest matter grew as rapidly as the number of new papers. Even the most isolated rural community developed an awareness of new social relationships, and of the active part county and state were playing in national growth. With this changing sense of national importance, Southerners took a certain pride in their localities and wanted to see them against the background of the rest of the South. The printed page was able to work wonders in giving the community a sense of importance.

But the feeling of membership in world and national society was hedged about with difficulties. It was paradoxical that as the world about the South grew smaller, Reconstruction caused Southern rural areas to grow in many respects more and more isolated. Antagonism toward the dominating national political system contributed to this condition and a sense of loyalty to immediate political alliances tended to focus attention on the precinct and county. As one Southern editor said, it mattered less to the Southern people whom the Radicals sent to congress than who was to conduct the county affairs. Thus at a time when industry and business in most areas were becoming nationwide, in Southern communities they were being constricted into tight local limits.

Courthouses became the storm centers of community political interest and sectional resistance. New political patterns were being formulated, and from these bastions of Democracy new personalities emerged to play subsequent roles in state and national politics. Once the storm of Reconstruction mismanagement was ended the New South sought its way to reunion and regional stability, and the country newspaper became one of the first major institutions to establish itself. Editors soon realized that their section was starting over with a fresh regional outlook which evolved naturally from the ruins of the old order. For the new and dominant Southern political principles to endure, a closely co-ordinated press was a necessity. The large daily paper was unable to supply this need. It spoke for the people en masse. Sections of states and of several states were lumped together, and editors wrote in broad terms. The daily paper's outlook had to include large segments of the South, but the country editor with his weekly paper spoke for and to a single small unit of homogeneous people. It was he who cultivated the traditions of the new order from year to year and supplied editorial justification for local attitudes. He more than any other individual implanted the idea that the South could maintain its regional integrity only through the predominance of the Democratic Party.

While the old stump of the ante-bellum South sprouted fresh political shoots, it likewise grew a crop of new economic ideas. Where once town and city storekeepers or factories supplied goods to farmers and planters there were now the local furnishing merchants. Legislators had created a new agricultural credit system in the lien laws. Although basic operating capital was largely of extraregional origin, the functioning of the new mercantile system tended more than ever to localize trade. Stores gathered about them a patronage which seldom went beyond the crossroads localities for goods. As lists of commodities for sale grew more diversified and places of origin more distant, these points of distribution tended to become more provincial. Thus it was that neighborhoods centered about churches and stores became increasingly a part of the Southern system. Provincial though they actually were, these tiny segments of society wished very much to be recognized, and the columns of the informal local newspaper supplied the only channel through which this desire could be satisfied.

Society and community pride, as important as it was, did not constitute a significant source of income to editors. The new system of farm credits did. There was a close connection among merchants, county officialdom and the country papers. The financing of production by use of agricultural lien notes created a new demand for local printing. First, there were blank notes, lien forms and other official papers connected with the new credit system to be printed. Later, when this procedure began to develop failures, there was a demand for an official advertising medium to publicize the sales of lands and chattels. County printing soon became a lucrative source of income, and it was not an accident that new weekly papers came into existence in the postwar South at an astonishing rate.

Editors in many cases financed the establishment of their plants and paid operation costs from public printing contracts and did not have to give too much thought immediately to subscription lists. Official printing was not the only source of profit for the newspapers. Almost continuously there was a political campaign in progress and editors sold space, cards and handbills to the army of candidates who sought election to office. It was true that editors remained steadfastly loyal to a single party in the South, but this did not prevent them from favoring a flock of card and handbill-buying candidates for every office. Shrewdly country publishers helped put New South local politics on a more formal plane and reaped an income for their trouble.

Editing a vigorous country newspaper was not a simple matter. An imaginative paper had to include much more than strict partisan politics, opposing the Republican Party and railing at public offenders. Readers were more interested in personal news, criminal cases and local industrial and agricultural improvement. They also looked for public discussions of issues as they arose and for the preservation of the Southern tradition.

As to news, the editor of the rural South was called on to supply only a purely local brand. The field of national and world news was not for him. By the time he could publish stories from distant places his material was stale. His responsibility here was that of abstracting the dailies and boiling down world news into concise opinionated editorial statements. Country readers were as much interested in what the editor thought as they were in reading the stories themselves. They expected him to read the daily papers and write in his weekly a suitable attitude toward the news of the outside world. An attitude was all they required.

The country paper needed only to confine itself to local happenings. People wanted to know of the social doings of their neighbors. They wanted to be informed when and where preaching services would be held, who was sick and expected to die, who ate dinner away from home, who strange visitors were, where the local baseball teams were playing and with what results, when there would be barbecues, who the candidates were, what had happened at court day, what was going on at the courthouse, what kind of weather prevailed over the county, what crop prospects were, who had been arrested, and whose cotton had bloomed first. They wanted to read circus advertisements, news of violence, hangings, lynchings, stories of curiosities, of big snakes, of big potatoes, big hogs, and the strange antics of animals, and all the social gossip of courtings, marryings and births.

The Southern common man lived simply and his interest was centered in the trivial happenings about him. It was to serve this everyday demand for local news that country papers resorted very early to the publication of names whether they made big news or not.

It was good practice to publish every birth, marriage and death, and to print obituaries in great numbers. It was part of the gloomy ritual of death in the South not only that a deceased individual be buried decently but that his memory be embalmed in printer's ink in a long and mournful obituary. Nearly every community contained at least one "literary" figure who could combine eulogy, sympathy and poetry in an expression of public sorrow. Even babies who lived scarcely long enough to be named were given publicity through expressions of sympathy for their parents. Country papers brought considerable peace of mind to bereaved families. The sting of death was materially lessened by publication of eulogies. These were features which readers clipped and preserved in scrapbooks for future generations to read. In fact, there were the morbid clippers who pasted every obituary in their scrap books whether they knew the deceased person or not; the grandiloquent praise of the dead satisfied their desire to be so remembered by the paper when they passed on.

Newspapers performed endless services in the vast field of human relationships. Perhaps none was more appreciated than the link they formed between persons who migrated to other parts of the country and their old communities. An army of homesick immigrants wrote long letters to local papers in which they described conditions in their new homes and inquired about persons and matters which they had left behind. The editorial shoulder was always a willing weeping post where the detached and lonely subscribers could rest their weary heads. They always found the editors willing to print even passable letters, and editors found nostalgic readers good subscribers from whom they collected important extra revenue.

There was no tie with a man's past which remained so constant and voluble as the country paper. It was a friendly, sympathetic weekly letter from home which revealed the activities of the whole community and which recorded the degrees of change more effectively than was ever possible in personal correspondence. Editors appreciated this fact, and they often ran special features to attract the attention of distant readers who had lost interest in detailed personal happenings. By doing this they converted their papers into pleasant doorways through which the reader was admitted to the historical past.

Many editors and subscribers alike were interested in local history. Frequently their research and writings in the field were so brief and restricted that they were not worthy of book publication and the next best outlet was the county paper. Nearly every paper at some time or other ran long series of historical articles reviving memories of old-timers, and creating new interest among the younger people. Always historical features were prime favorites, and generally papers gained subscribers during periods when they were being printed. Not alone did they stimulate a genuine reader interest, but often they stirred up controversies which brought out additional articles. Especially was this true where all the local forebears were not given what descendants believed were their deserts. Reflected in the country paper files is a keen sense of the reverence which Southerners have felt for their local pioneers.

It has always been a joy for local historians to trace the rise of counties from the dark moments in antiquity when Indians and animals prowled over the spots where courthouses now stand. They have searched religiously into the lives of those first small bands of pioneers who drove out the varmints and savages, cleared the ground, laid out the counties, built the towns and began to live like civilized people. Most of this material was personal and episodical. Because of this emphasis on the past, there lie buried in countless files of country papers many rich chapters of colloquial history. Though much of it is sketchy, poorly conceived and awkwardly presented, it is vital to the interpretation of provincial regional development.

To the modern historian the informal accounts of everyday events presented in the rural weeklies are much more significant source material than many pretentious essays composed consciously as histories. Scarcely a town or county in the South can produce public records that can serve alone as the basis of a satisfactory history. They are entirely too impersonal to give more than a skeletonized picture of the region. They seldom go beyond restricted subjects. There is, in fact, only one door through which the local historian can pass with satisfaction to much of the everyday world of the past, and that is the country paper. It was engaged in producing a crude chronological story of the community from week to week. The commonplaces of local news, sufficiently multiplied, take on significance and permit broad generalizations. In printing local news even more than in publicizing contemporary issues and public discussions, country editors preserved intact the materials out of which the student of today can construct again the living past.

Along with local news and history, discussion of local issues was demanded by readers of rural weeklies. Not even the most indifferent editor of a trifling "patent sides" weekly could avoid discussion of his community's problems. Almost every controversial issue which could beset an agrarian region was an integral part of Southern life. Here was a highly dramatic story which combined aspects of a raw American frontier with those of a well-developed and cultured society in a rapidly changing economic world. Fledgling editors who began their careers in hurriedly organized print shops attempted immediately in a homey way to analyze these conflicting forces. They fought back vigorously at Reconstruction exploiters—the Negro, the carpetbagger and the scalawag. They struck out viciously at the Washington politician and bared their teeth at the collective North. At the same time they struggled manfully to help re-establish Southern life on a native concept of order. There was a clear recognition that the region was faced with the serious responsibility of rebuilding itself along new lines which would allow the common man to assert his influence. The New South, the earlier country editors believed, was to remain an agrarian region, but it could look hopefully to the day when there would be industry and cities to supplement cotton fields and ramshackle farms.

Industrialization of the South seemed highly desirable, but means for accomplishing it were undeveloped. During the Reconstruction period, native Southern leaders worried about every aspect of the problem. Editors were disturbed about population. Although the thousands of letters which appeared in the weeklies describing the virtues of Texas and other Western states were highly interesting to readers, the editors did not like them. They could not refuse to publish these communications, but they recognized that they were very likely helping to reduce the white population of their communities. From 1865 to 1885 the South had more people than it perhaps needed at any single moment to operate its economic system but the time was coming when every laborer would be a decided asset to a community seeking industrialization. Because of this situation, maintaining the Southern population was one of the major responsibilities of the country press. Country editors clamored for immigration to their counties. They described Texas and the West in unfavorable terms, pounced upon every story of misfortune to immigrants—cyclones, epidemics, drudgery, droughts and insect invasions—to keep their people at home. They coined such expressions as "woman-killing in Texas," "godless country" and "rolling plains of buckshot mud" to offset the seductive descriptions of immigration agents.

Partly for a selfish reason editors wished to promote the growth of population in their communities. They wanted to retain profitable bodies of subscribers. They wanted schools and churches to thrive. Wisely they saw the need for sufficient population to insure adequate community functions. In sparsely settled regions, Southern resources lay dormant, awaiting the coming of industry to enrich the country. Thousands of editorials proclaimed the fertility of the land and the salubrity of the climate, the hospitality of Southerners and their friendly attitude toward new capital and labor. Everywhere the newly organized papers reflected a spirit of hopefulness for the future. They published columns of comments on the industrial future of the South, quoted freely from Northern and Eastern daily papers, courted Northern capital and pleaded earnestly for the location of manufacturing plants in Southern towns.

In all this vigorous campaign for industry there was an element of pathetic naïveté. Editors babbled constantly about the exploitation of natural resources and the coming of industry but few of them revealed a practical understanding of the problems connected with Southern industrialization. None of them grasped the sociological effects it would entail. Many editors expressed a bitter dislike for the Northern political system, yet they wooed industrialists who cunningly manipulated that type of politics. Despite their constant harping on sectional issues, they demonstrated little antagonism toward Northern capital. They drew a sharp distinction between the menial carpetbagger who sought picayunish personal advantages, and the energetic Yankee who came with cash to invest in developing the South. From 1865 to the present they have sought to cure their communities' economic ills by importing foreign capital and industries.

Immigrants, Northern, European and Oriental, were sought for the South. It was said there were 12,000,000 people in the region in 1867 and that there was ample room for 20,000,000 more. The great need of the South was an abundance of cheap labor which would replace the Negro in some instances and supplement him in others. Small farms were to be the pattern of the future and this called for owners adjusted to a simple scheme of operation. At the same time 80 per cent of the land, said some editors, waited exploitation. Forests had to be cleared and ground broken. An increased production of diversified farm crops awaited the coming of the thrifty immigrant. Possibly some editors sought Oriental and European labor with the hope of returning to the former days of the plantation, but if they did they retained a discreet silence on the subject. The small farm appears to have been the unit which country editors believed would bring the best results to the South.

According to the country editor, both the small-farm agricultural system and a type of industry utilizing the near-at-hand natural resources would bring about the economic development of the South. Most of the papers maintained that the ideal type of industry would be one which could be made to utilize Southern farm and mineral resources. It was desirable to bring cotton mills to the Southern fields, thus eliminating transportation costs on raw materials. Coal, iron, copper and lumbering could be prepared locally for the domestic market.

Between 1865 and 1910 this was to be an absorbing theme in Southern journalism. The weeklies discussed industrialization somewhat in the same vein as evangelistic religion. After 1880 they fell under the spell of such daily editors as Captain F. W. Dawson and Henry W. Grady. With the fervor of assisting revivalists in a warm Southern camp meeting they repeated the gospel of these power preachers in editorials proclaiming the South of the future. They spoke of the region as a sleeping princess who, when stroked gently with the magic wand of industrialization, would become an enchanting ruler in the national economy.

Country newspapers exhorted the staple-crop sinners, piny-woods adulterers and mountain ne'er-do-wells to hit the sawdust trail to the sacred altar of industrial salvation, and at the same time pointed up the hard fate of the unimaginative Southern farmer caught in the toils of one-crop agriculture and a ruinous credit system. Editors looked forward to industry with the naïve expectancy of the children of a tenant farmer on Christmas Eve. Column after column of statistical material, public letters praising the South, favorable Northern editorials on the region's advantages, excerpts from the *Manufacturer's Record* and travel accounts were published. This was the eloquent story of a New South in the process of being born.

Grady of the Atlanta *Constitution* and Dawson of the Charleston *News and Courier* spoke with loud, booming editorial voices of the better days to come. Their messages roared and thundered over the land. Their country colleagues echoed them with tiny peals in the local weeklies and busied themselves courting every industry which promised a cash income and employment of labor.

In a new role, with glittering new lines, fresh make-up and new properties, the region was presented as a grand spectacle of the art of making money. Editorials spoke of an abundance of land, inexhaustible water power, beautiful flowers, fields of white cotton, waving grain, sunshine, singing birds, freedom from "isms" and incendiary doctrines and a firm belief in the representative form of government. The admission price to this great spectacle was kept to a low and popular level. There was room for all: the aged patrons who had become gray and haggard and the young newcomers who sought inspiration in the modern setting. This was the New South so passionately described on the editorial pages of the more progressive country papers.

Industry and agriculture were two cardinal subjects in the press. But always along with them were the local domestic issues which kept the community mind in a constant state of flux. The South was still frontier country, and significant portions of its people were still pioneering just as they had been doing since the mid-eighteenth century.

They were still clearing the 80 per cent of wooded land which stood between them and a full agricultural exploitation of their region. As frontiersmen had always done they turned their cattle and livestock free on open range and fenced in their crops. The time came in more populous South Carolina when it was necessary to reverse this process. Timber resources became limited, fields grew larger and labor for splitting rails and maintaining long fence lines too costly. Like every domestic issue which has arisen in the South, this one moved slowly and in close correlation with the degree of community growth.

The emotionalism of the Southern demagogue was freely intermixed with the practical question of whether to turn cows free on the range and fence the crops, or to fence the pastures and leave the fields free. The ubiquitous widow and her ravenous milk cow paraded sorrowfully across the stage of the editorial page. Poor tenant farmers and the equally needy town householders were wept over by the ardent free-range reactionaries. The so-called "no fence" supporters were equally argumentative and perhaps more articulate.

From the Potomac to the Rio Grande the pages of the country papers were opened to full discussion of this issue. The argument and furious controversy over where the Southern milk cow was to graze kept pace over the South with the advance of dense settlement. No single question in the South has been more freely discussed, and at no time have editorial pages been opened more generously to anyone with an idea or a prejudice than they were during the years when the frontier practice was being crowded out by increasing settlement.

The range issue was only one of many which troubled the country editor. Education was a subject which reared its head continuously. Again editors approached the subject with a selfish motive in mind. Ignorant people were nonsubscribers to the papers. The only decent use to which an illiterate could put a country paper was that of lining his cabin, and blank newsprint would perhaps have been equally useful for this purpose. It went without saying that the country papers pleaded for better schools and higher teachers' salaries and sought more regular attendance and extended terms. Even the most poorly educated publisher understood that the magic key to community success lay in universal education.

The country press favored an appropriation of federal funds to subsidize Southern education, as was called for by the Blair Bill in the eighties. It was not until demagogues like Senator M. C. Butler of South Carolina, John Tyler Morgan of Alabama, and Robert Love Taylor of Tennessee dragged the red herrings of Negro equality, Yankee interference and the high tariff issue across its trail that the little journals opposed it. This subject was discussed in full for five years.

When the Blair Bill passed off the scene in 1888 other topics took its place. Since 1867 the Peabody Fund had worked as an educational leaven, and by the beginning of the twentieth century such matters as consolidation, compulsory attendance, teacher training, vocational education and the general lifting of Southern standards received ardent editorial support. Especially was this true in the first decade of this century when the famous educational publicity crusades were under way. In fact, the country paper can claim a material amount of credit for helping to break down the stultifying private-school tradition, and for dignifying the public school as an instrument of distinct advantage to the South. Its columns were a free sounding board where the whole idea could be explored in the plain language and within the simple thought structure of the common man.

Running parallel with the long crusade for improved schools was the plea for better social standards. Nearly every issue of every country paper published before 1920 was documentary proof that the South was a land of violence. The knife, pistol, brass knucks, razors, clubs and even fence rails took their toll of human life. Judges, preachers, editors, jurymen and community leaders fought the carrying of pistols. Crusades in court and out were aimed at unloading hip-pocket arsenals. Public hangings collected about the county jails larger crowds of drunken, brawling spectators than "Old" John Robinson's circus. To editors it was a matter of little wonder that lynchings were numerous. Many favored driving the lynchers into court, enclosing the public hangings within restrictive walls and dealing severely with those who chose to settle their personal differences in the physical manner of savages.

Perhaps no editor ever stopped to think what an impact his bound files would have on the historian. He doubtless never turned back through the columns of his paper to analyze the sordid record of carousing and ineffective law enforcement which he had compiled. For sixty years his current news came in from a frontier which was fighting its way forward. It felled its trees and its personal enemies with the same lusty vigor and lasting effectiveness.

Law enforcement in the South involved many problems. In fact the whole question of public correction was a baffling puzzle. Those culprits who were sentenced to imprisonment became enmeshed in a convict system which functioned with neither social planning nor humanity. A convict in many a Southern state became a soulless chattel in the eyes of the law. He was subject to sale to greedy and bestial private lessors to be worked and abused until he either served out his sentence or died. Constantly country papers dealt with this burning question. One nauseating and bloodcurdling episode after another was dragged across the weekly pages for readers to see the failure of their medieval penal system. The whip, the bludgeon and the booted heel of sadistic human beasts were brought before the bar of public opinion for a righteous people to condemn.

In Kentucky, the country press of the western part of the state cornered a politically-minded governor in an attempt to use the infernal convict-lease system. The B. DuPont and C. R. Mason and Company mining interests of Louisville had learned of the profits to be made from this source of cheap labor in the Birmingham area, and had sought to put the system into practice in western Kentucky coal mines. Alert editors took the fight directly to Governor Procter Knott and the prison commissioners, and when they publicized the action the convicts were withdrawn from the mines. The state was spared a lurid chapter of inhumanity. Doubtless this widespread publicity served to break up the convict-lease system in the states of Georgia, Tennessee, South Carolina, Alabama and Mississippi. Bad as some of the state penal administrations may have been, they were certainly preferable to the cruelty and inhumanity of the leasing system.

Equally fundamental were the ineffective and immoral law-enforcement officers. The sneaking, self-seeking and ignorant justice of the peace, the political sheriff, the jackal constable, the weak-kneed grand juror and the incompetent judge were all exposed in the country paper's pages. Some editors scorned them, while others made pitiful political excuses for their miserable pack. The publication of quarterly grand jury presentments most often revealed a story of the failure of the Southern system in local government. Filthy courthouses, ramshackle jails, illiterate officials, lazy road overseers, penurious almshouse keepers and owners of rowdy brothels all felt the sting of publicity. Where presentments were honest, a vital social record was compiled for the future analysis of the social structure.

One item in the grand jury reports perhaps received more attention than the others. Lack of roads kept most of the rural South isolated. Its backwoodsmen were prisoners within the very lands which offered them economic opportunity. The building of passable roads brought about a deep social transformation. Arguments for better highways ran the fence law and education a close race in securing newspaper space. Almost without exception, country editors kept up a continual appeal for better roads. They condemned the old spineless system of public workings and begged for specific taxation and responsible contractors. After 1895 they opened their pages to the good-roads campaign, and for more than forty years they have kept this issue alive. Good roads, next to spiritual grace, were the thing most highly desired in the South, and often editors preferred the improved highway to the sawdust trail as a path to salvation.

No phase of Southern life was overlooked by alert country papers. They listened enthusiastically to the first natal cry of future subscribers and welcomed them in their columns. They assumed their best party manners and stood about marriage altars and rushed away to write flowery accounts of commonplace small-town or country weddings. They knelt silently and tearfully at the bier of the dead, and dispatched the deceased to another world with highly commendatory obituaries. They patted native sons on the back for their accomplishments. They puffed and bragged about their towns and counties, and about everything else which promised any degree of happiness to their people. County journals were often the difference in their communities between complete isolation and a sense of membership in the larger region, with all its problems and progress.

They performed every conceivable service for their readers. One sympathetic patron said: "Your paper tells you when to go to church, to county, circuit and probate court, and when to send your children to school, and anywhere else you want to go. It tells you who is dead, who is sick, who married, who is born, and many other things you would like to know. It calls attention to business enterprise, advocates the best of schools, of law and order in town. Free of charge it records the marriage of your daughter, the death of your son and the illness of your wife. It sets forth the advantages and attractions of your town, it invites immigration, and is first to welcome newcomers."

Chapter 2

Country Editor

EVERY Southern paper reflected the personality of its editor. The term "personal journalism" was most accurately used when applied to the weekly press. Here the editor virtually was the paper. He formulated the policy of his paper, wrote editorials and news stories, edited locals, knew his readers personally, set type, ran the press, mailed the papers and smoothed over the ruffled feelings of irate subscribers. It was he who made financial arrangements for the publication of the paper, and it was his back that went bare if it was not a success. It was hard for the subscribers to think of the paper apart from the personality of its publisher. In a vast majority of cases it was not so much a matter of finding out what the Winston County (Mississippi) *Journal,* The Woodford (Kentucky) *Sun,* or the Sparta (Georgia) *Ishmaelite* said on an issue as it was to know what Will C. Hight, Dan Bowmar and Sidney Lewis thought. Mister Will, Mister Dan and Mister Sidney were important people in their communities.

To the editors their papers were vital things. They regarded every issue to come as a son after an unbroken sequence of daughters. Files might be preserved in rolls of tattered paper stuffed atop cabinets or packed away in the basement to catch soot and ashes next to the furnace, but the next issue was always a thing of promise. It came from the press a bright, fresh sheet smelling of green ink and was sent on its way to assure everyday Southerners that they were somebody. Their names were in print—and printer's ink gave them a coveted dignity. The editor's political and personal views were expressed in both editorial and news items. They provided the common man with a pattern by which he could think about politics and political personalities. They gave him an insight into social and economic problems which affected his daily life. It made little difference whether the country paper was ultimately shredded into bits by children with scissors, pasted on cabin walls as decoration and insulation or put to a humbler and less gracious end; it was respected for its services.

Though an active Southern press existed in 1865, never did the profession of editor seem more appealing than in the latter quarter of the nineteenth century. Publishing ranked along with storekeeping and mill management as desirable professions in the New South. Perhaps no other calling offered so much prestige and community honor in so short a time as did editorship. An ambitious young man possessing a common-school education, some gumption, imagination, business ability and mechanical sense could establish himself as a solid figure in a remarkably brief time. Many country editors lacked high-school educations, and few had been to college. Their writing frequently reflected hard common sense, but little grammar and cultivated style and only a sketchy knowledge of spelling and sentence structure.

Launching a weekly paper was a proud moment in an editor's life. When enough news was gathered to assemble at least two pages of print, the new editor saluted his prospective subscribers. He usually assured them that his paper would be safe politically, that it would boost its community, seek to attract desirable immigrants into the county, encourage local progress and attempt to correct certain faults of governmental administration. Important as these advance promises were, the selection of a suitable slogan for the masthead was perhaps just as essential. The new paper had to sail under a proud slogan. Many sentiments could be expressed—among them, "A Friend of Every Man, Woman and Child Who Toils for a Living"; "To Tell the Truth, Obey the Law, and Make Money"; "Talk for Home, Work for Home and Fight for Home"; and "Hew to the Line, Let the Chips Fall Where They May."

Just as no extensive amount of education was necessary in the editing of a weekly, so also only a limited amount of mechanical training and equipment was needed. It was possible to compose and print a paper in a remarkably small building space. A single room was frequently adequate housing. A Washington or Franklin hand press, a few cases of type, a foot-treadle job press, a pair of type sticks, a couple of iron chases, one or two galleys, a proof press, a supply of ink, a bundle of ready-print pages, a roller towel and wash pan were sufficient equipment. Perhaps it would not be wholly facetious to say that it was wise to include in this inventory a pair of knucks, a brace of pistols, a shotgun and a solid billet of wood, for editing a country paper was not without its hazards.

Once an editor acquired materials and established a paper, he assumed certain responsibilities. First, he had to protect his good name if his subscribers were to respect it. He inherited from his ante-bellum forebears an extremely delicate sense of honor, and it was not at all unusual for him to become involved in fist fights with subscribers and fellow editors. In 1890, P. B. Hamer of the Pee Dee (Marion, South Carolina) *Index* came to blows with J. H. Evans and W. J. McKerall of the Marion *Star* and was beaten and thrown down a flight of steps. Hamer was quoted as having said the *Star* editors were "politically a mite pro-Negro." Beginning the hard way, the editor of the Holly Springs (Mississippi) *Sun* was attacked twice on his first day of publication.

Much editorial battling resulted from a rural and frontier sensitiveness, but some of it was due to the clumsy, blunt expression and tactlessness of many half-educated editors, who were unable to campaign for an idea without writing personal attacks on opponents. They pitched headlong into battle, shouting bold and defiant words which invited trouble. Although there were, of course, editors who engaged in good-natured arguments with neighboring publishers just for the sake of enlivening their columns, such urbanity was rare.

Readers were at least as bad as the editors. People today can hardly realize how sensitive the old-time subscriber was. News stories and notices which seem perfectly innocuous now touched off emotional storms when they first appeared. If an editor confused a name, or located a tenant farmer on the wrong place, he was told to correct the error. Many a disgruntled reader stalked into the office and canceled his order for the paper on the spot. Occasionally an unreasonable subscriber demanded that the editor finish out his subscription period by sending a roll of blank paper each week.

When a paper was safely started and the new editor had time to feel at home with it, he gave serious attention to the objectives of the local region. The editor became the official community puffer and booster. His town and county were usually supreme in promise if not in progress. The land was fertile, the climate healthy and pleasant, churches were numerous and business on Main Street was booming, or would boom with some publicity.

This last note brought the editor around to the vital subject of advertising. Before a mercantile establishment could succeed it had to advertise its business, and only local newspapers offered this service. Here editors faced a difficult task. They had to destroy the provincial attitude that all the prospective customers needed to know was that stores existed—and this they knew already. Village-minded merchants believed there was no need to advertise staple merchandise. In consequence, literally thousands of stories were published to illustrate the benefit of advertising.

On one point, however, editorial and sluggish business minds met—in a stubborn resistance to mail-order houses. A stock moral story was published of a dollar bill which was marked by a Mississippi farmer and placed in circulation. The bill came back to him several times and was seen constantly in the community. Finally it was sent away to a mail-order house, and no one in Mississippi ever saw it again.

Both advertising and subscription rates were low. In the nineteenth century space averaged about twenty cents a column-inch, and thirty-five to forty cents for a double-column spread. Legal notices were fifteen cents a line, obituaries five cents a line and all other notices ten cents. Page advertisements were sold at thirty to one hundred dollars a page. These advertisements, however, were negotiated for on a special arrangement between the advertiser and the editor. It is doubtful that many papers had what is known to modern journalism as a "rate card." It would be practically impossible by a space analysis to arrive at anything like an accurate estimate of what advertising income the average country weekly received. Both the amount and the rate of advertising varied according to the size of the towns in which the papers were published and the spirit of rivalry which existed among merchants. Usually, before 1900, ads of foreign merchandise far outmeasured those of home products. Many small-town stores never bought an inch of advertising space.

It was this failure of merchants and business and professional men to support their local papers that caused friction between editors and their communities. Each week a paper was called on to publicize not merely the community but individual citizens as well. In provincial neighborhoods where social intercourse was either limited in scope or was stratified by a contradictory and emotional caste system, the editorial task was complicated. Any individual's success was measured somewhat by the amount of personal publicity which appeared in the paper. Publicity seekers were continually pestering editors for more, whether they deserved it or not. One ingenious publisher developed a scale of prices for delicate personal-vanity services. For bragging in public about a successful local citizen who was in fact as lazy as an army mule, $2.75; referring to a deceased neighbor as a man mourned by the whole community when actually only the poker players missed him, $20; writing delicately of a "gallivanting female" as an estimable lady whom it was a pleasure to meet, when it was a known fact that every merchant in town had rather see the devil (horns, tail and all) coming into his store than she, $10; calling an ordinary pulpit pounder an eminent divine, $60; and sending a hardened sinner off to the pearly gates with poetry, $5. Yet, aggravating as it was, this vanity factor helped make the country paper a popular institution.

Most editors accepted the responsibility of exposing frauds. Just as circus people uttered the famous cry "hey, Rube" when they were in danger, so the editors printed the warning phrase, "Pass Him Around!" Unfair and fraudulent advertisers were "passed around" through the exchanges; counterfeiters, board-bill jumpers, fake salesmen, labor agents, bogus preachers, quack doctors, kerosene safety salesmen and questionable itinerant females felt the sting of widespread editorial warnings. Peddlers appeared in Laurens County, South Carolina, in 1883, offering to trade new feathers for old, the new ones to be delivered at a later date. At the time feathers were selling at seventy-five cents. As evidence of good faith, the peddlers paid a deposit of twenty-five cents a pound. They collected hundreds of pounds of feathers this way. Then no one ever heard of them again. Papers warned readers of this racket all over the South. In stealing feather beds the rascals were striking a staggering blow at a noble Southern institution.

Other peddlers fed their horses, gorged themselves at country tables and paid for their keep with worthless brass pins, pretending all the time that they could speak little English. Counterfeiters passed both "green goods" and bogus coin. Everywhere editors exposed them. Horse thieves were active, and exchanges ran ahead to give them away and often to bring them to summary justice. "Cheap John" jewelry salesmen gulled naïve countrymen with their suavity and faked generosity. One such "salesman" worked the Georgia towns distributing "rare aluminum gold" watches and chains. His trick was to sell a few pieces of merchandise, then refund the purchasers' money, permitting them to keep the watches. The next day he was back and was surrounded by a flock of country gulls who bought watches and chains at an increased price, but when the peddler had disposed of his stock he packed up and left without refunding any money. Stories appeared telling of subscribers who went away to New York to deposit money in the ancient swindle of recovering treasure but were robbed and beaten for their troubles.

None of the swindles was more impudent than that of the marriage and mutual-aid associations which operated in Alabama, Tennessee and Mississippi in the 1880's. There were eight associations in Memphis, fourteen in Nashville, and at least a dozen more in other cities. Certificates were sold for one thousand to three thousand dollars with initiation fees of eight to twelve dollars. These certificates were claimed to protect one against marriage and, of course, they boosted the rate of marriage to such an extent that mutual policy holders were afraid to go to the post offices. It was the belief of the policy holders that if they married they would get the money guaranteed in the policy. Actually they got nothing but a swindling of initiation fees and early policy installment payments. In 1883 the Troy (Alabama) *Messenger* said, "And still the matrimonial assurance-Connubial-for-Everlasting-Happiness-and-Wait-for-a-Divorce-with-no-Possible-Prospect-for-a-Return-of-Your-Money Swindle thrives!" One policy holder was quoted in the same paper as saying, "Free, hell and damnation, the assessments are coming in two or three every day, and they are getting larger all the time. I think I will take my shotgun and go around to the swindlers and demand my money I paid in. Why, I am out over $1,000." Along with marriage frauds were the dishonest mutual burial associations, life assurance companies and other seductive schemes designed to swindle the gullible and ignorant. The papers took on the task of warning simple-minded readers of the oily pitfalls which awaited them in their attempts to get something for nothing.

The editor was not only the plumed knight driving out the cheating knaves who preyed on his people but also the critic rebuking the slovenly ways of the local people. He was ready to rap knuckles for shiftlessness as well as vice. For instance, up to 1910 the papers continually had to attack the practice of letting hogs roam loose in the streets. The editor of the *Messenger* was fighting an old battle when he pointed out that it was a mighty unpleasant experience to be homeward bound from church or a party and tumble over a flea-bitten hog stretched full length across the walk. "With soiled clothing," he wrote, "scratched hands and a general capture of fleas, an admiring public will, with uplifted hands, exclaim in unison: 'Blessed are the peacemakers, for they repealed the hog ordinance.' "

Dogs chased hogs into stores and upset merchandise. Dignified citizens were sometimes caught astride charging shotes and were made ridiculous spectacles as they were catapulted along in great danger to life and limb. Gaping holes were rooted in streets and wallowed out around public wells. In fact, public wells provoked almost as much editorial spanking as the droves of wanton hogs. Muddy water flowed in from the streets, and foreign materials from every quarter accumulated in them. The Greensboro (Georgia) *Herald* listed, in 1884, the following articles as having been taken from the town's well: tin cups, tin cans, old shoes, ax handles, popguns, bricks, bones, matchboxes, a chain pump, old hats, beer bottles, baseballs, the skull of a cow, three well buckets, a well wheel, a buggy shaft, vest buckles and lumps of coal. It is a wonder that any Southern town was able to exist, with so little interest in its sanitation, and a miracle that typhoid fever or some other epidemic disease did not destroy the population. The editors tried to clean up their towns but they had their troubles disciplining an irresponsible public.

Streets and sidewalks got in treacherous condition. On one occasion W. P. Walton of the Stanford (Kentucky) *Interior Journal* fell through a hole in a sidewalk and broke a leg. That he could do this was of itself a sharp indictment of the town fathers. From his bed he vigorously lambasted the city council for its apathy. Everywhere editors had to nag at indifferent officials about their failure to maintain walks, streets and roads. Public buildings were often allowed to become filthy from lack of care. No amount of oral fussing could accomplish the good of the printed word, which was sometimes effective in scaring the peculiarly apathetic official mind to the point that conditions were improved.

Not alone were sanitary affairs and the streets a constant cause of criticism, but likewise hitching racks, public shade trees and cemeteries. From the Civil War to the advent of the automobile, no problem ever roused more antagonism than hitching a team in a small

Southern town. Town officials erected indifferent hitching racks and then neglected them until they fell apart. Ordinances forbade farmers to hitch teams to fences, buildings and public monuments. Editors criticized careless drivers for leaving unhitched horses harnessed to vehicles containing children. Runaway scrapes were nearly as serious as automobile accidents.

By the same token cemeteries were neglected. Sacred village cows and unfettered hogs ranged at will over the graves of the fathers. Fences decayed, and honeysuckle grew in wild turbulent masses so that the tombs were lost in jungles of vines and briars. Hundreds of thousands of words were expended in the country press begging readers to show enough community pride and respect for the dead to keep the cemeteries clean and free of livestock.

Editors lectured their other readers just as they did public officials. Many of them commented often and unfavorably on the use of tobacco. It was not until after 1910 that a majority of publishers gave up crusading vigorously against the cigarette. They were forever condemning the cigarette smoker and citing occasional cases of horrible diseases in which both moral and physical fibers deteriorated because of the cigarette. One of these was "cigarette eye." The Newberry (South Carolina) *Herald and News* said in 1889 that Dr. McMartin would have to scrape the eyeballs of Henry P. Hatcher. His "disease is technically known as 'cigarette eye.' This case is a warning to all young men not to smoke the deadly cigarette." After 1910 cigarette advertising promised to return significant revenue, and anti-cigarette editorial observations became fewer in number.

Earlier editorial wrath was kindled against the citizen who chewed tobacco and spat where he pleased. As the editor of the Greensboro *Herald* said, "We wonder why it is some men can't do without its use while in company of ladies? It seems to us they could do without its use a few hours while at church or any public gathering as the stain does not look nice on the floor and walls of the house." An editor was caught in a rainstorm and forced to stop in a country church, where he observed the unbelievable desecration of the house of the Lord. Courthouses, hotels and sidewalks were as little respected, and even constant swinging of the editorial cudgel could scarcely maintain a semblance of decency.

Closely allied with public decency was the issue of public health. Since the introduction of serums and vaccines for the prevention of epidemic diseases, editors have prevailed on their readers to submit to vaccinations. In 1876 Dr. Luke P. Blackburn of Kentucky begged for "a white man's chance" to prove that pure cistern water would prevent the spread of cholera. In the yellow-fever epidemics editorials attempted to give the people the best possible advice about what they should do, and when finally state-health departments were organized country papers assisted materially in facilitating their work. This, however, was a long and arduous task in which local publishers often ran squarely into their readers' stolid folk resistance to new health ideas. Where local health boards attempted to clean up towns, editors did much to aid the campaigns. In later years various public and private agencies found country editors highly useful not only in seasonal community clean-up weeks, but in combating hookworm, tuberculosis and venereal diseases. In this respect editors usually proved themselves open-minded and willing, if not to take the lead, at least to give major assistance. It has nearly always been to their credit that their vision was not so obscured by ignorance and prejudice that they could not comprehend the promise of community improvement.

Other public matters came under editorial observation. The conduct of children remained in the realm of free and unrestricted criticism. It was the universal privilege of every American to set forth his views on how to raise children, and Southern editors exercised their inalienable rights. They were proficient in laying down rules for child guidance, and quick to criticize incidents of juvenile misconduct. Children loitering on the streets at night, carousing at parties, destroying property, scratching initials and bawdy verses on public buildings, stealing, talking and singing loudly or misbehaving in church were certain to bring down the editorial rod. The Americus (Georgia) *Tri-Weekly Republican* said, "Our streets [are] infested by a class of very small boys who use very indecent language and especially big cuss words. They smoke cigars, chew tobacco, drink whiskey, and play cards." Here, it was said, was a case where parents foolishly pampered children from birth and encouraged them to be no good.

Boys and irresponsible men were forever playing practical jokes which caused community troubles. Town watchmen were kept in constant panic over the antics of ill-trained youth. Occasionally some unthinking maniac exploded "booms" or large rolls of black powder in small towns, shattering windows and nerves. When one of these explosions occurred there was always fear that someone was blasting the bank vault. Boys tied cans to stray dogs. They awakened grouchy citizens and brought them to their doors in storms of anger. But worst of all was misconduct in public assemblies. G. H. Haight of the Fayetteville (North Carolina) *Observer* heard a boy whistling during a memorial ceremony. "We cannot tell," he wrote, "when we were more mortified," and he gave the boy's parents a stern lecture on public manners. For more than fifty years most editors believed that child training consisted of frequent applications of the hickory limb, and of allowing youngsters to be seen but seldom heard.

Adults, too, misbehaved and were called to task for their derelictions. Clandestine love affairs, whether actually discovered or merely suspected, were mercilessly flayed. Talking aloud in church prompted caustic observations with threats to publish names if offenses were repeated. Sometimes people who were not actively sinning were admonished for putting temptation in the way of their neighbors. For instance the editors had a good deal to say about the way ladies dressed. In 1901 Will C. Hight of the Winston County (Mississippi) *Journal* lectured the ladies of his cotton town of Louisville for deflecting the preacher's attention by their dress. "Ladies should take off their hats in church," he thought. "No preacher can inspire a man who is looking into a lob-sided aggregation of dead birds, stuffed weasels, chameleon skins, ribbons, beads, jets, sticks, straw flowers, corn tassels, and thistledown. It makes a sinner feel lost in the wilderness." Conduct in church was much on the editorial mind. In the 1880's an exchange contained the plea not to block pews. "Having entered a pew move along. Do not block up the end as if you did not intend to have anyone else enter it, or as if you were holding it for special friends. Do not rise to let others in, but move along and leave the pew invitingly open, so that they will know that they are welcome. If a pew holding six has five already in it, do not file out in formal procession to let one poor scared woman go to the farthest end next to the aisle. It is not necessary now for a man to sit at the end ready to rush out and kill Indians as possibly it was once."

It was never difficult for an editor to serve his community as a scold, but writing constructive editorials was more exacting. To be really constructive he had to know what was happening about him and in the bigger world without. This necessitated wide reading and sound meditation. He must also possess some analytical capacity.

Those who published the better papers often wrote extensive editorials in which they appraised political and moral issues, passed judgment on public personalities, criticized the course of government and pointed the way to happier local economic adjustments. During the periods when state legislatures were in session, editorial comment flowed freely. Seldom did a legislature please a considerable body of the country press. Any pronounced respect for, or confidence in, legislatures was lacking, despite the fact that they were political havens for many editors. Opinion prevailed that legislators were necessary evils who were often the tools of special interests. Governors were regarded in much the same light. Most of them at one time or another in their terms were bitterly attacked by large segments of the press. They have been charged with building up corrupt political machines, abusing pardoning powers, becoming demagogues, with being extravagant, stupid and unfaithful to campaign pledges.

Long editorials were by no means the rule. Some editors lacked time and ability to write them. Others believed a short epigrammatic treatment of an idea was the most effective way to bring it home to readers. Besides, if a man composed his editorials directly in type, without first writing them out, he found short, disjointed pieces easier to manage. Even many editors who could have turned out weekly essays turned to paragraphing.

Characteristic of this sort of editorializing were the paragraphs of W. H. Lawrence, editor of the Livingston (Alabama) *Our Southern Home.* He thought "nothing makes dress goods go up quicker than a mouse"; that "a woman's favorite glass is a looking glass, while most men prefer a beer glass"; and "a bolt of lightning recently struck a Negro in the head and didn't kill him. What it did to the lightning the paper didn't state." Putting in a good word for himself, editor Lawrence said, "There are two things in life which will make a man happy if he will only attend to them, one is to marry for love, and the other is to subscribe for this paper."

Editors made much of the commonplace. D. M. Wisdom of the Jackson (Tennessee) *Whig and Tribune* said he was fond of whistling. But whistling in the street by tireless amateurs was too much for him, and he sought assistance of the law to allay the discordant hubbub.

When Colonel W. C. P. Breckinridge of Lexington, Kentucky, became enmeshed in the famous Pollard case, editors throughout the

South exhibited a strong moral antipathy toward him. They argued that because of his alleged sex habits he was lowering the standards of Southern society. The cryptic judgment of the Macon (Mississippi) *Beacon,* "that it was hard to tell which was most to be condemned for his conduct, Colonel Billy Breckinridge, or his defense counsel, Colonel Phil Thompson," was expressive of the general press attitude. On the other hand, the editor of the Waycross (Georgia) *Herald* was of the opinion that the Kansas City man who married a forty-year-old woman thinking she was twenty-eight, and that a woman who had been married twice was a virgin did not need aid from the court. "A man fooled that easy," said the *Herald,* "does not need a divorce—what he needs is a guardian."

Many editors did their editorializing in their news stories, and they had little enthusiasm left for the more formal responsibilities of the editorial page. They strolled through the streets, talked with people, lingered a moment in the courthouse and talked with loafers in their own offices. Occasionally they took notes, but much of the time they set down from memory the facts they had learned. Few country reporters used sufficient care in checking their reports. Generally they knew everybody in the county or knew their connections and could guess the reasonableness of what they heard by the predictability of the individuals involved. Occasionally this was not true. Lycurgus Barrett of the Hartford (Kentucky) *Herald* heard a weird story on the street that a prominent doctor had committed murder, robbery and arson by squirting chloroform through a keyhole and anesthetizing a whole family. He published this preposterous yarn, and for the next year he had to submit to bitter abuse while he tried to correct his blunder.

Editors had to be careful not to be exploited by one side or another in malicious neighborhood quarrels. Nearly all of them had experience with spite news which was intended to even scores with enemies.

That editors got enough news in small, drowsy towns to bring out a paper regularly through many weeks is a matter of wonderment. There were anxious moments when it seemed that nothing would happen. T. Larry Gantt of the Oglethorpe (Georgia) *Echo* said that in one news famine he even watched a Negro curry a mule and hoped to see him kicked into "Kingdom come." Nothing happened. Nobody had a brawl. Every driver carefully hitched his horse and there were no runaways. No one was blown up while lighting a lamp; dogs refused to fight; there were no fires; gins failed to catch a man and mangle him. So he wrote, "Never within our journalistic experience, have we known local news to be so scarce. Everyone seems to be busily employed attending to his own business, and hence the drouth in this necessary essential to a live newspaper." The Abbeville (South Carolina) *Press and Banner* said Wednesday (August 3, 1871) was a day to gladden a reporter's heart: "a fire in the morning—a runaway scrape in the afternoon, a sleepy mule hitched to a Negro's buggy got frightened at a flapping parasol, caught by town marshall—a great day!"

Few country newspaper men used the techniques which are romantically attributed to the daily news room. There was never a breakneck rush to meet a press deadline. Press time was set for a day and not the split second of an hour. Editors regarded press day as a busy one, but their concern was the same as a conscientious housewife's for washday. Usually the papers were distributed so they would reach subscribers not later than Saturday, but sometimes they were held over until the next week. It was not an unheard of thing in the earlier days of postwar publishing for some editors to take a vacation and miss an issue or two.

Such was the case with the Springplace (Georgia) *Jimplicute.* On July 14, 1894, this paper was back in circulation after its subscribers had believed it dead. The editor explained, "The *Jimp* has never been dead, as some have supposed, we only took a month's rest through July mainly on account of financial depression around our sanctum."

Sometimes paper shipments were delayed and it was necessary to miss an issue, or occasionally there was so much material that much of it was carried over a week. It was not a matter of timeliness so much as it was satisfying subscribers by putting their local news into print.

Editors generally worked with small staffs. They ranged from one man to a crew of half a dozen. Tramp printers were both numerous and unpredictable. They appeared from nowhere and disappeared when they felt like it. There was a tacit understanding that every publisher would give them either work or a small sum of money. They expected to have the shops left open for them to sleep in at night. Sometimes these "birds of flight" remained only long enough to get out an issue of the paper, and sometimes they stayed for several months. Oscar Howard, a famous transient, remained in the office of the Franklin (Kentucky) *Patriot* long enough to become the lion of the village. He was engaged to marry a prominent girl. On his wedding day another printer appeared, and the two went off to celebrate. They got drunk and drifted away in a boxcar. The aroma of liquor always hung about the type cases. Many a dusty, dry editorial was set by printers whose minds drifted away pleasantly to the bottle hidden in a pile of waste paper in the shop corner. Usually tramp printers were efficient. Oscar Howard, it was said, could set up the Franklin *Patriot* in a day.

Besides the typesetter there were the devil, the pressman and the inevitable handyman. It is ironical that the army of brawny Negroes who pulled the levers of old hand presses or turned the cranks on cylinder presses, folded papers and made each issue possible were illiterate almost to a man. Devils learned the art as well as the bad habits of the tramp printers. They were general apprentices, expected to master both the mechanical and editorial sides of publishing, and were often sons following in their fathers' footsteps. Thus before schools of journalism were dreamed of, country shops were schooling their own people. Many editors now publishing Southern weeklies came up through an apprenticeship in their own shops.

The shops themselves were interesting places. In the brief inventory given at the beginning of this chapter there is missing a mention of furniture. Sometimes there were roll-top desks piled high with exchange papers, local reporters' correspondence and unpaid bills. More often there was simply a crude pine table which groaned under its load of newspapers, with just barely enough cleared space on one corner to put a half sheet of note paper. Along the walls stood at least one ramshackle cast-off cabinet crammed with odd books, pieces of equipment and dog-eared files. There was the inevitable stool, which symbolized the ivory tower from which the editor viewed the world. Papers were stacked everywhere, and every pigeonhole and crack bulged with files. Walls were lined with handbills, calendars, maps; and file hooks gave way under their burdens of notes and bills. There was a stove, and always a filthy wash pan and slick, greasy towel. To all this confusion was added the rather pleasing smell of printer's ink.

Just as the country store was a favorite loafing place, the country newspaper office was a gathering place for villagers. The editor of the Marietta (Georgia) *Journal* listed ten plagues of the newspaper office, which were loafing bores, poets, cranks, rats, cockroaches, typographical errors, exchange files, book canvassers, delinquent subscribers and the man who knows better than the editor how to run the paper.

Among the plagues perhaps the greatest were the poets. They blossomed at all seasons of the year. Spring, summer, fall and winter, the muse was active. There were poets of incurable love and of perpetual sorrow. A few sentimental souls turned to the classics for inspiration, while others preferred the more romantic periods of chivalry. Lycurgus Barrett of the Hartford *Herald* found that he had lost the manuscript of an original poem entitled "The Tattooed Knight." "The verses," he said, "abounded in pointed satire and overwhelming humor, were exceedingly Hudibrastic in spirit." The Dickson County (Tennessee) *Press* spurred the poets on to the fray in a long editorial on the spirit of spring by saying that this was the season for the local Shakespeares to sound their lutes. "Write only on one side of your paper, send the manuscript to us at once, by special messenger, as the mails are too untrustworthy to entrust such a document with, and upon receipt of it we'll—chuck it into the waste basket." W. P. Walton of the *Interior Journal* dealt literature in Lincoln County, Kentucky, an irretrievable blow. In his schedule of advertising rates he served notice that a charge of one dollar per word, payable in gold before the poem was written, would be made for poetry.

Another of the Marietta *Journal's* plagues taxed the patience of all editors. This was the delinquent subscriber. Subscription rates ranged from one to three dollars per year and circulation varied from 300 to 1,000 with an average of approximately 500 subscribers before 1900 and nearly 1,000 after that date. Often subscriptions made up the smallest part of a paper's earnings but sometimes they provided the margin between profit and bankruptcy. Patrons were indifferent about paying the editor and cash was difficult to collect. Always the local publisher appeared hard pressed for money and he used much of his own advertising space to scold delinquents. He begged for fire and stovewood, meat, potatoes, grain or anything else which could be sold or eaten. Often a subscriber paid over produce worth far more than the subscription price of the paper.

Publishing a weekly was never a lucrative profession. An editor could usually get a respectable living but little cash. It was said that when somebody tried to rob editor Willingham of the Georgia *Free Press* in 1881 he was much flattered by the compliment. The Marietta *Journal* thought "the fellow was evidently a stranger, or he would have never attempted to rob a newspaper man. We have heard of people robbing graves, but he who would attempt to rob a Georgia editor at once establishes his claim to a front room in the new insane asylum no matter where it is built."

The poor income placed a severe economic strain upon Southern publishers. Most of them seem to have been family men, and their broods demanded a reasonable amount of support. This situation forced many into other businesses as sidelines, or into politics. Constantly editors were serving in legislatures and in county and city offices. In fact, it was possible to go from the country-paper office to the governor's chair, as did W. D. Jelks of Alabama, James K. Vardaman of Mississippi, James Stephen Hogg of Texas, Robert Taylor of Tennessee, and Keen Johnson of Kentucky. Editors served in many other positions in state and federal governments. Josephus Daniels, who began his editorial career on the Wilson (North Carolina) *Advance*, became Chief of the Appointments Division and Chief Clerk in Hoke Smith's administration as Secretary of the Interior. Later he was Secretary of the Navy and Ambassador to Mexico. Urey Woodson went from the editorship of the Owensboro (Kentucky) *Messenger* to the secretaryship of the Democratic National Committee, and was for one term Alien Property Custodian. S. A. Jonas of the Aberdeen (Mississippi) *Examiner* was secretary to L. Q. C. Lamar when the latter was Secretary of the Interior. In nearly every state and national political convention there was a good sprinkling of country editors. They served as publicity chairmen for campaigns and were rewarded with political hand-outs.

Country editors often acted as reporters for city dailies and some of them became syndicated columnists. George Bingham of Mayfield, Kentucky, distinguished the profession of country reporting with his distinctly rural "Dog Hill Paragraphs," which burlesqued crossroads reports to country papers. Carey Williams, present editor of the Greensboro (Georgia) *Herald-Journal* contributes pungent fillers to daily papers patterned after the succinct paragraphs which have appeared in his paper for more than eighty years. Scores of editors and apprentices went on to higher rewards with metropolitan papers.

Notable among this group were Adolph Ochs, with his early Knoxville (Tennessee) *Chronicle* background, and one of his modern successors, Turner Catledge, who began his successful newspaper career on the Neshoba (Mississippi) *Democrat* and worked up through a series of weekly offices to be a reporter for the Memphis *Commercial-Appeal* and then Washington correspondent for the New York *Times*.

Editing a country paper was both a desirable profession and an excellent springboard into other callings. Lawyers, teachers and sometimes preachers found editing a paper a good side line. In this respect Brick Pomeroy was wise when he said, "Some think because they can describe a foot race, a funeral or a fire makes them an editor. The real ones come from colleges, caucus rooms, long apprentices in business."

Southern editors could take much pride in their accomplishments. Many of them speeded up industrialization in their communities. They fought for improved farming conditions, better roads and schools and a happier way of life. They passionately advocated the building of railroads and were down to welcome the first trains with genuine happiness. They recorded a vivid story of counties growing out of the woods and muddy-road isolation. Their papers were unofficial invitations to immigrants to move in and make themselves at home. They communicated the views of local constituencies to public officials and offered personal criticism with genuine courage. Constantly they warred with inefficient employees of the postal system before the advent of the rural free delivery—which they accepted as an interesting experiment. As the Schley County (Georgia) *News* said in 1898, "If the balance in the treasury is large enough each year let us have free delivery—but if it will require additional taxation in any form, let the scheme die in its infancy."

In every other field of human endeavor the country editor was an influence. He was rightfully accused at times of operating a free press for the benefit of the syndicates and their medicine company patrons, but this is another story, to be told in its place. Usually he was free of every kind of pressure except that of neighborliness.

Chapter 3

News from Chicago

SOUTHERN editors constantly urged their farmer readers to grow their own food. Whether or not they appreciated the evil of a one-crop agriculture, they felt it was a weakness for the South to be dependent on other regions for its basic foodstuffs. Yet the very papers in which they wrote their appeals for agricultural self-sufficiency were usually partially manufactured elsewhere and had to be imported. Probably many editors did not realize that they were no more independent than the farmers. Pushed financially in hard times and lured by a saving of labor, the publishers slipped easily into "foreign" servitude and thought of it only as good business on their part.

In the days before the linotype the biggest job in getting out a newspaper was setting by hand all the type needed to fill even four pages. And newsprint paper cost money. If a publisher could find an easy way to eliminate half the labor of typesetting, who could blame him for jumping at it? "Ready-print" or "boiler plate" would do it for him. In addition, if he used ready-print he could get his paper so cheaply that it was virtually free. But either one made him dependent on syndicates in Chicago or in the East.

Ready-print originated during the Civil War. While printers were away hurling lead at their enemies, ingenious Northern country editors searched for a means by which they could produce papers with limited shop forces. Ansel Nash Kellogg of the Baraboo (Wisconsin) *Republic* secured the co-operation of Horace E. Rublee and David Atwood, who supplied him with pages of their *Wisconsin State Journal* already printed so that he had only to add two pages of local news in order to produce his paper. This was in 1861. Four years later Kellogg was in Chicago publishing similar ready-print for a rapidly growing list of country weeklies. By 1890 ready-print services had become big business.

The syndicated services expanded rapidly after 1865, and it is certain that country papers could not have flourished so well without them. Perhaps many local journals never would have been organized had this facility not been available.

Ready-print sheets were available with either the two outside or the two inside pages printed by the newspaper union, and the other two pages left blank so that they could be used by a weekly for its local news, editorials and advertisements. The prepared material, by necessity, was "evergreen" and could be used any time and almost anywhere. It was as timely one month as another, like the Bible and Dickens' novels. If for some reason a bundle of papers was delayed a week in a freight office it could be used the next week just as well. Syndicate houses prepared this material undated and with no running head at the top of the page so that it was not only perpetually "in date" but also suitable for any location. The same sheets could be used by any number of papers without alteration.

Early ready-print compilers approached their tasks with scissors and paste pots. They clipped articles from daily newspapers and periodicals. Feature stories, useful hints, Biblical quotations, folksy observations, stale humor, sermons, agricultural and household hints, Sunday-School lessons, style notes and political matter were all crammed into the pages from Chicago. The compilers worked the whole field of human interest. So long as their material was undated and noncontroversial, they were free to skim the cream of American journalism and literature. It is a remarkable thing that even trained editors could turn out so much material for so many diversified localities without offending community prejudices or causing constant bickering with the weeklies they serviced or with the ultimate readers. The fact remains that they could—and did.

Before the advent of the linotype machine, ready-print had two advantages for most country editors. They were relieved of the almost impossible task of hand-setting four pages, to say nothing of gathering that much news. Home-set type was reduced from twenty-eight or thirty-six to fourteen or eighteen columns. On top of this, paper costs were reduced to an almost negligible factor.

Syndicates enjoyed a distinct advantage over individual newspapers in the field of advertising. Where most local publishers could guarantee only a few hundred subscribers, the newspaper unions, or syndicates, guaranteed from 500,000 to several millions. Consequently their advertising rates were high enough to justify their supplying sheets to weeklies at a nominal charge per quire of paper. There was a general understanding that ready-print material would carry no local advertising and would not compete with subscribing papers for the sale of space. Only products with a national market were advertised.

Ready-print proved to be a rich, cheap advertising medium for the medicine companies. Hundreds of nostrum sellers found the "patent insides" a godsend for the publicizing of their dubious products. Most syndicates refused to advertise tobacco and whisky in the days before the public accepted the cigarette, but they had little claim to virtue on this account. Proprietary medicines which they offered might well be more harmful than liquor or tobacco. Occasionally patent pages contained advertisements of pistols, often at the very time when local editors were crusading against them.

In its columns the syndicated page tended to bring the city advertiser, sharper or honest merchant, into closer communication with the countryman. Led by the Lydia E. Pinkham Medicine Company and W. L. Douglas, the shoeman, they offered every sort of article, as well as every sort of nostrum and gadget, to the rural subscriber. Pension and patent attorneys volunteered their services to veterans and inventors. Patent lamps, bicycles, air rifles, shotguns, garden seeds, tailored suits, books, electric belts, magazines, flower bulbs and scores of other items were listed for sale. Appeals were made to lonely Southerners, who felt insignificant and neglected because they received little or no mail, to send in their dimes and relieve their boredom by getting on sucker lists. Occasionally counterfeiters apparently picked up names in this way—at least stories appeared in many papers telling of local citizens who answered advertisements and were taken in by scoundrels.

Attracted by the profits of syndicated advertising, several competitors of the A. N. Kellogg Newspaper Company were in the field by 1880—among them the Chicago Newspaper Union, Sheffield and Stone, Kimball and Taylor, the Western Auxiliary Publishing House, Franklin Printing Company, the New York Newspaper Union, Cramer, Aiken and Cramer, the Southern Newspaper Union, the Publishers' Union of Atlanta and, after 1880, the Western Newspaper Union. Working furiously, these houses sought business all over the country, and their Southern branches helped to establish many new papers, a fact reflected annually in the revised listings of the several newspaper directories. It was rather easy for a prospective editor to secure a sufficient supply of type, an antiquated press and a bundle of ready-print pages and launch a weekly. The newspaper unions would supply the materials and equipment on reasonable credit terms. Ambitious editors founded little journals with brave promises but with the smell of the medicines they so abundantly advertised. The syndicates likewise stimulated the publication of spasmodic special-interest journals which lived through political and reform campaigns and then disappeared into well-merited oblivion.

Editing and distributing ready-print material was complicated. A large distributor like the A. N. Kellogg Newspaper Company of Chicago operated regional offices presided over by associate editors. Each editor had to be certain the material distributed in his region would not offend his readers in any way. The Southern editor faced a particularly tricky problem. His readers were of many sorts and it was next to impossible to find stories they would all find acceptable.

To begin with, in ready-print matter it was always necessary to maintain a gallant attitude toward women. Sex could not be mentioned suggestively. References to female underclothing were taboo. Vulgarity of any sort was prohibited, and so were profanity and rugged humor. On the positive side, the syndicate stories were definitely in favor of Christianity but in order to maintain strict neutrality, gave no recognition at all to denominationalism.

Politics presented one of the most complex issues of all for ready-print editors. They took great care not to let a bundle of Republican sheets go South. Those containing a Northern Democratic point of view were almost equally bad. Southern Democracy was sensitive and could be discussed best by those writers who had constant experience with the regional political system. Consequently ready-print stories were clipped from local dailies. Marse Henry Watterson and his *Courier-Journal* were constantly combed over, and so were the Atlanta *Constitution* and *Journal,* the Charlotte *Observer,* the Augusta *Chronicle,* the Arkansas *Gazette,* the New Orleans *Times Picayune,* the Nashville *Banner,* the Memphis *Commercial-Appeal* and other papers. It was safe to excerpt political matter from these papers because their news writers and editors were properly attuned to prevailing attitudes.

Although a great deal of care was given to editing syndicated political news, it is doubtful that much of this material actually influenced the Southern mind in any way. Southern politics fed on a greener and more nourishing diet.

By the 1890's the ready-print page had become much more versatile. It was made up in several forms. Local editors could send their own advertisements and professional cards and have them printed in the text. Columns were added in which the general weekly news of each state was summarized. This was perhaps one of the most popular features. Other columns summarized the "news of the world," but an analysis reveals that this world was little larger than the South itself. Much of the news was sensational and "unusual" in flavor. Criminal cases, murders, lynchings, hangings, calamities and scandals were recorded here. Announcement stories which outlined state-wide drives in public health, education and agriculture were given space. Frequently local editors preferred not to make unpopular announcements themselves and left them to the syndicates. This appears to have been the way many of them handled the hookworm campaign in 1910. Many editors were reluctant to face irate subscribers on this issue, and they permitted the "patent insides" to speak for them.

Newspaper unions, in their scramble for business, offered their clients the privilege of selecting from several styles of make-up. Pages were available with no advertising, or with much advertising and little text. Some formats carried state and local news, while others supplied a greater amount of purely feature material. In fact an editor could vary the form of his paper each week if he liked, so long as he made his wishes known early enough to permit changes in his headings.

After 1875 there was a second syndicated service called "boiler plate," which saved setting type in the offices of country papers. This new form of news matter was first offered for sale by the A. N. Kellogg Company. It was an invention of James J. Schock, who had assisted Kellogg in establishing his ready-print service. Boiler plate was prepared in column width on thin stereotype metal plates. The plates were drilled along the edge so as to permit their being mounted on "type-high" wooden blocks, or they had slots in the back which permitted their being fastened into the grooves of special patented bases. Boiler plate could be used anywhere in a paper, instead of handset type. It could be cut to any length to fill a gap. Since it was often interspersed with local matter and printed with it, it was not immediately recognizable as "foreign" syndicated stuff.

In the advertisements of the new service no reference was made to its content. It was quoted as containing so many running column inches of space-filler. It was understood, however, that the copy had come under the same strict editorial scrutiny as ready-print. No doubt many columns of ready-print were stereotyped into boiler-plate columns. Printers with space to fill did not worry much about the subject matter of the boiler plate they used to complete a column. It was not unusual for a desperate editor to cut a strip of plate the right length even if it left the last sentence incomplete and the point of the story unmade. Charges for the service were moderate. It cost only six to ten dollars to prepare the minimum.

Thus the mechanics of the stereotyped services was designed to enable shorthanded or green editors to publish their papers with a minimum amount of physical effort. Almost any publisher could find time to set a couple of pages of news and advertisements and he could use filler to complete a four-page sheet.

It is not easy to guess what appeal ready-print and boiler plate had for country readers. There was a marked difference between much of the "home-set" type and that of the patent pages. A reader needed little power of discrimination to distinguish between the two. Sometimes the textual contrast was comical. Ready-print editors gave the reader a wealth of knowledge on the lemur as a pet, or the nocturnal extravaganzas of the Edwards of England, or how the Queen of Belgium liked her breakfast, or how the natives of Tasmania regarded shoes, while the local publishers were offering columns of naïve reports from country correspondents.

Some patent features were widely read. Among these were the numerous religious columns, such as the International Sunday School Lessons and all the sermons of syndicate preachers. Appealing also were serial novels, the digests of state and regional news, and popular-science columns. Of the newspaper preachers perhaps none exceeded Dr. T. DeWitt Talmage in popularity. He was a clever writer who conveyed to readers of at least 3,500 ready-print papers some of the warmth of his sensational sermons delivered from his Philadelphia and Brooklyn pulpits.

On one occasion this famous minister created a stir among his country readers because in their eyes he appeared guilty of misrepresentation. He had told his followers of his approaching journey to the Holy Land, and said he would publish a sermon about each place he visited. He meant, of course, that he would prepare the material in advance and leave it with the editors. In one of the sermons he divulged this fact to the consternation of his literal-minded readers. They had envisioned the dramatic Dr. Talmage preaching before every sacred shrine he visited. Here was a holy swindle in which one of the most eloquent ministers in American church history had duped the people! Memory, however, was short, and before the ink of criticism dried on the ready-print pages, Dr. Talmage was again packing crowds into his famous Brooklyn Tabernacle, and Southern country readers generally continued to enjoy his sermons.

Among the many contributors and columnists who supplied material to the ready-print pages, J. L. and Kate Powers of Mississippi, and their modern successor Walker Wood, may be mentioned as successful state-news summarizers. Their columns brought readers up to date on what happened each week.

Henry W. Grady, Joel Chandler Harris and other Atlanta *Constitution* reporters and editorial writers became interested in the country syndicate field. Grady started his short-lived career as a columnist by writing of the idyllic Georgia rural life. He reminisced, as have all country columnists, about fresh milk in the springhouse, spareribs, the melancholy delights of fall and the full promise of spring. These nostalgic outpourings were completely out of line with his evangelizing for Southern industry, and his efforts to bring about pacification between the North and South. Harris enjoyed little more success than Grady in the syndicate field, despite the tremendous popularity of his stories.

It remained for their whimsical colleague Charles Henry Smith (Bill Arp) to capture the imagination of the South. He had grown up in a country store and had come to appreciate the peculiar interests of the rural mind. His later experiences as a lawyer only heightened his insight into the nature of his people. Like that other famous Georgia humorist-lawyer, A. B. Longstreet, Smith made himself a popular figure by being a literary man of the people. His career as a columnist began during the Civil War as a letter writer to the Rome (Georgia) *Southern Confederacy*. After the war ended, Bill Arp's occasional letters appeared in Georgia papers, and for twenty-five years before his death in 1903 he was a regular correspondent to the Atlanta *Constitution*. His writings were purchased by the Western Newspaper Union and distributed to country papers all over the South.

These letters usually fitted into a column or a column and a half, and dealt with almost every folksy or social subject which was a part of the Southern way of life.

Too long this significant figure in country journalism has been neglected in the history of Southern thought. Bill Arp, like many syndicated writers, spoke for large numbers of inarticulate people. He expressed a devotion to home and family. He loved the changing seasons of the year. He held a typical Southerner's views on religion, education, racial confusion and politics. Sometimes he wrote whimsical dialect, but perhaps his most effective columns were those in which he used colloquial English to express positive opinions. He spoke in ardent defense of the impoverished South. Arp revered the Democratic Party and often attacked Republicans with venomous tirades which caused them to appear as gory monsters. His observations on Teddy Roosevelt's racial attitudes were sharp and pointed.

Editors often read his columns before making up their minds on public issues. If the "Sage of Bartow," as they called him, was "agin hit," they were too. A subscriber of the Livingston (Alabama) *Our Southern Home* wrote: "I always read the general news and Bill Arp's letter on the inside of the *Home*. The Bill Arp letters alone will be worth much more than a year's subscription."

He expressed opinions on all sorts of subjects. Negro education took up much space in his letters. He always voiced the traditional Southern view of it. He believed that good Negroes learned from their masters, that the sorry ones were not worth teaching and that Booker T. Washington's efforts at Tuskegee would result in a colored aristocracy which would enslave the rest of the race.

The Georgia columnist discussed Southern textbooks and schools. He recalled with contagious nostalgia the days when his old teacher John Norton was whaling an education into him through his posterior parts. Modern schoolbooks, he said, were too expensive. It cost at least four dollars a grade to equip a child, and this was excessive in the hard years at the beginning of this century. The old sage read and criticized new textbooks. He favored those which were friendly to the cause of the South and was antagonistic to all others.

It was impossible for Bill Arp to keep away from the animosities of the war. He paid high tribute to Laura Talbert Gault who refused to sing "Marching through Georgia" when told to do so in the Louisville Girls High School. He thought that Louisville should forego the privilege of calling itself a Southern city unless it mended its ways and suggested that the children sing Joe Brown's version of the Yankee song with the refrain, "As We Went Thieving through Georgia."

Numerous letters of his were concerned with the Southern veterans. To a certain extent Bill Arp offered a sounding board for Confederate affairs. He encouraged the old soldiers to keep their organizations alive, to attend their reunions and to preserve Southern traditions. When the United Daughters of the Confederacy was organized he gave it abundant counsel as to what its objectives should be. Every organization interested in the past had his blessing, for his primary interest was Southern history, and he wanted its sources to be collected and used in writing the story of the region. After Judge Walter Clark's five-volume history of North Carolina was published Arp praised it on several occasions. He offered it to the other Southern states as a model.

For the ready-print editors, Bill Arp was a gold mine. His letters took up considerable space for them, were highly readable and thoroughly acceptable. They did not need to fear that an unfortunate sentence would cause a cancellation of subscriptions. They had no cause to worry lest a sentence with a hidden meaning would get them into hot water. Arp knew all the words and tunes of Southern prejudices and understood the limited framework of Southern popular thought. His writing was especially welcome to the newspaper syndicates servicing Southern weeklies because of its unmistakably native quality. Among dozens of imported articles his letters were straight from home.

There was only one Bill Arp. Usually ready-print editors had to go far afield for copy with which to fill their pages—sometimes very far indeed. For instance, it was fascinating that George Bancroft, the historian, loved roses! A vast majority of country readers had no idea who George Bancroft was, but it no doubt satisfied them to know that somewhere in this country there was a historian who loved something—even roses. Nearly a full column explained that the famous scholar had a passion for facts, and as he was putting the finishing touches on his monumental history of the United States he sat in a room fragrant with roses. "They are my children," he said, "the companions of my leisure hours."

Scores of stories were written on how common commodities were manufactured—needles, matches, paper money, stamps and what not.

Readers learned how the candy-striped barber pole came into use. A good deal of interesting information was sometimes given in a painless form. Other educational articles came under the heading of ephemera. For instance, it was hardly of great moment to an Alabama cotton farmer that keeping elephants was expensive! He was told in 1888 that it cost $17,197.40 to keep eight elephants for a year. Perhaps this served to make the upkeep of a cotton mule seem rather inconsequential. He was also informed that it was dangerous to fool with bear cubs; there was grave possibility that they would grow into unappreciative bears. If Southern subscribers had any thought of going into the North Woods in search of bull moose they were prepared for the venture by a feature story which told how to tempt the animals within gunshot.

Intimate accounts of authors, poets and musicians were published. There were sketches of Dan Emmett and "Dixie." Mark Twain and his writings were favorite topics. Augusta Evans Wilson, Thomas Dixon, James Lane Allen, Mary N. Murfree, George W. Cable, Thomas Nelson Page and all the other popular writers were subjects of feature stories. Southern folk stories and songs were discussed. Popular stories from Longstreet's *Georgia Scenes,* T. B. Thorpe's *The Hive of the Bee Hunter* and Johnson J. Hooper's *Adventures of Simon Suggs* appeared with some degree of regularity, and numerous versions of the "Arkansas Traveler" were published.

Following the Horatio Alger pattern, countless stories were told of poor boys marrying rich women, and of poor girls marrying their wealthy bosses. An American trick bicycle rider in Paris captivated a wealthy French heiress, and when he accidentally fell from a tight wire he landed in the arms of a wife and $300,000. If the modern reader knew no American economic history he would reach the conclusion from reading ready-print from 1865 to 1910 that all a boy had to do to rise in the world was to have a streak of luck in which he either married a fortune or dug up buried treasure in his backyard. The deserving boy got ahead, but the means of his success were not so easily predictable.

Always there was a humorous side to the ready-print page. The drabness of its commercialization was relieved by the modest humor of some of its stories. There was the account of a frantic throng of summer visitors at Cornwall, New York, who hurried aboard a Hudson River steamer. They had gone to a resort hotel. A baker there had prepared a pan of dough and put it aside to rise. A drowsy kitten crawled onto the warm mixture and stretched out to take a nap. The rising bread engulfed it and left no trace of its presence in the pan. The kitten was baked, and the bread was delivered whole to the table. This was more than delicate stomachs could stand and the guests fled the scene.

Kentucky has always loved rugged humor of a harmless sort. A greenhorn Virginian, traveling by train across an isolated section of the Bluegrass State in 1875, dropped off to sleep. When the conductor called out "Chicago!" and waked him and he saw before him a dirty, weather-beaten cluster of country village hovels, he exclaimed, "Great God! that shows what fire can do to a place!"

Equally addled was the Kentuckian who bought a drink of cider which contained a yellow jacket. When he swallowed the insect it stung him all the way down. He immediately bought the barrel of cider, saying that it had as much "snap" in it and was just as warming as fifty-cent whisky and 20 per cent cheaper.

A drummer said to a Kentuckian that the bicycle had brought the horse age to a close. The native son demurred. He admitted a bicycle was easier and cheaper to keep but held it was not nearly so dependable as a horse. When a man went to town on Saturday night and got tanked up, a horse would always take him back to the arms of his family, "but the bicycle ain't made that can do it, and I'm a man that goes to town on Saturdays."

There were columns of "humorous" stories on getting haircuts and nothing else in barber shops. Merriment was stirred over barbers who insisted that customers accept every service offered, including a generous amount of personal advice and community gossip. Just as funny, according to the ready-print standards, was the never-ending riddle of what relation a man would be to himself and his relatives if he married the daughter of his son's wife and both couples had children. There was almost no end to the involvements into which a clever ready-print editor could lead this miserable nonsense if he were short of satisfactory material.

Syndicate humor, labeled as such, might take the form of "middleman" dialogue. It was dreary stuff measured by the tastes of any period. A sample:

"George: 'So Rogers went fishing yesterday? I suppose he brought home a large string.'

"Charlie: 'No! Merely a big yarn.' "

Another:

" 'Was the count embarrassed when he proposed?'

" 'I believe he was—financially,' replied the millionaire's daughter."

Again:

"Mrs. Sharpe: 'They call the bell boy in the hotel "Buttons," I believe?'

"Mr. Sharpe: 'Because he is always off when you need him most!' "

Somewhere there must have been a senile jokesmith who thought up thousands of columns of this kind of trash. Occasionally moth-eaten cartoons accompanied many of these so-called jokes and were supposed to give added keenness.

Another type of whimsical filler appearing in ready-print material was the single-line philosophical observation. "A mule always has a kick coming." "A joke that requires an explanation is no joke." "Dress does not make the woman but it often breaks the husband." "Crabs and misers hate to shell out." "Silence may be golden, but the golden eagle talks." Syndicate editors were only tearing a page from the book of country publishers who took great pride in their numerous droplets of wisdom.

In a more serious vein the ready-print services undertook to bring instruction to their readers. They told about how people lived in other lands. This was an almost inexhaustible subject. The mode of life of the Laplanders must have been fascinating to many Southerners. They had never heard of Lapland and must have wondered why anyone would try to live in such a cold climate. All the peoples of the world were put on brief display. The Western Newspaper Union editors were among the first to sell the nation the one-world idea, though it must be admitted they emphasized the restless wanderings of mankind since the day of Cain and Abel.

As years passed, more attention was given to improved methods of agriculture. Just as ready-print editors knew little about local politics, so too they were at a disadvantage in understanding highly regionalized farming methods. They tried to demonstrate better methods of farming by illustrating mechanical short cuts and improved devices. They gave general methods of processing products, and of caring for livestock. Occasionally they discussed such revolutionary ideas as conservation of soil and timber. They undertook to apprise rural readers of the fact that national resources were rapidly being consumed by an increasing population. In a vague way they gave Southerners comparative glimpses of how other farmers lived, and of the success they were having with improved methods. They published pictures and stories of new types of farm implements, and of their practical use. Most of this copy came from experiment stations and from reports of the United States Department of Agriculture.

Other accounts illustrated the struggle of the nation to fulfill its dream of manifest destiny. Stories told of life in the Far West, of the expansion of rail lines, of the hardships of pioneering beyond the ninety-eighth meridian, of incidents of Indian fighting and of travel. Yarns were printed of trains which puffed their way through buffalo herds, of trains caught amid cattle stampedes.

One train was said to have been surrounded by 3,000 stampeding Texas steers being driven up the trail to Wyoming. The engineer ran his engine forward until he was unable to advance, and then he rushed backward grinding his bawling besiegers under the wheels. As the passengers were rushed back and forth through the maddened herd, they got out their pistols and had a thrilling time shooting the steers.

Other yarns portrayed life in the gold and silver camps, or travel across the deserts. Histories of the new Western states were printed as they were admitted to the Union. In later years old-timers would reminisce about the gold days when the West was young. Bad men loved to tell the public just how bad they had been, and stories of robbers and bandits, such as the James boys and Rube Burrows, who shuttled back and forth between the South and West never grew stale.

At Tombstone, Arizona, in the days when a ten-dollar bill would attract robbers, an imaginative courier boarded a train with a box labeled "rattlesnakes." When he reached his destination he deposited in a bank $80,000 worth of the green and yellow reptiles in the form of ten-dollar bills.

Patent pages were in many respects more accurate than the newspapers themselves in reflecting the changes of the larger national picture. By the late nineties they revealed the spirit of imperialism and expansion which was stirring America. Full pages of profusely illustrated stories gave accounts of the horrors of Cuban concentration camps. They told of European life as well as what was happening at home. The "big events" in American contemporary history were always publicized.

Much publicity was given to political events. Short and graphic biographies were written of the Presidents as they succeeded to office. An enormous amount of space was devoted to the assassinations of Garfield and McKinley. Life stories of Democratic presidential and vice-presidential candidates were published. The only knowledge isolated Southerners ever gained of their national officers as human beings might be through these articles. Not only were there notes on the careers of the various officers, but often there were accounts of their home lives and photographs of their families.

In the twentieth century more papers began to publish all their pages at home, and the syndicates had to offer new types of service. They provided Sunday School lessons, Washington columns, letters from New York and dozens of features giving advice on style, manners, morals and health. They even developed a weekly cartoon service.

With the changing times of this century the local paper's relations with the syndicates were soon governed by the attitude of the press associations. Soon after 1900 there was a distinct feeling that the Southern publishers were being exploited by the newspaper unions. Southern towns were expanding their populations, and local merchants were becoming more aware of the value of advertising. After 1915 the linotype machine came into common use and speeded up home composition. The tedious labor of publishing papers was much reduced. As "patent insides" were discussed less and less favorably in the annual press conventions, syndicate printing came to be regarded as the mark of either an old-fashioned editor or an indifferent and unimaginative one.

When the editor of the Pascagoula *Democrat-Star* criticized Mississippi editors for using patent insides, the editor of the West Point *Gazette* took him to task. In answer to the question whether a man had the right to run his paper as he pleased, the Pascagoula publisher said, "Yes, sir. But no newspaper which has half of the editing done in Yankeedom can lay any claim to legitimate journalism; it cannot win the full respect and esteem of its home people; it cannot consistently urge the patronage of a 'home institution' and honestly boast of 'being here to stay.'" He maintained that the surest sign that a newspaper is a stable institution is its ability to print all its material on its own press. When editors used patent sheets with advertising they surrendered 50 per cent of their space to outside publishers. In some instances press associations threatened to boycott publishers who were thwarting the local publishing business in clinging to patent insides and to refuse to allow them to excerpt clippings from other papers.

Eventually the business of supplying ready-print pages in the South dwindled. It is still a modest business, and especially during the last World War a number of editors used its service again to make up for the scarcity of linotype operators and compositors. But the old-style ready-print is on its way out.

Whatever the sins of the syndicates might have been, their material was well edited, and within a narrow framework of operation they gave their readers a fairly general but usually static news coverage. The patent pages were well printed and reasonably well illustrated. They brought into empty rural lives reading material which could never have reached them otherwise. Many Southerners learned to read novels in the syndicate pages. When pious mothers and fathers objected to their sons and daughters' reading novels in book form, they may not have realized that the banned literature was in the weekly newspaper.

The syndicates sinned unforgivably by permitting the proprietary medicine companies to prostitute their advertising columns with repulsive and fallacious claims. On the credit side, many Southern towns and counties enjoyed the benefits of a local press only because of the availability of ready-print and boiler plate.

Chapter 4

Go Tell Aunt Lydia

Two faces beamed benevolently at millions of American country newspaper readers. In fact, it is possible that these portraits were printed more often than any others in the country's history. They were Lydia Estes Pinkham and W. L. Douglas, the famous three and four-dollar shoeman. Lydia Pinkham became a famous woman, so famous in fact that a respectable amount of space is given to her in the august *Dictionary of American Biography.* She might easily be called a matron of panic. She was born in 1819 when the nation was feeling the pangs of postwar deflation, the daughter of a Quaker family. As a young woman she taught school and then married Isaac Pinkham, a builder and operator, in 1843. As Mrs. Pinkham, she compounded tonics from herbs which she found about her home in Lynn, Massachusetts, and gave them to neighboring women to relieve them of suffering from lacerations and weak backs. She had come to recognize the fact that the milestones in feminine health and life are filled with horrors, and she was interested in bridging the chasm from youth to womanhood, and from womanhood to the more matronly phases of life.

Mrs. Pinkham began a most successful career. Isaac Pinkham's real-estate business felt the pinch of 1873, and three years later the family was financially stranded. Mother Lydia was an ingenious soul, and in that strenuous period of 1875 she recalled her herb pot and suffering womanhood. This time it was to be for a modest price that she ministered to her ailing sisters. A job printer was hired to prepare labels, and her enterprising son Daniel went away to Boston, New York and Brooklyn to apprise the debilitated females in those places of the modern miracle of Lynn. In 1877 Daniel proved himself a master entrepreneur. The Lydia E. Pinkham Medicine Company began its long career of newspaper advertising. Its founder, however, did not live to see the business a success. She died in 1883, and her famous formula passed on to her sons to yield them snug fortunes.

The benevolent countenance of the saintly woman of Lynn smiled with gentle and motherly benignity at every female approaching puberty and promised to remove successfully the galling sting of womanhood's badge of original sin. In short, there were few female ailments from the cradle to the grave which this benevolent mistress of the herb pot could not cure. Her countenance was an epitome of American maternal love, and her advertising line was a famous chapter of American economic freebooting. She could easily have passed for the nation's mother of 1882, or as a crusading reformer seeking a second chance for wayward girls and motherless boys. Scarcely a country newspaper in the South was without her picture and her message. The year she died it was estimated that her portrait adorned the advertising columns of 6,000 journals.

Publishers wondered in the long hours when they were setting type by hand if there was such a person as Lydia Pinkham. The editor of the Burlington (Vermont) *Free Press* took it on himself to check this for the 5,999 other papers which bore her angelic countenance. In Lynn he found her at 225 Western Avenue in a bright and pleasant home. She appeared a trifle thinner than her portrait but just as sympathetic with her simple and trusting clientele. Pointedly she told the Vermont publisher that she spent her time answering letters from women who sought advice. She felt it her duty to mother every female with a pain, and she was happiest when immersed in the great care and labor of her mail. She answered on an average one hundred letters a day and kept two secretaries busy taking dictation.

So the fabulous Lydia E. Pinkham was described to the country press everywhere. In later years when the United States Congress became interested in the truth of medicinal advertising, the Lydia E. Pinkham Company must have become somewhat conscience-stricken. From time to time since 1883 it had published intimate notes about the personal activities of its patron saint. She had been pictured as a scholarly woman searching steadily into the diseases of the female organs. Once an enthusiastic copy writer boasted that she had had more training in the treatment of women's diseases than any doctor in the world.

The company was subtle in advertising its compound. After her death in 1883 the weekly spreads were made to read in such a way as to leave the impression that Lydia E. Pinkham still lived. In 1905, however, this misrepresentation was brought to light in Samuel Hopkins Adams' articles in *Collier's Weekly* exposing "The Great American Fraud." Quickly the country papers carried an advertisement which gave a partial biographical sketch of the founder. It was indirectly admitted that Mrs. Pinkham's daughter-in-law had worked with her and had taken over the task of answering the intimate letters which poured into the company offices. For twenty-five years young Mrs. Pinkham had written to women who doubtless believed they were communicating directly with Mother Lydia whose portrait had appeared with regularity above the admonition to address their pleas to her!

Lydia E. Pinkham's company was the most consistent of the hundreds of medicine companies that advertised in the country papers. It had contracts with ready-print distributors, and few if any issues appeared without the conventional advertisement displayed in a prominent place. Just as it was one of the most consistent advertisers after 1877, it was likewise one of the most appealing to suffering womanhood in its extravagant materials. Appealing to women who were denied medical care, it promised them impossible relief from their suffering.

The nostrum, it was claimed, "revives the drooping spirits, invigorates and harmonizes the organic functions; gives elasticity and firmness to the step, restores the natural lustre of the eye, and plants on the pale cheek the beauty of fresh roses of life's spring and early summertime." This just about covered the range of desires for a vast majority of women. If a fair dose of Lydia Pinkham's Compound, which was said to contain 20 per cent alcohol in 1905, could do it, was not that all right? Who could object to befuddled womenfolk taking a mild toddy, with some herbs for good measure? At least the public was spared the ordeal of having senators and congressmen recommend it from personal use.

There was more to the Pinkham story than bloom on the cheek and luster in the eye. To worrying females it promised children by rearranging their reproductive organs. Letters told of women in Iowa and South Dakota who had overcome the humiliation of barrenness. A Mrs. E. F. Hayes of Boston testified that Lydia Pinkham's Compound had cured her of a fibroid tumor which had baffled the skill of Boston physicians. By mail the "ghostly" Lydia had been able to prescribe the proper cure. Mrs. Hayes agreed to answer any and all letters asking about her case. "Mountains of gold," it was said, "could not purchase such testimony." To prove the validity of the testimonial, if not the cure of Mrs. Hayes' fibroid tumor, the medicine company offered to pay $5,000 if it could not produce the original letter.

The Cheney Medicine Company placed extensive advertising. It produced the famous "red clause" contract which provided that advertising could be canceled in a paper if the state passed a law detrimental to the nostrum seller's best interest. It was a brazen attempt to restrain the press from any crusade for pure-food and drug acts. An editorial construed as unfavorable would make a paper suspect.

Among the most active users of the country press was Dr. S. B. Hartman's Sanitarium of Columbus, Ohio. It advertised Peruna which was said to relieve almost every ailment that afflicts mankind. It contained 28 per cent alcohol, and its critics asserted that its victims were legion.

Public officials—Senators, Congressmen, governors, mayors and others—were quoted for weeks on the beneficial results which they had experienced from taking the medicine. Senator M. C. Butler of South Carolina, who had bitterly opposed the famous Blair educational bill, upheld the virtues of Peruna. Pictures of the Senator appeared in country papers everywhere. He who had long carried the banner of the Palmetto State wrote that he could recommend Peruna for dyspepsia and stomach trouble. "I have been using your medicine for a short period and feel much relieved. It is indeed a wonderful medicine besides a good tonic." The old bourbon might have added that it was excellent for chasing away the blues. Some alleged that Southern statesmen were prevailed on to endorse patent medicines in exchange for puffs in the Washington columns of ready-print and special-service reporters.

Dr. J. T. Ensor, postmaster of Columbia, South Carolina, and late superintendent of the state insane asylum, found Peruna a lifesaver for his large family; perhaps its general effects had helped to bring about the change in jobs for him! Governor W. J. Northern, a Georgia Populist and famous livestock farmer, expended a part of his literary talent in telling ruralites that he too had drunk deep at the Hartman wellspring of health.

Nearly all the medicine companies ran advertisements in series.

Lydia E. Pinkham displayed a veritable army of buxom females who draped their voluptuous forms over long and insipid letters about how they had been saved from the pains of womanhood. Fallen wombs, fibroid tumors, misplaced female organs, "that pressing-down feeling," childless marriages, and frightened mothers who awaited their daughters' approach to womanhood made commonplace reading matter for the country weekly's public.

Bearded preachers, bush-faced politicians and scores of women, including Sisters of Mercy, adorned the Peruna series. Of all nostrum advertisements, the one perhaps most symbolic of their true meaning was the Paul Bunyanesque hand of Peruna lying across the thigh of the nation. Five fingers grasped the map of the United States. The little finger, representing lung catarrh, tickled the Northwest, and the thumb—catarrh of the bowels and pelvic organs—gouged at New England and the South.

From Civil War times on to the first decade of this century, the medicine companies subsidized much of the free press. At first it was the bitters trade seeking a Reconstruction patronage by recalling the days of struggle. Already the quacks had learned to play upon political and social prejudices. One ingenious advertiser claimed that his product was the South's own. It had been used throughout her armies with amazing results. Attention was attracted by the picture of a Confederate soldier whose face bore a marked resemblance to Stonewall Jackson.

In keeping with times when Confederates straggled home years after the war to reclaim wives whom they had deserted, the bitters people advertised their wares as the stuff which kept women young.

There was the case of John who had loved and cared for a delicate wife in ante-bellum days. When the conflict began, "no persuasion could induce him to abandon his fighting propensities. He craved Yankee meat." John kissed his nervous and anemic wife good-by and went forth to do gallant battle. During the first year of the war he heard a rumor that his fading blossom at home had departed this life. Years after the struggle, John thought of home. "Oh," said he, "that sweet flower, so beautiful in failing, has gone, but I will stroll the walks where once we were so happy." At the door he was greeted by a full-bosomed and rosy maiden who screamed and fell headlong into the old Johnny Reb's arms. "My dear wife," gasped Johnny, "what has produced so great a change in you?" In one glad but tearful whisper, she said, "Dromgoole and Company's English Bitters."

CONGRESSMAN ALDRICH ENDORSES THE TONIC, PERUNA.

Says: "It Will Build Up a Depleted System Rapidly."

Hon. W. F. Aldrich, Congressman from Alabama, writes from Washington, D. C.:

"This is to certify that Peruna, manufactured by The Peruna Medicine Co., of Columbus, O., has been used in my family with success. It is a fine tonic and will build up a depleted system rapidly. I can recommend it to those who need a safe vegetable remedy for debility."---W. F. Aldrich.

H. S. Emory, Vice Chancellor and Master of Arms, K. P.'s, of Omaha, Neb., writes from 213 North Sixteenth street, the following words of praise for Peruna as a tonic. He says:

Catarrh of Stomach.

"It is with pleasure I recommend Peruna as a tonic of unusual merit. A large number of prominent members of the different Orders with which I have

Hon. W. F. Aldrich.

Another case which proves that no other medicine in the world accomplishes the same results as Lydia E. Pinkham's Vegetable Compound.

"Dear Mrs. Pinkham:—I was married for five years and gave birth to two premature children. After that I took **Lydia E. Pinkham's Vegetable Compound,** and it changed me from a weak, nervous woman to a strong, happy and healthy wife within seven months. Within two years a lovely little girl was born, who is the pride and joy of my household. If every woman who is cured feels as grateful and happy as I do, you must have a host of friends, for every day I bless you for the light, health and happiness **Lydia E. Pinkham's Vegetable Compound** has brought to my home. Sincerely yours, Mrs. Mae P. Wharry, Flat 31, The Norman, Milwaukee, Wis."

Actual sterility in woman is very rare. If any woman thinks she is sterile let her write to Mrs. Pinkham at Lynn, Mass., whose advice is given free to all would-be and expectant mothers.

$5000 FORFEIT if we cannot forthwith produce the original letters and signatures of above testimonials, which will prove their absolute genuineness.
Lydia E. Pinkham Med. Co., Lynn, Mass.

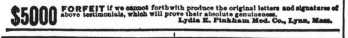

Recommendations Like These Carried Weight

Appealing to sentiment was the common practice. A mother holding out a chubby child asked, "Is your baby worth fifty cents? Then you should buy Dr. McGee's Baby Elixir."

Children were given narcotic-laden pacifiers which kept them quiet—but impelled them into a life of physical and nervous ruin. Parents were advised that they could rescue their offspring from croup and pneumonia by administering cough drops and ointments prepared by the great scientists of the proprietary-medicine trade. They were shown pacing the floor at night with limp children, and underneath the picture of woe a dramatic legend spoke of the saving powers of One-Minute Cough Drops, Teethina, McGee's Elixir or some other infanticide which was available for remarkably small sums of money.

Early in the game the nostrum merchants found that a girl's vanity could be turned into a real cash asset. Mothers and fathers wished to save their children, older people wanted to keep their backs straight and their kidneys drained, but maidens fair craved to retain the flush of youth. The Gentle Annies of the eighties and nineties were told that in the spring a young man's fancy lightly turns to thoughts of love. "But Gentle Annie," it was written, "with our changeable climate the bile soon begins to accumulate, and where love was what made the young man happy before, it now takes Hill's Hepatica Panacea." In other words Gentle Annie had to subject herself to a round of pulverized senna leaves and get her bowels open in order to be attractive to young men. Especially was this true with rural beauties. Country girls were behind their metropolitan sisters, so it was said, only because they did not know the value of a first-rate purgative. The surest way to retain attractiveness was to use Dr. Pierce's Golden Medical Discovery. Here was a tonic which would restore romance, cheer childless marriages, lead perennial bachelors to marriage altars and straighten the kink in Grandpa's back.

Learned doctors—they modestly acknowledged they were very learned—paraded their wares across the country newspaper pages. There were Dr. Tutt, Dr. King, Dr. Gretigny, Dr. Pierce, Dr. Kilmer and Dr. Bull. Most famous of them all, according to his own public admission, was Professor Edward E. Phelps, M.D., LL.D. Professor Phelps was graduated at Yale University, taught anatomy at the University of Vermont, lectured at Dartmouth and was then elected "to the most important professorship of all." Where this was he forgot to say, but at any rate he discovered Paine's Celery Compound, which was an "infallible cure for nervous and circulatory ills." By this wonderful scientific achievement he endeared himself to all the people of the world. Just as Lydia Pinkham rearranged the womb of civilization, Professor Phelps kept its nerves steady and its rich red blood flowing at high tide.

Although doctors and professors of every known type stared at the readers from behind whiskers, there was an antiprofessional vein in their advertisements. The quacks aimed a good bit of their messages at discrediting the medical profession. A Detroit husband claimed that for ten years his poor wife lingered between life and death, with the local doctors dawdling around trying to find her trouble, and then one day he saw a United States flag with the magic words "Hops Bitters" printed on it. Mr. H. W. thought he would be "a fool once more" and bought a bottle. The second bottle restored his wife to perfect health. Dr. Miles, the great Indiana specialist, said that physicians were ignorant when they advised patients that their heart trouble was caused by an upset stomach. Heart trouble demanded Dr. Miles' Patent Heart Cure, which would check short breath, fluttering, tenderness in the arm, irregular pulse and dropsy. Over and over advertisements showed an irate mother whipping a doctor out of her daughter's bedroom and then giving the girl some patent cure-all which would lead her again to the full bloom of maidenhood. The caption usually labeled the doctor a pious fraud.

Dr. Pierce wrote in his advertisement: " 'Yes, it pays,' said a big fat physician with a name which is known throughout the medical world. I have a practice worth $40,000 a year. 'Woman?' (sic) 'Yes, you have guessed it the first time. They pay $10.00 every time they come into my office. When one gets on my list I tell you she stays!' And Dr. H—— laughed long and loud. This is quackery—gilt-edged quackery—to keep suffering woman paying tribute year in and year out, and doing them no good." Dr. Pierce's plan was to remove them from the ten-dollar list and place them on his dollar-a-week list.

There was no disease that could not be cured. The surgeon's knife was a thing of holy horror. Cancer did not necessarily have to kill; Swift's Specific and a dozen other nostrums would cure it. Consumption could be as slight an ailment as a strawberry rash when treated with Allen's Lung Balsam, Dr. Pierce's Golden Medical Discovery, Ayer's Cherry Pectoral, Shiloh's Consumption Cure and many other varieties of bottled brown liquids. In all seriousness a Dr. Williams advertised his "Pink Pills for Pale People." They put real stamina in the corpuscles, a blush in maidenly cheeks and snap in the step. "Any girl can tell, and a physician who makes a test and is honest can see red corpuscles doubled."

Whether Mrs. Sam P. Jones was pale is not specified in a testimonial from her famous evangelist husband. The cures that came to the Jones' household were almost miraculous, and the most extraordinary among these was Germenter. In the tones of the campmeeting speaker Brother Jones wrote, "My wife, who was an invalid from nervous headache, has been entirely cured by Royal Germenter. I wish every poor suffering wife had access to that medicine. Two of my children were cured of nasal catarrh by it." There seems hardly to have been an important person in the South who at some time or other was not asked—and induced—to speak a good word for a patent medicine.

It was strange that such implicit faith could be placed in testimonials prepared by quacks and illiterate patients. Perhaps nothing begets success like proclaimed success. The allegation of cures was accepted as sufficient evidence. It was all part of a meaningful chapter in American social history. The South was not alone in its gullibility. The nostrum maker worked the entire country. He was careful, however, to regionalize his appeal. It was not worth while to advertise chill tonics in Minnesota or chilblain remedies in Louisiana. The Southern market was a particularly good one. A woeful lack of medical care prevailed there, and what was available was little above the level of some of the "doctors" who advertised their cures in the papers. The ills the medicines were said to cure were those of people overworked, poorly nourished, subjected to hard weather conditions, victims of bearing too many children and of bungling midwives. They were uneducated and without knowledge of scientific therapy. They looked on medical treatment and surgery as a sort of extreme unction, and they were reluctant to subject themselves to it.

Paid space in rural papers yielded unusually high returns on the dollar, because it led to an extraordinary amount of word-of-mouth advertising and so to chain sales.

It is a queer commentary on the sacred American guarantee of freedom of the press that it can be thought of in terms of medical advertising. Yet seventy years of the country journalism of the nation were one long dose of senna leaves, royal gentian, purgatives, narcotics and alcohol. Without a doubt the advertisers' filthy hands were clutched tight about the timid publisher's throat. Local advertising, public printing and subscription income were insufficient to free the local pages from them. The two types of income from the medicine trade, though meager, were more than many editors could resist. When they bought ready-printed sheets with advertising they got their paper stock for a negligible sum, as has been seen, and when they printed original ads themselves they were paid low rates for long runs. Advertising agencies were shrewd. They understood from the start that many an editorial hand could be reached with a subsidy, almost regardless of the validity of the product advertised.

Publishers yielded to an insidious practice which should have disgraced them even with their undiscriminating readers. Agreeing to locate advertisements in advantageous places, they agreed also to carry a certain amount of material in "home-set" print in the news and editorial columns. Local reports were freely interspersed with paragraphs telling how a couple in Tennessee stood over the cradle wringing their hands until they discovered Teethina. Headlines told of despairing husbands giving up wives until Peruna, Tanlac, Husky or some other toddy pulled them back from death's eternal door. Open graves yawned in the faces of readers who struggled to find out from local columns what the farmers in the Mud Creek Community had been doing the week before. The death notice of "Uncle" Joe Hunniecutt was followed by a paragraph saying that Dr. Pierce's Golden Medical Discovery had just cured the worst case of cancer ever known. Under the headline "With Sherman to the Sea," the reader was warned that Bucklen's Arnica Salve had taken over successfully where the doctors gave up. Pills, plasters and ointments greased the editorial offerings of many a shabby little weekly. Money-minded country printers even gave up their two sacred left-hand inside columns to the omnivorous panaceas.

Fully 80 per cent of the country papers were desecrated by medicine advertisements. It took a ravenous reader indeed to stomach them. They carried so many notices of *certain* cures for insidious diseases that they became nauseating. Editors who made the proud boast that they were publishing pure and innocent family newspapers did so in the face of the outrageous quality of their advertising. Scarcely anything could be more repulsive than to have chapter after chapter of female troubles spread out for the public to see. It was hardly a polite family matter that Miss Lillie Degenkolbe, treasurer of the South End Society of Christian Endeavor of Chicago, was having difficulty with her menstrual periods until she discovered Lydia E. Pinkham's Vegetable Compound, or that editor W. V. Berry of Lexington, Tennessee, contracted the piles while exploring Kentucky's Mammoth Cave, but was cured by Bucklen's Arnica Salve. Skin cancer victims were portrayed disgustingly one after the other in "before" and "after" pictures.

All this materially cheapened Southern country journalism. Editors who permitted free use of their papers by conscienceless exploiters could not deserve local consideration. What right would they have to think they could effect improvements at home from behind a hedge of liars and cheats? But it must be confessed that the reading public showed no offense.

In this brazenness is revealed a curious psychological inconsistency on the part of both editor and reader. Had an editor attempted to discuss in original copy some of the subjects covered in medicine advertising, he would have been ostracized by his patrons and possibly his paper would have been bankrupted by irate withdrawal of support. No editor would have dared to refer himself to the fact that certain matrons were suffering from fallen wombs or disarranged organs, or that some petite miss was having trouble of an equally intimate nature. Up to the last fifteen years the reading public resented a frank and sane discussion of venereal diseases, and sterility was taboo in news and editorial columns. Yet medical advertising, both open and disguised, contained the most repulsive discussion of female diseases and masculine impotency which obviously resulted from syphilis and gonorrhea. If any large number of readers had ever given serious thought to the foul trash which was printed after the Civil War, if indeed it had struck them as the loathesome thing it was, journals would have been denied the privilege of the mails by the pressure of indignant public opinion. Editors maintained a front of rectitude, but ostentatiously avoided the slightest suggestion of vulgarity in their own editorial writing and in local news, yet in their advertising columns and the free reading space they gave advertisers, permitted—and profited by—vulgarity without restraint. The public was just as squeamish—and betrayed its prurience by the ways it responded to the ads.

A few discriminating editors refused to let medical advertising appear as reading matter and either limited or excluded altogether the more blatant frauds. Where this occurred the quality of journalism was high. Perhaps no single phase of journalism reflects the dangers of uncontrolled and unregulated enterprise better than the abandon with which fraudulent nostrum sellers robbed the public from 1865 to 1905. Only the most reckless defender of that period of unscrupulous advertising could say that had it not been for this source of revenue the country never could have developed such a widely dispersed press. That would obviously deny a sense of proper values.

From 1900 to 1906 the so-called muckrakers and an important segment of the national press expended great energy to expose the patent medicine quacks. Little or none of this important campaign was publicized in the country papers. In a large number of cases the famous "red clause" provisions had silenced the editors. Equally significant is the fact that a remarkably small amount of publicity was given the passage of the pure food and drug acts. While this legislation was driving free-spending advertisers from the flesh pots of weakness for patent medicine, some editors were too timid to express opinions.

As early as 1895, a bill was introduced in the Tennessee legislature which proposed that compounders of patent medicine print the ingredients on their labels. This caused a minor battle among the editors of the state. There were those who contended that this was a free country, that men had a right to their trade secrets and that any attempt to make them reveal these secrets would be tyranny. One editor with more wit than social consciousness said, "The Memphian is right. When a compounder gets together some good bitters and bad gin that will fill in the morning a long felt want in the stomach of a prohibitionist, the originator of the drink should not be compelled by law to give the Scnapp away."

After 1906 the country press grew bolder. It spoke with more freedom on narcotics and was a little more circumspect about advertising. Those self-respecting editors who sought legitimate local advertising and freed themselves of the Eastern and Chicago advertising agencies were able to publish effective papers. Once the ready-print pages were attacked by the state press associations, and organized editors began writing uncomplimentary editorials about those rugged individualists who wished to continue to receive the frugal handouts of the agencies, the country journal became a less offensive advertising medium. More significant was the reflection of a growing medical profession, and a semi-intelligent attitude toward more adequate public health care for the Southern common man.

Book Two

THOSE WERE THE DAYS

Chapter 5

Names Make News

For seventy years after the Civil War, country life in the South progressed at a nonchalant pace. One thing followed another in leisurely succession which permitted each one to be savored to the full. The routine was one of duty generously intermixed with pleasure. By a standard editorial jest the spring schedule went in this fashion: "Fish, grass, spring, snakes, lizards, fish tales, news scarce, loafers lazy, fine weather, picnics coming, trees budding, spring chickens, delinquents fat, peach crop safe, paint your house, farmers plowing, small boys fishing, seed ticks coming, corn-planting time, editor a mere skeleton, wheat and oats a-growing." This was a quarter's work for the country editor. Somehow he had to cover these varied activities and to enjoy some of the more agreeable phases of life himself. The other seasons were as crowded.

Weekly editors learned early the ancient newspaper adage that names make news. Enterprising publishers attempted to print the name of every white man and woman in the county at least once a year. Always there has been something magical about seeing one's name in print. An isolated and bedraggled Mississippi cotton farmer found it so as much as a society matron. The only fundamental difference between the two was that the modest countryman was satisfied with a statement of plain homely facts, while the matron demanded a half-column of ridiculous flattery and hypocrisy. It was impossible to fill a country paper with acceptable material unless one made it both informal and highly personal. Editors chose rural correspondents from crossroad stores and country churches and encouraged them to send in news of everything which happened. They gave them free subscriptions to the paper and supplied stationery and pencils. Reporters recorded news accounts with all kinds of pencils and pens, often on miscellaneous bits of paper. Sometimes it was a major task to translate these communications and rework them into sentences which could be understood, or to fish a news item out of a flowery paragraph.

"Our printers," advised the McMinnville (Tennessee) *Southern Standard,* "can get along very well with bad handwriting and bad spelling, but they can't waste time trying to read copy written with pale ink or a pencil which makes a dim mark. Correspondents will please keep this in view, and use only good black ink, or a soft lead pencil, and if they would leave off all flourishes in writing, write as plain as possible, we are always willing to correct any little inaccuracies in spelling and grammar, but we request all our correspondents to be as accurate as possible in all their statements."

Standard instructions were that the reporters write legibly, avoid sweet little sallies, say it in a few words, refrain from disturbing religious groups, keep personal affairs at home, write moderately fair English, use the dictionary occasionally, avoid predicting the death of a neighbor just because he was sick, and get all material in by Wednesday night. Outside of these simple instructions they were free agents.

Next to getting one's name in the paper, being a crossroads reporter was one of life's great satisfactions. For the bossy soul this was an opportunity to be a social arbiter. The reporter might sit in his ivory tower and comment freely on life about him. He could pass judgment on the merits of social events in his own inimitable way. He could even carry on a petty spite war against those individuals whom he considered beneath notice, or who antagonized him, by keeping their names out of the local "dottings."

It was not world news, nor even national news, that rural subscribers wanted to read. They looked for "what the paper had to say" about incidents that occurred round about them in the county. Often they enjoyed reading an account of something they themselves had seen happen just to confirm their notion that they had witnessed an important event.

Weather was always a significant item. If rain broke a drought, that was of more immediate local significance than the passage of the Hepburn Act or the sinking of the *Titantic*. During a rainy season a fair day in Mulberry Grove was worthy of publicity. As the seasons changed, reporters wrote of the cycles of farm labor. Spring columns were so filled with news of farming that readers could almost smell the mellow smoke of burning log and brush heaps, or the fresh, pungent fragrance of freshly turned soil. The columns left no doubt that farming was the central theme of rural life.

News of these things gave country papers a wide appeal. Every paper had subscribers outside the counties and states in which they were published. The distant subscribers wanted to read of the happenings in their old home communities. Countrymen never quite severed connections with their native soil no matter where they went to live. Those who moved to the cities dreamed of the day when they would return to the land, and news of farming activities and country events brought them a singularly intimate and vicarious enjoyment. Thus it was that local papers have been sentimental ties with the past in restless nomadic America. Homesick patrons read them to keep up with farmer friends and neighbors, and to observe the evolution of the old communities. They wanted to know how romances turned out, who had borne children, who was still running for office, who had died. The reading of a country paper over a period of years has proved the happiest tie with the golden past—and on occasion the gentlest way to break the sentimental thread. In the country newspaper business the emigrants have always supplied an appreciative audience and have been a source of worth-while revenue. Distant subscribers sometimes became encrusted in acquired sophistication, but seldom lost appreciation for the crossroads report—if for no other reason than that it confirmed their self-satisfaction in a new state of mind.

Country reporting was a special art. It called for acute perception of news values. If Harrison Van Cleve went to Pursely Ridge Sunday night, that was news—maybe to no one but Harrison, but this was the stuff of which good locals were made. When homefolks gathered for Sunday dinner and to spend a long afternoon gossiping, or when children came home from school, the neighbors were interested—this was an ideal way of letting word get around that the children had been away to school. When John Wolfe of Shelby City, Kentucky, went to Chattanooga and was robbed of $270 in a bagnio, that was indeed news. The Stanford *Interior Journal* stated that Mr. Wolfe "has been on a spree." For the moment it did not matter how the editor was to make out with the unfortunate Wolfe when he got home. Interest in the story justified its publication.

Less libelous but equally interesting was a story about little Vic, the daughter of J. M. Sublette, who swallowed a toy pewter spoon. A local reporter for the Chatham (North Carolina) *Record* said her family was frightened, but Little Vic's digestive system took care of the matter in the course of time. "Her parents were in much anxiety until the spoon was passed. It was about three inches in length with carved handle and dipper at end. She was standing in a chair with the spoon in her mouth and must have swallowed it as she jumped from the chair. The spoon is right black, burned so by the acid in her stomach. Her parents have the spoon and will preserve it. As for Vic she is still jumping."

Accidents and sicknesses were frequent, and reporting them was a joy. Local correspondents seemed to get a sadistic delight out of writing gloomily of neighbors' ill fortunes. "Miss Minnie Crosby is out on crutches," wrote a Kentucky correspondent. "Little Bettie Lewis is no better, fears are entertained for her recovery. Miss Bettie Martin is daily sinking, a few days more will close the earthly existence of one of the earth's fairest daughters." The same writer reported that one of Kentucky's most estimable citizens, Moses Sweeney, was seriously ill. His recovery, in fact, was extremely doubtful. But Mose, unfortunately, was still able to read that he was soon bound for glory, and because the paper said so, he presumably knew that his demise was bound to happen.

Bob Cleveland from near Marietta, Georgia, said a local column in the *Journal,* was out on crutches. He had been "gently patted on the left foot by an affectionate mule." Lew Daly of Springplace, Georgia, "had the hard luck to get kicked in the face by a mule. However, he sustained only facial injuries and will soon be all right," or at least this was the studied opinion of the *Jimplicute's* reporter.

Far more serious than accidents with mules was a fatal epidemic of measles which swept through the same community. Snowden Hill, an infant son of Hill McGee died, and the reporter paused in his news column to drop the verbal tear:

"As they laid their darling Snowden down,
Beneath the grave's cold sod,
They gave his little form to earth
But his spirit went to God."

Sore eyes, whooping cough, measles, typhoid fever and, earlier, yellow fever competed with grippe and rheumatism as newsworthy ailments. From local columns it would be possible to construct a pattern of Southern disability. Every illness got into the paper, and often follow-up notes appeared until recovery or death occurred.

Many of the correspondents were women and young girls. Their emotional directions shifted as readily as spring breezes. One moment they were breathing a reportorial sigh over the grave of a child, and the next were delving maliciously into some community love affair. Nothing surpassed love-making for outright public interest. Local reporters were everlastingly spilling romantic beans for the young folks, particularly for boys who assumed latitude in their amorous activities. For instance, a young bachelor walked slyly into a Marietta, Georgia, hotel to meet a jubilant young lady who grasped his hand and exclaimed, "God bless you, Papa! I am glad to see you!" Papa, no doubt, was glad to see the girl, but he disliked an account of the meeting printed in the next issue of the *Journal*.

Ignoring editorial admonitions not to write juvenile "guess-who" paragraphs, local correspondents kept right on asking veiled questions which were understood by only one or two readers, and which were always embarrassing to their victims. "Guess what young lady looked so very lonesome last Sunday afternoon," wrote "Red Bird," in the "Granite Hill Dots" of the Sparta, Georgia, *Ishmaelite*. Such a note obviously was devoid of news value, but it possessed a nuisance quality which satisfied some spiteful people. This vigilant guardian of community affairs assumed the role of Madam Grundy and pointedly advised a gay blade that the rock quarry was a mighty poor place to keep a horse and buggy on Sunday night.

A young man was passing the house "of a certain young lady" in Oconee County, Georgia, and stopped to pay a brief social call. The priggish young woman, dressed for a frolic, saw him coming and was afraid he would ask her to accompany him to the party. She rushed back to her room and changed to everyday clothing. After a moment the boy went his way and left the girl to get dressed up all over again. The next week a full account of this petty affair was set forth in the Oconee *Enterprise* in such a way as to start a neighborhood fuss.

More exciting to feminine readers was a statement in the Springplace *Jimplicute* that Burton Moore was considered by the experienced local girls as the best "sparker." It was tough on Charlie Cochran that someone went home from church on Sunday with his best girl. A boy named Eddie was accused of going through the village on Sunday night in an unusual hurry—which implied his girl's father had excused him at an early hour.

Prospective weddings were given a lot of jocular publicity. They were indeed outstanding news items, and news-hungry scribes were alert for information which would lead to a juicy report. If a wedding happened to be formal there was much commotion, but if it were a quiet justice of the peace or a whirlwind preacher affair, not much could be said. A Georgian reported one of these brief weddings in which J. H. Whittle and Mollie Adair were happily married on the spur of the moment at the bride's home. The couple then went to church, and later accompanied a friend home "where dainty nuptials were lavishly spread—but your humble servant didn't get to go. Well never mind there's going to be another one this week! Maybe I'll get an invitation to it—I'll write you next week about that wedding if I get to go."

"Oranges blossomed" all the year round for the country papers, and the local columns kept the public fully informed on who was to marry whom, and in what circumstances. When Walter West of Springplace, Georgia, said he was short a rib and was going to bring one home, the reportorial decks of a local correspondent for the *Jimplicute* were cleared to wait for him to make good his word. An anxious neighbor wrote the Erin (Tennessee) *News* that she was all ready to report a wedding the next week "if the girl's father will only stay away for a few days, so it will give T. D. a chance." If the old man read that his daughter was about to acquire a new mouth for him to feed, the wedding did not come off.

Where there were orange blossoms, in time there was bound to be fruit. A crossroads writer lamented in the McDuffie (Georgia) *Journal* that he could hear of no "blossoms" to report but there were a great many little oranges which had sprung from those of last year. The little oranges were always numerous, and they too found their way into print. Perhaps they were known simply as "bouncing" boys and "sweet blue-eyed" girls, but their arrival in the world was significant enough to be greeted by the county paper. So it furnished a semilegal birth record to many a person who could produce nothing more authentic. Such entries have been especially valuable in recent years when in most Southern states individuals could prolong a feeble existence with a quiet dignity on an old-age pension and needed to establish their birth dates. People find it a sentimental satisfaction to turn through fraying files and uncover accounts of the flirtatious frivolities of their parents, a story of their marriage and finally a birth announcement—information published as weekly drops from "Dripping Springs."

Reporters and editors gave local columns alliterative titles—"McHenry Movements," "Whitesville Whispers," "White Run Rumors," "Sutton Syrup," "Horton Hash," "String Ridge Racket," "Beech Springs Bubbles." Reporters used quaint pen names—"Red Hair," "Dad's Little Pet," "Blue Eyes," "Too-Whit-Too-Whoo," "Wide Awake," "Little Emma," "Little Tom," "Crinkle," "A Villager," "S. E. X.," "Beefstaker," "Big Texas," "Little J.," and "Uno." Some reporters accumulated over a period of years a following almost as large as the paper itself.

Correspondents were of three general types. There were post-adolescent girls and devilish boys who found reporting vicarious release for their emotions and, too, a golden opportunity to keep social affairs stirred up and moving. There were preachers who wished to report the sober news of the community and write sermons with the strictest puritanical interpretation of human behavior. One pious columnist admonished a young man who had persuaded a girl to leave prayer meeting and go to a dance, to read Acts VIII: 21-23.

There were frequent complaints about hunting and fishing on Sundays, and threats that something drastic should be done about it. "It doesn't speak well for a county," said an Allardt (Tennessee) *Gazette* local, "to have the sabbath occupied in hunting, yet no longer than yesterday we could hear shot after shot of rifles and guns—somebody had better go slow, as there is danger in such business. . . ." Other persons were reprimanded for abusing their livestock and racing teams heartlessly up and down public roads.

Occasionally these moral lectures changed from admonishing individuals to behave themselves to brief dissertations on the kind of morals a community should cultivate. A local reporter could editorialize or preach, and so long as the responsible publisher gave him loose leash this was a good post for self-important watchdogs of the neighborhood.

Church affairs, revivals, camp meetings and baptizings always made news. The emotional influence of a vigorous revival can be sensed in the degree to which the local "corresponder" was aroused. If by chance he "got religion" his column overflowed with saving grace.

If, however, he went just to enjoy the crowd then his eye for news ranged to the buggies and wagons of courting couples, and his ear to the farm talk of their elders who, whittling and spitting, squatted about in circles. All reporters felt called on to list preachers' accomplishments in terms of converts and candidates for baptism and, usually, to give a general statement on the degree of emotion which they had generated.

There was a type of reporter who volunteered his services because he felt his community—as well as he himself—was being left out of the paper. His pride and vanity would get the better of him, and without having made previous arrangement with the editor he would submit a column of material, prefaced with, "I haven't seen anything about Siloam in the paper for a long time, so I have decided to write up the news from this place." When this sort of report came in, usually from a neighborhood elder or schoolteacher, it was pretty apt to indicate editorial yearnings. It was not in an altogether unselfish spirit that he had gone to the trouble of garnering local news and dishing it up. The column would comment on the stock subjects of weather, the conditions of crops, the farmers, illnesses and activities of neighbors, and then turn to brief editorials on the New South, religion, the Negro and politics.

One of these sober writers declared in a local column of the Schley County (Georgia) *News,* "It will be new industries that will restore prosperity to the South." Make the South the home of the cotton factories and other industries and "soon the American Eagle will be turning from the New England States in this direction." This note voiced the sentiment of the cotton and tobacco-ridden South. It revealed a naïveté characteristic of much Southern thinking: that all would be well if only a community could secure a textile mill.

On the subject of the Negro the local reporters were often blunt. Macon (Mississippi) *Beacon* "driplets" said the main difference between meetings of the whites and the Negroes was that the Negroes climaxed their affairs with fancy razor waving. On September 14, 1889, "the sons of Ham" cut and shot several of their fellows "at some sort of a jollification meeting on J. R. Windham Harris' place."

When news was scarce elder reporters resorted to argumentation. A country paper might have several disputes going at once among its columnists. They challenged one another over trivialities and feuded for weeks. If a correspondent boasted of seeing a large onion, potato, or fruitful stalk of cotton, or an unusually large ear of corn, then his fellow writers would belittle his prize-winning produce. Arguments would become intensely personal, and the editor would have to step in and moderate them to keep the whole county from getting into an uproar.

Country editors had to remember that they were publishing newspapers for a literal-minded public, and that matters inconsequential to educated subscribers were vitally important to less well-informed readers. Such a simple mistake as misspelling a man's name, mixing his initials or attributing to him a child not his own would almost surely bring a call at the office. At no time could news appear to ridicule an individual in a sly or subtle way. It was quite all right to be jocular and whimsical about a neighbor in a broad and blunt way. It was even all right to tease a young man about his girl and complicate his social affairs, but this teasing must never take form which could be construed as casting aspersions on the character or social standing of those involved.

Editors had to be keenly alert about social relationships. From the community standpoint the best editor was he who had the surest understanding of local happenings and who knew everybody. Quarrels sometimes got into news columns in a covert way, and editors had to spot this inflammable material. New and unsolicited local correspondence might result in copy which had no other purpose than getting vengeance in a fit of personal jealousy.

At least one editor was tremendously embarrassed when he printed, in perfectly good faith, an account of the wedding of a girl of good standing to a boy much beneath her in character and gentility. He had to make a humiliating apology and admit that he had used the report of a relatively unknown correspondent.

An editor had to watch out that reporters did not abuse their privileges to further the interest of clans and cliques and annoy everyone else. Likewise, he had to make certain that irresponsible jokesters did not willfully falsify news and say, for instance, that a well-known old maid had given birth to twins, or that a perennial bachelor had committed some unorthodox act which clouded his reputation.

Fortunately relatively little local reporting was of a venomous character, and most of it delightfully reflected the gentle tempo of life. Consider, for example, the contemplative attitude of a church congregation which speculated from Sunday to Sunday on how much longer its precarious stovepipe would remain intact. It was February 1897, and a visiting lecturer was earnestly discussing Sunday School work in the South. "The stovepipe at the Methodist church, which has been threatening to fall for some time," said the Schley County (Georgia) *News*, "came down with a crash Tuesday evening during Mr. Witham's lecture. Fortunately it fell across the pulpit and no one was hurt, though it narrowly missed knocking down a large lamp. With the exception of soot and ashes scattered over the floor there was no damage done, and the speaker hardly paused in his address."

He was no doubt a kindred soul to the president of the Americus, Georgia, "Do-Nothing Club," which was organized in pursuance of the Southern tradition of doing as little work and as much talking as possible. This energetic organization of steadfast idlers argued daily from nine o'clock to dinnertime, and from two o'clock in the afternoon until supper, on such weighty subjects as "how much molasses will it take to sweeten the Atlantic Ocean enough to make it potable."

A local column in the McDuffie (Georgia) *Journal* described the simple tastes of men and boys. Draughts and marbles had their attention during warm weather. "From early morn to dewey eve," said the *Journal*, "the unemployed citizen humps his spine over the fascinating board, or stands at 'taw' and plumps the middle man, while the familiar cries of 'vence,' 'roundance,' 'taws, at the middler,' 'fat, boy golly;' etc. etc. float on the summer air."

More exciting were political speakings, barbecues, big dinner meetings, spelling bees, quilting parties and other folk gatherings. "From what I can learn there was a large crowd at Usey's Mill Saturday. Amusements of various kinds engaged them, some fishing, some dancing, or, I believe these days they call it 'Tucker' especially when church members are in the majority, and some went to play ball, so you see," said the reporter, "the chances were very good for a big time generally though I was not there."

During summer months newspapers noted frequent barbecues and basket meetings. Springs, lakes and water-mill sites were favorite places for these pleasant gatherings, and they all followed the same procedure. Mornings were filled with speakings to which the old folks listened, while the young ones danced until they were exhausted. Even the narrowest-minded preachers and deacons were willing on these occasions to sign a truce with the devil and let the young folks be gay. Generous neighbors brought wagonloads of watermelons and gave them away. Preparations for the barbecue had been in process for at least two days and nights, and there came from narrow charcoal-filled pits the most succulent mutton, beef and pork imaginable. Dull care was forgotten, and old as well as young cut loose. These public feasts partly accounted for the South's reputation for hospitality.

Winter evenings afforded their counterpart. "They have spelling matches very badly hereabouts," reported *Volens Bene Omin* in the "Sunrise" locals of the Hickman (Tennessee) *Pioneer*. People met every Friday night at the Campground Church to spell, gossip, court and frolic. Two interesting professors appeared of the type that infested Southern communities when there was little danger of their having to work for a livelihood. Professor Bumpass from Lawrence County, Tennessee, was one. He was a master of the pen and could draw birds' nests, scrolls and curlicues all in the first letter of one's name. To him the art of writing a fancy Spencerian hand was a major accomplishment of life. He lectured on the virtues of good handwriting and tried to organize a class in penmanship.

Rivaling him was Professor Shires, who had drifted in from Texas with a tuning fork and was a master at "histing" tunes in a country church. Professor Shires was a center of attraction. At a quilting party in the residence of "Mr. P. B." the young folks ate a big supper and then proceeded to lift the roof in song, "Thus on this occasion," wrote *Volens Bene Omin,* "your correspondent saw the idol of his heart:

> " 'May Friendship's flowing wreath entwine
> Its sweetness on her brow;
> Not like the flowers of Time,
> With passing years depart.' "

Not only was the local reporter ensnared by a good supper and smiling eye, but so also was the tuning-fork professor. In February 1897 the *Pioneer* locals said that the matrimonial market was bullish. "Somebody gave Professor Shires a Nichol(s) that weighed 160 pounds, so he is no longer a candidate." No doubt he was now in a situation where the simple art of "histing" a tune on the tuning fork was an insufficient means of keeping his Nichol(s) weighing 160 pounds, but the romance was good while it lasted.

There were other relatively harmless professors who appeared on the country streets and at the crossroads professing to be able to do everything except an honest day's work. One such itinerant was a tight-rope professor who showed up in 1883 at Dallas, Georgia. His ropewalking excited the crowd. F. M. Gann, a merchant, got drunk and tried to walk the rope himself—"except he walked head downward and broke his jaw."

At the time when electricity was first publicized and before the backwoods boys knew anything about it, men who sought easy pickings would take a galvanic battery around the countryside and sell shocks at ten cents apiece. These fellows got into the local news. One such vagabond came to Pittsboro, North Carolina, and, after shocking the local gentry, decorated his rig with flags and took his departure for Raleigh. The Chatham *Record* said the outfit caused so much excitement that the circuit judge adjourned court to let the lawyers bid their ingenious friend good-by.

Medicine men exploited the Southern villages but brought to isolated people one thing which they craved—music. It was not so much the magic spell of the windy barkers that sold their worthless medicines as it was the captivating airs with which they gathered a crowd about them. Medicine shows were so highly regarded in some quarters that correspondents reported them as if they were reputable entertainments for cultural improvement.

J. S. Hall, editor of the Fayetteville (North Carolina) *Observer,* gave a puff to Dr. J. H. West, Frank Gordon and James McCormick's Kickapoo Indian Show. There were two wonderful things about this performance: it was free and its rendition of the "Feast of the White Dog" was beautiful. The editor estimated that as many as 5,000 persons were in attendance. Elsewhere in the South these clever mountebanks convinced local reporters that both their shows and their medicines were wonderful.

Equally appealing to reportorial taste were items about ordinary farm animals. Horses were often as well-known and dearly loved as human beings. Always there has been a close affinity between the Southern farmer and his animals. The Zeno reporter for the Yorkville (South Carolina) *Enquirer* stated that a familiar figure in the village was no more. G. L. Riddle's horse Charlie had died from an inflamed stomach. "It has been said that he was the best horse, in all his qualities, ever raised in Bethel. So now he is dead, your readers will pardon the mention of one so well-known on the streets of Yorkville as was this noble animal."

A livelier animal was Zeb, the cart horse of J. A. Davis of Yorkville. He was frightened by a passenger train and ran down a road parallel to the tracks. He cleared a fence with the cart and then stopped and stared at the fiery monster. Colonel Davis, a courtly gentleman, alighted and bowed low to the passengers as they were whisked by.

Animals were forever getting into trouble. Jim Frazer of Schley County found "his lost cow advertised for in our last issue [of the *News*]. She had fallen into a deep gully and was too dead to skin." But not so S. E. Brook's cow in the Murray neighborhood. In some way she lost her tongue. Her owner was puzzled over how it happened, but he told the local correspondent that he thought the cow "was licking through a crack of a stable where he had fed his mule, and the mule bit it off. He can't account for it any way, as the cow was in the lot at the time. The tongue is about well. The affair is a mystery, but a Georgia-raised mule is full of mystery." Then there was Marvin Pillow, down on Mud River, in Kentucky, who had a serious mishap. His cow jumped a "bobwire fence this week and severed one of her teats smooth with the udder," said a local correspondent of the Russellville *News-Democrat.*

Most favored of all favorites was a dog fight. Jip, a little feist of Lewis Thomas, went down to defeat and came near being mortally wounded by a band of "canine assassins on Maiden Lane last Monday night," said the Sparta *Ishmaelite.* In the same neighborhood there was a rip-roaring fight between a medium white bull and a black cur. When the bull was pulled loose less of the cur walked around than before. Down on Mud River the correspondent came up with a bit of wonder. Misses Gertrude and Pearl Crowder's milk cow gave birth to a calf "last Friday night which has eight teats on a full developed utter; four of normal size, four a little shorter, the calf is a normal full developed calf."

No news fit to print was excluded, and many items unacceptable in more formal journals were included. The strange antics of animals supplied some of this news matter. It was with genuine pathos that a schoolteacher reporter for the Edgefield (South Carolina) *Journal and Review* recorded the passing of A. J. Fulmer's brood sow Bet. "Bet would have been five years old the 25th day of next April. She took the first premium at the Johnston fair, weighing 800 pounds. Bet has had several litters of pigs." She attracted many encomiums;

among them, that she was "the largest hog ever seen in that part of South Carolina." No doubt the editor of the *Journal and Review* regretted Bet's passing, for the story appeared in the society column.

One never knew when a human-interest story would break. A colorful reporter kept the *News-Democrat* (Russellville, Kentucky) well informed on the happenings in her vicinity. She arrived at the unhappy conclusion that there is no such thing as complete joy in this life. "A prominent woman of the county" had finished washing dishes and was ready to enjoy that lazy moment when a hot Southern sun pitches gently over the first slant of afternoon, as visitors arrived. They had not had dinner, and there was nothing left in the house to serve guests. Only one thing could be done in the emergency: get a ham from the smokehouse and give the company ham and eggs. In her haste to be hospitable the hostess climbed atop a cask of molasses to reach the ham. Unhappily the barrelhead was air-slacked and it caved in, dropping the good lady up to her armpits in thick sorghum syrup. "Now this is not all the picture," wrote the alert correspondent. "It took two men to pull her out of the barrel. You had better be careful where you buy your molasses."

According to the same reporter poor Marvin Pillow, a good news source, went out "in the backyard the other night and did just what he didn't go to do—stepped on a rusty nail." Claude Johnson "was returning from his barnyard last Sunday morning with two buckets of milk when he accidentally fell to the ground (too bad for the milk) receiving minor bruises and injuries. It was thought at first that he had dislocated a shoulder." Such items enlivened dull rural conversations.

Local columns gave the countryman a sense of dignity. He saw his name in the paper and took pride in the fact that he was somebody. Occasionally publicity seekers brought baskets of fruit, hams and watermelons just to get "puffs." "Our friend, W. J. Donaldson," said the editor of the Dickson County (Tennessee) *Press*, "has our thanks for a very fine lot of nice, ripe persimmons. Will always has a warm spot in his heart for the poor editor." "Puffing" readers was remunerative in another way. Subscribers would come in and pay for their subscription ahead of time just to get mentioned. Occasionally a solicitous patron would pay several years in advance and then ask the editor to write a real story about him.

The country paper had the time and the will to be an informal human institution. Editors and their local reporters understood the taste of their readers and often mixed news and advice with hearty sentiment. When an aged neighbor, W. S. Jamison, began a sentimental journey to his old home in Baltimore, the local reporter for the Stanford (Kentucky) *Interior Journal,* knew that he had planned over the years to make this visit and sent him away with the poetic wish: "May he be protected from robbers, and pimps, and broken rails, and collisions, and cyclones, and all the ills that the flesh is heir to, and sweetly singing 'My Maryland' may he gently glide into the monumental city, and unfold his patriarchial beard in the home of his boyhood!"

There is no way to estimate the personal influence of even the poorest little "patent-sides" county weekly which ran the major portion of its "home-set" matter in the local columns. It was this pyschological aspect which made it both a personal publicity and opinion factor in the Southern scene. The more loyal friends it made, the better chance it had to influence readers socially and politically. The editor's spirit of genuine human warmth and neighborliness went far toward erasing much of the crassness of the more maladjusted aspects of life reported.

Chapter 6

The Ladies, God Bless Them!

IN 1891 Sidney Lewis of Sparta, Georgia, sat near the door of his *Ishmaelite* office with his famous writing board across his knees. He was writing an editorial on the character of the Southern girl. To him the daughter of the South had every womanly virtue. She spoke softly and sweetly with a warm cordiality of manner. From birth, said the old Georgian, she was taught not to say unkind words and to be horrified at any form of crudeness. She was taught to select soft feminine clothes, to learn more about men than Shakespeare, to love God and her ancestry and to be a comforting nurse. In short, "she is the strongest power in the South, that sweet-voiced, gentle, womanly creature that we call the Southern girl."

On no other subject did Southern weeklies indulge in more hypocrisy than on that of women. A large portion of social reporting obviously revolved around this tantalizing theme. Editors played all the keys from idolatry to gross jest. The Linden (Tennessee) *Times* exemplified the extremes to which simpering writers went in the publication of studious nonsense. It contained a story which had appeared in the Boston *Transcript* and drew a "moonlight and roses" picture of social life in the South. It was said that when Southern girls prepared for a party they would not think of sending invitations by the vulgar post. They packed a picnic lunch, assembled a company of neighboring beauties in family carriages, went out for a day's outing and incidentally left personal invitations along the way. "It is a delicate personal attention almost unknown to Northern customs." This was utterly ridiculous for one reason because the editor knew that in 1902 the average family carriage had difficulty in getting over Tennessee roads.

Perhaps a carriage full of giggling girls, munching sandwiches and delivering personal invitations to parties was in sharp contrast to a story of the Boston girls published twenty years earlier. It was said that the Eastern belle lathered and shaved her arms just before she went to a party, and this accounted for the electrical shock a man got when she put an arm around his neck. It also explained why young Bostonians were chafed around the collar the next morning. "If they keep shaving their arms," said the Southerner, "they will be able to raise quite a beard on them in a few years. There is tickling enough in ordinary hugging without shaving the arms we hear."

Much gallantry toward Southern woman stemmed from the downfall of the Confederacy. A sentimental editor could always raise a tear by referring to the sacrifices of womenfolk during the war. Furthermore, he could plead with the same gallant women to accept unhappy postwar conditions and to help rebuild the South. In 1869 the Columbus (Mississippi) *Index* expressed fear that Southern girls might not be entirely loyal to ex-soldiers. An editorial advised girls how to treat Confederate veterans. Most of the girls had not learned to work and they were at a serious disadvantage. When they married men whose only wardrobe was a suit of gray and a canteen they would have to work. Too many men, thought the editor, were having to say of a local girl: "Well, she is all right for an evening's entertainment, but she will not make a good wife." Clearly the New South was to make a new appeal to women. Music, art, painting and embroidering were ideal pastimes for girls, but the time had come when sweeping the floor, washing clothes, darning socks, cooking, patching breeches and saving money were more important. A girl's kisses could be just as sweet and her smile just as tender in the kitchen as under the parlor chandelier.

A modern reader of the earlier weekly papers realizes that editorial appeals to the loyalties of Confederate women had a suggestion of subjugation in them. The ideal Southern belle became a work horse in the kitchen and a drudge with a scrub broom. Dancing, said some papers, was a gracious art indeed, provided it was performed in the kitchen around the meal barrel and the dish pan. Nevertheless editors continued to memoralize the past with the tenderest sentiments. The Fayetteville (North Carolina) *Observer,* in 1904, expressed the belief that life was not to make money but rather to reverence the past. "To successfully move forward," it said, "one must have an appreciation of the past. What people ever had a grander past than those of the Southern Confederacy? Of such people, who acted a more heroic part than their women? All honor to them! Let us show this not in empty words, but in such imperishable forms that all coming generations in the South may know that they sprang from such noble women. Let us show by our deeds that we are worthy of such parentage."

This, with some deviations, was the general theme of the weekly editorial attitude toward women. They were placed on a pedestal. At times they allowed themselves to be enslaved to an artificial ideal because of their indiscriminate acceptance of the empty court paid them. They lost certain personal freedoms in accepting the gracious flattery of their menfolk. In 1869 it was proposed by a number of Georgia papers that the state's young ladies compete at the Macon fair for the equestrienne championship. Some of the editors thought it would be a tender sight indeed to see the fairest of Old Georgia riding forth on their mounts before the judges' stand, and to have one of them selected queen of the saddle. This proposal, however, aroused the opposition of some of the more refined gentlemen of the press, among them Columbus Heard of the Greensboro *Herald*. He considered the proposal fit only for the stronger-minded women of the North. Surely no Southern girl would exhibit herself for money before a band of pickpockets and rowdies. "We take it for granted," wrote the Victorian-minded Heard, "that every *southern gentleman*, who might be present on the grounds, would veil his eyes to so disgusting an exhibition. Should the proposition, however, be accepted and any number of *southern women* should be so lost to decency, so void of modesty and refinement which has ever adorned the ladies of our section, as to appear as contestants for the prize! Then we should respectfully propose that they shall be required to appear *a la* Anna Dickinson, or Mrs. Dr. Mary Walker, in *male attire*." This was not all, editor Heard proposed that they mount their horses and keep riding until they arrived in the "land of New England saints."

Riding horseback in an equestrienne contest was bad enough, but riding astride was unforgivable. Any woman who did so was in a sense advertising herself as lewd and immoral. Editorial wrath on the subject flamed bitterly from Virginia to Texas. The idea was so repulsive to the genteel Southern mind that surely no woman would ever have the courage to withstand the bitterness of public opinion. When women finally ignored this taboo, their editorial guardians screamed like scalded dogs.

In other fields women were under the ever watchful eyes of local journalists. Politics was at best a thing for white men and, possibly, Negro men. It was unthinkable in 1870 that a Southern white woman would disgrace herself by expressing a desire to participate in governmental affairs. Woman suffrage was considered as degrading as free love. "In spite of all that has been said by Mill and other distinguished advocates of woman suffrage," said Hugh Wilson of the Abbeville (South Carolina) *Press and Banner,* "it seems to be at war with the first principles of our nature, and to divest woman of the crowning attractions, and chief graces of her sex." In Kentucky the Flemingsburg *Democrat* belligerently condemned politically ambitious women. A Mrs. Bush applied for the state librarianship, and the editor said he opposed everything which smacked of "woman's rights." During the balloting in the legislature on Mrs. Bush's application, the halls were filled with women "all eager for the contest—using their best endeavors as 'lobbyists' to secure success of their favorite. We are free to say it would have been better taste for the ladies to remain at home."

In subsequent years country editors were sorely tried by their womenfolk. Militant leaders among them demanded equal political rights. When Mississippi revised its Reconstruction constitution, and delegates were engrossed in the famous "educational clause" debates, their womenfolk asked for recognition of "women's rights." Over in Georgia, the Hamilton *Journal* bitterly assailed the proposal. It thought that if the women were allowed to vote, then Negro women would run the country. Mrs. Mary Lease was the aggravating little shrew back of all this disturbance. The "old hell-raising Kansas heifer" was called immoral. Editors did not appreciate her penetrating sermons on the plight of women and farmers. When she shouted in a speech that "man will walk on all-fours," the editor of the Schley County (Georgia) *News* agreed with her. "There is little room to doubt the assertion if the coming woman follows her example," he wrote. "The men will at least be ashamed to look up and acknowledge their mothers."

How much to educate women was a problem. There was some danger that the trained woman might force the woman's rights issue. Education was worldly and might introduce vices to young women. Colonel W. P. Walton of the Stanford (Kentucky) *Interior Journal* felt that schools opened the way for the social "upper ten" to invade a community. If such a thing happened it would bring the wickedness of high life, including lotteries, hopping, gaming, horse racing and drinking. Woman would learn the secret of becoming wasp-waisted. She would paint her face and burn her hair to a crisp with curling irons. There were those, however, who disagreed with the Colonel. For instance, the editor of the McMinnville (Tennessee) *New Era* said that a girl's education was useful, provided she would settle down after graduation to guide a home circle. Education of women should prepare for the care of a home and children, and not for the world. "Let her have a share in all the widening circles of duty in the home, and then we shall see her reaching the highest type of womanhood, competent to meet any demands that may be made upon her."

Georgia weeklies expressed the opinion that women should be educated for the home and for business. Fathers, however, were urged to be careful to keep their daughters' education as nearly within a framework of ante-bellum tradition as possible. Many papers said the South had become a region of poor people, and that many girls could not enjoy the leisure and security of the ample past. If a girl wanted to earn money then she should teach school for this was most akin to the environment of the home. Women proved especially successful at teaching children in their first years of school.

As the decades passed, editors saw the old traditions swept aside. Most states established women's colleges and the doors of universities were opened to them. Education rapidly destroyed the old taboos. Women in jodhpurs were riding astride in horse shows; they put on shorts to play basketball and other sports. Suffragette stories and finally news of the League of Women Voters crept into the columns of the papers. Older editors swallowed their ancient pride and prejudices and published the news as it was made. In fact, the only recourse for old-line editors was to crawl off in a corner and whimper that maybe it was bad for Southern manhood to come too much under the influence of women teachers.

Education and suffrage might change women and their place in society, but the editors maintained Victorian attitudes and trumpeted praise of unsullied womanhood "and the double standard." Woman's character was likened by the editor of the Schley County *News* to a postage stamp—to be ruined by one black mark. But he compared man's character to a treasury note: "no matter how many stains it has it will pass at par. When a woman falls from grace her character is generally ruined forever, on the other hand a man may straighten up and be received into the best society again."

Country editors were eloquent in their defense of virtuous womanhood. Lewis M. Grist of the Yorkville (South Carolina) *Enquirer* spoke for the editorial brotherhood when he said that seduction in Southern society meant instant death. There was no time to parley when a stain of reproach which would lead to evil whispers for many generations was placed against a fair family name. There were perhaps skeletons in every family closet, but for a century and a half woman's virtue was dearer than life itself to the South. Any man who violated the established social code should die the death of a coward, and if he even came within the suspicion of wrong he was obligated to justify himself by marrying the woman. By the same token he was obligated to live with her the rest of his life so as never to leave her to bear alone the stigma of a sullied name. The shotgun or the marriage altar were the only alternatives; the gun was quick and final in its decision, while the altar meant a lifetime of repentance for the sensual act of one passionate moment.

Even though manhood was in theory solely responsible for the Southern woman's virtue, there were astounding reports of seduction, fornication and adultery printed in the weekly papers. Such a case was that of John Tyler, a transient bigamist. His sordid story of hasty marriages, ill-gotten children, and moral misadventures streamed across the South like the flaring tail of a comet. The Eufaula (Alabama) *Times and News* (1882) said in the past three years he had "ruined three girls" by leaving each with child and blighted reputation, to be cared for by grief-stricken parents. From Georgia to Mississippi at least six wronged women wondered what had become of their red-headed lover who had vanished in the heavy shadows of night.

Two notorious shootings to avenge wronged women startled the reading public of the '80's. These were the Thompson shooting at Harrodsburg, Kentucky, and the Lanier-Love tragedy in Greenville, Mississippi. The wife of "Little" Phil Thompson accompanied him as far as Cincinnati on his way to Congress, and there she met a friend who, it was said, got her intoxicated and then seduced her. When her husband received news of the affair he came home and shot his wife's defamer. Stories of this tragedy appeared in many of the Southern papers, and every sordid detail was reviewed. The shooting of D. L. Love in Greenville, Mississippi, in 1881 by John T. Lanier was also widely publicized. These two men were keen rivals for the hand of Ida Johnson, and when Lanier won, Love withdrew to Mississippi. On the wedding day he sent notes to Huntsville, Alabama, reflecting on the lady's character, saying that his intimacies with Ida were well known to her mother. Silently the Laniers, father and son, left Huntsville to follow Love's trail. They pursued him to Greenville and accosted him in front of a livery stable. John Lanier emptied a load of buckshot into Love, and ran him back into a mule barn where he was cornered and received a second charge. There he fell bleeding in the filth of the stable. He died a coward's death atop a pile of manure. The Laniers were praised by the county press for acting like men. The Hazlehurst (Mississippi) *Copiahan* commented, "It is therefore an honor to the chivalry of our manhood that every impulse is fired to defend woman's character. Our social life and institutions depend upon it. Every man, if he have the soul and is worthy of the name man, is a guardian and defender of female virtue. A man therefore, who carries the tongue of a slanderer deserves to die. Like a ravenous, roaming beast of prey he is too dangerous and deadly to live."

Although editors reiterated the code every time a community scandal became public, they often took sly liberties with the sacred subject of women. It was the opinion of Columbus Heard, that staid knight of the pen of the Greensboro (Georgia) *Herald,* that when a girl cropped her front hair and pulled it down over her forehead like a Mexican mustang, and tied a red ribbon around her neck, it was no wonder young men threw away their ambition and passed sleepless nights trying to raise a mustache.

Other subjects treated in editorial columns were not entirely conducive to young men's thoughts of business. In 1882 when Lily Langtry visited this country she set editorial tongues a-wagging. Where they had been talking such sweet nonsense as "a young lady in her pristine purity, elegance and charming naïveté is only a little lower than angels anyway," they turned to more mundane discussions of this lady's experiences in the higher realm of love. An interested speculation ensued as to the exact texture of the "Jersey Lily's" bosom. Someone said it was boneless, and editors wanted to know who told on her. "Did the Prince of Wales tell? Who told?" they asked. "The fellow who betrayed her confidence ought to be shot on the spot."

Many an editor inserted sly little "observations" on this beautiful but wicked continental charmer. Lewis M. Grist examined a woodcut of the famous beauty and arrived at the conclusion that it had little sex appeal—he called it charm. Whatever might have been the difference between the "Lily" in a crude woodcut, and the lady in person, the Yorkville editor was still willing to take his chances on the local girls. A long article in the McMinnville (Tennessee) *Southern Standard* continued the purely academic discussion of the beauties of a woman's bust. How large should it be anyway? asked the *Standard* in a purely objective manner. Did corsets affect it, and was it necessary for women to engage in gymnastics for the sake of more voluptuous development?

Discussion of female anatomy, couched in foxy editorial lingo, was only a part of what the papers offered on sex. Editors seemed to have feared that inexperienced boys would make a mess of courting. Periodically they published instructions on how to kiss a girl. It mattered not that these basic stories originated in boiler plate, the principles were as applicable in St. Francisville, Louisiana, as in Chicago. Women, said the account, were growing weary of having their hair torn down, and their corsages smashed by clumsy beginners. It was not necessary to grab a girl as though she were a fleeing shote, or to walk on her feet as if they were the courthouse steps. It was not even necessary to get a deathlike grip on her dress and try to turn her over inside it, or to yank her head forward as though it were a sack of oats. Kisses were not to be fired promiscuously at an eye, ear or neck. There was no telling where they would land. Remember, boys, said one adviser, the girl is not trying to get away. Keep cool and bear in mind that you have the sympathy of your victim, and that your aims are identical. When you have calmed down, "insert gently your right coat sleeve about her directoire costume and turn her gently toward your manly form. Place your other, and as yet unoccupied arm, in such a position as the exigencies of the occasion seem to demand, and give a gentle and soulful pull, as Amelia Rives Chandler calls it. By this time the 'rosebud' mouth, as you see fit to call it, is turned toward you. Lean over gently and let nature do her work. That's all. Girls don't like it any other way, boys."

Boys were given additional advice on their conduct around the ladies. In 1883 there was a change in the fashion of taking a girl's arm. "The Southern gentleman of culture bends his arm at the elbow, the latter member resting on his hip while his hand is allowed to run straight out in front of him," said that gallant old Virginian, Colonel W. P. Walton of the Stanford (Kentucky) *Interior Journal*. Thus a niche was formed and the lady's fingers were delicately slipped into it and she was afforded all the support she needed. The old-fashioned method of grabbing a girl by the arm as you would the mane of a horse was passé with everybody but dudes.

A few clutching dudes were extant at Stanford. Their etiquette was deficient but the girls were good teachers. A local belle was strolling with a young blood when he grabbed her arm in the "old-fashioned" way. She asked to be unhanded and then showed him how to be a gentleman. "Such a girl," wrote Colonel Walton, "deserves honorable mention by name, but we are not at liberty to disclose it. That she is a sensible one there is no doubt and it will be well for others to emulate her example. 'Touch not' should be the motto of every young lady in so far as it applies to masculine hands and those who will adopt it will receive greater respect from the gentlemen."

Editors gave social advice freely, but they were unable to enforce obedience. Like fathers, they learned with difficulty that criticism of women's clothing was useless in the face of changing styles. Always in the weekly press a long-faced moral crusade was in process about what the "careful" female should wear. Had the first two generations of postwar editors designed feminine wear, instead of, as they said, the prostitutes of Paris, Southern women would have worn shapeless, somber weeds, and would have presented the doleful appearance of the mother of all mankind in mourning for the sins of her sons. Men would have been able to get about as much impression of the shape of the female figure as that of an ear of popcorn in a heavy shuck.

Actually the weekly press had about as much influence on the feminine-dress issue as a thin mist upon a summer morning. When "tie-back" skirts appeared in the stores, the editors took one look and sent up a loud whoop of disdain. According to that astute old Georgian, T. Larry Gantt, it was "a fashion that sharply defines the outlines of the lower limbs, and busts, and exaggerates posterior protuberances; imitates the stage costumes of tights that one can almost see the play of the muscles as she walks—such a costume might do well enough for the nude drama, or possibly might be tolerated if worn exclusively at home." For a woman who would walk the street in such clothing the editors had just one descriptive word—indecent! But tie-back skirts became the rage, and editors could do nothing but wail.

"Pin 'em back, ladies," said the Oglethorpe *Echo* in 1875. "Pin 'em back; don't be ridiculed out of darling fashion, even if it did originate among the *demi-monde* of Paris. Draw 'em tight and tighter. Take short steps, sit sidewise, resent impertinent stairs—in short, have your own sweet way as usual, we can stand it if you can. Pin 'em back. Make 'em look as much like an umbrella closed, or one leg of a pair of pantaloons as possible."

Girls defied the editors and pinned their skirts back, and the boys went on loving them. At least, an army of brides and grooms appeared annually at the altars. Weddings were special social occasions and country editors were called upon to write about them like a combination of the vaporous political orator, the maudlin poet and the emotionally aroused female. It mattered not that the groom was like a wrinkled treasury note, or that the bride, like a postage stamp, bore evidence of a faint cancellation; the editor had to report the wedding as though it were the tinkling of sweet angelic harps just inside the celestial gates.

In true country-newspaper style, the editor of the Elberton *Gazette* wrote of a Georgia wedding, "Around the house sways the majestic pine forest—hence the name Pine Hill. The majestic sentinels on this occasion sighed at times, for their beautiful young mistress was to leave the old homestead, but as the winds passed on they would raise their tall heads and don an air of rejoicing, for that night, also, the fair young lady was to be a happy bonny bride. If there are any three things in the world that we think prettier than anything else, they are, orange flowers, bridal veils and brides, and on this occasion we beheld the loveliest bride attired in the prettiest dress of white with the most beautiful veil, and the sweetest flowers we ever saw. . . . Burns must have seen in his mind's eye this young lady when he wrote:

"Fresh is the rose in dewey morning,
And sweet is the lily at evening close;
But in the fair presence of this lovely bride,
Unseen is the lily, unheeded the rose."

There was a standard decoration for formal weddings in the changing decades of the postwar South. The bride's home was decorated with flowers from kitchen to porch; and living room, parlor and dining room became veritable bowers of floral beauty. Above the altar the initials of the bride and groom were worked into delicate rose-petal hearts, and frequently between the hearts a design of clasped hands symbolized union. Church weddings employed virtually the same decorative plan, sometimes with a floral inscription. When William Chapel married Georgia Adams in Pulaski, Tennessee, in 1881, the *Citizen* said that festoons of evergreens extended across the folding doors; from the center an evergreen horseshoe was suspended, and there were white roses and silver leaves and sprigs encircling two hearts of white and pink roses. Above all this and extending the entire length of the room was the scriptural quotation: "Thy people shall be my people."

A wedding in such a setting demanded high-flown description. Most editors soared high but Colonel S. A. Jonas of the Aberdeen (Mississippi) *Examiner* outdid them all. Lavish and elaborate as a wedding might be, Jonas' account of it made it three times as wonderful. He was in his element when he described how all Aberdeen bowed its collective head while a bride and her attendants approached along a flower-strewed path to the bower of Hymen. Gallant attendants helped their selected beauties to their places, and then stood by while the handsome knight of a groom charged love's jousting place to claim the hand of his beloved. The bride was described as looking lovelier than a poet's dream in the "airy folds of her bridal veil. As she passed under the wishbone, of natural flowers," said the *Examiner,* "and stood under the umbrella of roses, over-arched by a rainbow, a silent prayer of good wishes ascended that their life might be typical of the same, and that God's smiles might disperse the storms should they approach and encircle the pathway with the wings of his eternal 'bow of promise.'"

Everywhere Southern reporters struggled to convey a romantic impression of love which would surpass all other accounts. Adjectives were heaped up until castles of love towered and trembled beneath their own saccharine weights. Every hackneyed phrase was squeezed dry. The South had cultivated a tradition of fair ladies and gallant knights, and country newspapers worked to continue it with an ever-fresh stock of idolatrous tributes. In fact, editors seemed not to be so much concerned with launching a newly-married couple as they were in preserving an ideal which they thought of as one of the proudest traditions of their region.

As desirous as editors were to be both original and flattering in their reports of weddings, they were often bored with this particular chore. Often they published fake stories of what they would like to say of some marriages. A model outpouring was published by the Wilson (North Carolina) *Mirror.* Amidst the ringing of glad bells, and the twittering and chirping of song sparrows, it paraded its imaginary bride and groom "up the perfume-swept avenue of love and under the roseate archway of Hymen. They passed into the joy-lit realms of that higher and ecstatic feeling and hearts touched hearts through the blended channels of lips, and their souls must meet and swap-a-swap of labial endowment, and, now, how can we describe that osculatory performance? It was not a spasmodic kiss, like a stopper flying out of a champagne bottle; or a suctionary kiss like a cow pulling her foot out of the mire; neither was it one of those long, lingering, languishing kisses, which lovers give when hidden by cluttering vines from the glances of the moonbeams. No, none of these, but it was, to be alliterative, a kind of slaunchwise, slandicular, soup-sucking meeting of the lips, which went for the whole hog of endearment or none; and that is the way two hearts began to beat as one."

Although it was true that editors felt they had a romantic tradition to guard and nurture, it applied principally to the elaborate weddings of the well-to-do. When humbler folk were wed the papers were content with brief notices that they had gone before a justice of the peace to have the necessary legal words pronounced, or had routed a circuit rider out of bed in the late hours of night to beat the bride's father to the shotgun. For a period of twenty years, 1880-1900, runaway marriages were almost as common as courtships. Couples living within reach of the Ohio River dashed to Cincinnati or to Jeffersonville, the Gretna Green of southern Indiana. Kentucky and Tennessee editors gossiped continually about these hasty affairs. Everywhere Lochinvars snatched up their ladies and hastened across county and state lines to the consternation of sober parents.

Buried away in the files of the country papers are numerous stories of blighted romances which came to unhappy endings. There are accounts of unfortunate and broken marriages, of marriages of gallantry and of convenience, of old men running away with young girls, and old women robbing cradles for husbands. Some of these forgotten stories—with the addition of a few details never made public—could have explained the half-sinister, half-romantic cloak of mystery that clung to couples living in many Southern communities. These men and women appeared outwardly as husbands and wives, but they concealed some secret. Older settlers of the community kept alive veiled gossip that their marriages were nonexistent, spurious or somehow blighted and wrong.

Marriage was always a good news subject. Occasionally there were comical angles to weddings which editors were quick to report. Too, there were unusual intermarriages which created social complications. Such was the case of the so-called "marrying Hambys" of Jonesboro, Georgia. The Widow Hamby had five boys and Widower Starnes had five girls. The Hamby boys began marrying the Starnes girls, against the wishes of Father Starnes, and in a short time the two families were almost fused. When the last young couple ran away, Starnes got in his buggy and called on the Widow Hamby. As the McMinnville (Tennessee) *New Era* said, "Starnes, seeing himself thus outwitted, went to the house of Mrs. Hamby, the mother, and almost by force, put her into his buggy and riding off to Fayetteville, married her, thus completing the circle of family union."

Along with the marriages entered into intentionally or at least knowingly, there were an unbelievably large number of prank marriages. Young people in much of the South often found it difficult to entertain themselves, and they resorted to practical joking. Like children with loaded guns they were fascinated at playing marriage and were tempted to go through bogus ceremonies. In 1890, the Schley County *News* said that Rosa Skellie and W. H. Harris of Fort Valley were in a most unhappy predicament. They and some young friends had prepared a fictitious marriage license and the Reverend B. L. Rose had married them in good faith, not realizing that the wedding was a prank. The next day the couple discovered that under the laws of Georgia they were legally married despite the unofficial license, and apparently they had to accept the situation. Occasionally practical jokers worked up romances in which a coveted lady said yes to a proposal but a devilish boy was substituted in the ceremony.

Exploiters found it convenient to use bogus licenses to marry innocent girls and then skip out and leave them in disgrace. Editors were forever exposing these rascals. Such happenings indicated how much of a frontier the New South was, and how defective were the state marriage laws. Professional sharpers and sly local scoundrels took advantage of parents' ignorance of the law as well as the eagerness of their simpering daughters to marry. It was with real justice that the editor of the Calhoun (Georgia) *Times* said that women would consent to marry men about whom they knew nothing. A merchant would refuse to sell a total stranger a hundred dollars' worth of goods, and no man would buy a house encumbered with first, second and third mortgages, yet there was not a day or night in the South when some woman was not entrusting her future happiness to a strange man. Girls, he wrote, were determined "to leap headlong over the barriers of parental common sense and forethought."

Editors tried to print all the social events of the South. These stories record both social customs and attitudes. They reveal a New South undergoing rapidly changing conditions but trying desperately to cling to the genteel traditions of the Old South. It is clear that editors were trying, by means of printer's ink, to give dignity and majesty to ordinarily drab work-a-day social relationships. In many instances they appeared to labor hard to create and maintain a dream world far removed from material actualities.

Few Southern editors revolted against the prevailing custom of praising everything and everybody. Colonel A. G. Horn of the Meridian *Mercury* scolded the Mississippi press for its habit of writing about every woman as though she were a candidate for office. He said it was abhorrent for a decent woman to run afoul the professional "woman puffer." All sorts of females were associated in these adulations, and any woman who was pleased with such flattery was too cheap to be called a lady. The Vicksburg *Commercial* agreed with Colonel Horn's point of view, saying that it detested having to swear that every daughter of Eve was as beautiful as every other one. Social writing for the country press for four generations grew monotonous, yet much of it persisted in following the pattern detested by the *Commercial.* Editors are still writing that "Miss Araminta Spriggins is temporarily on a visit to Miss Angelina Muggins and both are pronounced beautiful and accomplished."

Chapter 7

An Egg was Laid on the Editor's Desk

COUNTRY editors felt obligated to give readers not only the local news but also a reasonable amount of entertainment. They could always count on human-interest stories to catch readers' fancies. These stories were of many varieties. Perhaps it is impossible to draw a precise line between Southern folklore and Southern folk interest. Certainly editors never bothered themselves with such an academic distinction. They believed the scope of their coverage should be as broad as nature itself.

Nature was often fantastic and human beings were oftentimes equally strange. The average country newspaper office presented the appearance of a rural museum. All sorts of freaks and unusual things were collected there. Human beings have been selfish about almost everything except displaying the oddities they find. If a hen laid a strange egg, or a three-legged chick hatched from the shell, its owner hurried to the editor's door to show it to him—and to the world. If a litter of pigs contained a three-eyed or five-legged monstrosity, the editor was supposed to class it as a wonder and its owner as a great man. If a Georgia sow farrowed fifteen pigs but had nursing facilities for only eleven, the event provoked a discussion of pig feeding and what was to become of the four little pigs left over. Hens with one wing, eyeless kittens, babies with tails or six toes and fingers, two-headed calves and every other imaginable caprice of nature were publicized in the paper. Sometimes people assisted in the creation of oddities. A man covered a setting of eggs deserted by a fickle hen with a litter of young kittens and hatched the chickens. A woman took another deserted setting of eggs into her bed and kept them warm—and unbroken—until they hatched.

Rural readers relished this type of news. The more fantastic the stories, the better they liked them. A good many papers carried columns of news from over the state, in which they rounded up happenings from extensive exchange lists, and much of this material was of the unusual variety. Sometimes these "gleanings" were taken from papers all over the South.

Tree roots that grew in curious shapes were chopped off and taken to town. Sometimes slender blades of grass grew through solid tree trunks, vines penetrated impossible barriers, and pieces of metal or coins were found in bolts of wood with no trace of evidence as to how they got there. Balls of human hair were discovered pegged in ancient holes in trees. There was much speculation on the meaning of such discoveries.

Sex was ever a mystery. Occasionally stories appeared in which roosters and turkey gobblers adopted the natures of hens. They sat on nests of eggs and fed and brooded their fledglings. Other farm animals displayed curious sexual transitions, and crowded the local columns with accounts of their unorthodox behavior. Even human beings were mentioned among these abnormalities. Sometimes a man or youth exhibited the characteristics of the opposite sex, and the earlier newspapers ran stories about them.

Not all the curiosities were found on the ground. The sky supplied its quota of wonders. People were forever seeing things overhead. Perhaps the commonest aerial phenomenon was the perennial belled buzzard. He drifted from one county to another, attracting attention wherever he went. The tinkling of a buzzard bell alone was not significant but the mystery of who had belled it was subject for speculation. Other curiosities sailed about the heavens. The strangest of all were the showers of flesh which came down like rain. A story went the rounds in 1876 of the deluge of bloody tissue which fell in Bath County, Kentucky. So-called scientists examined this strange rainfall and concluded it was frog eggs. One facetious editor observed that the Kentucky legislature had just adjourned, and possibly it had exploded. In Georgia swarms of spiders toppled down like sheets of rain. Everywhere stories were told of fish falling in heavy rainstorms; in fact, it was believed that stagnant ponds were stocked with fish in this way. Balls of fire shot about the sky and over marshes as ghostly warnings. Perhaps the sky phenomena which produced the most news-copy were the comets, especially Halley's brilliant spectacle in 1909.

Not all of the wonders were abnormalities. Large stalks of corn loaded with numerous well-developed ears wilted in editorial sanctums. Spreading stalks of cotton with their limbs drooping under the burden of mature bolls, prized stalks of sugar cane, big radishes and turnips, forked ears of corn, fancy peaches and large watermelons were contributed to the editorial museum and table. Subscribers who went to Florida sent back coconuts in their heavy fibrous covering and strange tropical fruits and plants to be exhibited and to call attention to the fact that the senders were on a trip.

The proudest of all exhibitors were those ambitious farmers who were first with any crop. They brought in early peaches and apples, first cotton blooms and squares and the earliest tassel on the corn. They reported the first ripe watermelons but seldom brought in the evidence. A triumph of many a Southerner's life was to produce the first cotton bloom and to gin the first bale of cotton. Editors understood that they were expected to publicize these facts in highly complimentary stories. Many a wise country publisher made warm friends and stabilized his subscription list by the simple trick of giving space to things which seemed insignificant to more sophisticated readers. An experienced editor knew how a lonely farmer treasured a clipping describing his achievement.

Less pleasing but more exciting were the perennial snake stories. The growing crop season was also the season of snake yarns. Since the rattlesnake was one of the most venomous of the common snakes it received a tremendous amount of publicity. Every spring editors divided their attention between farming news and rattlesnakes. Hair-raising tales were told of mothers finding timber rattlers in bed with their children and of their desperate efforts to remove them without disaster. Frequently there were stories of the discovery of long established hibernating dens of rattlers in which large numbers of snakes were killed. A landslide on the Chilhowee River in Tennessee laid bare a den of snakes from which 892 were killed. A moonshiner in the great Smoky Mountains was operating a wildcat still in a deep gorge. The walls of his stillhouse backed up against the rocky wall of the gorge, and the heat from the fire warmed the ledge. When the moonshiner failed to appear after one of his periodic visits to his wildcat distillery his family went out to see if the revenue men had at last caught him. They discovered that the heat from the still had awakened a den of rattlesnakes, and they had attacked the moonshiner. His bloated body lay on the floor and the room was crawling with snakes. The door of the building was securely fastened and the place burned down, cremating the moonshiner and his attackers. In the Alapaha bottoms of Berrien County, Georgia, a rattlesnake was said to have jumped from a bush and struck a deer hunter. His companions rushed out of the swamp to secure help. When the rescue party returned they found the victim sleeping quietly with a half-bushel of dead mosquitoes scattered about him. They had drawn off the venom and died for their trouble.

Southerners living in a frontier country liked snake stories. When editors did not print them, subscribers asked for them. In 1884 the editor of the Eufaula (Alabama) *Times* said in an editorial that he was not always willing to indulge his subscribers, but when his neighbor J. E. Ray of the Lumpkin *Independent* found seventeen rattlers in an old chestnut log he was willing to give in and print the story. T. Larry Gantt of the Oglethorpe *Echo* concocted a rattlesnake story to end all snake stories. He claimed that Richard Ives of Kentucky had located a rattlesnake den in the side of a cliff, and the biggest snake had its head out of the den holding a grown hog in its heavy jaws. This snake was said to be ten feet long, a foot and a half in diameter, and it had 110 rattles. The snake story in the rural paper had just enough suggested danger to captivate the rural frontier mind. Editors considered themselves fortunate if their offices were not cluttered with the overripe carcasses of numerous reptiles.

Anything of an unusual nature had definite news value. A couple in Nelson County, Kentucky, exchanged engagement rings. After they were married the woman dropped her ring and it disappeared. Two years later, in a rat extermination campaign, the ring was found looped about the neck of an emaciated rat. No one could be sure what had happened but it was easy to imagine a story to fit the circumstances. A mother rat had stolen the ring and brought it back to her nest. One of the baby rats had worked it over his head. He was growing very rapidly and soon it was impossible to get the ring off. As he grew still larger the ring almost throttled him. Tantalizing as this story was, it did not cause as much talk as the tale of a Georgian who had apparently worn shackles on his ankles for years. This man died suddenly and when his body was prepared for burial an iron band was found around each ankle. His early history was unknown. He had appeared in the county years before, without explanation. He had married a local woman and was regarded as a good citizen. The wife claimed she had never seen the leg irons before and she was not able to explain how her husband happened to be wearing them. This was a mysterious and romantic story which led the reader into dark byways of imagination.

Mysterious human stories always received editorial attention. The accidental opening of an unknown grave in making a railway or highway cut or in digging a cellar was reported in exciting accounts. Sometimes streams cut across cemeteries and bore ghostly cargoes away on their currents. On occasions skeletons were exhumed from the sites of smokehouses, but perhaps the most famous of the mystery stories were those of skeletons found in hollow trees. Three men from Tallapoosa, Alabama, were hunting stray horses, and at night camped on Iron Mountain near Birmingham. They chopped down a hollow tree which unexpectedly contained a skeleton and a bowie knife with the name B. B. Turner engraved on it. The victim had evidently attempted to cut his way out. In Gilmer County, Georgia, near the Cohutta Range, a party of hunters ran a fox into a hollow tree. When they chopped down the tree they discovered a skeleton, a powder horn and a bullet pouch. Occasionally the skeleton of a murder victim came to light years after the commission of the crime. At Villa Rica, Georgia, the bones of Mary Bagwell were discovered at the bottom of a coppermine shaft seventeen years after she had been murdered. Mary had borne one illegitimate child and was pregnant with another. There was an ugly story of miscegenation connected with her, and it was said she met death at the hands of her dusky paramour.

One tragedy after another flavored Southern news. In 1871 the tax collector of St. Clair County, Alabama, received a large sum of money and left it with his wife. He and two confederates, all three of them wearing masks, robbed his wife of the public funds. The three then demanded that she prepare their supper. The woman assented readily to this and proceeded to poison them. When they were dying she removed the masks and discovered that her husband was the leader. A tragedy of another type reflected the news interest of the more or less morbid subscriber. Five men were raising a barn in Rowan County, North Carolina. One of them, John Held, threw an axe at Peter Josephus and split his head open. In throwing the axe, Held lost his balance, fell and broke his neck. Two men on a scaffold, in their excitement, dropped a log on Richard Wiley and killed him.

Thus three men were killed in a twinkling of an eye. This theme was repeated many times in varied settings.

In Kentucky a sorrowing widow who had just buried her husband took her three small children to a spring to wash clothes. The pet dog treed something near by and the two little boys went to see what it was. One of them rushed up to the tree and was attacked by a rattlesnake. He was killed immediately. The second child undertook to save his brother and when his mother reached him he was dying. A scream at the wash stand recalled the mother and she arrived to find her baby girl scalded to death in the wash pot.

In Murray County, Georgia, a man named Johnston undertook to drive his wagon across a swollen creek. The wagon bed floated away with five of his children and they were drowned.

An aged brother and sister, George Pieratt and Elizabeth Goodpaster, lived together near Pulaski, Tennessee. George threw a large piece of wood on the fire, and pitched forward dead from a stroke. His sister was a paralytic, but she, by superhuman effort, managed to pull her brother's body away from the fire, and then got back in bed. Before assistance arrived she was forced to lie helpless and see their pet cats tear the corpse to pieces. This was an extreme horror story which was first published in the Pulaski *Citizen,* and then exchanged over the South.

Morbidity was an important element of the Southern mind. Accidents and murders almost too horrible to be true were given detailed treatment. Some of these crimes and accidents became community legends. In Georgia a man was killed by a dog in an extraordinary manner. A young couple living near by had depended upon an older neighbor and his family for advice and company. On one occasion the young husband had gone to Atlanta on business and left his wife alone. She asked one of the neighbor's girls to stay with her, but the girl's father would not allow his daughter to spend the night away from home, nor would he allow the young wife to come and stay with his family. The only thing for her to do in this emergency was to remain at home alone with locked doors and a dog for protection. In the night a marauder undertook to beat down the doors and get at her, but he was attacked by the dog. The young woman fled into the night. In the morning when she led neighbors to her home they discovered that the dog had killed her would-be ravisher. On examination, the dead man turned out to be the father of her young neighbor. These local stories or legends of unbelievable crimes originated all over the South and they grew in proportion to their repetition.

Newspapers gave a large share of their space to death. The subject exerted a morbid fascination. But in feature stories prior to 1900 even death paled beside the horror of being buried alive. New versions went the rounds periodically of the famous South Carolina case of cremation. Henry Laurens of Charleston almost buried one of his children alive. The youngster had apparently died but was actually in deep coma. During the wake a neighbor discovered that the child was breathing. Before Laurens died he provided that his body should be cremated. This was one of the earliest cases of cremation in America, and it continued to attract attention in the press until the turn of the present century.

Lack of any proper medical examination doubtless sometimes accounted for the fact that persons in coma were believed dead. The papers printed many news items that told of supposed corpses found to be alive just before casket lids were fastened down for the last time. Sometimes they sat up in their coffins during funeral services. Stories were common about people who were dead enough to be buried but who, it appeared when their bodies were exhumed, had struggled in their coffins or even turned over.

These stories, so often repeated in the weekly papers, give a clear indication that the people of the South were unreasonably frightened. The medical profession tried to lay this fear to rest. Long medical essays were printed locally and in ready-print columns saying that it was practically impossible for a person to be revived by the limited oxygen contained in a hermetically-sealed casket. If the flame of life burned so low that a patient did not come to in an abundance of fresh air there was no chance of his revival after burial. One physician said in order to make sure death had occurred it was only necessary to inject a drop of ammonia under the skin and if it failed to produce a red spot then death was certain. A boiler-plate story said the French government had developed a sure test which would insure against premature burials. If a candle was held to the flesh and a water-filled blister appeared then it was a sure sign the patient was alive. If the blister filled with gas the patient was dead.

Edgar Allen Poe never wrote more gruesome stories than many of those appearing in the country papers. Coffins were struck by lightning, horses ran away with hearses and mangled the corpses. Preachers died in the midst of preaching funerals. People insisted on being buried with some type of signaling device inclosed in their caskets so they could make a noise if they should happen to come alive.

Henry Berry of Marion, South Carolina, was a wealthy man. He owned 20,000 acres of land and other property. Before he died, in 1876, he followed Henry Laurens' example and ordered that his body should be cremated. It was said that about fifteen years before his death he exhumed the bodies of two of his children and found that each had been buried alive. He provided in his instructions that $500 should be paid a trusted mulatto servant for burning his body. Berry's corpse was to be placed in a plain box, hauled by mule cart to a designated spot, there to be covered with a pile of six fat pine logs from trees described in the instructions. The whole pile of logs was to be ten feet high and twelve feet wide, and torches were to be applied at each of the four corners. All male members of the family were to attend and to remain until the funeral pyre was reduced to ashes fine enough to be blown through the woods. These instructions were to be carried out to the letter of the will before the heirs could inherit his rich property.

Occasionally a morbid sentimentalist stirred his readers with an account of death. Especially was this true with ready-print authors who wanted to arouse their patrons with more imaginative stories than "How Matches are Made." A good example of this type of popular news story was that of the discovery of the body of a young miner in a coal pit where it had remained in a perfect state of preservation for a generation. The face was peaceful and handsome. The black curly hair and full mustache had remained glossy. No one knew who the handsome mummy had been. But as word spread of the strange young cadaver, an aged woman hobbled to its side and burst into sobs. Before her was the form of her fiancé. He had gone into the mine on the day before they were to be married and had been the victim of an accident. His body had not been found. As the decrepit old lady stood by the crude bier, looking into the face of her dead lover and whispering words of tenderness, the eyes of strong men standing about filled with tears. Her endearments fell upon the deaf ears of eternity, and the editor climaxed this sentimental story with the observation, "they had both been young those long years ago, but time had gone on with the living and stood still with the dead."

Death, like life itself, was accompanied by errors. A Georgian was borne to his grave clad in a favorite suit of clothes. In his pockets were large sums of money and several promissory notes which had been overlooked by the obliging neighbors who laid out the corpse. A few days later a child of the family died and was buried beside the father, and while the grave was open the money and notes were recovered. Other stories were published telling of misers who wished to carry to their graves the material gains of life. The Crawford (Georgia) *News-Monitor* reported the death of a local money-worshiper whose will was upsetting to the practical editorial mind. He provided that all of his property be given to relatives, except for $1,505 in cash which was to be placed under his head. It seemed a shame that the executors observed literally this man's last ridiculous request. The editor of the *News-Monitor* thought they should have invested the money in bonds, or written out promissory notes and rested his head on them, leaving the money in circulation.

Occasionally people wanted to take not only their money with them but also their jewelry, fine clothes and sentimental trinkets. Seldom, however, was anyone willing to depart this life so modestly as the Kentucky woman of the Knob section of Lincoln County. Her wishes were simple and childish. She proposed to prepare herself for the day of judgment by taking to her grave several favorite photographs and a cherished lock of hair, and clutching a stick of peppermint candy in each hand.

Country editors made a rule of printing the unusual and the morbid. Although they always ran the danger of being taken in by wild stories, it was good to please subscribers and to give them something which diverted their minds from politics and local gossip. Often their news stories were as fantastic as the fabulous advertisements they ran for the advance agents of circuses.

Chapter 8

Type Lice

PUBLISHING a country paper was somewhat like being the father of a rollicking and intimate family. Despite the circumspection of ready-print editors many off-color stories were printed by local publishers for the delectation of friendly readers though they might not be altogether acceptable in more formal journals. Just as a father sometimes told racy stories for the amusement of his children and frowned upon telling vulgar yarns in public, editors published stories which enlivened what they called "family journals." In fact some of the stories published from time to time were Rabelaisian. Just as Southerners liked a generous dash of spice in their food, so they did in their reading. Country editors knew this to be true and they were always tucking in spicy paragraphs to give color to their papers, and to fill up blank space in copy. There was nothing so exasperating to a country printer as to be ready to go to press and to discover that he lacked about two inches of type to fill his chases. In this emergency a witty exchange could always be mustered into service.

The general tendency has been to regard the late nineteenth and early twentieth centuries in Southern history as staid Victorian years in which great care was exercised that nothing at which the politest lady could take offense would be uttered or published, but such was not always the case. Buried in the files of country papers are some excellent pieces of broad American humor which indicate a robust frontier love for this type of wit.

Printing newspapers was not without its humorous moments. Printers had favorite practical jokes as well as all the tricks of the trade. A favorite stunt in a "hand-set" country office was to show greenhorns the type lice. Since lice infested nearly everything else in the South, it was reasonable to believe that one species thrived on lead. In moving type about in galleys printers sprinkled it generously with water to make the slugs stick together. Each victim was told that the lice were very small and that he would have to lean down close and look hard to see them. When his face came within a few inches of the wet type, a wiseacre printer slammed the lines together, spraying water and ink up into his eyes and mouth. This was the first act in initiating a devil, and frequently it was an excellent trick for driving off loafers.

Not all the type lice were sprayed into the faces of the unwary in the shops. Readers were regaled with witticisms of every sort. Women, animals, religion, greenhorns and all the foibles of human nature were fair game for editorial wit. An editor said that a Washington society lady remarked at a reception, "If you men would let the women's dresses alone, there would be much less foolishness and misery in the world." He observed, "A painful silence followed, and we suppose it proved the truth of the remark." At any rate, women's clothing for the last eighty years has provoked the writing of countless columns of newsprint. At first, editors thought women wore too much clothing, and in later years not enough. In those affluent decades, 1870 to 1910, when the contour of the female figure was a sinful thing and an uncovered ankle was indecent exposure, country newspapers poked fun at women for bearing up under their discomforts.

Ladies of the nineteenth century were supposed to be most uncomfortable because of the ridiculous dictates of style which governed their lives. Editor John K. Spence of the Greensboro (Georgia) *Herald* conveyed to his male readers some slight notion of how a fashionably dressed woman felt. All you had to do, he wrote, was "to take a man and pin three or four large tablecloths about him, fastened back with elastic and looped up with ribbons; drag all his own hair to the middle of his head and tie it tight, and hair pin on about five pounds of other hair and a big bow of ribbons, keep the front locks on pins all night and let them trickle down over his eyes all day; pinch his waist into a corset, and give him gloves a size too small, and a frill to tickle his chin, and a little lace veil to blind his eyes whenever he goes out to walk, and he will know what a woman's dress is."

Women were teased for many things besides their fashion of dressing. There was a virtuous young lady who listened indignantly while a temperance group passed a resolution to cut out all spirituous liquors. She was highly disturbed by this action because she believed only cider could quiet her nerves enough for her to go to sleep and dream good and virtuous dreams. In her moment of perplexity the maiden arose and addressed the temperance supporters thus: "Brethren and Sisters, cider is a necessity to me and I must have it. I shall have to eat apples and get some fine young man to squeeze me; for I can't live without that delightful nectar, the juice of the apple."

Cider or no cider, there were many maidens who liked to be squeezed, or so the editors said in their nonsense columns. There was that schoolmistress of no specific geographical location who undertook to "whale" a nineteen-year-old male scholar into obedience. The boy, however, disarmed his teacher and returned kisses for blows. Being a stern woman, the teacher looked her pupil in the eye and said, "William, I will give you precisely fifteen minutes to stop hugging me, and if you disobey me I will punish you severely."

A little more positive even than the belabored schoolmistress, was that "energetic lady" described by the Greensboro (Georgia) *Herald*. She was an ambitious woman who believed that the way to get a job done was to keep steadily at it. She had married four times and seemed bent on doubling, if not tripling, the country's population. She had borne twenty-four children, and when the editor expressed surprise and wonderment she said, "Stranger, I coulda beat that—I'd a made the other dozen if I hadn't lost so much time a-courtin', menfolks is so slow." Of course only a few of the men folk of the whimsical stories were slow. There was the well-meaning benedict who in the process of dressing needed a pin. He stepped into the kitchen and asked the buxom cook to supply it. Her hands were covered with biscuit dough, so she arched her bosom and told the man of the house to search for one. Colonel W. P. Walton of the Stanford (Kentucky) *Interior Journal* said "the poor awkward man would have been fumbling around for that pin yet, if his wife hadn't happened to step in and bounce the rolling pin off his head."

The subject of women weighed heavily upon the country editorial mind. Perhaps an exact space analysis would show that at least three-fourths of the ephemeral material centered around this subject. Some of it was copied from exchanges and some was original. No doubt a majority of the Southern editors agreed with the Marietta (Georgia) *Journal*, "There is no place like home, especially if it is the house of a pretty girl, when they keep a good fire during the cold weather in the parlor, and turn the lamp down low to save expenses."

The subject of love was evergreen, and editors wanted to see it bear fruit, but occasionally the belief was expressed regretfully that nine-tenths of the sparking was done by inexperienced youths. It was said, "They haven't generally a second shirt, and they are no more qualified to get married than a steer is to preach." Certainly the debating society at Rome, Georgia, had ideas, even if not altogether original ones. At least the society could come to the point. Its young men, just on the verge of raising mustaches, debated the question, "Is the mental capacity equal in both sexes?" An ardent negative speaker left the general impression that, intellectually, all women were morons. Realizing before he sat down that he had generated considerable heat among his fair listeners he apologized with the practical statement that he "intended to marry a woman, and nothing else but a woman, and any man who did not marry a woman was no gentleman."

Marse Henry Watterson supplied the country journals with a marvelous exchange story of the mourning wife. A Mrs. Wagner lived in Louisville with her husband and when he died she dutifully hauled him away to be buried in that most peaceful of all spots along the Ohio, Cave Hill Cemetery. Mrs. Wagner was not satisfied to let the fading flowers and the sod keep silent watch but added her own vigil. Every day she wept bitterly by the grave for a love that was gone. A tombstone salesman capitalized on her extremely sentimental state of mind and sold her an uncarved marker. A stonecutter named Ferguson was employed to chisel on some original sentiments from the pen of the mournful wife, and when he began his task the widow inspected each letter as it was developed. As the dexterous craftsman worked, his employer developed an admiration for him. As for Ferguson, he uttered sweet words of comfort in the sorrowing widow's ear. On the second day, a second line of the sentimental inscription was begun, but romance was too strong. The chisel fell at the head of the grave, and the hammer was dropped beside it. The tearful Mrs. Wagner was now on her way to the justice of the peace to become Mrs. Ferguson. The lines of the tombstone went unfinished, and the tools were later gathered up to be used in cutting inscriptions for those outside the family.

Editors shifted easily from the frivolity of fickleness to the realism of rural courting. Nothing was more thrilling yet more painful to the shy and green country boy than being in love. Girls confused and disturbed him. He stood off and admired them, but he was frightened at courting, especially in the presence of older people. Editors understood perfectly this frame of mind because most of them had been country boys, and they made good use of their experiences in nonsense backwoods stories.

Courting was like taking a dive into an icy stream. Once you were in, it was not so bad, but preparing to take the first dive was a time of anguish. One Kentucky editor advised the girls to get an album if they wished to encourage young men. "It's the first thing a bashful young man grabs when he enters a strange house where there are girls. We've seen them look through one until they knew every picture by heart from page one to General Grant in the back part," said an experienced Kentuckian. He believed an album "is the best thing in the world to occupy a young fellow's hands, and it's a sure-cure for bashfulness." He might have very well added that there was nothing like an album for encouraging the holding of hands. Many a bashful country boy who could not have otherwise been encouraged to hold a girl's hand found an album bridged the gap for him, and soon he did not know whether he was looking at Uncle George's picture when he was in Texas or courting his niece.

A favorite story in many newspapers told of the troubles of bumpkins who were caught in unexpected rainstorms and were benighted in their girls' houses. A country swain caught in a rainstorm was in a serious predicament indeed. At best his sleeping wardrobe was strictly a shirttail affair, and his privacy in the house was a matter of grave uncertainty. After a harrowing night in which he conjured up every embarrassing thing that could happen to him, one of these imprisoned Romeos was invited to breakfast and reluctantly agreed to eat with the family. Sitting opposite a mirror he discovered that he had failed to comb his hair. Then he dropped his fork, scattered food on the floor and spilled coffee down his shirt front. Frantic attempts to correct one blunder resulted in others. Finally the flustered youth crossed his hands in his lap where he felt the table cloth resting across his legs. He mistook it for his shirttail and tucked it tightly into his belt. When the family left the table, the young man jerked the dishes onto the floor. At last, after freeing himself with difficulty from some three feet of tablecloth, he fled home. He went into hiding and "the girl," said the Edgefield (South Carolina) *Chronicle,* "is looking for a less bashful lover, who can tell his shirttail from a table cloth."

From joking about the girls and human blunders it was but a short step to the writing of tall tales. Stories of Baldwin, Longstreet, Thompson, Hooper and a host of others found their way into the little weeklies. Over and over the old frontier story, "Cousin Sally Dillard," was published as an original. Sam Slick made periodic appearances, and so did Major Jones, and at least a half-dozen hardshell backwoods sermons drifted around among the exchanges. Country people were living for the most part in the raw backwoods, and they loved its rugged humor. A Mississippi story which the old folks carefully put aside to read when they wished a good chuckle was printed many times. It began with the traditional theme of the courting boy getting caught in a rain storm at his girl's house. Cover was scarce and before daybreak the chilled but ingenious visitor undertook to check the draft by stuffing his trousers into cracks in the log wall. Calves in search of salt chewed up his pants in the night. When the old man called the young visitor to breakfast he feigned illness and remained in bed until he could figure out some mode of escape. In the meantime the girls went out to milk, and when they returned to the house they left a pail of milk near the bedroom door. The hungry lad heard them and was determined to slip out when the coast was clear and steal a drink. In order to be as inconspicuous as possible he got down on all fours. Just as he tilted the bucket up to his mouth the bail slipped over his head and he was trapped like a raccoon in a log.

Another complicated tale was the account of the pathetic end of Colonel Welby of Arkansas. He was a mixture of the old border and the Old South. The Colonel was an enthusiastic sportsman who loved the woods and his dogs. Real poetry to him was the sweet sonorous baying leads of a Walker "redbone" hound, and the rumbling bass responses of a langorous "blue tick." For more than fifty years, the melancholic notes of the hound had led the agile sportsman over the Arkansas hills. To him, the mournful note of the hound, like the notice of an overdue note at the bank, was an imperative call to duty. In March, 1883, on a "night so dark that a black cat shined like a new moon," the colonel's favorite hounds treed near his house. The first notes disturbed his sons, and they begged their aged father to desert the dogs just once. The day had been hard on him, and he was in no physical condition to spend a March night in the woods. He paid no attention to his sons and went out to join his dogs. When he reached the hounds they were circling a monstrous gnarled beech.

Nothing would do the old man but he must fell the tree. It was a long task of "night chopping." He hit a lick with the ax and then felt the gash to determine where to strike next. Chopping and panting, Colonel Welby worked away the night hours. Sitting in a circle the dogs alternated between thunderous roars and disturbed frightened little growls. To George Welby, a son, it seemed the dogs in their inarticulate way were trying to persuade their master to go home. But he was a determined man; he had never failed his dogs and would not do so now. At the moment when a thin light streak formed a jagged tear between the inkiness of night and the sullenness of predawn, the grisly old beech toppled down, but in its falling there was no smashing crescendo. As the exhausted Colonel rushed forward he discovered that he had labored all night chopping down a tall stump. That was too much. The day before he had buried his third wife, and now his dogs had treed up an empty stump. The old man stumbled home on the arm of a son and crumpled into bed. Tugging at the coverlids, the gaunt old fingers signaled that life was unendurable. Those gnarled old hands had kept faith with the dogs at the butt of many a monarch of the swamps, but this night's deception was too cruel. At ten o'clock in the morning Colonel Welby's wan ghost soared out to meet those of three wives, and George, the oldest boy saddled a horse and rode into town to buy a coffin and to give the story of his father's unexpected death to the editor.

As long as there are woods in the South there will be hunting dogs, varmints and incurable liars. Thousands of stories circulated through the papers about strange tracks which were seen in creek bottoms and along sandy hillside roads. If some of the chimerical animals believed responsible for the footprints had appeared in reality, whole communities would have been scared to death overnight. In addition to the imaginary animals, an amazing army of bears prowled the countryside. Along with springtime and moonlight nights came a rash of the perennial bear stories. Regions as devoid of bears as of unicorns were frequently upset by rumors of the appearance of large and presumably bloodthirsty bruins.

Occasionally a real bear walked through the countryside scattering people before him and paragraphs behind him. One was reported in Union County, South Carolina. A party of two hundred men and twenty dogs trampled cotton fields for miles around hunting him. When they found him, some dogs were killed and the men ran away home. Other and more courageous pursuers took up the chase, shouting that they would run him "to Charleston or Atlanta or catch him." In Lancaster County the bruin crossed a field where thirty Negroes were chopping cotton. The minute they sighted him they took wings and almost flew to the tops of the near-by trees. At Fort Mill the bear was killed, and the Newberry *Herald and News* said it weighed 335 pounds. It furnished enough newspaper copy to fill its weight in country columns for months to come.

Running bears across upper South Carolina, or trailing Christians across the Mississippi River were of equal news interest. The Jackson (Tennessee) *Whig and Tribune* reported the experience of a young man on the road to Little Rock, Arkansas, who overtook an elderly traveler and asked him where he was going. "I am going to heaven, my son, I have been on my way eighteen years."

"Well, goodby, old fellow," replied the youngster, "if you have been traveling toward heaven eighteen years and got no nearer to it than Arkansas, I'll take another route."

Religion was ever a source of humor. Editors were careful not to make direct thrusts at local preachers and churches, but without indulging in personalities they enjoyed writing comic paragraphs about the indecorous happenings in church meetings. They liked especially to discuss the various doctrines of the churches. Modes of baptism were subjects for whimsical newspaper humor. A favorite story was that told by the *True Witness* of Texas of the denominational cattle. It was said that in the great Lone Star State where there was "not only a large, growing mixed population, every variety of climate and soil, game and stock," but the very oxen became denominational. A stranger overtook a native driving four oxen. As he approached he heard him say, "Get up, Presbyterian! Gee, Campbellite! Haw, Baptist! What are you doing, Methodist?" When the visitor asked the Texan why he had given the strange names to his team, he explained, "I call the lead ox in front Presbyterian, because he is true blue and never fails—he believes in pulling through every difficult place, persevering to the end, and then he knows more than all the rest. The one by his side I call Campbellite; he does very well when you let him go his own way, until he sees water, and then all the world can't keep him out of it, and there he stands as if his journey had ended. This ox, behind, is a real Baptist, for he is all the time after water, and will not eat with the others, but is continually looking first on one side and then the other and at everything that comes near him. The other, which I call Methodist, makes a great noise and a great to do, and you would think that he was pulling all creation, but he don't pull a pound."

Ordinarily editors little relished disputing with preachers and denominationalists. Readers who were rabid in their denominational views were humorless, and they took jocular reference to their churches as personal slights and called on publishers to recant. Publishing humorous church stories, however, was a good way of getting in criticism and occasionally such a good story appeared in the exchanges that it was worth a good row just to have the satisfaction of printing it. The editor of the McDuffie (Georgia) *Journal* enjoyed telling the story of the attempted baptizing of a Miss Wilson in Pineville, North Carolina. She was a maiden lady of mature years and had long before laid aside any ambition of marriage. Unfortunately, said the editor, this attractive lady had "unintentionally inserted her leg under the wheel of a heavily loaded wagon and she found that once shapely limb so completely ruined that she consented to have it cut off and thrown away." If it had been merely a matter of misplacing a leg, thought the Georgian, many a young man would gladly have gone in search of it, but Miss Wilson's leg was thrown away. In a long dissertation on marrying a woman with one leg, the editor concluded that "it would be a bold man who could calmly look forward to marrying a woman who might some morning interrupt him while shaving by asking 'James, would you mind handing me my leg? I think you will find it behind the rocking chair.' "

Miss Wilson saw her chances of matrimony vanish and she became embittered at her two-legged fellows. But while attending a camp meeting she fell under the persuasive spell of an "Eleventh Day Baptist" power preacher. Her heart was softened and she joined the church. Announcement was made that she would be immersed on Sunday morning, and everybody was invited to attend the ceremony. The minister, a Brother Waters, had a fine reputation for the speed and facility with which he could baptize the faithful. A Presbyterian minister had on one occasion incurred Brother Waters' wrath by trying to deny that John the Baptist had engaged in total immersion because he had baptized his followers at the rate of two and a half a minute. Not to be outdone by a Presbyterian logician, the Baptist brother had publicly put twenty-five candidates under the water in the remarkably short time of eight minutes, thus bettering John the Baptist's record by fully two minutes for each immersion.

Whereas Brother Waters was a fast worker, said the editor, there was a neighboring Baptist minister, "who would sometimes be carried away by his emotions, and would sing an entire verse of a hymn in long meter while holding [his victim] under water." But Miss Wilson had nothing like this to fear. She had placed herself in the hands of a skilled craftsman who worked quickly. The new convert had made the one condition that she be allowed to go down into the water on her cork leg. She weighed 200 pounds, and the artificial leg was a precise mate for her live limb. As Brother Waters led her deeper into the water she experienced great difficulty in keeping her artificial leg down. Each time the great baptizer undertook to immerse the girl, the buoyancy of her leg stood her on her head. After a dozen futile attempts to submerge her, the minister called for a fifty-six pound weight to ballast his victim. Miss Wilson refused to stand for it; she strode forth from the water and joined the Presbyterian Church, where the buoyancy of a lady's leg was not necessarily a bar to her accepting with dignity the rite of baptism. The Georgia editor proposed that artificial limbs makers create a perforated metal appendage for the use of Baptists.

Immersion as a mode of baptism caused much joking comment. Constantly editors discussed the subject. A mule near Thomson, Georgia, stepped into an open well. His groans brought help, and after much hauling and pulling the animal was once again on top of the ground. The McDuffie *Journal* said, "this mule, we dare say, is decidedly in favor of sprinkling instead of plunging."

There were others, however, who contended "plunging" was the answer. One ardent advocate of immersion made the boast that he could preach on any subject found in the Bible. All he had to do was to open the Scriptures and the first words he saw would serve as a text. He was challenged on this proposition, and he opened the Bible, and the first words he saw were: "The voice of the turtle is heard in the land." The brother was stumped at first. He said, "Brethren, at first thought one would think there was not much in this text, but on a little consideration you will see there is a good deal in it." Preaching eloquently on the voice of the turtle he maintained that the turtle had no voice so how could it be heard in the land? The only sound the turtle could make was a splashing one when he fell off a log into the creek. Therefore his voice, such as it was, suggested immersion. Much of this nonsense about baptism was the kind of humor to keep an editor in hot water. A large number of readers were on edge about their church affiliations, and those denominations which practiced immersion were on the defensive. But the editors felt a desire to bring to public notice humorless preachers who were as limited in breadth of vision as the one who was stumped momentarily on the literal subject of the voice of the turtle.

Another subject as good as the denominations was Negro humor. The editors usually handled it with a sentimental touch. Often the Negro was placed in an inferior position, but in this the publisher was following a simple rule for good folk humor. He profited in the long run by this practice. Much of the light material he published was dredged from this rich and inexhaustible vein. A story could be found to point up almost any moral. For instance, the irritating trick of bragging about one's lineage and aristocratic background was made fun of in a story of a Virginia lady and an old colored man. The lady, who was visiting in Louisville, Kentucky, sought to cover up her personal shortcomings by boasting about her home county and her maiden name. She told an ancient and dignified Negro of the Uncle Remus type that her maiden name was Morson. The old man replied, "I b'longed to Mars' Hugh Morson. I knowed we was related!"

Poking fun at false vanity came easy for the editors. They were clever at the art of subtle deflation. It amused them to take sly digs at pretense and to explode the myths by which many people lived. A man landed in Louisville looking for a Colonel Smith. A polite native pointed out at least a dozen Colonel Smiths but none of them was the right one. In desperation, the visitor stated that he had served in the Confederate Army under Colonel Smith and wanted very much to see him again. The Kentuckian hastened to explain that there was no such person by that name in Louisville, because none of the many Colonel Smiths there had been nearer a war than the bar of the Galt House.

As famous as Kentucky's perennial colonels were those two eminent Southerners who started a legend, the governors of North and South Carolina. One of them is credited with saying to the other, with intent to imbibe, "It has been a long time between drinks." Surely the two must have met and the historic words been uttered, but when and under what circumstances is one of the puzzles of history. Editors all over the South have tried to unravel it but in their attempts at clarification they have succeeded only in confusing matters. The editor of the Pulaski (Tennessee) *Citizen* made as good an attempt as any to get at the actual truth. He said the Governor of South Carolina visited the Governor of North Carolina to adjust some interstate matters pertaining to turpentine and rice. Between them sat a demijohn of fancy double copper-distilled North Carolina corn whisky, and each governor was equipped with a capacious tin cup.

Interestingly the men appeared to be of somewhat the same physical type, but actually there were several fundamental differences. The Governor of South Carolina was "a square drinker," and a man with a great warm heart. His skin was perforated by millions of pores, and he could "hist" liquor all night without overheating. The Governor of North Carolina was a tight-skinned man who retained every drop of whisky he swallowed.

The two sat on the piazza of the executive mansion at Raleigh and argued first about turpentine and then rice. First one dipped into the demijohn and then the other. When dinner was announced the pair moved their jug into the dining room and feasted on jowls and greens, sweet potatoes, spareribs and buttermilk. Again the cups went into service. At the end of the meal the loose-skinned South Carolinian settled down for a comfortable evening of talking and drinking, but soon the tight-skinned North Carolinian was asleep. The Governor of South Carolina waggled his cup under the nose of his host and got no response. After a second waggling of the cup, the Governor of South Carolina murmured to the Governor of North Carolina, "Governor, don't you think it's a long time between drinks?" There was no response. George, the butler, knew his master was asleep for the evening and that the liquor was exhausted. He took to the woods in humiliation. The gallant South Carolinian mounted his horse to ride away and a bystander heard him mutter in a hurt tone "that there was coming to be a hollowness in friendship, and that human nature was in danger of drifting into a condition of mockery."

Light pieces of Southern local color and traditions gave the editors great pleasure. They also furnished genuine enjoyment to both contemporary and future readers of the paper. These luscious bits of journalism have become seductive "booby traps" for serious research students. They have more appeal and oftentimes more value to modern readers than the so-called important stories. A few isolated paragraphs of "editorial observations" sometimes had greater contemporary interest than much of the news material, which was often stale before it was ever printed. Papers edited by long-faced old-time partisans are like their creators, dull and unimaginative. In contrast, papers that studied the tastes of their readers and carried a reasonable number of lighter stories have flourished through the years. On their mastheads today they carry high volume numbers in proud Roman numerals.

Bragging about the South often resulted in humorous bits. Editors were always conscious that the South was their first love, and they often wrote of the region with the same glowing warmth they bragged about new brides and babies. Perhaps no Southerner put his feeling more eloquently in words than an effusive justice of the peace in Sandersville, Georgia. According to the Choctaw (Mississippi) *Plaindealer* he concluded a marriage ceremony thus: "By the authority vested in me as an officer of the State of Georgia, which is sometimes called the Empire State of the South; by the fields of cotton that spread out in snowy whiteness around us; by the howl of coon dogs, and the gourd vine, whose clinging tendrils will shade the entrance to your humble dwelling place; by the red and lucious heart of the water melon, whose sweetness fills the heart with joy; by the heavens and earth, in the presence of these witnesses, I pronounce you man and wife."

Nothing so clearly indicates the turn of the Southern rural mind for approximately seventy years as the character of reading matter in the weekly papers. Whether the easy pace at which Southern life progressed during the period from 1865 to 1930 was economically sound for the section is beside the point. Life did go on at a leisurely pace in many sections and the people enjoyed it. Loafers around P. C. Cheaver's livery stable in Lebanon, Kentucky, discovered a spider "no bigger than a pea" performing an engineering feat of enormous proportions. At eleven-thirty in the morning the spider looped a strand of web around a mouse. By nine o'clock the next morning the mouse, more dead than alive, was three inches off the floor. "The news of the novel sight soon became circulated," said the editor of the Marietta (Georgia) *Journal,* "and hundreds of people visited the stable to see the sight." The spider's Lilliputian struggle became a great topic of local speculation. Here was a baffling question. How could a tiny spider lift a mouse off the floor? To the people of

Lebanon it was a more formidable engineering problem than building the Brooklyn Bridge. Perhaps it was.

Philosophically, the editor turned his mind to speculations upon the foibles of humanity. To Will C. Hight of the Winston County (Mississippi) *Journal* life seemed a series of ridiculous contradictions. No one had discovered the secret of contentment. One man was building a house at an exorbitant price while another was trying to sell one for less than it cost him. One man was spending every cent of money he could rake and scrape together to give flowers to his sweetheart and to take her to shows in the hope of making her his wife, while a neighbor was mortgaging everything he had to get a divorce. One man cursed the fate that made him work indoors at a desk, and another wished that he could work inside protected from the weather. The man in business hoped for the time when he could retire, while his neighbor struggled to get into business. The farmer looked for the day when he could sell his farm and move into town, while the town businessman was slaving to get enough money piled up so that he could sell out and move away to a farm where he could have a big bell at the kitchen door and play at being a plantation owner. Perhaps the editor himself dreamed of the day when he might slip away from his cares and take life easy digging worms and catching catfish in a neighboring creek.

Whatever the editor's dreams were along this line, actually he was kept busy catching type lice and passing them on for his subscribers to enjoy in their idyllic moments of "setting on the piazza" in the shade.

Chapter 9

The Southern Mind in Thralldom

MUCH of the material that passed over the editorial desk was neither news in a strict sense nor humor. It came from a rich vein of Southern folklore. Country editors everywhere recognized the value of these folk stories and they printed them often. It is difficult to determine how much of this material was seriously regarded by the publishers and how much was merely space-filler.

From the mass of published folk stories which had recognizable relation with actual conditions of life, it is possible to establish some elements of regional thought. Fear and uncertainty are basic themes in much of this material. People had a vague dread of divine visitations, alien races, disease, failure, reptiles, insects and disaster always in the back of their minds.

The remedies people used to treat illness show not only the general lack of medical care but also the primitive attitudes they had toward disease and its causes. Oftentimes only folk medicine was employed to combat all the malnutrition, unsanitary conditions, infections and parasites that caused suffering in the South. Medicines, however, were strong for people believed that illness resulted from some violent force at work in the human body, and the cause of trouble had to be removed by use of powerful remedies.

The influence of superstition and common folk belief upon the Southern mind is great when measured over a period of five decades. It is difficult to estimate the influence of the newspaper in fostering beliefs of all sort. Much preposterous material was certainly disseminated by the press. The formal editorial attitude was of little actual consequence so long as the papers continued to offer this sort of story. Inadequately schooled readers lacked the discernment to distinguish truth from legend. To them the printed word was gospel, and they were not equipped to detect facetiousness or subtlety in it.

As reflected in much of this basic news material, the rural mind was not a rational one. Collectively it gave evidence of not having the capacity to follow through in its process of reasoning. It accepted the idea that man functions in the universe under the direct power of a series of supernatural controls. It is true that this concept is of ancient origin, but perhaps it was never more pronounced in a civilized society than in the New South. Progressiveness was always in conflict with established local order, and outside influences had to filter slowly through the social structure. Many new ideas had their origin in Europe or at least outside the region, and both sources were suspect in the South. To effect material change in local custom and usage required tolerance, courage and well-directed energy, none of which was sufficiently prevalent generally to make appreciable departures from old ways of life.

To the country editor the conservatism of the region constituted a problem. He was forced to choose between drifting with the strong current of the folkways of his patrons or struggling to haul his readers' intellectual interests into unfamiliar fields, often against their inclinations. Many editors believed leadership was their responsibility and sometimes for their pains they found themselves battering their heads against the rugged barriers of community prejudice. To be effective, every published line had to be tempered with foreknowledge of the restricted intellectuality of the community. Because of this elementary block to free expression of ideas, many a publisher paid feeling tribute to a departed colleague with the wistful sentiment: "His real ability lay in knowing what not to print."

Out of the great mass of folk material published in the country papers it becomes clear that a powerful guiding force in the rural Southerner's life was his stern evangelical religious faith. Fundamentally it was presumed that his religious ideals were based upon the gentle and humane teachings of the New Testament, but history as recorded in the papers eloquently refutes this. It is to be seriously doubted whether an appreciable number of literal-minded Southerners read their Bibles understandingly beyond the authoritarian Book of Job. God, as reflected in much of the weekly press, was a highly personal and jealous master. He observed and judged each individual act upon its merits. For sixty years after the Civil War this seems to have been the only system of accounting which most agrarian Southerners could understand. It was the stern God of Abraham, Isaac, Jacob, Moses and Job who kept vigilant watch. The slightest personal default was marked against the transgressor. Thus it was that revival singers everywhere cherished the ancient hymn "Give Me That Old Time Religion."

Of all the sins man can commit, blasphemy was regarded as one of the worst. It received much publicity in the country weeklies, and according to some editors it was immediately punishable. The Princeton (Kentucky) *Banner* told of an old man who complained of dry weather. He cursed the Lord because of the drought and was instantly struck dumb. At Marietta, Georgia, said the *Journal,* a young man sat astride his horse chatting with his companions. He too was embittered by the drought and criticized God. As he did so, lightning played around him in a menacing fashion. Frost came early in Shelby County, Kentucky, said the Oglethorpe (Georgia) *Echo,* and John Cotton was much agitated. He swore bitterly until he was suddenly struck dumb. In Oglethorpe County "a pious good man" bought a pen of shucks from a profane neighbor. Before he could move them a cyclone blew away the sinful neighbor's property but the shuck pen remained unharmed.

During Reconstruction the Selma (Alabama) *Southern Argus* published a story of the "trooly loil" who whipped a Methodist preacher in Blount County, Tennessee. Six men were involved in the crime; three of them died tragically, a fourth was injured when he fell from his horse, a fifth was struck by lightning and the sixth was in jail awaiting trial. In addition to the retribution visited upon the human tormentors of a man of God, the tree to which the preacher was strapped was struck and destroyed by lightning.

Preachers themselves were not immune from Divine wrath. A Reverend Davidson of Raytown, Georgia, said the Warrenton (Georgia) *Clipper* "was warned of the error of his way. He had occasion in a sermon to refer to the incident where Christ applied clay to the eyes of a blind man in order to restore his sight. He commented that this was 'very foolish of Christ' when he was suddenly stricken with paralysis of the tongue, and remained speechless, utterly unable to articulate for several hours." In Texas there occurred "a most singular and melancholy affair. A man named Sibley argued with his wife 'Big Jennie.' " As the row grew warmer the husband became extremely blasphemous, once calling upon God to paralyze him if he were wrong. He was struck dumb "and has not uttered a word since."

Ten miles from Washington, North Carolina, there stood a longleaf pine which served as a landmark. This old tree was spared when the country was cut over; in fact, it had never been chipped for turpentine, nor were there any carelessly inflicted ax marks on it. Near by were eight sharply defined prints of a horse's feet. For seventy years those tracks had remained distinct. When leaves and dirt fell into them they were mysteriously cleared overnight. "On the best authority," the editor of the Washington *Progress* recited the story associated with the defiant old tree and its miraculous horse tracks. In the early part of the nineteenth century, Jesse Elliott had attempted to organize a Sunday horse race on a neighboring church ground. No one would accept his challenge and he rode away in a gallop. Over his shoulder he shouted stinging oaths at his righteous neighbors. As Elliott rushed toward the old pine, his horse swerved suddenly to one side and dashed him against the tree. His brains were smeared on the bark. Soon that side of the trunk died, though the tree as a whole lived. For a long time the ghastly bloodstains and portions of the brain remained as nauseating testimony of Divine wrath. All who saw this gruesome sight were reminded that country church grounds were not to be desecrated by blasphemy and horse racing.

It was a simple transition in the folk mind from punishment of individuals guilty of capital sins to predictions of the destruction of the whole human race. Calamity howlers told country editors that the world would end on certain dates. In 1874 Cyrus Holmes of Illinois created a sensation in Georgia by predicting the world's end in 1878. He was a "Second Adventist" who was sure that hell was in the middle of the earth for he had seen it. Cyrus claimed he understood thoroughly the Book of Revelation, and that it was revealed to him that Abraham, Isaac, and Jacob represented the human organization. Isaac portrayed the mind, Jacob the soul, and Abraham the body. Samuel P. Quins of the Athens (Tennessee) *Post* regretted that Brother Holmes could not move the date of destruction up four years and save him from having to get out the paper.

Prediction of the Second Advent in 1878 was merely a beginning of this type of story in country papers. By 1882 calamitous prophets were certain that the world would not endure through the year. Scriptural passages were cited to prove the point, and Lycurgus Barrett of the Hartford (Kentucky) *Herald* said resurrection robes were being added to his list of subscription prizes. The Covington

(Georgia) *Enterprise* reported the people of Cedar Shoals were excited over a curious spider web spun across Beaver Dam Creek. It was filled with strange symbols and letters, and people came from miles around to see it for they believed it an evil thing. This same kind of folk prediction of calamity was transferred to the erratic markings which appeared on eggs. Occasionally some frightened subscriber rushed into a country newspaper office with an egg bearing a crude "W" which he was convinced foretold war. The same superstition applied to the "seven-year" locusts which roared out one stage of their septennial metamorphis with "W" on their wings.

Sometimes the earth itself created wild rumors. With people believing firmly that hell was not far underfoot, any surface disturbance of the earth was enough to throw a community into hysterics. Frequent notices of tremors left the impression that it was only a matter of time until flames would belch forth from inner chasms and consume the universe. Large cave-ins of the ground attracted crowds and spread horrendous tales that civilization would be swept away. Especially was this true in the Appalachian highland area. Predictions appeared in 1874 that a volcano would spout forth along the whole eastern mountain chain. The editor of the Athens *Post* said one theory was that the devil was being released for 1,000 years and that he was working his way up through Bald Mountain, and would soon appear on the promontory "to take a survey of the empires, kingdoms, principalities and powers of the earth." This Democratic editor living in a Republican community took a dark view of the Bald Mountain tremors. Speaking of theories that the devil was causing the rumblings he said, "This, however, is reasonable only upon the premise, which few well-informed minds attempt to controvert, that there is no country in the world where the father of sin has more near and dear relatives and friends [and] subservient and faithful followers than in the United States, and it is perfectly natural that they should first receive his personal attention." North and South Carolina, Tennessee and Georgia weeklies contained frequent mention of earth tremors.

When the earth was not misbehaving, human beings who walked upon it were exhibiting strange manifestations of unusual powers. There was an astounding amount of poltergeist material of local origin in the country papers. A long feature story of the strange powers of Little Clara Richardson of Memphis, Tennessee, appeared in the exchanges in 1871. She was a student at Brinkley College and was outwardly a normal girl, but she began to have visions. A spectral visitor told her of a secret which lay buried before the college. So specific were the apparition's instructions that a group of men began digging for the object. When they tired and stopped the ghost admonished the girl to dig for the secret herself. When she had removed a few spadefuls of dirt she reached over and picked up something and then fell to the ground in a dead faint. A medium called up the spirit who said the girl must continue to dig. For an hour the exhausted Clara labored with the spade until she unearthed a glass jar which contained a long yellow envelope, but the apparition said it would have to remain sealed for sixty days. *The Tri-Weekly Republican* of Americus, Georgia, published two accounts of this weird case. Suspense was created by the provision that so much time had to pass before the jar could be opened. Robbers appeared, however, before the time elapsed and stole the jar. Country editors no doubt knew that this type of story was utterly fantastic, but they continued to publish them as serious news stories without explanatory notes.

Somewhat more valid than the account of the Brinkley College ghost were those of boy and girl preachers. Generally these misguided souls became preachers because they had once been given up for dead, or had entered a state of coma, and were considered to have returned from death to preach an inspired gospel. Characteristic of these child prodigies was J. Harry Shannon of Eufaula, Alabama, who could preach, speak and play any instrument. W. D. Jelks of the Eufaula *Times and News* said the boy was "a talking machine with a good memory." A six-year-old Arkansas girl could go into a trance and predict a person's future. In fact, she made one neighbor well-to-do. She told him where to find a purse containing $20,000. Thirteen-year-old Jimmie Cook of Carroll County, Georgia, was a power preacher of the "old time" variety who kept his audiences spellbound with his knowledge of the Bible. A blind neighbor, Sally Foushee, was able to compete with the best of the heaven-inspired juveniles, but unfortunately she proved to be of unstable character and was turned out of the church on a morals charge.

The army of boy and girl preachers whose thin little voices echoed on Southern church grounds had only their visions and their neuroticism to captivate audiences. They were not so well-endowed to entertain as were the "electric girls" publicized in the weekly newspapers. These girls were able to do astonishing things by a seemingly miraculous use of physical power. Electricity baffled most Americans of the eighties and unusual physical phenomena were at once attributed to this strange source of energy. Among the more famous Southern "electric girls" was Lula Hurst who lived in Collardtown, Polk County, Georgia. She defied physical force, laws of gravitation, logic and reason. At least three editors visited this young woman and saw her demonstrate her magical powers. A 180-pound man was unable to hold a chair to the floor when she touched it even with her finger tips. She hurled two men out of bed, tore up an umbrella, bent iron rods and broke pieces of wood without apparent physical exertion. Lula could lie perfectly still and make melodious music sound around her. She could stand on tiptoe on one foot and two men could not shove her over.

Articles in widely dispersed papers told of the wondrous Lula; even the metropolitan dailies became interested. Editors of the Paulding (Georgia) *New Era* and the Marietta *Journal* agreed that the times were out of joint. There were earthquakes, severe cyclones, strange quirks of weather. Now people were exhibiting weird and inhuman powers which enabled them to master force by the simple process of laying on hands. Colonel Freeman of the Cedartown (Georgia) *Advertiser* said people were afraid of Lula Hurst and the other electric girls because they were believed to be manifestations of evil spirits.

Whether or not Lulu Hurst had any intention of adding to the woes of her already downtrodden neighbors was unknown. On her elaborate tour through the South she was interested in relieving them of money for admission tickets to witness her public demonstrations. In Alabama she excited the weekly editors by her appearance. Several columns of Lula's activities appeared in the Eufaula *Times and News*. It was believed there, said the editor, that the Georgia girl was a strange force loose in the world. Mayor Comer of Eufaula, appearing on the stage with a boutonniere in his lapel and a diamond stud in his shirt, said he believed God was showing his omnipotence through the medium of the girl from Collardtown. Lula tossed the local gentry about the stage, broke a number of chairs, caused a supernatural orchestra to play and walked away with a nice sum of money. Elsewhere, however, she had trouble. A New York physician said she was a fraud, and the irreverent Detroit *Free Press* poked fun at her in a facetious article on woman's electrifying power.

Other magnetic females competed with the Polk County wonder.

Mattie Lee Price of Murray County, Georgia, demonstrated that the tips of her fingers possessed the power to lift men off the floor. She took sticks away from strong men by laying her hands upon them and tossed them about the stage and broke chairs for the fun of it. Daisy Robinson, said the Sumter (South Carolina) *Southron,* did startling things to household furnishings. When she was around, "cups, saucers and other frangible articles about the room committed suicide." Sewing machines toppled over, and an organ tied securely to a wall with strong cords danced a hornpipe. Mirrors jumped about on the wall and crashed to the floor. Brickbats tumbled into the room from nowhere. Equally interesting was the mail which came to Daisy from the East. New York and New England cranks wanted the girl to describe her experiences to them so they could be used in studies of clairvoyant powers and in the writing of books.

People grew tired of the electric girls, and when the world failed to end and cyclones and earthquakes again became normal phenomena, the girls lost their appeal. "Whitfield County now comes along with an electrical wonder," wrote the editor of the North Georgia *Times,* "she is quite young and, of course, very beautiful. We are of the opinion that Eve and all her beautiful daughters possess this same magnetic influence, and while some lift chairs with awful fat men on them, others content themselves with lifting the captured hearts of the sterner sex into the elevated bowers of love. This is where romance reigns, the queen unrivaled."

It was easy to change pace from describing strange human phenomena to repeating hoary folk tales of the stinging hoop snake. This serpent was a horned, jointed, stinging monster which curled head to tail and rolled across the land like the rim of a cart wheel. It did not matter that herpetologists refuted the idea that such a snake existed. Those rural Southerners who doubted the hoop-snake story had never lived near swamps where such things could be seen; neither had they read their country papers. W. H. Inloes of Asheville, North Carolina, wrote the Smithsonian Institution in 1885 about the possibility of these horned, stinging snakes' existing. A Dr. Reims replied that there was no such thing. This failed, however, to convince the editor of the Lenoir *Topic* who declared a man named Eagle brought into Black Rock Springs, Virginia, a four-and-a-half-foot hoop snake with black rings and two horns in its tail which, if pressed, exuded poison. The *Topic* editor assured his readers that their only protection from a hoop snake was to get behind a tree. Papers everywhere published a lot of nonsense on this subject. Some of them sincerely kept the legend alive, while others deflated it with tall yarns of how they had seen jointed India-rubber hoop snakes come to pieces and then collect their fragments, reassemble themselves and crawl away.

No amount of scoffing was able to destroy the stinging hoop snake folk belief. It appeared in exchange columns with perennial freshness. In fact, the snake was a source of much Southern folklore. A characteristic story was reported by the Salisbury *Carolina Watchman.* It was said that Dr. Pleas Henderson and Dr. Samuel G. Boynton were riding along a country road when they discovered a black snake crawling up to a nest of young blackbirds. The parent birds were highly excited and were busy bringing white ash leaves to cover the nest. When the nest was covered, they apparently felt it was protected and awaited the downfall of the snake. As it came near enough to attack the young birds, contact with the leaves caused it to relax its hold and fall to the ground dead. When this drama of life and death was complete, the old birds removed the leaves and resumed feeding their young. The doctors failed to explain why the white ash leaves killed the snake but did not harm the birds.

There was a great body of folk matter published about the ability of snakes to hypnotize their victims. Tales were recited of rattlesnakes' charming house cats, rabbits, chickens and other animals. They were said to be able to keep up a nerve-tingling whirring of their rattles, and to focus their beady eyes on their victims until they were within striking distance.

All snakes and everything which had to do with snakes made gripping news. Every year most papers felt duty bound to publish enough material on this subject to keep interest at a good pitch. Rattlesnakes were given almost as much space as most county officials. Fantastic accounts of human accidents with snakes and of the unusual places into which the reptiles wormed their way always gave spice to locals. Some editors, when they were unable to uncover a legitimate snake story, proceeded to make one up. This, however, was seldom necessary, because that unfailing spring of country journalism, the exchange, could always be tapped for enough hair-raising material to bring a period of dull news to life.

Snake stories were usually sinister as well as fantastic. As an example take the one published by the Wadesboro (North Carolina)

Herald which claimed that two Negro children found a nest which they mistook for that of a quail and ate the eggs. Unfortunately these were snake eggs and the children died.

Perhaps the strangest and most incredible stories were written about the cabbage snake. In 1904, the weeklies of Tennessee, Alabama, Mississippi and Georgia told of the appearance of this remarkable, almost microscopic serpent. In Greene County, Alabama, said the Selma *Canebrake Herald,* persons reported snakes in their cabbages. These were said to be about four inches long and the size of a sewing thread. They ranged in color from green to dark brown, and were extremely difficult to see. As usual with such stories, some unnamed doctor declared these creatures were deadly poisonous. Accounts were published about an entire Negro family dying as a result of eating cabbage soup which contained the tiny reptiles. Tennessee papers said that the cabbage fields of Trousdale, Cheatham, Smith, Franklin, Coffee and Bedford counties were infested, and at Cookeville, according to the Fayette (Mississippi) *Chronicle,* Mrs. Z. T. Hinds found a small pink snake about the size of a number 40 thread. This was enough to set off rumors wherever cabbage was grown.

These irresponsible stories made people afraid to eat cabbage and the market for this vegetable was seriously affected. Grocerymen, truck farmers, vegetable brokers and the United States Government were disturbed by the falling off of sales. Immediate steps were necessary to restore public confidence. A search by Department of Agriculture officials failed to produce a single cabbage snake or to locate anyone who could make oath he had seen one. Graves of the people supposed to have died as a result of eating contaminated soup could not be found. Publication in country papers had given the story credence, and only by their publishing a denial could it be discredited.

Those superstitious Southerners who survived the cabbage snake scare were still exposed to horrors. Too many people in the South believed that live reptiles took up residence in the human body. White and black alike were victimized by this ancient folk legend. Three full columns of the Jackson (Tennessee) *Whig and Tribune* quoted a fantastic story originally published in the Murfreesboro *Record* of the extraction by Dr. J. M. Burger of a mature water moccasin from the stomach of Thankful Taylor. It was said that this girl might have picked up the snake in drinking water, or perhaps it had crawled down her throat while she was asleep. As the reptile grew it needed air, and every time it came up to breathe Thankful had fits. Dr. Burger's extraction was described in nauseating detail. To give validity to the story, the old mountebank produced three affidavits and these were published in full in the *Record*. Significantly, two of these statements were signed with cross marks. Thankful Taylor was only one of many people who appeared in country doctors' offices with live things in their systems. "Lizard leg," as one such disease was called, was said by some editors to be common.

Folk treatment of disease was of major importance in the rural South. Something has already been said of the scarcity of properly trained physicians, the lack of pure water supplies, sanitation and facilities for the care of the sick and the general ignorance of the people as to all matters of health. With this condition prevailing, country newspapers inevitably became conscientious sources for disseminating folk medicine and cures.

One of the most frightening calamities which could happen to anyone before Pasteur's discovery of a serum for rabies was to be bitten by a mad dog. Southerners liked dogs and kept them around in packs. A poor white or a Negro, even though too impoverished to own a gun, often had a pack of half-starved dogs. So long as communities swarmed with dogs there was constant threat of rabies. Editors were always on guard, and they tried to keep communities warned of danger.

Both country and city newspapers published annually many columns about mad dogs. "We scarcely pick up an exchange," said the Toccoa (Georgia) *News* "that we do not see some account of the terrible work done by rabid dogs. Dr. Dozier of Jasper County, died a few days ago from the bite of a mad dog; a Mr. Mahone, of Talbott County, was recently bitten on the thumb by one of these rabid animals, and forty sheep and two pigs known to have been bitten, and which showed unmistakable signs of hydrophobia, died within the past few days."

Before the common use of the Pasteur treatment, there was no sure remedy but there was treatment. Some authorities held that the madstone was the only chance the victim of a mad dog attack had of escaping a death too horrible to be described. The Newberry (South Carolina) *Herald and News* reprinted a two-column story which appeared originally in the New York *Herald*. A man in Missouri had willfully permitted a rabid dog to bite him in order to prove that the madstone would extract the virus. Doctors, thought the *Herald,* should give scientific attention to the madstone. There was grave doubt in the New Yorker's mind whether the madstone belonged in a geological or a medical and chemical museum. Chemists and doctors were called upon to locate a stone and to determine scientifically its healing power.

In the South there was little doubt about the power of the madstone. A report in the Calhoun (Georgia) *Times* disclosed that Mary Skates was bitten by a dog on the hand and in the face. She was taken to a Dr. Rudicil who applied a madstone and she was healed. The Paulding (Georgia) *New Era* said W. L. Cochran, postmaster, storekeeper and farmer at Ackworth possessed a stone which was taken from the maw of an old doe forty or fifty years before.

Madstones, said the Calhoun *Times,* were used by the ancients. They possessed porous characterictics which gave them an adhering and extractive or capillary quality. Traditionally, these stones were flat and oval, were bluish in color, somewhat resembling the old Southern "thunder rocks" which were burned in fireplaces to keep the hawks away. It was said that if an individual was actually bitten by a rabid dog, the stone would adhere to the wound and remain there until it had absorbed the poison. If the dog was not mad the stone would not adhere to the wound. Proof positive that a madstone would work was published in the Newberry *Herald and News* as part of an account of a bitter struggle between a jack and a maddened stallion in William Thomas' Mercer County, Kentucky, barnlot. The stallion had gone mad after being bitten by a rabid dog. William Thomas, Jr. was bitten by the same dog and was treated with a madstone. The stone adhered to the boy three times, and there was every indication that he had thus avoided hydrophobia; no thought was given to the jack.

One skeptical voice was raised among Southern editors concerning the power of madstones. At Lenoir, North Carolina, the editor of the *Topic* thought it should be accepted only as an extreme treatment. "The 'madstone question,'" he wrote, "has been generally discussed for the past week. Some say that it is all tomfoolery to believe that there is any such thing as a madstone with any curative virtues in it, while others contend that it is all a matter of absorption and chemical attraction and that it is possible there may be substances which have the property of drawing out the virus of a snake or a rabid dog by suction. As for us we are inclined to look upon a madstone as a humbug, but if we should be bitten by a rabid dog we should not hesitate to apply one. Just so did Captain Fawcette and Captain Moore view the matter when they applied madstones to the wounds from the bite of a dog upon their children."

Newspapers reflected the folk mind at work in other scientific fields. Farm animals suffered from the strange medical aberrations of their masters. Cows lacking sufficient food in the winter were treated with regularity for hollow tail and hollow horn in the spring. Hogs were given cures which were more debilitating than the ailments they suffered. In fact, it was not until after 1920, and then through an intelligent campaign in the rural press, that much of the frontier folklore about farm animals was replaced with scientific information. One of the reasons the South had failed to produce more meat at home was the prevalence of disease among animals. Farmers lacked information on how to keep them healthy and free from disease.

Untrammeled by fact, the folk mind roamed through other fields. Periodically weekly papers published stories of the appearance of wild men and women. One such story in the Hart County (Kentucky) *Three Springs* told of the fantastic adventures of William Bowman. This humble Kentucky husbandman was a modern backwoods Romulus whose parents deserted him in the North Carolina mountains. He was suckled by a bear. "At the age of ten he was captured, tied hand and foot, and then his captors found that he could not talk. Nor could he be persuaded to take any food but milk, which he sucked from a bottle, showing that he lived solely by nursing the bear. Bowman is now a farmer near Omega, and anyone doubting the truth of this statement can have it verified by seeing him."

Near Chattanooga, in 1883, said the Warrenton (Georgia) *Clipper,* a wild man was seen eating the carcass of a horse. His body was naked. His beard was from four to five feet long, and his hair was down on his shoulders. He had been seen once at Acworth, Georgia, and at Chickamauga. By accident the wild man climbed into an empty freight car and was captured by a train crew. Perhaps more fantastic was the Trinity (Louisiana) *Herald's* story of the wild girl of Catahoula. Two travelers saw her first at Hemp's Creek. She was the "most ferocious being human eye had ever seen." The travelers could get no closer to this wild woman than fifty feet. When they approached she leaped a "clayroot" seven feet high and was fleet as a deer. She spoke no language but made instead a gibbering sound. She was powerfully built and about sixteen years of age. This lady of Catahoula wore no clothing and had long brown hair which hung to her waist. It was estimated by the traveling men that she was strong enough to outdo three men at once. A committee of fifteen scouts was organized and sent into the woods with two weeks' supply of food to capture the woman.

Folk stories of wild people and wild animals, strange physical manifestations and diseases constituted a large part of what editors loosely classified as "material of interest to our readers." Publishers differed radically in their opinions of the validity of this kind of news copy. Some of its was accepted as factual, while the remainder was labeled fantasy. Sometimes it is very difficult to determine whether the editors themselves believed there was truth in their folk material. Whatever their attitude, the fact that this stuff was published is significant. It is interesting to observe how well this mass of folk material fitted into the superstitious pattern of rural thought and encountered willing acceptance. Its appearance in newspapers only confirmed the ignorant opinions and beliefs which prevailed among an astounding portion of the weekly's constituency. When the country editor said that the times were out of joint because of abnormal seasonal changes many of his readers quickly took his judgment as established fact. Editors and some discriminating readers naturally realized the more fantastic stories were not true but they were probably a rather small minority. Both the gullible and the skeptical read them with avidity.

What should have been of concern to the realistic rural editor was the enormous economic loss which his section suffered because of superstition and folk belief. Backwardness, illiteracy and reactionary attitudes are wasteful and expensive. No thinking editor could observe the dense smoke pall hanging low over the South each spring and fail to appreciate that his community was destroying its resources. Ignorant and violent local people believed that forests were alive with snakes, varmints, insects and miasma, and the surest way to destroy these was to use fire. Spring after spring they set fire to the woods.

Millions of dollars were lost annually to the section because of such twisted beliefs, perhaps more than enough money to maintain a first class medical school in the South. Hidden away in the musty files of the country papers is this weird, wasteful and virulent chapter of social life in the New South.

Chapter 10

The Roar of the Lion is Heard in the Land

IN addition to the native wonders publicized in the country newspapers, there were the circuses. Barns, walls, trees, warehouses, fences and everything else which would hold posters were covered with lithographs of marvels to come. Circus publicity men were liberal with their seductive posters but they also used the newspapers to draw customers. There was a good-natured camaraderie among country newspapermen and circus agents. Almost every town large enough to support a newspaper had sufficient population to be visited by some kind of a show at least once every two years. In the South the circus season was longer than in most other sections, extending from April to December. The shows liked to hit the Southern towns toward fall because by then they were moving toward winter quarters.

For the countryman whose drab life was a repetition of work, crop seasons, protracted meetings, court days and uncertain weather, the gaudy notices promising the appearance of a circus offered a welcome break. When the average Southerner opened his county paper on Saturday morning, after the first hint of the circus had reached him and read that soon "the roar of the lion" would be heard in the land he was happy. Spread out before him were streamers two or three columns wide, which listed in the most extravagant language the wonders of the world which would be hauled into towns and shown under sizzling (130°) canvas tents.

The countryman could look forward to seeing a show, and also a parade in which he would be an integral part. Sometimes there would be a balloon ascension. Occasionally he could see some fighting among his neighbors and he could count on hearing some gossip.

Nothing ever caught the attention of the perennially juvenile American mind like the circus. It was an exotic world which was dragged from place to place. It made extravagant promises to extract money from the yokels. Somehow the Southerner adjusted himself to this fine bit of sham and hypocrisy and accepted it as a natural portion of his entertainment.

Editors begged for shows in many instances. The offering did not have to be original and clever. People liked the red and gilt paint on wagons, fancy colored velvet clothing, the stodgy humor of the clowns and tricks performed even by animals as commonplace as dogs, mules and pigs. Their pulses responded to the rhythm of the raucous music of a circus band, which was gay and loud even though it was not good. Elephant tracks in sandy streets, the roar of lions, the sharp nasal pleading of the barker, the smell of the cook wagon, all of these combined to weave the magic of the circus.

Since about 1840, when Seth Home introduced colored bills, advertising a circus was important. In 1843 the big top became a symbol of the circus, and about the same time newspaper advertising first appeared. Artists who made the lithographed placards had to be imaginative. They had to picture human beings and animals in acts which were impossible but interesting, and to offer twice as much show as the management could deliver. It was not enough to picture a man being fired from a prosaic cannon; he had to be hurled far above tent tops from the flaming mouth of a monster field gun and the expression on his face had to be pleasant. In fact the purpose of the poster was to make the stingiest strait-laced cotton farmer in Mississippi relent in his determination not to attend the circus.

Newspaper advertising was denied the use of color, except in a few minor instances. Artists depended on black and white figures. These they placed in hair-raising positions, defying physical law. Wild animals they showed grouped in their natural habitat and in such numbers that many trains would be needed to haul them. The real artistry, however, in newspaper publicity was in the composition of the descriptive material. The copy writers had to get effects as vivid and violent with nothing but words. The spiels they achieved made parents feel that it would be almost criminal not to take their children to the show. And the editors helped the press agents spin their magic.

Rural and small-town Southerners liked the circus, despite their occasional religious scruples. They looked forward to its coming with the same happy anticipation with which they wait for watermelons to ripen, for laying-by time and the beginning of political campaigns and camp meetings. Although farm people had little cash in spring and summer, they somehow got together astonishing sums to pay admission to the circus, to buy popcorn, candy and insipid lemonade. A day ahead of the arrival of a circus, dusty country roads as far as thirty or forty miles away were dotted with crowded wagons headed for town. Some families slept in or under their wagons during fair weather and cooked their meals over open fires so as to be on hand for the unloading of the circus and to get good positions on Main Street for the parade. Excursion trains moved populations of towns and villages to the show and local reporters for country papers made a fuss over these visitors.

Wagon lots were crowded. Fences, poles, tree limbs and every other place to which a mule could be hitched were pre-empted. Barking and fighting country dogs swarmed over the towns. Horses, restless under the heat and excitement, sometimes cut through wagons and buggies in blind runaway dashes. Carefree men and boys heightened the glamour of the moment with whisky, and had the notion in their convivial state that they, rather than the more highly decorated clowns, were the comedians. Like some of the menagerie they usually wound up in cages, but far removed from the circus grounds. The next week these miscreants were painfully reminded of their disgrace by ironic accounts of their indiscretions in the paper. For instance, Frank Ball, "a neighboring brother went to town and got a little high on lemonade and various other little things. He jerked out his pistol and saluted his friends in the parade. Frank was sent back to his country estate with a $50 bail bond and a hang over."

Mothers worried during circus days for fear their brood would be lost or injured. Sober and frugal fathers remained on constant guard to see that their families did not get excited and spend too much money. Some men were careful not to be too much in evidence, especially where preachers, deacons and creditors could see them. Rawboned and sun-tanned country boys, their upper lips just beginning to sprout downy mustaches, and their bodies ill at ease in clean clothes, high collars and shoes, had their attention divided between the circus and the girls. Uncounted couples remembered years later how they had flirted or even met for the first time at a circus. Showmen made thousands of dollars out of young couples. Here was a ready-made sideshow, candy, popcorn and concert trade. No young man with enough courage to ask a girl to go to the circus refused to offer her everything the shrewd barkers suggested.

Of all the circus patrons none was more comical than the elderly man or woman who pretended boredom with the whole idea but consented "reluctantly" to take the children to see the parade, and then enthusiastically followed it to the show ground. Editors appreciated this human foible. The Eufaula (Alabama) *Times* said, "Circus coming, old fogies are relaxing in their views and some even propose to take their children to see the animals which the Lord made." Will C. Hight of the Winston County (Mississippi) *Journal* wrote, "The roar of the lion is in the land as the big circus wends its way southward, and the children (with such chaperones, guardians and nurses as are needful to properly escort each one) are consequently happy."

Circus managers understood the moral scruples that held some people back and the professed boredom of the older folks, and a good manager had a dozen ways of drawing everybody in. Parades were trade-getters of the first order. Old John Robinson's advertisement of his street exhibition was characteristic of the others. He assured his patrons of a "procession of dazzling splendor, unsurpassed as a moving panorama of brilliant chariots, wagons, cars, cages, carriages, dens of animals, two bands of music, horses, wild beasts, fifty ponies, a team of ponderous elephants drawing a golden chariot forming a picture of bewildering beauty." Customers generally cared little that some street parades were hoaxes. Showmen knew the art of dragging gaily painted wagons through drab country towns so as to make them appear spectacular. A few gilded wooden figures on top of a wagon became a dazzling spectacle against a backdrop of weather-beaten and snaggled-toothed buildings. Cages labeled "lions" in glittering letters were as exciting as exhibitions of the beasts. Clowns driving donkey carts in and out among the heavier vehicles drew attention away from the tawdry quality of the procession and focused it on themselves. No matter how indifferent the display, it appealed to a basic human love of a parade and always served to lead crowds to circus grounds.

There was one spectacle which circuses offered free during the latter part of the nineteenth century. Balloon ascensions could not very well be confined within a paying arena, except for filling the gas bag. Consequently most shows used this feature as advertising. It was often a disappointment to the crowd and always a tricky and troublesome stunt for the showmen. Balloons were expensive and their upkeep difficult. There was always danger of an explosion which would mean certain death to the personnel of the act. The Imperial European Circus announced in the Stanford (Kentucky) *Interior Journal* that Professor Windy Kintz would give his "grand free balloon ascension." "It will be a sight such as it may never be your good fortune to witness again." A week later Colonel Walton wrote, "The circus bills said that Professor Windy Kintz, would go up in a monster balloon. It was a rather windy affair, anyhow—so far as the balloon and Kintz were concerned." Perhaps the circus managers did not mean to make false claims when they advertised they would have balloons with their shows. Uncertain weather conditions and frequent accidents prevented them from keeping promises printed on bills before the show season began. At Columbus, Georgia, Professor Vandygrift ascended a half mile in a hot gas balloon and it exploded just as he was kissing his hand to the audience. Women and children screamed, and men stood in fright as the Professor fell into the Chattahoochee River and was drowned before help reached him. Balloons were always ungovernable. One dragged Emma Colter from central Kentucky to a height of two miles above mountainous Rowan County, where it caught on fire. She was able to bring the burning bag down but was almost dragged to death against the mountainsides. Eventually this risky attraction was abandoned.

Before the monopolies got control of the circus, the South was visited by many individual shows. Perhaps the most famous was Old John Robinson's. John started in the show business in the thirties, and in 1840 he was billed as a "four-horse" rider. He made a trip to England with the Van Amburgh Circus and acquired for himself an international reputation. Old John was an excellent performer, and frequently in his later days took part in one of the equestrian features. In his many years he grew wise in the show business, as well as in the ways of the South. Early Southern editors favored him and happily gave him space. It was true that Old John had a good circus and willingly showed in the smaller county seat towns, but much of his success came because he had good publicity sense and a facility for giving tickets to the right people. The editor of the Abbeville (South Carolina) *Press and Banner* said after forty-five years the approaching date of Robinson's show still made everybody happy.

In 1869 Robinson was parading through South Carolina with large numbers of wagons marked "trained animals"—"a good many of which, by the way," added the editor of the Chester *Reporter,* "have nary an animal in them." Six years later three full columns of brisk advertisements proclaimed his organization to be "the largest show on earth," at least the largest traveling in the South. Advertisements claimed an unrivaled menagerie and aquariums that filled several special trains, which conveyed the show on its travels. Robinson's agents had ransacked the sea, the air and the land for wonders and monsters. There were likewise skilled horseback riders, double-somersault leapers, tight and slack rope walkers, trapeze performers, four-horse riders and twenty clowns, including John Lowlow, a former student at the University of North Carolina and one of the great clowns of all time. Robinson, "King of the Showmen," knew the value of a good copy writer, and his lists of animals were made to sound like the roll call of the universe. His only handicaps were the inadequacies of the English language, which often failed to convey his sense of the superlative. One thing could be said for Old John—he knew the Southern people better than they knew him. With great care his dazzling advertisements sobered up sufficiently to say, "The public, particularly the ladies, children and families are assured that this department is without a blemish, and nothing said or done that can offend the most fastidious taste of a refined or high-toned community."

Thomas H. Clark of the Selma (Alabama) *Southern Argus* said, "The readers of the *Argus* will find in another column the advertisement of John Robinson's Circus and Menagerie, which will exhibit in this place and at several other points in the neighborhood in the course of a few weeks. It has not been our custom to admit advertisements of this kind to our columns, as we are generally crowded for room for matter of more interest to our readers, but the persuasion of Colonel Davis, the agent, and the display pictures of lions, tigers and other furious looking beasts won us over." The sincerity of this statement may be doubted, for few papers were ever so badly crowded that they could not include a circus ad in the last three columns of the second or left-hand page. John Robinson's copy paid well in cash and complimentary tickets, and many editors were flattered if they were given an opportunity to interview him. Characteristic of the feeling of country publishers toward this showman was that expressed by the Clarksville (Tennessee) *Tobacco Leaf*. In a long story its editor said John Robinson's word was as good as his circulars.

Old John was by no means alone in exploiting the Southern amusement trade. Earlier there was Colonel C. T. Ames, a Confederate veteran who owned the "Grand New Orleans Menagerie and Circus." The Colonel publicized the fact that when his show played Atlanta in 1869 he gave the proceeds of one performance to the Ladies Memorial Association. News of this generosity was spread over the South. The Abbeville (South Carolina) *Press and Banner* said this was a "graceful charity and commendable liberality which should bespeak him a kind reception everywhere in the South." His notices promised a show composed of "150 men and horses." After listing the usual menagerie, clowns, athletes, leapers, trapeze artists and horseback riders, the Colonel offered a grand and glittering tournament in which the carriage of the Rajah of Egypt, surrounded by live royal tigers, was the center of attraction. A unique feature of the Ames show was uncaged lions and tigers led by Mademoiselle Eugene parading through the streets. Advertisements promised that streets of towns would become jungle paths where slinking beasts would prowl like hound dogs.

Rivaling John Robinson and Colonel Ames were W. C. Coup, S. H. Barrett and Company, Sells Brothers, Miles Orton, W. W. Coles, Adam Forepaugh and even the Great Barnum. W. C. Coup's United Monster Shows advertised in the conventional style in the country papers, except that they had a striking colored sticker pasted in by hand, of the great aerialist Zulu flying through the air above the tent. Editor Jelks said Coup was "a sterling man of sterling worth." He claimed to be the head of the largest show ever organized, which gave the most extensive exhibition ever seen in America. Among the wonders which he proposed to show in the eighties was a series of grand historical tableaux representing Guiteau's assassination of Garfield, with a life-sized figure of Guiteau dressed in the identical suit of clothes which he wore at the time of the assassination. The suit Guiteau wore when he was sentenced would also be exhibited. Scenes of the incidents from the time of the assassination to the sentencing of the murderer would be depicted. The public was promised that more than 500 figures in this national tragedy would be shown, some of whom would be James G. Blaine, Judge Cox, Judge Porter, Lawyer Corkhill and George and Elizabeth Scoville.

Roughest and toughest of the whole group of circus managers was Adam Forepaugh. He specialized in elephants and highly descriptive profanity. His advertisements claimed that he exhibited more elephants "than any other individual in the civilized world." Dexter Fellows described "Old" Adam as looking like Chauncey Depew, but employing a very different strain of oratory. Forepaugh stirred the dust of many Southern towns with his vaunted 1,500 animals, birds and beasts. Though he used the language of Billingsgate, this old Roman was conscious that at times he had to be circumspect, and his publicity was written in language which was supposed to be acceptable even to the more religiously inclined patrons. He was not, however, a satisfactory press agent or a good diplomat. At Pulaski, Tennessee, he left an irate editor behind him. John Boatman, of the Pulaski *Citizen* wrote in 1881, that he found "Mr. Hugh Coyle gentlemenly press agent, prince of politeness," but that Adam was "an insulting old braggart. . . . We hope this may come to his eyes, and teach him that it is at least good policy to affect manners, if he is too brutish to be polite; we have no cause to grumble though, for we found everything else all right except the miserable old proprietor."

John Boatman was not the only person to find Adam Forepaugh a "miserable old proprietor." On the night of November 2, 1882, his circus was loaded on two Louisville and Nashville trains at Columbia, Tennessee, and headed for Pulaski. Later in the night, at Lynville, the first section stopped to take on water, and while it was standing, the second section plowed into it and demolished an engine, a caboose and a sleeping car and crippled two elephants, doing in all $16,000 damage and causing the show to miss the "biggest circus crowd ever gathered in Pulaski." In a long letter to the Pulaski *Citizen* Forepaugh accused the train crews of being drunk when they left Columbia. They had appeared at the circus earlier in the evening in a state of drunkenness and demanded admission to the show. An argument had occurred before the trains left Columbia, but the telegraph operator refused to call the division superintendent to secure new crews. One of the conductors, in a highly intoxicated state, surveyed the wreckage at Lynville and said, "it was good enough for a d—n Yankee — — a —." A general fight ensued between the circus and railroad men. Later a newspaper battle developed between the circus management and the railroad. Forepaugh accused the L. & N. of trying to win its suit in the newspapers.

Getting newspaper publicity for a circus was a precise art. In the immediate postwar years some editors accepted advertisements reluctantly because they disliked publicizing popular entertainments.

FORMERLY ROBINSON & ELDRED'S.

SOUTHERN SHOW,

THE LARGEST

COMBINATION IN AMERICA

Greensboro Wednesday Nov. 13th

John Robinson's

GREAT COMBINATION

CIRCUS & MENAGERIE

Ten Shows

ZOOLOGICAL DEPARTMENT

WILD ANIMALS

Features of the ten Shows,

GRAND GRATUITOUS EXHIBITION

UTZ'S

Cattle Powders

LUNG FEVER, GLANDERS,

UTZ & BRO.,

GRIFFIN,

M J. SHARP'S

Billiard Tables,

ATENT CUSHIONS,

W J SHARP

43 Barow St. New York.

D. R. BUTLER,

& BUTLER,

n Warehouse

ion Merchants

gusta, Ga.

Sale of Cotton and

her Produce.

usta Hotel,

GEORGIA

NES, Proprietor.

BARNUM'S MUSEUM COLLECTION

VAN AMBURG'S

GREAT

Menagerie,

GREAT COMBINATION OF THE BARNUM & VAN AMBURGH MUSEUM & MENAGERIE Co. AND DAN CASTELLO'S GREAT SHOW

IN CONJUNCTION WITH

DAN CASTELLO'S

GREAT SHOW

Greensboro', Tuesday, Nov. 5th, 1867

Barnum's Department—Natural History.

Dan Castello's Department.

SPECIAL ANNOUNCEMENT.

Mademoiselle Pauline,

LITTLE MINNIE.

Two Circus Ads

Some of them believed part of their function was to keep public morals pure. There were also some early fears that publishing circus advertising would make local preachers indignant. Circus press agents found that their first task was to secure acceptance of paid publicity. It was complimentary to the power of the rural press that the agents seemed to believe newspaper advertising governed the size of crowds which attended the show.

Fortunately for press agents, that perennial boy at heart, Marse Henry Watterson of the Louisville *Courier-Journal,* wrote a classic circus editorial. He brushed aside the carping moralists, grabbed up the ringmaster's whip and fell into step with the calliope. Marse Henry believed going to the circus was a moral obligation for purposes of self-rejuvenation. Showmen appreciated the Louisville editor's boost. Many a country editor, prodded by an advance agent, published this "free reader" just before the appearance of a circus in his town.

Press agents sought four kinds of publicity from the country editors. The first, of course, was paid space for their regular advertisements. Second, by handing out some complimentary tickets, they tried to induce the editor to write a local piece on the circus. Third, they could often persuade him to run complimentary "free readers" exchanges from papers where the show had appeared. Finally, after the show was over, they wanted a favorable review that they could send ahead to be published in papers on the show's itinerary. Press agents worked on the theory that the best way to do this was to court favor with the editors' womenfolk. If they could only get them to the circus and see that they had the time of their lives, they could forget the editors.

One limitation on fraudulent advertising was a genuine fear of the bad effect of exchanges. If a circus advertised an act and failed to present it an editor was quick to make the fact known. The Eufaula *Times and News* said that John B. Davis' circus was well attended, "animals good, would compare with Sells Brothers, but the white spotted elephant failed to appear." There were a trained elephant, a black camel and a good concert, and Davis and his staff were polite and pleasant. In short, the show was good but the absence of the much-vaunted elephant was pointed out.

In 1882, Edward Sheafer of the Toccoa (Georgia) *News* said of S. H. Barrett and Company's Show that he liked the trained dogs, bareback riders, tightrope walkers and trapeze artists. Behind this approval was the fine hand of the press agent Willis Cobb. "During the performance," said the editor, "and while upon the grounds, Mr. Cobb bestowed upon us many appreciated attentions which are kindly remembered! And we feel that we hazard nothing in confidently recommending Mr. Cobb to our brethren of the press." At Marietta the editor of the *Journal* felt inadequate to describe the show. The strong man did astounding things, and so did the educated dogs. Never in his life did he expect to see a trapeze artist do such breathless dives. But best of all was a hand-kissing balloonist who sailed away toward the sun to land later in Mr. Charles Rogers' garden on Church Street.

Miles Orton made up with promises what he lacked in animals. After he showed his animals in Elberton, Georgia, the *New South* said the show was good, but "it is a mistake to call so small a collection of animals a menagerie." Before this show reached Elberton it was advertised to be "The Last! The Best! The Great Show You Have been Waiting For! Best circus ever in the state!" This was tall advertising which, pehaps, would not have been tolerated in connection with any other business. Many editors felt the circus was a childhood tradition which it would be sacrilege to abuse. No doubt they realized from the beginning that they would not see everything promised them. As D. M. Wisdom of the Jackson (Tennessee) *Whig and Tribune* said, when a highly advertised daredevil failed to appear, "The fictitious and daring trapeze acrobat failed to put in an appearance, and the thrilling spectacle of a man hanging by his feet in mid-air was wanting, but we suppose no disappointment was felt by the humane crowd."

Less humane in his attitude was Sidney Lewis of the Sparta (Georgia) *Ishmaelite* who reported that his town had just been visited by the Cole Brothers show, "and, incidentally, a gang of cut-throats and pickpockets gave one performance here Monday to a large crowd. Possibly there were more people here than had been here in years and the attendance at the show was good. . . . The show carried away from the county not less than $5,000 and the best compliment we can pay either show or those in attendance is that 'they have gone.' "

Sidney Lewis mentioned a sensitive subject when he referred to the pickpockets and cutthroats who followed the circus. Managers were divided into two groups when it came to controlling the "grifters." Honest managers tried to keep the scoundrels away from their grounds, while others permitted the conycatchers to operate not only on the grounds, but sometimes within side shows. On one occasion the editor of the Pulaski (Tennessee) *Citizen* accused that tough old Spartan Adam Forepaugh of doing a little "grifting" of his own. His regular admission price was fifty cents and seventy-five, but the official ticket wagon was so located that very few people could reach it. Out in the open and easily accessible were two wagons at which tickets were readily available for sixty and eighty-five cents.

Small-town and country people were completely absorbed by the sights immediately before them. They gaped before animal cages, or were captivated by peanut-consuming elephants, and became oblivious to what was going on. Sometimes they were pushed, or people crowded against them momentarily, and in a twinkling of an eye their cash was gone. An old man in Pulaski, Tennessee, fell for the old gag of a man screaming that his pocket had been picked and felt to see if his own money was safe. In a few moments his roll of $107 was gone. Picking the "gillipin's" pockets was as much a part of the circus as were lemonade and swindling side shows. Sells Brothers' manager announced in the papers that his show was being followed by two clever crooks, and that the management would pay $50 apiece for their capture.

It was an astounding thing that flocks of plain Southern people took so much money around with them. Apparently the excitement of circus day caused even the tightest miser to dig up his cash from the garden and strike out for town to display it. Many a man who could not be cheated in a horse trade found himself on the little end of a perfectly innocent-looking gambling deal. In 1881 Mr. Sudsary, a piano tuner of Winston, North Carolina, was involved with a three-card-monte sharper. He won $40, and lost it along with his other cash. Then he rushed to the bank, borrowed $1,000 and lost that. Only with the aid of friends and a half-dozen lawyers did he force the gamblers to repay him.

An ancient story often published in the country papers, and attributed to the *Anglo-American Circuit,* was that of a slick "grifter" who appeared in a community ahead of the circus, located a well-to-do farmer and informed him that he wished to buy a farm. Reluctantly he accompanied the farmer to the circus, advised him against sharpers, but maneuvered him into a shell game to be fleeced by his partner.

The farmer won a few times and he was persuaded to check $500 out of the bank. He lost that and also his cautious friend. Despite newspaper warnings, smart country jakes went right on betting and losing their savings on the turn of walnut hulls and thimbles. A clever racket, not as profitable as "lifting leathers" or taking in large sums at three-card-monte or thimble rigging, was that of telling fortunes and reading heads. Characteristic of this type of swindling was the picking of a yokel in Jackson, Tennessee, who became so dazzled by fat ladies, pretty ladies and snakes in a side show that a phrenologist relieved him in a moment of $2.50 for reading his "bumps."

Not all of the robbery and trickery occurred on the circus grounds. At Sparta, Georgia, while the circus was in town, H. F. Rozier, a local merchant, was blackjacked and robbed of his money and belongings. This crime created a most unhappy community scandal. Three local citizens were arrested and jailed as suspects. Two of them were convicted on circumstantial evidence and sentenced to long jail terms. John Wright reported after the trials that he heard "hangers-on" of Coles' Circus say that they knew where they could make some easy money. Defense counsel for the local citizens followed the show over the South looking for the criminals and was finally able to find them and free the local men who had been sentenced.

Always drunks constituted a menace. Sidney Lewis said his town was full of intoxicated men. "We have never before seen so much dissipation in such a complete form as at the circus. The circus did the work. One young man in Milledgeville paid, besides the admission price, and the price of whisky, $38.75 because he was unable to decide who was performing, he or the lady trapeze artists." Ticket sellers and special circus guards were masters at defeating local bullies who attempted to raise a row. A skillful slap across the mouth, often powerful enough to knock out a handful of teeth, quieted a bad man. Local red-neck constables and police always bustled around circus lots, puffed up with self-importance and a false sense that they were the "law." Constables were often as great buffoons as clowns. Wearing large pistols at their hips they snooped around to make certain that everybody was behaving. Sometimes they made fools of themselves by interfering with the circus acts. At Camden, Tennessee, a horseback rider pretended drunkenness and a band of heavily armed assistant constables arrested him. Only by the most persuasive argument was the performer released and permitted to go on with his act. B. E.

Harris, editor of the Dickson County *Press,* was infuriated. He said since Noah led the animals out of the ark this had been a standard feature in every circus performance. Some states, it was said, passed laws forbidding circus performers to pretend drunkenness in the art of producing laughter.

At near-by Jackson, Tennessee, there was a veritable outbreak of cases of the right of self-determination. In April, before Adam Forepaugh's circus was to appear in May, a Jovelike, handshaking evangelist raised a pertinent issue of freedom of personal choice. He asked all in the congregation who wished to go to Hell to stand, and a boy arose. He was arrested on a charge of disturbing public worship. The court held that "if the boy wanted to go to hell he had a perfect right to do so, and that such conduct did not necessarily disturb the meeting within the meaning of the law."

With the victory of the hell-bent young man fresh in the memory of the entire community, two young blades decided they would test the right of self-determination a little further. They appeared at Forepaugh's Circus with two notorious local prostitutes clinging to their arms. "They were arrested by the police and fined, but gave fictitious names, and hence our inability to publish them to the world. Such violations of public decency, such parading of the vilest of all vices, and such public insults to virtue and morality are wicked beyond the power of words, disgraceful to the extent of boasting in shame, and disgusting to the fullest depths of the vilest depravity, and the names of the guilty should be heralded to the world as boldly and publicly as they have confessed their own want of decency, self respect, regards for virtue and personal honor. This we would have done and will do yet if in our power."

Circus managers had to use care in their advertising and performances not to stir up the local bigots. Frequently preachers and conservative community leaders were prejudiced against circuses. They questioned the personal morality of the performers. It was popularly believed the circus performers were without morals, and that every circus train was potentially a den of adultery and fornication, that gambling was permitted wholesale. Women were improperly dressed in their public acts, and they violated local taboos against riding astride, performing athletic feats and making public spectacles of themselves. Men performers suffered similar opprobrium. Circus managers were clever enough to keep the effects of these moral objections at a minimum. Shows were advertised as highly educational. Children would have an opportunity to see and study the Lord's handiwork as exhibited in his animal kingdom. The hippopotamus became the Biblical behemoth described in the Book of Job. Then, there were the unicorn of Job, the lion of Judea, the prodigal's swine, or just plain wart hog, the wild asses, "the hind that calved," and camels or sacred ships of the desert. All of these were reminiscent of Abraham, of Noah and of Job. Tableaux of Biblical scenes were popular. In 1878 Van Amburgh and Company advertised a street parade of dens, vans and cages exhibiting animals of every sort. "Every cage, wagon, chariot, etc., is gaily painted or decorated," said the publicity man. "Biblical paintings from the famous collection of the eminent artist, Gustave Doré, are prominent upon every cage."

Appeal was made to a combined love of the classics and the Bible. Many of the shows advertised Roman and Greek chariot races, tableaux portraying some classic story or incident, or ancient Egyptian scenes in which sultans, queens, slaves and highly gilded carriages played a leading part. Not all prejudices against the circus could be allayed by such gaudy veneering of the true end of the show. Not even that clever old master of local sentiment John Robinson could make complete peace with the religious people. In Tuscaloosa, Alabama, a Methodist power preacher, Brother Alonzo Monck, had stirred that community to a fever pitch. So powerful was his emotional storm that almost everything in the world seemed profane to his hearers. At this high pitch of the revival, Old John advertised in the Tuscaloosa *Gazette:* "An honest show on honest principles by honest men" was coming to Brother Monck's front door on sixty railway cars. There were ten big shows, five monster menageries, fifty cages and lairs, a female brass band, one hundred knights in full armor, and a full program of entertainers, including a tattooed woman, the Twila family of unicycle riders and a three-horned three-eyed bovine.

This glowing advertisement was in keeping with Brother Monck's concept of the subtleties of hell. After a vigorous sermon he called on those who believed religion was a practical thing and who did not expect to attend the Robinson circus to come forward and shake hands with him. The result was not unlike the troubled marching of the Hebrew Children across the Red Sea. Brother Monck shook hands with most of John Robinson's potential customers. He boasted that the circus would not have four adult patrons for every child, and that the young men had organized a prayer meeting for the hour of the show. Even the editor of the *Gazette* was repulsed by the obscenity of such worldly entertainment and wrote against it, advocating instead prayer meetings and lectures sponsored by the Y. M. C. A.

The next week, the editor observed, "The circus has come and gone. It is said that it was the smallest crowd that ever assembled under a circus tent in this city. It was attended by the usual crowd of thieves and sharpers that always follow up such concerns. We have not heard of a single young person who pledged himself during the meeting, breaking his vow, but a few of the older ones did, 'Had to carry the children, you know.' The Y. M. C. A. held a prayer meeting at the time the circus was performing, and a great many young men went to prayer meeting instead of the circus. Mr. Monck's attack on the circus cost Old John Robinson fully $1,000 at the lowest estimate."

Others attacked the circus. Edwin M. Poteat, a Furman University professor, and "the brainiest Baptist in the South," acting as guest editor in 1905 for the *Pee Dee* (Bennettsville, South Carolina) *Advocate,* condemned this type of entertainment for its gambling tendencies. A week earlier, in the same paper, Brother W. H. L. McLaurin opened a fusillade against circuses and carnivals. He contended they kept men from communing with God by creating evil passions and desires. No honest man, he said, with knowledge of the Bible could attend a circus, and still work for the glorification of God. Towns where shows appeared, thought this preacher-editor, would feel the blighting effect for the next ten years. Poteat and McLaurin were, however, the feeble voice of a minority. Advance agents with complimentary tickets worked wonders in getting editors to look upon the circus as a highly instructive institution.

Happy-go-lucky billposters and advance agents sometimes stirred a community. Of all the irresponsible and amoral vagabonds who wandered over the South, some of the circus bill-posters topped the list. All they desired was a tree or a building, with a side toward a "big road," on which to post their flamboyant signs. It was not unusal for one bill-poster to cover up the handiwork of another, or to overlay those of local businesses. An agent for Colonel C. T. Ames almost nullified any advantage his employer enjoyed in South Carolina as an ex-Confederate soldier, by posting a garish bill on the side of the Ebenezer Methodist Church, five miles from Abbeville. The irate editor of the *Press and Banner* wrote, "These circus men, some of them neither fear God nor regard man. They are a sort of gypsies, half-civilized Arabs, who verify the curse of Ishmael, 'Their hand is against every man, and every man's hand is against them.' " W. W. Scott of the Lenoir (North Carolina) *Topic* accused advance agents of having more brass "than ever was on the old andirons that used to stand in the hall fireplace." One had offered R. E. Blakey, business manager of the *Methodist Advance,* $75.00 for a single insertion of a two-column advertisement. Scott, despite his statement about brass, thought it must have been difficult for Blakey, an ex-country editor, to refuse so lucrative an offer.

Circus stories flowed into the country papers in season and out. A show went broke and left its people stranded, and their plight attracted attention. F. B. Meigs, a little operator, reached the end of his financial rope in Jackson, Tennessee, and his people were forced to secure labor to obtain food and shelter. Among the unfortunates were two fat ladies who weighed 550 pounds each. The editor of the *Whig and Tribune* took a look and felt sorry for them, but he believed a little honest and steady labor would perhaps give them a wonderful perspective on life. Sometimes a stranded actress could see no sense in patience and took her troubles to court. Madame Hecke, the dog woman, asked the defunct Stowe and Rome Circus to pay her $402. Madame Hecke had a troupe of dogs which could do about everything but live on promises and empty seats. Some were hoop jumpers, some could ride horseback, one or two could pedal a tricycle, and the most captivating of all could stand on his head. They had been asked to travel from Manchester, New Hampshire, to Troy, Tennessee, to help save the show, but at Van Cleuse, South Carolina, it was discovered that not even the eruptive Madame Hecke and her yipping canines could fill the seats. In court her antics resulted in the composition of several columns of local print, and she acquired the name "the dancing dog woman from New Hampshire in tights." Her chief witness was a "boss gymnast" named Mexican Joe, who could speak just enough English to create a storm of laughter, and to lose the case.

Occasionally circus employees were fatally injured in accidents and were left in towns to be buried. A young nameless roustabout was killed in Tennessee when a center tent pole snapped off, and local citizens saw him decently buried. The editor said he had the appearance of being a young gentleman. William Burt (or Kincaid), a double-somersault leaper, died of injuries at Pulaski, Tennessee, while performing in Forepaugh's circus. The mayor made Old Adam pay for a coffin. A large crowd of townspeople were present to shed tears for this friendless boy who was being laid to rest in a foreign but hospitable soil. This was not an unusual type of story. Editors and their patrons operated on a stationary and unhurried principle, and when a neighbor was injured they stopped their labors long enough to give him ample care. The circus moved on a strict time schedule, and no man was so important to it that the show could afford to miss an engagement.

Sometimes animals escaped. At Cartersville, Georgia, a general free-for-all fight broke out among circus roustabouts, Negroes and constables. Shots were exchanged, a Negro was killed and two roustabouts wounded. A lioness and a bear were turned loose, and the countryside was left in a state of terror. At Rocky Mount, North Carolina, a boa constrictor escaped. Occasionally elephants got mad, broke for freedom and frightened people. In fact, some elephants were unpredictable. John Robinson's famous bull, Chief, had a bad reputation for going on sprees of anger. At Charlotte, North Carolina, Chief pulled up his stakes and departed. He spent a night roaming and upsetting things as he went. This was not the first time the old bull had appeared in print because of misconduct. Once when the Robinson show moved southward on an Ohio River steamer, Chief became angered. When he refused to squeal at being pricked with goads and pitchforks, the boat was landed and the bull led ashore. His keepers jerked his legs into the air, lassoed his snout and dropped flaming cotton padded hoops saturated with kerosene over his legs until he begged pitifully. It was said that Chief hated showmen, and when one got within reach of his snout he made news copy for country editors.

Moralists argued aimlessly against the circus. Old fogies fooled no one in pretending boredom. Young men even continued holding short-lived prayer meetings in Y. M. C. A.'s, but the last three columns of the inside page of most country papers were the accepted property of the circuses. A majority of the editors regarded advance agents as warm personal friends, and gave them what they wanted if they could. Publishers knew their communities would be from three to five thousand dollars poorer, but they believed their people would relaxation in a fantastic world of make-believe. It was worth five thousand dollars just to give small town and country boys and girls something new to talk about. They usually picked up enough Bowery and circus slang to corrupt a community's speech for a year. Almost universally the country editors agreed with the Greensboro (Georgia) *Herald* in proclaiming: "Get ready your dimes, and let everybody go. Let all the teachers give a holiday, and the stores and workshops close doors, and for once let us all *laugh and grow fat!*"

Book Three

LOOK TO THE FUTURE

Chapter 11

An Old Order Dies

SOUTHERN people by nature and custom have a liking for memories and things long gone. To them history is not so much an academic interpretation of events as a source of personal enjoyment and diversion. The past has often excused the present, and the Southern country newspapers have helped nurture this philosophy. There was no place where sectional history thrived more abundantly than within the files of the weeklies. The rural papers have been a convenient medium for reminiscent subscribers who wished to have their memoirs published, and for those who wished to read local history without having to wade through long volumes. It was natural that the newspapers of the post-Civil War years should be concerned with events of the immediate past.

The country press of the New South was born in an age of social and political reconstruction, and it assumed as one of its many protective responsibilities the guardianship of Southern traditions. Editors were never to forget that their region went through four extremely difficult years of war and was plagued for ten more by Reconstruction. There was always evidence that the editors realized that the South was undergoing a radical change, if not outright revolution. Some of them, including the rabid Confederate editor of the Greensboro (Georgia) *Herald,* were ready in 1875 to question the wisdom of the war. In moments of objectivity they professed to see that neither side had won a distinct victory. "A new era is evidently dawning," wrote editor Shipp. "The bitter animosities engendered by a civil war of four years duration, and kept alive by the malevolence of Radical spleen, are gradually giving way to better feeling."

As to Reconstruction itself, the attitude of the country press was varied. There was open and constant opposition to Northern political invasion of the South, and the resulting failures of local and state governments. Editors wrote freely and bitterly of much of the political manipulation of these years. To them the exploitation of the region meant simply that liberty had been snatched from the people, and until the excesses of political piracy had run their course there was no hope for a return to local autonomous control and decent government. But even though there was extreme bitterness toward the North and its politicians and carpetbaggers, the weekly editors exercised remarkable restraint.

There is a notable difference between what many students of Reconstruction have written about the South, 1865-1876, and the reflection which appears in many of the country papers. Southern life went on at a fairly even pace in most places. Aside from purely political activities, there were few stories which portrayed any real dissension in communities. Occasionally a Ku Klux Klan story, or one of a commotion among Negroes, appeared in the papers. Advertisements, on the other hand, indicated a rather quick return to normal commercial conditions. There is a sense of expansion, an awareness of general economic change, but this is treated as a matter of national progress. Even the poverty-stricken South appears more as a strait-laced Victorian society than as a devastated region. Doubtless large segments of rural people in the South were little affected by Reconstruction. The larger issues of the period, which involved the constitutional amendments and the reconstruction acts, were too technical for a majority of the readers to comprehend in their full meaning. Even military governments failed to disturb the provincial tenor of the Southern mind in a considerable part of the region.

As for the papers themselves, the editorials were almost always critical when references were made to President Grant and his official family. Occasionally editors became overwrought at local mismanagement and graft and railed out at their section's oppressors, or they rushed to the aid of a colleague who was threatened with maltreatment by the military government.

The most famous case of this type was that involving Colonel W. H. McCardle of the Vicksburg *Herald,* out of which grew the classic *Ex parte* McCardle case. Negro voters, jackal scalawags and carpetbaggers were scoffed at. "Cuffee" was frequently regarded as a pitiful buffoon involved in a civic travesty, and the country editors did little to make him appear otherwise. There were frequent accounts of riots, and racial confusion, but aside from these life progressed at a pace as normal as possible under adverse economic conditions.

Two attitudes in respect to the South's position in postwar America stand out in the country newspapers. There was the deep-seated feeling that the region had been sorely abused by calculating and scheming Northerners who intended to outdo the devastation done by the United States Army by destroying the last vestige of political morality and order. The other was the more conciliatory one which looked toward a restoration of national harmony. For the next sixty years after the end of the war, news stories and editorials reflected the conciliatory attitude, and especially was this true in the discussion of national politics.

Every four years in the presidential elections the angers of Reconstruction were to be stirred anew. Issues involving the South were examined to determine to what extent they were tinctured with the philosophy of radical Reconstruction and Yankee machination. Radical political and racial confusion cut deep gashes in the Southern editorial mind which have never completely healed. Thus any consideration of the reunification of the South with the nation must be tempered with knowledge that the Southern press has preserved this fundamental skepticism. Nowhere was this more nobly demonstrated than in the passionate manner in which the newspapers almost unanimously guarded the fortunes of the Democratic Party.

These were the marks of history which have required decades of national development to erase. They were the gaping wounds slashed in the side of the South which could not be altogether healed with the sweet-smelling ointments of centennial celebrations, joint reunions, and frequent visits of distinguished military and governmental officials. But the application of these salves was pleasant to the patient, and it gave the country press almost unlimited copy.

While Reconstruction was ebbing, the nation celebrated the centennial of the signing of the Declaration of Independence. Possibly for the first time since the war, here was an occasion when the North and South could come together in peace and understanding. Country papers heralded this affair as a great patriotic moment and encouraged the Confederate States to join in its observance.

The Philadelphia centennial was only a beginning. There were many similar events which demanded attention. While Reconstruction was still in process in South Carolina, Southern white troops marched up Bunker Hill under the leadership of Fitzhugh Lee to join in the centennial celebration of this famous Revolutionary battle. General Lee rode in an open carriage and it was halted several times for him to receive loud ovations. South Carolina in Boston was a novelty, and stories coming southward on boiler plate and in personal letters warmed sentimental hearts.

Within a decade the North and the South joined in patriotic celebrations of many famous events in American history. The states sent fancy-drill militia companies with distinguished-unit state flags and brass bands to march in the grand review at Yorktown. Here the Confederate gray was as common as the Union blue, and men marched, visited, joked and reminisced throughout the celebration, except when they were quelling internecine fist fights in some of the companies. New Hampshire troops were camped between those of Virginia and South Carolina, and there was much intermingling. South Carolinians attached palmetto pins to the chests of the Green Mountain boys, and the boys from Dixie accumulated an assortment of fancy buttons and New Hampshire souvenirs. Nights during the encampment reverberated with the strange commingling of "Dixie," "John Brown's Body," "Marching Through Georgia" and the "Battle Hymn of the Republic." When a Yankee band played "Dixie," Southerners had hysterics, and there was wild and ungoverned cheering when Southern musicians struck up tunes which were anathema to them prior to the celebration. Editors throughout the South watched anxiously for news of the Yorktown centennial. Some of them had opposed the idea, but when stories came back that all was well, and that militiamen on a lark had bridged the chasm which politicians had opened and could not close, they were quick to write editorials praising this spirit of good feeling.

Only one note of disharmony was to disturb the grand affair at Yorktown. The Ninth Massachusetts Militia arrived in Richmond with the mistaken idea that their visit constituted the second taking of that city. Country papers copied their reports from the Chicago and Boston dailies, and both sources were critical of the militiamen's misbehavior. It seems that this organization was composed of the roughs and toughs of Boston saloons. In Washington they had caused trouble, and when they arrived in Richmond and were invited to an official reception they responded by calling every woman in sight "sis," and they proceeded to kiss everything wearing a skirt. In desperation the mayor was forced to give his obstreperous Yankee guests just four hours to depart the city. Governor Ezra Cornell of New York became so enraged at the "Bay State Bummers" that he volunteered the services of his Thirteenth Brooklyn Regulars to assist in reopening the battle of Richmond. The so-called Boston Bummers jerked down street decorations, ransacked a store at Chickahominy, raided Negro houses of prostitution and created havoc in general. Later at Williamsburg, the "Roughs" created pandemonium, brought a carefully prepared official reception to naught and almost caused open war between Virginia and Massachusetts. When news of this reached Boston, the national press carried stories from both sides of the line describing and condemning the unhappy occurrences. The Bummers were at Yorktown on their own initiative and in no way officially represented their state. In fact, their presence at the celebration was said to be a matter of surprise. The Independent Cadet Corps, traveling with the Governor of Massachusetts, was the official militia organization invited to attend the review. Southern country papers publicized the outrages of the saloon toughs, and also the Boston *Citizen's* apology in which it was said that "the better class is heartily ashamed of the regiment, and trusts that the citizens of Richmond will not judge our people by unprincipled fellows for whom we have no word or excuse."

Where the wild Ninth Regiment from Massachusetts had upset both sections of the country, the genteel First Regulars of Connecticut won high praise. This unit went from Yorktown to Charleston to help celebrate the centennial of the activities around Fort Moultrie. Editors, both North and South, felt that this was a cementing bond, and the Southern weeklies carried Northern editorials commenting on the affair for several weeks. This practice of military companies' and of individual veterans' visiting between the sections became a regular thing during the eighties and nineties. Northern soldiers visited the battlefields, or held joint reunions with Confederates who had opposed them in battle. In the Shenandoah Valley a Pennsylvania Guard unit re-formed and marched into the Virginia country to visit old scenes, and to listen to long patriotic speeches by both Northern and Southern orators.

Only one of the numerous intersectional celebrations backfired seriously. In 1889 when the states sent their militia units to New

York to observe the centennial of the inauguration of President Washington, a comical misunderstanding arose between South Carolina and its ancient enemy, William Tecumseh Sherman, over the flag carried by one of its militia units. Proudly the Charleston Washington Light Infantry carried to New York its sacred old palmetto flag which had been used at the battle of the Cowpens. This was the only Revolutionary banner which was strong enough to be exposed to the breeze. In New York the marshal of the parade instructed this company to display its old ensign in an honored position and unaccompanied by the national colors. When the South Carolinians marched proudly in the procession with the palmetto unfurled in the breeze, General Sherman hopped up and down and shouted sulphurous words on this breach of patriotism by the late rebels. Like all hotheaded and overzealous patriots he rushed to the press before he determined the facts and hurled fiery blasts against the South. He claimed that Benjamin Harrison had turned his back on the South Carolinians, but the President later said there were so many soldiers and flags that he, unlike General Sherman, did not know one was missing. It mattered not to General Sherman that the second South Carolina unit carried the United States colors. His impetuous contention was that the Carolinians were insufficiently penitent, and that the Washington Light Infantry was made up of brazen men who were flaunting their impudence in the face of the President of the United States. The General succeeded only in renewing the war between himself and the Southern country editors. When he discovered his stupid blunder it was too late, the editors were not willing to drop the matter.

Flags were the source of an enormous amount of publicity in the rural journals. Almost every time some one dusted one there was a public furor. Perhaps the most innocent of all these was the famous row started by Adjutant General R. C. Drum. A cabinet full of Confederate unit flags was discovered in an attic room of the War Department Building, and he suggested to Secretary of War W. C. Endicott that it would be a good house cleaning move, and a friendly gesture, to return them to their units. In the past Union flags had been returned with happy results. As a purely routine matter both Secretary Endicott and President Cleveland approved the idea. When this story appeared in the papers, General Lucius Fairchild of the Alexander Hamilton Post of the G. A. R. became excited and shouted, "May God palsy the hand that wrote that order. May God palsy the brain that conceived it, and may God palsy the tongue that dictated it." Governor Joseph B. Foraker of Ohio raised the national roof about this unpatriotic gesture of the Democrat in the White House. He wrung streams of blood from the battered old shirt of the Grand Army and employed Samuel Shellenbarger and George S. Boutwell as lawyers to stay the rebel hand of Grover Cleveland. Other Republican state governors were caught up by the hysteria of Fairchild and Foraker and wired tearful pleas to the President not to placate the rebels. They would display the flags in every capital in the South and erase from the Southern mind the fact that the section had lost the war. In Massachusetts Charles Sumner proposed to erase the name of every battle represented by these flags. Even old "Beast" Butler pitched headlong into the fight, but the New York *World* observed that perhaps he came into the argument too late. The newspapers and the G. A. R. were talking about returning flags; "nothing has been said about a general surrender of spoons, silverware, bijouterie and articles of virtue; there seems to be no apparent reason for him to go wild."

So much publicity was given the flag incident that President Cleveland was provoked into commenting upon it in his Fourth of July (1887) speech on the battlefield at Gettysburg. Just as Lincoln had so eloquently done before him he reminded his hearers that the battlefield should again be consecrated to the cessation of bitterness and strife. Insincerity and hatred through a profession of kindness should be erased, and it should be remembered that most of those who had fought had learned to forgive. It was wicked, said the President, to traffic in sectional hatred under the guise of patriotic sentiment.

In calmer moments the hysteria aroused by the innocent gesture of friendliness in the return of the flags quieted down, and everybody concerned felt ridiculous. Private negotiations went on, and flags were returned by both sides without futher commotion. For many years country newspapers contained stories of these ceremonies. A Mississippi woman living in Minnesota discovered that several Southern companies' flags were in that state, and she began negotiations which led to an enormous amount of correspondence and expressions of love by pompous orators on both sides before the tattered old banners were sent home to pass into dusty oblivion in county courthouses.

Occasionally editors started private disputes with Yankee fanatics and kept their readers amused at the new battles of the Potomac. One such case was that of A. B. Williams of the Greenville (South Carolina) *News* and Colonel Elliott F. Shepard of the New York *Express and Mail.* For lack of anything better to occupy their time, these "old die-hards" conducted insulting arguments about the Civil War. When Colonel Shepard pretended that he had never seen a Confederate flag Williams sent him one express-collect, but enclosed fifty cents in the package to pay the cost. Colonel Shepard wrote back that he had seen Confederate flags before, but that he had taken them from captured posts and had lacked time to examine them carefully. He added that express charges were only twenty-five cents and that he contributed the extra money to the Grant's Tomb Fund.

Other editors watched this juvenile banter between the professional Confederate and quarrelsome Union publisher and enjoyed the sport. The war was well on its way to becoming a memory by 1885, and the weeklies were engaged in printing scores of recollections of soldiers. Almost immediately following the cessation of hostilities, Confederate soldiers grew reminiscent. Officers and privates alike wrote voluminous accounts of battles and experiences in the war. Local veterans, urged on by friends, recalled the battles in which they had fought and wrote of their experiences for the local papers. A modern reader can refight almost every battle and skirmish of the Civil War guided by old-soldier memoirs. In 1881 the Marietta (Georgia) *Journal* asked the rhetorical question, "Cannot some member of our legislature introduce a bill making it a penal offense to publish reminiscences of Confederate generals in newspapers? They sheathed the sword sixteen years ago. So come, now let's muzzle the pen on 'general subjects.' Don't reminisce any more."

Old stories of Jackson and Lee were published repeatedly. Some of these were written by local soldiers who fought with them, while others were prepared and distributed by ready-print and boiler-plate services. Repeatedly accounts of Jackson's dashing raids and prayerful attitudes, as well as the story of his relationship with his Unionist sister, were told. He became a veritable golden knight on horseback riding boldly through the pages of the country weeklies. Lee, on the other hand, was less the bold knight scrambling up and down the angular ridges of the valley of Virginia, and more the personification of the tender spirit of Southern courage and patience. He enjoyed a distinct place in the news coverage of the reminiscent war, and no story seems to have forgotten the fact that he was a man of great dignity. A few editors caught the significance of General Lee's attitude toward the war, and were able to translate into conciliatory editorials his philosophy of the task of rebuilding the South. In gloomy moments of Reconstruction many editors were able to point to Lee's striving to restore the section for which he had so gallantly fought. Occasionally a sentimental story crept in to deflect the serious lesson which this noble leader tried to teach his people. Accounts were published by the "patent" services of General Lee's return to Arlington. In a heart-rending bit of nostalgic writing he was described as visiting his old estate unannounced, and it was only by accident that he was recognized by one of the Negroes working there. He rode around the farm, walked through the grounds, visited the house and finally stood on the front portico and looked across the river to Washington and the capital. These stories of Lee expressed a fine sentimentality. Never were they underlined with bitterness as were some of those relating to Jefferson Davis.

General John B. Gordon and many lesser soldiers wrote stories of the final day of the Southern army at Appomattox. Country editors and their readers appear never to have tired of reading about this disheartening incident of the war. General Gordon wrote grandiloquently of great events while humbler veterans told their more restricted stories of personal hardships and disillusionment. Even Grant was quoted at length on the surrender. He explained that he had been riding across country and was muddy and disheveled and had no other clothes, while Lee was clean and neatly dressed. In this same interview Grant gave a lively estimate of some of the Southern officers. He admired Jackson and the Johnstons but thought poorly of Floyd and Pillow.

In addition to General Gordon, other Southern officers, Ben Hill, Jubal Early, Nathan Bedford Forrest, Wade Hampton and scores more, found time to write of their experiences or to speak of them in letters and addresses before Confederate reunions. Some of their writings attempted to explain situations which had arisen in the army, to compare the damages done each army or to revive, for sentimental reasons, the memory of the days of Confederate military service. Many of them were written to eulogize the South and its gray-clad soldiers. The tone of the more moderate pieces was always that of tenderness. In the fading years, the war became a sacred experience which bound Southerners together with a bond of unity stronger than all other ties.

Occasionally General Jubal Early enlivened a column of print by railing out at the evil forces of Yankeedom. Especially was this true when some old Johnny Reb touched him off with a letter complaining of Yankee abuse. In response to a request for the address of a Mississippi veteran named Captain Wilhonnes, the General said he was dead and gone to heaven: "I believe all good Confederate soldiers who will hold out faithfully to the end and not join the radicals or re-adjustors, or any other band of thieves, will go to same place." Four years later, in 1889, General Early, while speaking to 10,000 people at the decoration of Confederate graves in Winchester, Virginia, said that if ever he repudiated the cause for which Lee fought and Jackson died he hoped heaven would blast him, and that he would be scorned by all humanity. It was his opinion that Confederates who had deserted the cause since the war were more traitorous than those who had left the army in the heat of battle. His words were given Southwide distribution in the country press and were perhaps more heeded than the pacific words of Lee at Appomattox, which were often repeated as a historical footnote to war.

One curious aspect of the war received more than its share of publicity and editorial comment, the execution of Mary E. Surratt as one of the Lincoln conspirators. From 1865 to 1910 her ghost appeared frequently in the news columns of the Southern papers. S. A. Jonas, secretary to L. Q. C. Lamar of the Cleveland Cabinet, wrote in his Aberdeen (Mississippi) *Examiner* in 1887, that the hanging of Mrs. Surratt was "as cruel a spectacle as ever stained the escutcheon of a nation." This attack was aimed at Edwin Stanton. Editors were certain the true facts were kept from President Andrew Johnson, and that General Hancock acted under orders from Stanton alone. Stanton went to his grave with this anvil chorus of Southern journalism ringing in his ears—he died the murderer of an innocent woman in order to cover up his own guilt.

The country press was important in keeping alive a sense of popular regard for the war, and general denunciation of the Reconstruction Period which followed. Many memoirs and historical articles were published widely, but without doubt the stories of Jefferson Davis were given the most complete coverage. From 1865 to 1890 his name trailed through weekly newspapers like a dark and restless ghost seeking solace of an approving Southern opinion. He existed only as a reminder of a South which had passed.

By September 1865, articles began appearing in the weekly press in defense of the President of the Confederacy. The old local criticisms and rancors had largely disappeared, and now that Davis was paying a bitter personal price for the failure of the South he became an almost saintly figure. Columns without end attempted to analyze the Federal Government's reasons for imprisoning him. What was the basic intent? Was it to establish a *casus belli* or was it to humiliate the South? Some editors were of the opinion that Davis' trial was dragged out because President Johnson wanted to avoid responsibility. When the Confederate President was finally released, the weekly press responded with a bitter note that his case was not decided on the basis of the validity of the charges lodged against him. His release, said the Southerners, resulted from the cowardice of officials saddled with disposing of a prickly case instituted in the heated passion of the war's end.

Whatever might have been the true reason for the treatment Davis received at the hands of Johnson and Chase and the court, his arrest came to seem a virtual Calvary to the South. The incarceration of Davis at Fortress Monroe takes its place among the most stupid acts of any conqueror. Imprisoning him was enough but putting him in leg irons was unforgivable. Had Davis been ignored by the military authorities, or had he been given the humane treatment due a gentleman, doubtless he would have been virtually forgotten by the end of the Reconstruction Period, but persecution made him a martyr. Editors were to cry out in ringing phrases which caused thousands of Confederate hearts to bleed, and many sorrowing female voices were lifted in prayer for the delicate frame confined within the walls of "cold and dank" Fortress Monroe. There the personified cause was dying from the tortures of a bestial victor.

It caused virtually no change in Southern attitude to publish stories of Davis' comfortable quarters, Captain Howe's pleasant company and the humane treatment he received after General Miles's arrant blunder of putting irons on him. The idea of torture was already indelibly traced on the Southern mind and it remained there. As an example of the hatred of those who were responsible for Davis' imprisonment, the Southern papers never spoke of General Nelson Miles again without sneering at his cowardly treatment of Jefferson Davis. Even after his services in the Spanish-American War this bitter attitude prevailed. When the General was presented at court in England, the little weeklies barked, "A sorrier cat never looked at a king." His military activities in the West were but the puny acts of a man trying to hide from his conscience. As for Davis, he lived to enjoy many years of adulation.

Patriotic Confederates of Bourbon County, Kentucky, wished to see the President of the Confederacy settled in comfort and proposed to buy him a ten-acre plot near Louisville and to erect a comfortable home on it. This brought forth a bitter roar from the press farther south. A Georgian rebuked the Kentuckians for their niggardly attitude and proposed that the Southern people present the old Chief with a well-improved plantation, and that he be given at least a quarter of a million dollars with which to purchase the comforts of life. These were fine outbursts of Southern enthusiasm, but Davis got neither the ten acres nor the plantation and the quarter-million dollars. Actually, the press's gift was abundant personal publicity.

Apparently it was highly acceptable. Davis and his family moved about the South, visited people, were the idols of Confederate reunions, gave out interviews and answered critics. All of these activities were freely publicized. When he visited Columbia, South Carolina, in 1871, on business for his insurance company he was asked his opinion on Negroes, politics and the South generally. He refused to talk politics, but did express the belief that the Negro would eventually move away from the South. The Confederate chief was in an unhappy situation in giving interviews. Even journalists with the friendliest intentions got him into hot water.

At New Orleans, in 1882, he was reported to have said in a speech to the Association of the Army of Northern Virginia that the Confederate cause was not dead but sleeping, and Southern editors were quick to respond that such sentiments were dangerous. Neal and Massey of the Marietta (Georgia) *Journal* voiced the opinion of a considerable segment of the weekly press in a heated paragraph on this speech when they said that "young America wants no more cripples or orphans or widows. They want good government, peace, happiness and prosperity—they are bent on recuperation—and no bugle blast can call them to arms again, and only the defense of a common country, and no one need apprehend but what our people will continue buying their provisions in the West, their guano on a credit, wheat and meat, the same as ever. No, Mr. Davis, the 'Lost Cause' after its heroic struggle sleeps well, and its hero [sic] dead, Robert E. Lee, Stonewall Jackson and its host of others embalmed in the hearts of a brave people who have no desire to renew a fruitless and unnecessary struggle."

After this powerful blast was set in type, the Georgians discovered that they had misread the report of Davis' speech. He had spoken in defense of the Union, and "a Yankee Republican Associate Press reporter had bungled the story." Instead of throwing the type back into the cases and starting anew, the editors felt they did not have time to make up the paper again, and it was just as well to let their readers know how they would feel if Davis were so unreasonable in his attitude. Definitely the South was back in the Union and it meant to stay there if a majority of its weekly editors had their way about the matter. Though Reconstruction and its moral turpitude were a fresh and bitter memory, the South certainly wished to look to the future so far as its political and material welfare was concerned.

Northern papers frequently ran stories about Davis' capture. The age-old story of his being disguised in feminine dress periodically went the round. Not infrequently eyewitnesses told of his capture and described how he was dressed in a hoop skirt, an old straw hat, a shawl and other feminine clothing. One Indiana captor claimed that Davis had written a letter thanking him for his services. This provoked a hot reply from Davis in which he branded the Hoosier cavalryman an unmitigated liar. Many Northern soldiers wrote in defense of their Southern prisoner and denied the legend of his disguise. James H. Parker of Ellburnville, Maine, said that he was the first person to see Davis and that the fugitive was not dressed in woman's clothing and he defied a single veteran to produce proof that he was.

For twenty-five years scarcely a season went by without a story of some kind about the unhappy Mississippian. He was pressed for opinions on many subjects. When the Liberty Bell made its tour in 1885, Davis was asked to accompany it across Mississippi to New Orleans. He responded with the fervent sentiment, "Glorious old bell; the son of a revolutionary soldier bows in reverence to you, worn by time in the sacred memories." Prohibitionists undertook to get him to make a statement on the issue. A Mrs. S. F. Chapman spoke at a Beauvoir camp meeting favoring prohibition and Davis was present. She tried desperately to get him to sign her book, wear the ribbon and make a public statement, all of which he refused to do. Then she tricked him into delivering a badge to a member of his family. Mrs. Chapman pinned it to his lapel, but Davis let it be known that he believed prohibition an invasion of individual rights.

If he had been willing to remain in seclusion, it is doubtful that Davis could have kept his name out of the press. He was sought as a speaker, North and South. Committees for every important Confederate gathering invited him to attend and then reported their action to the papers. Occasionally he agreed to come for their meetings. Perhaps the most notable function of this sort was one held at Macon, Georgia, in 1887. There he became the unhappy victim of a bitter rivalry between that place and Atlanta. Grover Cleveland was to visit Atlanta, and Macon undertook to steal the show. The aging Confederate chieftain was in delicate health, and his appearance in Georgia was to be as unostentatious as possible. He was to be excused from shaking hands and he was to be protected from the crowds. No precautions could save him. Once the tide of tattered gray swept close and the first old soldiers in the line reached out for the delicate hand of their former commander-in-chief, pandemonium broke loose. Mrs. Davis, Winnie and Mrs. Hayes, along with General John B. Gordon and Senator Alfred Colquitt, shook hands with the mob in an effort to protect Davis. Seldom did emotions run so high in the postwar South as on this occasion of October 24, 1887. It was among the last of the large-scale demonstrations in the South.

As the old-timers on both sides began to die, newspapers sought Davis' opinion on their worth. Often he was asked for his attitude toward the North and its leaders, and these interviews were published. He spoke kindly of Lincoln, Grant and others. Only General Sherman drew his wrath. His dislike for Sherman stemmed partly from events of the war, but just as much from the General's frequent public utterances about the war and its Southern leaders. When he accused Davis, in an official Senate document, of saying that Davis would have been willing to use Lee's army against any Confederate state trying to secede from the Confederacy he stirred up a hornet's nest. Davis was provoked to the point of calling the Union general a liar and demanded that he produce his source of information. In the same outburst, he berated Sherman for reviving the bitter contention that General Wade Hampton had burned Columbia. In all of his communications, Davis seemed to be attempting to justify the existence of the Confederacy, and thereby to justify himself personally. The country press carried an abundance of publicity on his book and its explanation of the South's course of action. Perhaps this book received more attention in the rural press than any other published prior to 1900.

In 1889 Davis' health failed. The press rallied to him and defended his past before the nation. It was said that for twenty-five years he had served as a target for Northern animus. On December 6, 1889, he died in New Orleans. Southern weeklies mourned for him. Every detail of the Confederate chief's death and burial was related in full-page stories, and he was eulogized in double-column editorials. His funeral was an occasion for the United Confederate Veterans and the Grand Army of the Republic to join hands in grief and friendship. Everywhere the weekly press was touched by the generosity of Northerners in this sad moment. He had achieved in death what he had failed to do in life. Editorials were highly laudatory. Some of them regarded him as next to Washington and Jefferson. Others were content to call him a patriot and to praise him for his unswerving fidelity to the South. Editorials and news stories from other sections of the country were reprinted. In 1890, when the papers recovered from this flood, an era of Southern history came to a close.

Just four years before Davis' death the North and South had met to extend tearful condolence over the casket of General Grant. Joseph Johnston, Simon Bolivar Buckner, John B. Gordon, Fitzhugh Lee, Wade Hampton and Matt Ranson were present. Some of them were pallbearers. The Southern press's attitude toward changing times was reflected in the Lenoir (North Carolina) *Topic's* observation that after this display of unity at Grant's funeral, the Republican waver of the "bloody shirt" would be a marked man. An appraisal of Grant by the moderate Southern editors was not too far out of line with that of sounder historical scholarship. Figuratively they laid two men in the same grave, "Grant the soldier" and "Grant the president." Southern editors regarded him as a worthy soldier but a "bad, very bad president," and for his failure they made the halfhearted excuse of rascally advisers. As to his political career, the kindest service history could render him was to draw the veil of oblivion over it after the magnanimous moment at Appomattox. His terms of surrender were generous, and his heart was ever kind. A year before he died the ailing old campaigner had to decline an invitation to attend the fair at Richmond where funds were being collected to build a soldier's home, but he sent a contribution and a tender message.

Though Grant was gently laid to rest by the editors, Sherman was sent to an editorial potter's field. Too many times he had incited the South to wrath. He could never forget the war and salute his former enemies as worthy foes. His passing removed from the scene one of the three or four bitter sectional enemies at whom editors hurled vitriolic invectives with complete abandon. No gray-clad brigadiers rushed northward to stand with bared heads about his casket, and no black borders were wasted on the announcement of his passing. Notices of his death were so brief and bare that they scarcely identified him.

Among those who passed on about this time was Alexander H. Stephens. The Vice-President of the Confederacy died in the Georgia Governor's Mansion, and papers everywhere in the South carried stories of his life and death. Georgia weeklies told the story of Robert Toombs's last journey to see the face of his famous contemporary. As Toombs stood by the casket and stared at the immobile features of Stephens, the editors felt certain that the end of an era had come to Georgia. The famous old orator and fire-eater was himself standing figuratively with one foot in the grave and waiting for the end. Little Aleck, unlike Davis, was active in postwar Southern politics, and the country papers carried many hundreds of inches of news about him. Unlike Davis, he had incurred the wrath of some of the local editors.

When Davis and Stephens and many of the other leaders were gone, the United Confederate Veterans and the newly organized Daughters of the Confederacy kept alive the memory of the cause. Stories of reunions and dedications of monuments appeared in an unending procession.

It was not unusual for an old soldier to spit up a bullet or a Minié ball long after the war, and to revive the memory of the day in battle many years before when it had been lodged in his flesh. Some of the old boys remembered that they had buried money during the war and dug up peach orchards and gardens looking for it. Occasionally stories were circulated of large sums of buried Confederate gold and months of arduous labor were spent looking for this treasure. The only significant caches uncovered were those of human interest stories. Confederate gold remained safely in the ground or in the faulty memories of those who claimed to have helped bury it.

Impostors traveled over the South impersonating the fabulous Belle Boyd. Some of these fakers secured considerable money and entertainment wherever they went, and some of them were guilty of behavior unbecoming the famous heroine. One of these females, riding in the ladies' car of a Georgia train when a Negro insisted on the privilege of riding in the same car, drew a pistol and sent him hustling. Stories of the true Belle Boyd were published frequently in an effort to save the gullible, but they seemed to have had little effect.

To anything about the Lost Cause the country papers were willing to give their space freely. But after 1890 they treated the war only as a glorious memory. Its merits lay in the mellow recollections of the old veterans in their reunions and in the activity of their daughters who sought to preserve the spirit of the other age in their chapter meetings.

Occasionally the women of the Confederacy appeared in the news with something more exciting than a routine meeting. The ladies of Camden, South Carolina, worked faithfully to secure funds to erect a Confederate monument in that town. When at last they were ready to unveil it, they ordered badges from the R. H. Macy Company portraying a shield of the Confederate flag overprinted with a photograph of Jefferson Davis. Their order fell into the hands of an order clerk who had perhaps never heard of either Davis or the Confederate flag. With bland innocence he wrote that Macy's could supply badges with a shield of the United States flag overprinted with a portrait of Washington.

This provoked a wrathy editorial from the editor of the Camden *Journal.* He wrote that they should have gone all the way and suggested that they supply badges with General Sherman's likeness on them. "But to throw out so foul and dirty a reply as this to the noble women who, with hearts sincere, have surrendered the jewels of their souls in a cause which they believe sacred," said the editor, "and which though buried today carries along with it only the most precious memories of right is cruelty known only to the heartless and not to the brave." There were few outbursts of this kind. Editors looked seriously to the future. Their South was one of the coming years and not of the past.

After the Civil War many a textbook interpretation of the four years of bloodshed disturbed both veteran and public mind. A. S. Barnes and Company distributed packages of school texts to Southern editors and received a ferocious blasting for their trouble. Barnes's *History of the United States* was considered a slur at Southern integrity. The Marion (Alabama) *Commonwealth* thundered, "And when Messrs. Barnes and Company (or any one else & company) come into our southern schools, and say to our children 'Your fathers were rebels and fought to destroy the nation,' we meet them at the very threshold, and in the language of one of their most adored leaders exclaim 'You lie, you villains, you lie!' " Superintendent McKee of the Alabama schools was called a "Sut Lovingood kind of a fool" for adopting the books. Willard's, Quackenbos', and Goodrich's histories were placed in the same category, and later the American Book Company was berated for publishing and offering to Southern children the Eggleston histories. Just before the Spanish-American War the Buffalo encampment of the Grand Army of the Republic uttered a hysterical outcry against Southern texts. But carousing was more exciting than patriotism, and the responsibility of bringing the Southern textbooks to Grand Army standards was assigned to the auxiliary, while the veterans got on with their drinking.

When the United States went to war with Spain in 1898, the Southern press was diligent in encouraging Southern boys to join the army. Here was an opportunity to prove Southern patriotism and fighting ability. Ready-print pages carried extended stories of the war and of the part the Southerners were playing. There was editorial criticism of the casualness with which the allegedly moribund War Department dispatched Southern regiments to Cuba, but Fitzhugh Lee and "Fighting Joe" Wheeler were on hand. After wearing the gray with so much distinction they were now equally courageous in the blue. Their names were spread indelibly upon the annals of both the Confederacy and the Union.

On numerous occasions the Blue and the Gray met on the old battlefields to hold joint reunions. In 1894 they were together again on the once-bloody field at Shiloh as guests of the Shiloh Battlefield Association. There were 10,000 persons present. General Lew Wallace of military and literary fame came with a surveyor and measured precisely the area over which he fought, and discovered that he had covered the astounding distance of eighteen miles on April 6, 1862. While the general measured the ground he had covered in the past, veterans in blue and gray argued, reminisced, swapped tobacco and drank themselves into a delightfully misty state of mind in which the booming of the ancient Shiloh guns became the romantic lullaby of history. The author of *Ben Hur* spoke long and eloquently of a division which had closed. He admonished his hearers ever to cherish the spirit of the Union and peace. The last pallid drop had been wrung from the ancient bloody shirt and new issues were before the people to turn attention from a cause which had grown stale as a political stock in trade. To the strain of "Home Sweet Home" the old actors, who in the bloody April of 1862 had made Shiloh a carmine drama in Civil War history, tottered homeward happy in the thought that nothing more devastating than oratory was heard at this ancient scene of blood and war.

The two old armies met in 1910 in joint reunion at Atlantic City, New Jersey. Hilary Herbert and Commander Van Sant of the United Confederate Veterans were anxious to consolidate with the Northern group. At the head of the Unionists was that ancient enemy of the South, General Daniel Sickles. So conciliatory was the spirit of the Atlantic City meeting, however, that when General Sickles appeared at the door of the hall, with his empty trousers leg neatly pinned over the stump of his leg, every man arose, and as the band played "Dixie" four men gathered the old soldier up in a chair and marched to the stage with him. Before old Dan were the Union and Confederate colors. When quiet was finally restored in the hall he arose and said, "If I had been told when I was in Antietam that in years to come I would stand side by side with Confederate soldiers and grasp the Stars and Bars and the Stars and Stripes with them I would have been insulted. But I love the old flags now."

This was the sentiment of the country press. The term "Yankee" occasionally raised a fever, and sometimes heedless professional Confederates galloped off to war in the best style of one of Sir Walter Scott's knights, but on the whole the country press was willing to let the dead past be buried along with the old veterans. They agreed with Will C. Hight of the Winston County (Mississippi) *Journal* who wrote, "But pshaw! What's the use of scratching old sores! Let them scab over. Are we not brethren since the Spanish War? Did we not all fight and bleed and die together in Cuba? Don't the editors and political orators tell us fraternal peace prevails between the sections?"

Chapter 12

Children of Freedom

SOUTHERN country editors were confronted with many peculiarly regional problems. None, however, was more perplexing than that of the relationship of the white and black races. From 1865 to 1880 there was general confusion because of Reconstruction. Editorial judgments were never free of resentment caused by the immediate political revolution. When the Negro was active politically or otherwise showed an air of independence he aroused the opposition of his white neighbors. When he behaved with the humility of a slave, he received expressions of genuine love. Many postwar editors assumed the role of adviser to freedmen and quietly lectured them on their new situation. They gave their counsel freely on such subjects as manners, morals and New South economics, even though a limited number of Negroes either saw or could read the papers.

Characteristic of this fatherly advice was that given the Negroes of Holly Grove, Mississippi, in 1867 by Albert Gallatin Brown. He outlined the slow steps necessary for them to achieve social and economic security. Their primary needs were tools, feed, livestock, cabins and land. The tenant system would supplant slavery, and eventually, the Mississippian hoped, farm ownership would displace tenantry. But to acquire a farm of his own the Negro needed to live frugally and industriously. Two years later South Carolina editors were presenting conflicting points of view on the subject of the future of freedmen. The Horry County *News* believed that they needed to learn to behave themselves, and to forgo excesses, especially at Christmas time. They were warned against exploiters who would abuse them. It was said, for instance, that Preacher Jacob Wilson was selling from the pulpit a paper purported to be a letter from Jesus Christ. He charged the Negroes a quarter for it though it cost only half a cent to print. In upcountry South Carolina, the Abbeville *Press* was of the opinion that the Negro caused all the postwar tumult in the

South. He was trying to throw into reverse the laws of God and Nature by attempting to rule his former master. Universal suffrage had made him a legislator.

Two months later the *Press* again aired its views on the Negro. On Saturdays and court days Abbeville was crowded with drunken, quarreling black hordes. The editor saw them as deluded and misguided folk whose inevitable destiny was to be hewers of wood and drawers of water. Colored militiamen were called cowards who would stand only when the points of white bayonets were pressed to the seats of their pants. They were advised to beat their swords into plowshares and to open attack upon "General Green."

Within fifteen years after the end of the Civil War, so far as the editorial mind was concerned, the race problem in the South began to crystallize. In 1880 it seemed to the editor of the Elberton (Georgia) *Gazette* that certain failures were evident. Negro education was a necessity. Fifteen years of freedom had proved that freedmen were the South's most useful laborers, and it was imperative that employers take an interest in their moral and mental development. There was no time to be lost in laying a foundation for the social improvement of the race. He advocated local schools and colleges for Negroes supported by taxes on whites.

Across the line in South Carolina in 1883 the issue of Negro education agitated the local weekly press. The Georgia legislature had failed to heed the Elberton *Gazette's* plea and wished to place responsibility for educational support on the shoulders of the Negro. "It is hypocritical," wrote the editor of the Greenville *News,* "and a cowardly beating of the devil around the bush, and is intended to shift the responsibility and a duty." He predicted that a South Carolina legislator would attempt the same thing at the next session of that state's general assembly, and he condemned the act in advance as that of a demagogue. He hoped that such a legislator would be returned immediately to private life. "The Negro is poor, dependent on us and ignorant, with undeveloped and unknown capabilities," wrote Louis M. Grist of the Yorkville *Enquirer.* "We owe him an opportunity to improve his condition and elevate himself above the level of absolute ignorance. If we deny him that opportunity we are false to our saxon traditions of generosity and magnanimity, blind to our own interests and recreant to our solemn pledges."

These were indeed liberal views on the race problem. They by no means expressed, however, the opinion of the entire weekly press. Where a few farseeing editors believed education and patience were solutions of the South's problems, there were many who disregarded them as unimportant. Perhaps the only clear-cut fact to be dredged from the avalanche of printed material is that there were many conflicting emotions and cross currents of thought in the Southern mind. No one seems to have worked out a solid basic premise of racial relationships, nor to have conceived a set of principles by which whites and Negroes could live harmoniously and by which both races could progress socially and intellectually. One reason no thorough solution was ever found was that the problem had many angles which touched all aspects of the Southern social structure.

Education was believed by the more enlightened editors to be a major aid in lifting the Negro's standards. In the 1880's when the Blair Bill was pending before Congress, many editors advocated its passage, even though it would give material assistance to the Negro. The statement was repeatedly made that the states would receive $77,-000,000 in federal aid. Senator Blair made a speech in 1888 in which he spoke critically of the South and strongly advocated public schools for the Negro. Unfortunately this bill became entangled with race and tariff issues and aroused sectional jealousies. Local press sentiment became strong against it, especially when men like Senators M. C. Butler of South Carolina and John Tyler Morgan of Alabama advocated its defeat.

Locally editors were caught on the horns of the dilemma of taxing white property holders for support of Negro schools, or of allowing Negroes to grow up in ignorance. Many editors agreed that Negroes should be educated but believed they should shoulder the burdens of supporting and directing their own schools. In this latter contention the editors were often critical of the lack of ambition shown by the colored race. Its local leaders were usually illiterate preachers who exhibited almost the identical shortcomings of many of their white ministerial colleagues. There was no way for the Negro to pull himself up by his educational bootstraps. In 1875 "Old Silver Eye" wrote in the Oglethorpe (Georgia) *Echo* that the Negro could never be a good citizen and should not be educated. The moment he learned to spell he began to preach and organize "his infernal societies." He is good enough as he is for the purpose for which he was intended." G. H. Haigh of the Fayetteville (North Carolina) *Observer* was of the opinion in 1888 that "circumstances beyond control of man had placed black and white together; question, 'Shall we live in direct opposition, at dagger's point as it were, or shall we try to shape our ends that by united action mutual benefit shall be the results?' "

On one point most editors agreed: few or no Negroes were capable of taking a literary education, and their efforts should be confined to learning a trade. In this respect they approved the theory behind the Tuskegee experiment prior to Booker T. Washington's dining with President Roosevelt. Those who were sufficiently well-informed about the Alabama school believed its educational policies were in tune with their philosophy of Negro training. Even in 1904 the Selma (Alabama) *Canebrake Herald* was able to praise Booker T. Washington for his sound plan at Tuskegee. Editors believed the same policy should govern the establishment and operation of state-supported Negro colleges. There was no place, it was thought, in Southern society for the literary Negro. Bill Arp's column did much to shape editorial thinking on the subject of education. He was dubious of the Negro's ability to assimilate an education. He was extremely suspicious of the efforts of Andrew Carnegie to assist Negro schools. Arp turned a bitter attack on the Steel King and his apparent generosity. He felt that his money should have been given back to the laboring people who earned it and not used to disturb the racial situation in the South.

Most country editors revealed a poor understanding of the working of social forces among the races. Characteristic of this was the view of the publisher of the Paulding (Georgia) *New Era,* who thought that after sixteen years Negro education was a failure. He accepted the race problem as unavoidable and believed it could not be solved. People lived by excitement, and the race issue was as adequate a disturbance as any. "The negro question," he wrote, "may be a new kind of a meteor shooting athwart the horizon of politics that, like many others, will burst and leave a deeply profound darkness. Still it would perhaps be well to keep one eye upon the course the current is taking. It may yet require more statesmanship to adjust the problem than has been manifested in the leaders of the parties for the last score of years, and the part our leaders will have to play will be to study the vessel. G. O. P. [sic] will have to be responsible for adjustment."

One question seems to have stood out above all others. How was the Negro to fit himself economically into the new order in the South? Several ways were open. He could become a share cropper. As such, he would enjoy a little more economic freedom but less security than he had had as a slave. If he possessed either capital or credit he could buy a farm. He could hire himself out as a wage laborer or he could leave the section. This last solution, if it can be called a solution, stimulated constant publicity. Negro migrations ranked with the defects of Southern agriculture, education, the open-range issue, good roads and religion as news copy. On the whole Negro question editorial thinking was emotionally confused. Generally editors believed the Negro supplied abundant cheap and locally adapted labor. Some publishers thought the share system of farming was best, while others favored the wage plan. All agreed in thinking the Negro had to be supervised by a white man.

Editors sincerely believed the Negro lazy. Before the end of the nineteenth century papers were discussing the subject of efficiency of Negro laborers. Aiming an indirect criticism at the work of Dr. Charles Wardell Stiles in combating the hookworm menace, the Okalona (Mississippi) *Messenger* said it was not necessary for the "professor" to travel all the way to Africa to search for the germ of laziness. It was to be found among Mississippi Negroes. Sidney Lewis of the Sparta (Georgia) *Ishmaelite* wrote that the efficiency of the Southern Negro had decreased to such an extent that he should be moved out of the South. The Fayette (Mississippi) *Chronicle* regarded Negro labor as a weak reed on which to lean. Good white immigrant muscle was the solution for a labor supply.

In advocating the replacement of Negroes with white immigrants, weekly publishers had many misgivings. It was true that the Negro disturbed the Southern white mind, but he did not threaten the orthodox Protestant churches and the commonly accepted social stratification. Always the Negro had followed rather closely the religious pattern of the white South. Socially, he had formed gradations within his own race similar to those of his white neighbors. Politically he had caused some disturbance. There again the editorial mind indulged in stocktaking. If the Negroes moved away and were not replaced immediately by white immigrants there was grave danger that several Southern states would suffer a reapportionment of national representatives as a consequence of population loss. On the other hand a flood of immigrants threatened the local Southern political system by reducing native majorities.

A common Southern fault was to regard social problems from too limited a perspective. Too many editors demonstrated a marked tendency to weigh every human problem in the light of what was happening within the purview of their own small vantage points. When they stood in their office doors and looked up and down streets, or loafed in courthouses, post offices and corner drugstores they felt they were sufficiently informed to speak. When they saw streets crowded with carefree Negroes they were convinced that the colored race was neither downtrodden nor dying out. Provoked by an editorial on this subject in the Philadelphia (Pennsylvania) *Times* the editor of the Winnsboro (South Carolina) *News and Herald* wrote, "Judging from the immense throngs that can be seen on Saturday on the streets of the towns in the county, we think, therefore, that these alarmists who periodically get into a flutter on account of the dying Negro need worry themselves no longer." A common editorial belief was that a white man might just as well try to catch a comet by the tail as to keep Negroes out of town on Saturdays.

A question which the weekly editors could never answer was what should be done with the Negro. Should he be absorbed in the community social system, kept apart from it, made a responsible citizen or sent away from the South? They agreed on only the point that was clearly stated by the Albany (Georgia) *Herald,* "If the Southern darkey would elevate himself, his first step upward should be on the round of employment." The Negro had a partial solution of his own, to move away to new scenes of activity. Because of this situation, from 1865 to 1920, the press was seldom without stories of migrations either away from the South or from one area to another within the region.

In the 1870's the exodus was to Kansas. The Negroes were lured there by clever agents who passed the news around by word of mouth and printed cards and handbills that Kansas offered free land and golden opportunity. In 1879 a near-catastrophe occurred when 1,200 Mississippi and Louisiana Negroes were led to believe they were about to be re-enslaved if they remained in the South. Lycurgus Jones, president of the Colored Colonization Society, distributed circulars and letters reciting white abuses. The back of each page carried the warning: "Show this circular to none but colored and keep its contents secret." When a rumor was started that Southern Negroes were about to be shipped back to Africa, many of them refused to plant crops and gardens for fear they would not be able to gather them. Many others were duped into buying tickets on the "African Special" train. They waited in vain on given dates for its appearance.

When the movement to Kansas resulted unhappily, Negro migration changed direction. New delta lands in Mississippi, Arkansas and Louisiana beckoned to the excessive population of the older cotton belts. Hundreds of news stories from 1880 to 1905 told of the activities of labor agents among the Negroes. So long as the movement away from the older sections was gradual there was little anxiety among the weeklies, but when there was mass movement, North and South Carolina and Georgia papers were greatly agitated. Editors were quick to call attention to the activities of labor agents and to request that they be required to pay prohibitive license fees in every county where they operated. In the South Carolina counties of Edgefield and Fairfield, it was said nearly twenty per cent of the colored population departed within a month. At Christmas time in 1882 the Augusta, Georgia, railway station was crowded with a singing, howling mob of displaced field hands awaiting the "Rackansas" special train to haul them away from the place where they had failed to make a living.

The press was frightened. Editors were willing enough to admit that lien laws, lack of privilege, poor housing, illiteracy, poor land and general social uncertainty were drawing the Negro from the Old South. His going, however, robbed the region of its most satisfactory and abundant source of cheap labor. The best evidence of the editors' fear was the vehemence with which the South Carolina and Georgia weeklies commented upon the plan of Senator M. C. Butler that the Negro should be colonized in Liberia. After much publicity on this subject in 1889 and 1890, the editor of the Newberry (South Carolina) *Herald and News* wrote, "Liberia and Africa still sit crownless and voiceless in her [sic] desolation and so it will be with Senator Butler's measure. It will be buried with his impractical plan for working the roads." Never has the Southerner dreamed up a more impractical scheme to solve his race problem than African or South American colonization. Occasionally editors pretended to believe their communities could adjust their racial problems in this way but when they faced the practical matter of establishing such a colony they always reneged.

Railroad agents were busily engaged in organizing immigration movements. They worked secretly in cabin, field and pulpit. Inevitably their presence became known to the editors, who branded them a new type of carpetbagger. Once they were discovered, there was a hue and cry against the agents. Any *sub rosa* white activity among Negroes at once provoked the wrath of the press. The Pulaski (Tennessee) *Citizen* thought labor agents should be kicked out like rabid dogs. It was said people of that section had little idea of what was happening. "Do people of Giles County know what labor agents are doing? Every few days sly wretches are in Negro cabins pouring out their venom into the ears of listeners."

Perhaps the most famous of the labor agents was that crafty one-legged Confederate veteran R. A. (Pegleg) Williams, who had ridden with General Nathan Bedford Forrest. In the black belt of the Old South he was called the "modern Moses of the Mad Mississippi Exodusters." He served in the employ of the Illinois Central Railroad, and his name was anathema among planters from North Carolina to Mobile. At the turn of the century he appeared in Greene County, Georgia. Yellow-fever epidemics had depleted the Negro population of the Mississippi delta lands, and the old Confederate was out to restock it. When he first arrived in middle Georgia, the Greensboro *Herald* rather favored his visit. In adjoining Hancock County Sidney Lewis' *Ishmaelite* said the Negro should be free to go where he pleased so long as he had not made a contract with a planter to grow another crop. Both papers doubted the wisdom of continuing the plantation system, and they believed so long as there was abundant Negro labor there was little chance either to conserve land or to maintain stable white communities. But before the year was over "Pegleg" had created a storm in both South Carolina and Georgia. He was arrested, a trainload of his Negroes was halted and unloaded in Madison, Georgia, and he was prosecuted for violating the Georgia labor-agent license law which required the payment of $500 in each county where solicitation took place. Before the argument ended his case was appealed to the Supreme Court of the United States.

Despite the fact the Illinois Central Railroad and its labor agent lost their case, the Negro exodus from the older sections of the South kept up. By 1918 hundreds of gaunt, deserted cabins stood bleak amidst fallow cotton lands. Their former occupants had moved on to the taller cotton of the delta or they had gone North to booming industrial cities. Occasionally weekly papers referred to changing conditions, but after 1900 resistance to the dissolution of old labor patterns was not ardent. By that time the entire plan of Southern farming, farm credit and marketing was changing, and the loss of labor and the breaking of lien contracts were less publicized. Most of the editors had ceased to fear that one of the probable results of shifting population would be reduction of Southern representation in Congress.

A significant internal change occurred in the South after 1890. Lumber men tapping the region's timber resources built hundreds of local sawmills which drew large bodies of agricultural labor to the logging camps. Sometimes the farmers resented this home-grown competition which materially increased the labor difficulties on the farms. Another feature of the Southern lumber business tended to lower old Southern social barricades. Negroes and whites labored together, both of them detached from the land, and sometimes the Negro surpassed the white man in competition for jobs. Certainly there were noticeable changes in race relationships in communities where white men and Negroes labored and lived in close proximity.

Every aspect of the Negro question discussed in the country papers was merely part of the whole racial issue. It is true that nearly every editor loved some individual Negroes. Frequent stories recounted the faithfulness of old retainers. "Uncle Henry Youngblood died here Saturday," wrote Sidney Lewis in his *Ishmaelite*. "Uncle Henry belonged to that class of Negroes, the faithful ante bellums, who we are sorry to see, are fast becoming extinct in the Southland." The papers, however, reflected a general fear of the Negro. An unbelievable amount of space was given to discussions of race riots, plots and conspiracies.

Radicalism and the Reconstruction debacle no doubt contributed to tension between the races. Too much editorializing pictured the Negro at best as a wild, ignorant animal whose civilization was to come in the future. At worst he was a black sensual fiend, whose intense hatred of the white race would cause him to strike with wild demoniacal fury at an unguarded moment. Scores of incidents reflect the general press attitude toward this subject in the Reconstruction

Period, and the later attitude in the eighties and nineties and first decades of this century. Early conflicts, such as the famous Cainhoy and Hamburg riots of South Carolina between whites and Negroes, were the results of animosities growing immediately out of war and the first chaotic years of freedom. Friction in the later period, however, was caused by political conflict, inequality before the law, a sense of economic frustration and the general failure of the Southern agrarian system.

In August 1888 a Negro named Tom Broadfoot led an assault against the Cumberland County, North Carolina, jail. A rumor was spread abroad that colored prisoners were to be removed from the jail and lynched. The situation was frightening to both white and colored, and for weeks the community was upset. There was some indication that the entire Negro population might rise up in a class war and that much bloodshed would result. The editor of the Fayetteville *Observer* wrote: "White men of Cumberland County and North Carolina, what is in store for us, with the conditions of things as here indicated, to be followed by the dire consequences of Negro supremacy! All issues of the moment sink into insignificance in the face of the race issue, especially when Negroes stand up in solid rank and threaten to overthrow law and order." Ten years later North Carolina was thrown into panic by a hot white-supremacy political campaign which provoked at least two inflammatory editorials by the Negro editor Manly of the Wilmington *Record*. He had asked white men to be more careful about protecting their women and implied that many Negro men had been lynched on charge of rape when really they had allowed themselves to be caught in clandestine love affairs. As a climax to this editorial and the political campaign, there occurred the famous Wilmington riot in which the *Record* plant was burned, and the black and tan city officials driven from the state.

A second notorious riot scare was the so-called Jack Turner incident of Choctaw County, Alabama. In 1882 a band of Negroes under the leadership of Jack Turner planned to wipe out the white population in a surprise attack. They were more diligent than discreet at plotting. A written record of their discussions was kept and one night after a midnight session, the drowsy secretary carelessly dropped his book in the road where it was found by a white boy. News of its contents caused immediate consternation in south Alabama and Mississippi. The plotters were captured and hanged, but the germ of suspicion was planted and there was widespread fear of an uprising. Negro meetings were regarded with apprehension, and even colored revivals were suspect. It was feared that the ravings of a highly emotional preacher only obscured a plot to strike at the whites. Editors sometimes were guilty of keeping alive the groundless belief that the Negro possessed a strange, dark bestial nature, coming from the jungle, which made him a potential brute. They claimed a deep surge of savagery in his soul made his nature unfathomable and unpredictable.

As late as 1904, the Sparta *Ishmaelite* made the startling claim that there was a Negro maffia society operating in Hancock County, Georgia. Its members, he said, were arrested and sentenced to be hanged. They had murdered a family named Hodges and had attempted to burn the evidence of their crime. In this sort of reporting, the country editors offered no common-sense leadership. There is evidence that they were stampeded by local hysteria into encouraging a mutual hostility between the races. It is doubtful that the society was much more than a bogey man conjured up by local rumor.

A lack of consideration for the Negro's pride and feeling was a common failing of editors. They poked fun at him because of his habits. Frequent comparisons were made between the Negro and the mule. An exchange said that a German scientist had discovered a way to get rid of the mule by crossing jackasses with zebras to produce "Zebrulas." The editor claimed the Negro and the mule were blood cousins, bound together by hoops of steel. They were "two souls with but a single thought, two hearts that beat as one, hence the inexorable logic of the situation is: no mule, no Negro; no Negro, no mule. Therefore it is a dead moral." Physiologically the editor catalogued the Negro by certain of his less attractive characteristics. His heels were long and widespread, his nose was flat, his lips were thick, his wool was kinky, his odor offensive, his skull thick, and he was "ape-armed." Numerous references were made to his thick skull. Will C. Hight of the Winston County (Mississippi) *Journal* said that a local justice of the peace had ruled a Negro's head was a lethal weapon, and that a defendant was within his rights in using a pistol for self-defense. Rather frequent stories told of bullets bouncing off Negro's heads, of sling shots failing to make dents and of heads warding off other blows. The Fayette (Mississippi) *Chronicle* in 1904 claimed the Negro's skull was growing thinner, for a young Negro suffered a fracture from a blow with a stick.

A Georgia editor reported a Negro jumped off a moving train near Ellaville but fortunately landed on his head. It was said a hole was blasted in the ground as if a bomb had fallen there.

It was believed generally that the Negro was without sex morals. There was no such thing as fidelity in marriage, and indiscriminate cohabitation was to be accepted as a matter of course. The Negro male was considered an oversexed and sensual animal with the morals of a billy goat. Negro women were said to submit readily to the entreaties of both black and white, and many editorials and observations centered about this point. Somewhat characteristic of the popular belief about Negro morals was the announcement by the Americus (Georgia) *Tri-Weekly Republican* that a twelve-year-old Butts County Negro girl had given birth to a baby and the editor remarked facetiously that the race was not dying out. In 1899 "L. A. G." of the Murray (Georgia) *News Letter* said much had been written about the corruptness of Negroes. He reported that he had found a sixteen-year-old Negro boy who had "never taken a drink of whiskey, never smoked a cigar or cigarette, never engaged in a game of baseball, never tried to dance a step, never cussed an oath, and doesn't know one card from another, but does chew a little tobacco when he can get it." "I remarked to him," said the reporter, "that I thought now was a good time to kill him, that maybe we could get one Negro in Heaven."

Negroes were described as "goat-scented," "Sons of Ham Noah," "Fifteenth Amendment contrabands," "Suffrage slingers," "burr heads," "niggers," "coons," "odoriferous wenches," "of the colored persuasion," "Fifteenth amendments," "colored niggers," "ginger cakes," "dusky gentlemen," and "darkies." Perhaps the derogatory term which caused most resentment was the common "nigger." Seldom did this word appear in print without a suggestion of bitter vengeance or scurrility behind it. Scores of editors, of course, were careful not to use it but many others did. The Elberton (Georgia) *Gazette* quoted a boiler-plate article from the *Iowa Sentinel* commenting upon the Negro's squeamishness over the use of the term "nigger." The *Sentinel* said, "You may kick a nigger from New York to St. Paul and back if you only call him a 'colored gentleman.' Nothing on earth riles a nigger, like calling him a nigger. The literary niggers are the worst of all. We get several nigger newspapers in exchange, the fellow talks about colored papers." The Northerner added with a snort,

"A colored individual may be any tint from a yaller dog to a black snake."

Non-Southern views of the Negro were often quoted or commented upon. Nothing infuriated the local publisher so much as adverse comments by outsiders on the South's racial attitudes. Especially was this true when a New Englander undertook to set the region straight in its thinking. In 1904 several incidents plus the general confusion resulting from some of Roosevelt's appointments created a commotion both North and South. Robert Lewis, editor of the Woodville (Mississippi) *Republican,* wrote that Northern people were doing their utmost to insult the South. "We will continue to draw the line down South," said the Mississippian, "but to save the female Negro-loving agitators of New England the heart hunger of spinsterhood, we will gratuitously furnish them with addresses of some of the mahogany-hued bucks who would likely be willing to exchange their satisfied existence on Southern plantations for a position in society composed of those vilifiers of the Southern people."

Another outburst against an outside opinion was provoked in 1894 by the report in the London *Sun* of Ida Wells's triumphant English visit. This Memphis girl had figured prominently in efforts to better racial conditions in that city through her writing and publication of the paper *Free Speech.* She had campaigned vigorously against lynching. Apparently she was forced to leave the city and she went to England to solicit assistance. The *Sun* described her as "a graceful, sweet-faced, intelligent, courageous girl." A fantastic story was told that she could not go back to Memphis because the white people had planned an elaborate lynching bee for her. They were "anxious to hang her by the neck in the market place, and burn the soles of her feet, and gouge her beautiful dark eyes out with red-hot irons. This is what a Southern white does with a Negro or Negress for preference, when he wants a holiday sensation, and when he finds a charming victim, such as this sweet girl would make. The mayor of the town orders the schools to be closed, and the little scholars turn out in holiday ribbons, and their Sunday-go-to-meeting best, and lead the youngsters out by their hands. They go out to see the fun, and have their photographs taken at the scene of Martyrdom, and there is much rejoicing over the black sinner that repenteth not." Southern editors almost reopened the American Revolution because of this farfetched English fabrication.

Ida Wells's English story was reminiscent of that famous New England woman, Harriet Beecher Stowe, who was lionized abroad and praised in the North. Down almost to the present editors were still breaking a lance on "Aunt Tommy," as they called her. The Greensboro (Georgia) *Herald* said Mrs. Stowe did have a conscience but it was located in a peculiar place. In her book *My Memories of Foreign Lands* she remarked, "Suddenly, so suddenly that it was quite mysterious, conscience smote me in the deepest centre of the pit of the stomach." Not much could be done with a conscience of this sort, but the editor thought the "little woman" should be given "a puke and purge" and wound up again, and if she ran down then she should be thrown away as salt which had lost its savor. Constantly local friction was being developed over the play *Uncle Tom's Cabin.* Traveling stock companies were run out of one Southern town after another, and the editors sanctioned such treatment.

Southern publishers were pleasantly aware of criticism of the Negro which appeared in Northern papers. These articles were excerpted and published throughout the South. Reports of racial tension in the Ohio schools in the eighties caused Southern papers to watch for editorials criticizing the Negro. When the Cleveland *World* commented that "10,000 bobtail gorillas trained to put folded paper in a slot would exercise as much judgment and understanding as 10,000 Republicans in Louisiana and Georgia," Southerners agreed this was a correct view. The Negro was believed to be encroaching upon the Northern white man's rights, and the *World* was again quoted as saying, "A darky does not know his level, he bobs up where he is not wanted like an inflated bladder. Prick the bladder and down it goes. Cannot this question of color line be settled by forcing the Negro to seek his level?"

In the face of outside criticism Southern editors were generally convinced that Northern people did not know how to deal with Negroes. Paradoxically, they believed that Southerners had an inborn understanding of the Negro, despite all his mysterious African background. A story was told many times through the region of this mutual love between the two races. It was said that a Negro named Sam moved from Texas to Iowa in search of brotherly love and free political expression. In the North, however, he found that the "friends of the Negro" were also businesslike, and that it was almost impossible for him to find work. Disheartened and hungry, Sam headed south for the rugged understanding of Texas. He asked for food at the home of an ex-New Yorker but was turned away because times were hard. At many other back doors he was given the same inedible excuses. At one house the homesick Negro found a man cutting grass and he told him his long and unhappy story. When he was through the grass cutter said, "You black idiot, why didn't you have sense enough to stay in Texas?" Immediately Sam was on his knees shouting and clapping his hands. "Boss," he exclaimed, "you don't know how glad I is to see you. When did you leave the Souf yo'self? Oh, Boss, I is glad to get among friends agin." "Go in the house there, you black fool, and git some chuck," said the Southerner. "Perhaps you will know enough another time to stay where you belong."

Segregation was a major issue. Frequent news stories and editorials from 1865 to 1947 recorded the history of it. Negro travelers caused no end of social friction and editorial comment. Many editors believed that although railroads should be forced to supply decent accommodations Negro passengers should be restricted to special cars. Perhaps the first opposition to Negroes riding with whites arose over the use of the old-fashioned ladies' cars. Negro men were said to be forever trying to force their way into these cars, and they were nearly always engaged in fights and abused for their efforts. Numerous fights in which guns were drawn occurred aboard Southern trains. Even one of the numerous Belle Boyd impostors was involved in a dispute with a persistent Negro passenger in a ladies' car.

An outburst of righteous anger was directed at Bob Gleed, a Mississippi Negro senator, in 1872 for trying to invade the privacy of the ladies' car on the Mississippi Central Railroad. "Old Bob Gleed, the flat-nosed, thick-lipped, long-heeled, goat-scented, state senator from Lowndes," said the Forest *Register,* "undertook to make a pile out of the Central Railroad one day last week, but utterly failed in the attempt. He packed his stinking carcass into the ladies car." Bob was hit between the eyes by a passenger and was knocked cold as a wedge. The *Register's* editor stood by and cheered the fight. Negroes, senators or not, felt the editor, had no business around white women, and violence was always justifiable in enforcing this kind of racial segregation.

From 1885 to 1905 weekly papers reflected the efforts of Southern legislators to pass segregation laws. In the public mind the Negro was to be separated from whites not only in institutions, stores and public conveyances but likewise in occupations. In 1887 a rumor was afloat in the South Carolina press that the Abbeville *Press and Banner* employed a Negro compositor. The Newberry *Observer* asked, "What does the state press think of this move in the direction of cheap labor and of crowding young white men out of a field of industry peculiarly suited to them?" The paper believed that it would undermine an old and honorable profession. "We say this in no unkind spirit, but as an humble protest against what we regard as a lowering of a profession that needs above all things to be kept on a high plane." In the adjoining county of Fairfield, E. B. Raggsdale of the *News and Herald* took issue with the *Observer*. The liberal Winnsboro editor was of the opinion that no profession was degraded when a practitioner made an honest effort, regardless of the color of his skin. Professional success rested upon intellect, not upon one's race. "The color line," he said, "may be drawn at the door of the drawing room. It cannot be drawn at the door of the workshop."

In other ways the Negro was handicapped by prejudice in earning a livelihood. He had difficulty getting work which brought him into any kind of association with white women, especially if this association left him alone with them. No subject in all the tangled skein of Southern racial relations was more explosive than this, and nothing was fraught with more danger for the Negro man than his manners toward the white female. A reflection of this attitude regarding white women and Negro men in occupational relationships was expressed in 1905 by Will C. Hight of the Winston County *Journal* when he condemned livery stable owners in the neighboring town of Ackerman for sending colored drivers to convey white women about the countryside in single-seat buggies. This was an exceedingly delicate subject, and an injudicious discussion of it was apt to provoke an unpleasant racial incident.

On the other side of the racial ledger, miscegenation between white men and Negro women was perhaps a social blot, but miscegenation between Negro men and white women was under the strictest of all Southern taboos. Numerous accounts of intimacies between white men and colored women crept into the news, and occasionally a white woman was exposed to community wrath for interracial lewdness. Numerous editorials, bordering close to libel, scolded white men for their casual illicit relations or for living with common-law Negro wives.

Perhaps the most famous case of this sort in Southern history was that of David Dickson and his mulatto wife of Hancock County, Georgia. Dickson was one of the most progressive Southern farmers and livestock breeders. He accumulated a comfortable fortune of over $400,000 which he left to his common-law wife Amanda and their mulatto daughter Amanda, making them the richest Negro women in Southern history up to 1887. Elsewhere this problem of white men and Negro women was given legislative attention. A bill introduced in the Tennessee General Assembly in 1881 proposed to stop cohabitation between white men and Negro women. The author was a Memphis Negro, and the Woodville (Mississippi) *Republican* agreed that if marriage was illegal then so was concubinage.

Perhaps the most important single issue in the entire field of racial relations was the Negro's place in Southern politics. Through the late decades of the nineteenth century the Southern country press was outspoken on this question. The editors believed that the entire Southern social system could not be maintained if Negroes were permitted political rights on an equal basis with whites. The Negro minority was regarded as an ominous threat. Negro suffrage, said the editor of the Selma (Alabama) *Southern Argus,* was forced on the country to elect Grant. It would be better for the Southern people to be sentenced to the Dry Tortugas than tolerate it. "But the 90,000 Negro voters in the State [Alabama] will devitalize the numbers of all parties; and from the poisonous fountain, corruption and death will penetrate to every extremity of the administration."

Poison and corruption did penetrate every extremity. In the last seventy-five years no major social issue has been discussed in the press free of, and apart from, the race issue. In South Carolina alone, from 1865 to 1947, the press has printed enough on the Negro's political future to fill a score of encyclopedia volumes. A reporter for the periodical *Methodist,* writing in Reconstruction times about exploitation of the Negro by demagogues, said "South Carolina is absolutely ruined; no statesman on earth, no angel in heaven can suggest a solution of her financial problem," because of the debauchery of Negro politics. Most papers were filled with condemnation of Negro suffrage.

Most editors wanted the Negro to secure fair trials in the courts, and they believed that in many instances juries leaned over backward to give colored people lenient treatment. They favored reasonable economic opportunities for Negroes, but political participation was not for them. Almost unanimously the country press declared the South a white man's country. The Negro was said not to be ready to participate in political affairs. He needed education, poise and experience before he could be prepared. The most fantastic explanations were offered the Negro as to why he should forgo his recently gained political rights. He was reminded that he was subject to exploitation which corrupted his race and Southern politics.

The poll tax and constitutional limitations on colored voters were hailed by the editors as reasonable restrictions. Some of them went so far as to declare with vengeance that white supremacy had come to stay. The Alabama press was openly jubilant in 1901 when the Negro was disfranchised in that state.

A sample of the rejoicing over final victory of white supremacy was the editorial tirade in 1901 of the Weekly (Alabama) *Enterprise* which gloated, "The day of the long-legged, lantern-jawed, slab-sided, pigeon-toed, jangle-kneed, box-ankled, turkey-trotten, unforgotten political polawog has gone, the day of white supremacy dawneth and the black clouds of Ethiopia are receding from the American horizon." Alabama was to be divested of the Negro vote, and no longer would officers get elected by the intrigue of counting "dead niggers and dogs." Editor T. J. Carlisle, like most of his fellows, was ready and willing "to bow to the behest of caucasian rule."

The country press is of great consequence in determining racial attitudes. Unfortunately too few mature studies of this complex subject have approached an understanding of the regional social system through this course. Editors nearly always exhibited a definite love and respect for individual Negroes, as has been said before, but they often indicated a fear of the Negro collectively. The speeches of demagogues like James K. Vardaman and his more arrant successors convinced the publishers that Negro excesses were of jungle origin. Africa had been transferred to the South, and the mysteries of that dark continent were unfathomable to the white man. It was believed by many that the Negro was a fiend and an inveterate thief.

This attitude is well illustrated by T. Larry Gantt of the Oglethorpe (Georgia) *Echo,* who said that the "Negro church (or pen) near the village has blown down, and most of the material used up thus rendering its resurrection highly improbable. 'It is an ill-wind that blows nobody good.' We are opposed to Negro churches. When a darkey 'jine de church' or ties up his wool in cotton strings you had better watch your hen roost." The *Journal and Review* (Aiken, South Carolina) said a Mississippi editor had proposed the best plan for solving the political issue. His scheme was to make petit larceny grounds for disfranchisement, and build hen roosts low to the ground. Everywhere there was much discussion of the Negro's fondness for chicken. An editorial in the Americus (Georgia) *Union* said that a "Gentleman of color" had "a weakness for chickens peculiar to his race," and got into a hen house in Charleston. When he left he walked across a turnip patch, and everywhere he stepped the turnips came up and grew bountifully.

Whether editors engendered prejudiced beliefs about the Negro's character in their readers or whether they merely reflected a popular attitude is debatable. At any rate the Negro supplied an immense quantity of newspaper copy. In the discussion of the race question, as in that of almost every other public issue, editors realized the limiting factor of their patrons' preconceived opinions. No doubt many papers would have expressed a far more progressive attitude had their publishers felt the public mind was conditioned for it. It must be remembered that most editors were born and reared in the counties where they published their papers, and in their mature years they were thrown in such close associations with their readers that it was often difficult for them to think independently even on major public issues.

Sometimes colored editors published pitiful little "patent-sides" sheets of their own, but these were often edited by preachers who never dared voice opinions on any subjects. They were content to follow the worst journalistic practices of their white neighbors by printing semiliterate locals, church and lodge notices, reports of meetings and social affairs. A few Negro editors succeeded in getting themselves into trouble by criticizing self-conscious white men for their illogical relationships with colored women. An occasional attack on the white economic system drew fire, and sometimes a Negro paper was threatened with destruction because of its bold editorial views.

In more recent years country weeklies which exhibit any real understanding of social conditions have ceased bitter and scurrilous tirades against the Negro. They have discontinued use of the distasteful term "nigger," and given up other crudely offensive words. The Negro traits and actions which they emphasize have undergone some significant changes. With this new attitude there appears a more wholesome understanding between the races. In the modern weekly publicity is thrown on injustice to Negroes and inequalities in the law. Negroes are accepted as participants in general civic improvements. Their activities are reported in columns which deal with agricultural work among their race, or in special local news columns. Their agricultural clubs receive publicity, and so do some of their special social events. Later twentieth-century papers do not carry the bitter tirades of the nineteenth.

Other changes are at once noticeable in the press. Although migrations have drawn off large numbers of Negroes from many areas of the South, there are no longer conflicting editorial emotions on the subject. A major portion of Southern lands and resources have been either exhausted or exploited, and the use of ingenious farm machinery is enforcing idleness in fields where once cheap Negro labor was a necessity. The native white population has expanded rather rapidly, and the social and economic problems are now fairly evenly distributed among the tenant, laboring white and the Negro. Sometimes editors revert to the old question of what has happened to domestic help. Once Republican politicians were blamed for draining the countryside of Negro household servants and concentrating them in the towns. Labor agents were lambasted for taking away the white man's servants and field hands, and threatening farmers with having to pay higher wages to those who remained. In the 1930's the New Deal supplanted the agents and was accused of spoiling the Negro domestic servant. For a brief period rumors of "Eleanor Clubs" agitated the editorial columns. Problems of coracial political and social opportunities are again persistently demanding solution.

Some modern editors show a remarkably clear insight into the question of black and white men living harmoniously in the same community. They exhibit liberal points of view and appear to be willing to go well beyond the conservative policies of their immediate predecessors. There seems to be a genuine sense of social responsibility on the part of many of the publishers who believe the broader social needs of their communities will not be served properly by allowing this lack of adjustment to remain a public secret. Occasionally an editor shows a wholesome courage in pointing out this fact to an indifferent local reading public. Others are hopelessly confounded by the age-old Southern questions, and show a defeatist tendency to shrug off the need for solutions of racial problems, apparently regarding them as some sort of infernal machination of the enemies of the South. But they are dwindling and the liberals are in the ascendant.

Chapter 13

Saddle Leather Hip Pockets

A LIGHT snow fell in Marietta, Georgia, on Friday, March 10, 1881. By noon that day it was slushy underfoot. A tightrope artist had stretched his rope across the street and was performing his tricks to the amusement of a crowd of crudely dressed, noisy bystanders. Occasionally the crowd sent up loud whoops of coarse, nervous laughter, or some smart aleck made quips about the death-defying showman. The mind of the crowd, however, was not so much on the tightrope walker and his act as it was upon the more important event of the day which had brought them together. Near by two facile-talking street medicine men were displaying their quack nostrums to a shivering throng of rural hypochondriacs.

In all, six or seven thousand people milled about the streets of the north Georgia town. Most of them were grim, hatchet-faced countrymen whose beards had grown long during the cold spell. Their bodies smelled of a winter's accumulation of dirt and grime, and their lips were smeared with thick coatings of tobacco and snuff. Added to the earthy smell of unwashed humanity was the odor of raw corn liquor.

Bottles and jugs were turned up to soiled lips in plain view. Neighbor was treating neighbor in an attempt to calm the nerves and cast off the cold. Everybody was talking loud, bantering his fellows, swearing and firing off his pistols. As the liquor began to have its effects men stopped being peaceable and became brawling rowdies. By noon the "law" had filled the jail and city calaboose and was holding more lawbreakers in makeshift places of detention. Everywhere one turned were pistols and shotguns, and the noise of the crowd suggested an intermittent battle.

In the streets and crowded about smouldering coal stoves in the stores harassed women were hugging babies to their breasts while they kept an eye on restless older children. They were waiting for the big show to take place. Dogs ran barking and fighting about the streets. Like their masters they were excited by the gathering. At hitching racks cold mules and horses stamped their feet in the slush and relieved their emotions by braying and blowing their nostrils clear.

This was a big day in Marietta. Pink Pratt was to be hanged in public at twelve-thirty, and the show was free to everybody. A large plot had been cleared off on the west side of College Hill, and there was ample room for the six or seven thousand curious spectators on hand to see the law take its course. In the midst of the open space stood the heavy wooden gallows. The trap was in place, the trigger was set. The rope with its greased noose was still in the sheriff's custody.

The only unhurried thing in town that Friday was the courthouse clock ticking away the minutes in its methodical way. The sheriff, his deputies and the Marietta Fire Company were at the jail ready to begin the death march. Waiting in his cell, Pink Pratt was enjoying his last and most thrilling day on earth. He was cocky and self-assured. There was to be no intermittent screaming and fainting for him. Not every man in Georgia could expect to arrive at the place of his death accompanied by a sheriff, a flock of officious deputy sheriffs and the Marietta Fire Company.

When he began his journey to College Hill he lighted a fresh cigar, climbed into the waiting buggy and sat erect in its seat like a proud African king. When he arrived at the scaffold Pink examined the gallows with considerable care. He seemed to suspect that some carpenter's error would rob him of his moment of glory. He then climbed to the platform and took his seat with regal calmness. Near him stood three ministers, one white and the others colored. Pink's eyes traveled over the large audience as though to make sure everything was ready. Then the ministers began their prayer. The Negro's lips moved in unison with the ministerial plea for his salvation. The sheriff had brought the audience to its feet and the people stood with their heads bared, and some of the more devout knelt in reverence.

When the prayer was ended the dramatic moment of the occasion came. It was the prisoner's privilege to address the audience for at least twenty-five minutes. There was an old Southern adage that a guilty man would not hang with a lie on his lips, and it was his inalienable common-law right to confess before being executed. Even lynchers gave their victims an opportunity to pray for mercy and confess their crimes. Pink delivered an eloquent statement of his guilt and exhorted members of his race to heed his sad plight and rectify their sinful ways short of the yawning drop of the gallows. From the crowd came jeers and catcalls. It greeted the prisoner's speech in a shameless and profane manner. When he was through speaking the boy stepped forward and said he was ready to die. The nervous sheriff slipped the waxed noose about his neck, fastening the knot directly behind an ear, bound his hands at his sides and slipped the black hood over his head. A pull on the trigger and the trap door fell open, dropping Pink Pratt to eternity.

The prisoner's body fell three feet before the rope snapped tight and broke his neck. Mercifully the boy died without a struggle. A hush momentarily held the crowd, and then there was a roar as the throng released its nervous tension. Some onlookers had fainted, some had turned their heads as the body hurtled downward but others had stared with vulgar amusement. For twenty minutes the limp body twirled at the end of the rope. Then it was cut down to be examined by two doctors and given to the grief-stricken parents for burial.

This was the ending of a type of Roman holiday all too common in the South prior to 1920. Pink Pratt had raped a young white girl and left her hysterical, lacerated and bleeding. He was brought to trial in court and sentenced to be hanged after a jury had found him guilty of a crime which was ordinarily expiated by lynching. Scores of similar public hangings occurred each decade, and each one attracted as much attention as John Robinson's perennial circus performances. Some prisoners were dramatic and some sheriffs were adept at arranging an exciting show. Often prisoners were tied astride their coffins and hauled along. At the gallows they offered prayers while thousands of strangely pious spectators knelt with them. They led in group singing, greeted their friends, lambasted their enemies, confessed their sins and proclaimed their assured salvation. If their wives, children and parents were present they were marched up to the platform for tearful farewells. It is easy to imagine the bizarre spectacle of a Georgia father standing on the gallows with the noose about his neck and his wife and children about him. Just as the sheriff was ready to pull the hood over his head he screamed hysterically, "I must have one more look at my little Florida."

Thousands of the curious, drunken spectators who milled about

WHO IS THE AUTHOR?

Our friend, Rev. W. C. Baber, of Texas, sends us the following article clipped from a Texas paper, and asks us if such assertions as are made in this article are facts. Now, we do not know anything about who the correspondent is that sent this dispatch, but whoever he is, he is certainly a bigger liar than any of the political liars in the present campaign. It is a fact that our Board did make a mistake, in our judgment, in making this hanging public, but so far as anything else in this article being true, it is not. There never has been less interest displayed in our State in a hanging. There are no preparations or demonstrations of any kind so far as we can find out about this coming hanging, and we simply brand the whole thing as false. We reproduce the dispatch as a matter of information to our readers:

Louisville, Miss., July 22.—The board of county supervisors has acted favorbaly on petitions for the execution in public of Bell Gage, a negro convicted of wife murder.

When Gage was convicted and the date of his execution set requests began to come in from many prominent citizens of the county for a public hanging. Objection was raised by some residents of the county, but those favoring pulicity argued that it would serve as a warning to other negros and would give the rising generation of both races a wholesome dread of breaking the law.

The supervisors seem to have an economical idea in granting the request for a public hanging. They argued it would cost considerable to build an enclosure for the hanging to keep the crowd from the jail yard and the chances were the crowd would break down the enclosure and see it anyway.

Hanging the negro in the open, they argued, would save the county the expense of building the high board fence and would also save the people the trouble of tearing it down.

The people of the county seat are not united on whether it was a wise move to order the hanging to be public, but merchants who did not quite approve of it have been solaced somewhat by the prospect of a large trade from crowds that will come to the city to see the negro hung.

All over Winston and adjoin- counties parties are being made up to go to the hanging. Reports indicate Louisville will have the biggest crowd of its history that day and preperations are being made to feed the visitors at temporary restaurants. Thrifty residents of Louisville are planning to erect refreshments booths and several street fakers have made plans to interest the crowd while it waits for the execution.

A legal hanging is a novelty in Winston County, for there has not been an authorized execution here for thirty-five years. This is one of the arguments used to induce the board of supervisors to make the execution public.

They were told it had been so long since there was a hanging in this county that the people ought to have a chance, none of the younger generation ever having seen such a spectacle in their home county.

There have been some hangings in the county since the last legal execution, but they were not formally announced, and only those who happened to be in the lynching party were present. Details of those hurried executions told with labored attention to minute details, have made those who did not see the sight envious, and publc execution of Bell Gage will give all citizens an even chance to witness the taking of a life.

SHOULD HANGINGS BE PUBLIC?

the public gallows were subscribers to country papers. Details of every case had been given them by their paper from the moment news of the crime became public until the last spectator had dragged himself reeling from the scene of the hanging. White and black alike paid the penalty for their crimes at the end of the hangman's noose. Like so many acts of violence, a public hanging made exciting news. Probably no other kind of story had quite the morbid appeal of an account of a hanging. As a result nearly every paper played up every detail of a local hanging.

Frequently earlier editors showed some slight disapproval of public hangings, but they went right on publishing every nauseous detail for a sensation-loving audience. A vast majority of the stories gave minute descriptions of the fall through the trap, the contortions of the body, the heavy snoring sounds made as the struggling victim gasped for air, the precise time at which the prisoner ceased to struggle at the end of the rope and was declared dead and finally the appearance of the corpse.

Few of them seemed to have sensed the terrific shock which their people were experiencing. To the Southerner hangings were an ancient English institution for the punishment of enemies of society. Onlookers were warned to give up their ways of crime and to obey the laws of the state. In the South the ancient ritual of hanging was made a bold, colorful ceremony, rousing a broad range of the most intense emotions. The bloodletting of the war and the unhappy period of social adjustment which followed gave the rural Southerner an appetite for strong punishment. His frontier mind and his strong racial animosities often added a thirst for vengeance unconnected with morality. Both hatred and fear caused drunken crowds to rush into towns on hanging days, to fire off their pistols and shout profane and vulgar jeers at the victim. Although a genuine religious feeling made emotion-charged mobs of thousands kneel in prayer with a condemned man and join with him in singing sacred hymns, it was a bitter spirit of social vengeance that sent him to eternity with volleys of profane oaths and vulgar jeers ringing in his ears.

In time thoughtful editors began to realize that publishing accounts of hangings was perhaps only encouraging the practice and might be leading to the commission of new crimes. The public execution stirred the passions of the spectator and often made heroes out of criminals. As evidence of this, after many hangings folk ballads appeared recounting the heroic deeds as well as the executions of criminals and immortalizing them in local literature. This was more than the most upright citizen could hope for when he died quietly in his own home and was carried off to the graveyard in the usual conventional manner.

By the mid-eighties occasional editorials indicated a changed point of view. A syndicated column originating in Macon, Georgia, appeared in many neighboring papers in that state. Its author was a bitter opponent of the scandalous public executions which caused so much demoralization in the South. This critic condemned the drunken carousing and morbid curiosity of the crowds gathered to witness the public hangings. Instead of carrying out the solemn intent of the law, these Roman holidays were actually circuses or public entertainments. There was little real sense of the awfulness of the crime or the extremity of the penalty which the victim was paying.

Hangings where the victims delivered long religious harangues and assured their hearers that the best life was the virtuous one bore the earmarks of a victorious revival meeting. Criminals often stated that whisky, women and money had been their downfall. The Warrenton (Georgia) *Clipper* said of the hanging of Taylor Bryant in Monroe County that "most people in attendance were drunken animals babbling in senseless jargon who had only animal's fear of death, and no sense of the awfulness of crime." Bryant was hanged in a blaze of glory. As the editor said, "Bryant's sins were forgiven, as is usual in such cases, and the ignorant and superstitious left the scene thinking, no doubt, that the surest and speediest way to heaven was by the gallows."

From the platform witnesses were charged by the convicted man with lying, or they were forgiven the injury they had done him by testifying before the court. Sometimes the friends of the murder victim were on hand and engaged in open and shameless arguments with the prisoner. The dignity of the law was dragged in the mire, and the sanctity of the trial by jury was reduced to a carousal. Occasionally prisoners sold their bodies to doctors or medical schools and spent the proceeds for food and tobacco weeks in advance of the hanging. Sometimes they had their pictures printed on postal cards, which agents and relatives sold through the crowds to secure funds to support their families or to pay burial costs. Pieces of the rope and noose were often peddled by shrewd promoters. The hood was sometimes sold and so were pieces of the gallows.

By 1900 there was widespread journalistic pressure for private executions to be witnessed by only such people as the law required. Death by hanging, said the editors, should be made austere and fearful. It should be made impressive through mystery and secrecy. There should be no crowd pyrotechnics to make a public hero of the condemned. In many instances publishers began their campaigns against such miscarriages of decency the moment a prisoner was condemned to die. They urged that the sentence be executed in absolute privacy, and no doubt this public opinion campaign contributed materially to the almost complete abolishment of public hangings.

Hangings, sensational though they were, constituted only a minor part of the violence which was minutely described in the papers. Lawlessness was general. The explanation of this trait lies partly hidden in the influence of the region's frontier condition. The violence of the Civil War and Reconstruction Period contributed heavily to a lack of respect for society's laws. Four years of bloodshed had left their mark. Men who perhaps would never have learned about guns in any other manner had grown familiar with them. On the field of battle they had become inured to bloodshed. They came home to find state and local governments ineffectively administered at a time when law enforcement was especially needed. Distrusting the authorities, Southerners in many places became their own family defenders.

Tempers were short, and pride was deeply hurt because of defeat in the war and the following disorganization. Old sores remained unhealed in many places because of guerrilla and bushwhacker activities. Honor was as delicate a thing in the New South as it had been before the war. The code of honor underwent a change only in the manner of execution. A keen feeling of personal dignity kept alive a sense of obligation to secure vengeance and personal satisfaction for wrongs done one's feelings or family prestige. Men became unreasonably touchy about their veracity and good names. A personal slight was not to be accepted lightly, and the offender was to be whipped or shot for his insults. Never before had resentment of personal affronts been so essential to a man's standing in his community as it was in the postwar South.

There were other reasons why the New South became a land of violence. It suffered from some of the same growing pains the nation did. There was much of the spirit of the lawless West in the growing South. In fact the population movement from the South to the West tended to link distant areas in blood kinship. There was a difference, however, between the physical conditions of the West and those of the South which led to different patterns of violence. The South had vast areas of heavily wooded country. People living in them were usually isolated, and criminals found it easy to cover their tracks. It seems that there was something about the wooded isolation which spurred the criminally inclined Southerner to acts of the basest sort which he would have lacked courage to commit in open country. Men were robbed, women raped, families murdered and houses burned down on them. Innocent persons were shot wantonly by lonely country roadsides. People were slugged and whipped, livestock was killed and maimed and scores of other crimes were committed in the obscurity of the wooded country.

Much violence resulted from fights over land lines. The confusion resulting from the adoption of stock laws in the various states provoked a tremendous amount of bickering and shooting. The logging of forest lands frequently led to violent disagreement over ownership of timber. Later, dissatisfaction with the failure of agricultural prices resulted in sporadic extralegal movements, known as "white capping," to control the price of cotton by regulating the operation of gins. Bands of disgruntled farmers reverted to the tactics of the Ku Klux Klan or adapted the more modern Western idea of vigilantism, and rode about the countryside terrorizing their neighbors and burning gins and cotton houses. In Kentucky and Tennessee the "night riders" or "black patch" warriors campaigned under cover of darkness, from 1906 to 1910, to raise tobacco prices. They scraped plant beds, intimidated unco-operative growers, burned warehouses and issued threats of violence throughout the dark tobacco belts of the two states. These movements became big news, and papers outside the immediate areas affected gave generous news coverage to these incidents. The Kentucky-Tennessee tobacco war was one of the biggest news stories of the early twentieth century.

Even the pleasant pastime of baseball, which was enjoyed so generally in the South, provoked many local rows, and pistols were brought into play. A ball game on a church ground at McBean Station in Burke County, Georgia, ended, as the editor of the Warrenton *Clipper* said, "in a holocaust. Three people were shot, two were killed, and a fourth was saved by 'a muscular woman.' " In fact, reported the *Clipper,* "the affair seems to have been a general battle with the nimble pistol." Added to these causes of criminal acts was the eternal race conflict which had existed since the earliest days of freedom. The Negro criminal was aided both by the cover of darkness and the forest in seeking vengeance for his grievances.

In too many cases the Southerner lacked proper recreational outlets for his energy and passions. He was too much alone where he had an opportunity to brood on his injuries and to imagine personal slights and abuses which under other conditions would not have caused him to pause a moment. He had too little access to mechanical things to divert his attention from guns. The woods and fields afforded abundant game, and hunting became the chief sport of most Southerners. Success at hunting depended to a very large extent upon the quality of the gun. Thus ordinary recreational and mechanical interests were combined to overemphasize the importance of firearms in everyday life.

At the same time that the pistol and its wanton use created such a problem, the Southern press recorded an excessive consumption of whisky. War and Reconstruction had served to lower all restraints. The fears and uncertainty of the new age were drowned in the bottle. In 1883 the Paulding (Georgia) *New Era* commented on the fact that the consumption of whisky had dropped off locally and so had the sale of pistols. Less encouraging, however, were the signs of peace in Fayetteville, North Carolina. In the same year that the Georgia editor was pleased with the reduction in the sale of whisky and pistols, Fayetteville was being kept in a state of nervous tension because of the continual firing of guns in the night. Nearly everywhere in the South editors complained of the reckless use of guns.

Saturday afternoons in many Southern towns were full of excitement. Although the Negro was berated for his habit of coming to town on this day, he was only following the long-established behavior of his white neighbors. Roads leading to town swarmed with country people flocking in for a day of shopping and gossiping. There were always fights and hard feelings. Factions in local feuds gathered on the streets hoping they might get a glimpse of their enemies and shoot it out with them before frightened but appreciative audiences. Boys fought over their rivalries for country girls' favors, tenants and landlords quarreled over the divisions of crops at settling-up time. Drunken bullies stumbled about through crowded streets trampling feet and jostling sensitive countrymen, swearing before women and calling men fighting names. Saturday was pistol day in many Southern towns, and there was no end to the petty provocations which would cause armed bullies to reach for their guns. Correcting this state of affairs was a task at which the editors labored. In spite of the fact that they preached almost continuously against pistol-toting, an astounding number of people went armed with pistols and unreasonably long-bladed pocket knives.

An exchange in the Bardstown (Kentucky) *Standard* said a revolver was a nickel-plated substitute for bravery. This makeshift excuse for personal courage had almost driven the real thing off the scene. "The revolver," said the editor, "gives the puny man with a 5/8 inch brain and the pluck of a grasshopper a 100 yard reach and makes him more deadly than a Sioux Indian. There was a time when this country had no more dangerous animals, except bears and wolves, and life was safe, except on the frontiers, but now vast hordes of 16 year old boys who use their skulls for dime novel bookcases, roam the streets with cigarettes in their faces and portable cannon in their hip pockets, producing obituaries with the skill and enthusiasm of a cholera microbe, while it is at all times possible to meet a personal enemy who has been chasing you for a week, and who is reluctantly compelled to defend himself when he catches you by filling you so full of lead that your remains will require eight pall bearers."

W. P. Walton of the *Interior Journal* said that a local judge had asserted that the man who habitually carried a pistol was a coward, and that Kentuckians almost universally indulged in the habit. Public gatherings were disrupted by men who came loaded to the gills with revolvers and ready to shoot at the drop of a hat. The habitual pistol-toter was condemned by editors everywhere as a contemptible coward who was beneath the dignity of brave men.

Many accounts appeared in the weekly exchanges telling of the number of pistols discovered in open courts. A Florida judge charged a grand jury to search out the cowardly pistol and to make the county safe for peace-loving people. During his impassioned plea one of the jurymen caught a glimpse of a pistol butt sticking out of the judge's pocket and he was the first man disarmed. Perhaps one of the most frequently quoted exchanges was the account of a Judge Lester's disarming the attendants and spectators in his north Georgia courtroom. He had the sheriff lock the doors in the midst of a trial, then announced that he had seen a pistol on a man in the room. If the culprit would come forward and lay down his pistol and a dollar bill, he said he would not have him prosecuted under the stiff law of the state. When the first man came up with his pistol and dollar bill, the judge claimed he was not the man. Repeating this process Judge Lester collected twenty-one pistols and dollars before he was satisfied with the harvest.

Editors prodded state legislatures to pass laws to empty hip pockets, but seldom did the lawmakers respond with adequate legislation. It was pretty well known that the Southern legislatures contained men who belonged to the pistol-toting element themselves, and they had no wish to pass laws against themselves. Many halfhearted and ineffective acts were passed by general assemblies, but no one believed they were serious. An excellent example was the bill passed by the South Carolina legislature which provided that it was an offense to carry a pistol weighing less than three pounds and having a barrel shorter than twenty inches. Immediately the South Carolina lawmakers became the butt of scores of scoffing editorials from one end of the South to the other. In Georgia and Kentucky, blundering legislators attempted to impress their constituents with laws which made it an offense to point loaded guns at individuals.

The "unloaded gun" was a genuine menace. Many people met their deaths by them every year. Many a heartbreaking tragedy was related in the columns of country papers because someone had been careless with his gun. In 1884 John Bowers of Georgia called on his sweetheart, and while the two were courting in the parlor the boy picked up a pistol on the mantel and pointed it at the girl, demanding that she hold up her hands. The gun went off accidentally and the young lady sank on the sofa dead. Young Bowers lost his mind. Allen Wheeler's thirteen-year-old son near Toccoa, Georgia, was playing with an old gun when it went off accidentally and killed his grandmother and wounded his mother and baby sister. Wives and daughters were wounded and killed by shotguns which had been carelessly thrown across rumpled beds, and numerous children died by their own hands from having access to loaded guns. Even that army of bad men who swarmed into country photographers' galleries to

SEPTEMBER 1. 1911. SUBSCRIPTION $1 PER YEAR

BELL GAGE HANGED IN THE PRESENCE OF LARGE CROWD

Last Wednesday was an exciting day in town for many people from the county. People began coming in early in the morning, a report having gained currency that Bell Gage, the boy convicted for murdering his wife, would be hanged at 6 o'clock a m instead of 1 p m. By the noon hour there was a crowd estimated from 1200 to 2000 people in town. Many of them seemed very impatient for the hour to arrive when Bell would launch out into the unknown world. At 1:30 p m Sheriff Hull and deputies repaired to the jail and brought the prisoner on the scaffold in the presence of the large crowd. Prof Singleton, a colored preacher of Kosciusko, who happened to be in town, together with Rev Jim Thompson, who had been administering spiritual food to Bell for several days, accompanied Bell to the scaffold, and made short talks relative to the occasion. Singleton's address was along the line of law and order, and right living, especially among his people, and was conceded by all who heard it to be the best thing of the kind they had ever heard from a negro. His advice to his race was excellent, and couched in good language. He was highly complimented upon his remarks. Sheriff Hull asked Gage if he wanted to say anything, and while he showed a desire to talk, he could not say much, only advising the people to do right and meet him in Heaven, where he said he was going. He had nothing to say about his crime. He thanked Sheriff Hull for his kind treatment and shook hands with all who were on the scaffold, asking them to meet him in Heaven; and had Smith and Shuford, white prisoners, to come out and tell him good-bye. He showed wonderful nerve, standing throughout the half-hour service without a quiver, but seemed rather in an ignorant state of mind as to the real thing he was up against until the Sheriff placed the black-cap on him. About 20 minutes after the trap was sprung by Sheriff Hull, Drs Parkes and Dempsey pronounced him dead Gage was a mulatto boy of about twenty-five years of age, and looked above the average negro in intelligence, He killed his wife while under the influence of cocaine, and was convicted at the last term of court

Only for the guards at the jail Tuesday night, Gage would have effected his escape, and the vast crowd would have been disappointed in the hanging With a wire he slipped the latch on the cell door and liberated himself from the cell, and was in the act of picking a hole through the brick wall when Messrs H J Gammill and J B Webster discovered it

This is the first legal hanging in our county for about thirty years. Below is a note Gage gave the writer for publication, which we print verbatim. It is of no little importance, however.

Bell Gage Hanged.

By oversight in making up the front page, the note written by Belle Gage was omitted, and appears below:

Aug. 30 1911

"to my Friends Both White and Black I exvise you all to live to worship God lay Down you Bad habets al kinds take up the rite habit that leads From erth to Glory Dont take nothin no one ofer you unless you no what it is unless you no it will do you Good and meet me in heven For that where I am gon Goodbye

Bell Gage."

BELL GAGE HANGED IN 1911

have themselves photographed with their revolvers crossed over their chests were not free from accidents. A young man posed in a Western cowboy outfit for his picture in Marietta, Georgia, and he became so excited at his own toughness that he pulled the trigger of his gun and shot a hole in his shoulder.

Gun accidents were reported in the papers almost as frequently as were weddings and weather changes. Murderers broke into homes, robbed and killed. Dogs ran out to the roads to bark at passing strangers and were shot. When their owners protested they too were shot. In 1882 James Dorothy, returning from Thomson, Georgia, after dark, met a man who demanded to know his name. Dorothy replied that he was "a man who attended to his own business and didn't interfere with the affairs of others." This infuriated the inquisitive stranger who drew his pistol and said, "Damn you, I'll find out," and shot the Georgian just over the heart. A Mississippian, traveling from Louisville to French Camps to attend a Baptist association meeting, met a drunken man. He greeted him with the usual "Good evening, sir!" The drunk replied, "That's what I say, but don't shoot." Even innocent bystanders were not immune to wanton shots from irresponsible men. Excursion trains often passed through villages and towns with pistols blazing through their windows. Fights aboard trains were sometimes serious because of gunplay. On a few occasions passenger trains pulled into stations with battles raging in the coaches.

Silencing the pistol, and halting violence were perhaps the editors' most pressing responsibilities. W. P. Walton of the Stanford (Kentucky) *Interior Journal* explained the reporting of crime stories by the fact that "as journalists we owe it to the people amongst whom we live and from whom we derive our support, to aid them in its [crime's] suppression. We cannot afford to be 'mealy mouthed' about crime or misdemeanor which may occur within our section. To be so would be to falsify our trust and stultify ourselves. If men desire to keep their names out of the paper they should govern themselves accordingly."

When the Gibson (Georgia) *Enterprise* lashed out at the pistol and its cowardly owner he pretty well expressed the antipistol sentiments. It was this editor's opinion that a pistol did not make a grown man of a boy, and that grown men who carried pistols added something which God had not intended to strap on them. As he said,

"God made us, and he made us right, if he had needed a revolver attached to us he surely would have done that." Men did not need pistols to make them pretty, said the Georgian, any more than a Hottentot needed a ring in his nose to make him kissable. A man who carried a pistol either bore a mark of Cain or was an incurable coward and prepared to defend himself against imaginary enemies.

Perhaps few editors were conscious of the criminal history which they and their colleagues recorded throughout their region. If the black story of the weekly press's crime report had been assembled and handed in a block to a regional press association it would no doubt have been branded as an infernal attempt to indict the South. Yet the country editor lived faithfully by the rule that his readers should have all the news. At the same time, they were not unconscious of its adverse effects upon the reputations of their counties.

In 1889 Columbus Heard of the Greensboro (Georgia) *Herald* published a brief analysis of capital crime in Richmond County. Fifty-six murders were committed in thirty-four years. Four Negroes were lynched for rape, but the murderers got off with sentences from seven to twenty years.

This analysis led the Greene County editor to a careful search for an answer to the question of why the South was victimized by crime. His figures could be duplicated in almost any Southern county. For instance, the Aiken (South Carolina) *Journal and Review* said in 1890 that the court of general sessions, sitting for eleven days, handed down indictments for almost every known type of crime. There were murder, arson, rape, larceny, housebreaking and assault and battery with intent to kill. The *Journal and Review* editor agreed with editor Heard that whisky and pistols were to blame. Columbus Heard thought that if every Southern county should fine all violators of the concealed-weapons laws on the same Sunday, the combined fines would pay off the local debts and leave enough cash to operate without taxes.

In 1885 the Breckinridge *News* reviewed Kentucky's criminal record for the past six years. There were 1,340 murders, or an average of 223 per year. Only eight murderers were hanged, four white and four colored. The pistol had worked overtime in the mountains and in the bluegrass country.

The editors were convinced that the courts were ineffective. They did not believe that courts and juries dealt severely enough with criminals. They often expressed doubt as to the intelligence of jurymen. The Troy (Alabama) *Messenger* told of a case of assault and battery on J. B. Sperry tried in Fincastle, Virginia. Although Sperry testified himself that he was the victim of nothing worse than assault, the jury after two days' deliberation returned a verdict of manslaughter. The editor of the Breckinridge *News* believed the jury system was breaking down in Kentucky. He assured the lawmakers and courts that the people were getting tired of murder and crime. They were ready to revert to the mob law of early Mississippi and the vigilantism of the West. He thought when it came, wholesale hangings would result.

He deplored such a method, but it seemed to him to have some advantages. The mob administered law which never tangled itself futilely in technicalities. "From its verdict," he wrote, "there is no appeal. The murderer it condemns will find no friend, no savior, in the court of appeals. It cannot be corrupted with money. Its eyes are not blinded by the glamour of family prestige. It is impartial as the sun that shines and the rain that falls. It simply does the work the law should perform. And it does not increase the burden of taxation. Its judges draw no salaries, its juries no fees, its processes cost no money. The law would be preferable to the mob if it could be depended upon. But it cannot be—no dependence can be placed in it. It reads well in the books, it sounds admirably in judges' instructions, but there praise of it must end. It is a promise destitute of performance—the ghost of a shadow." Of course the Kentuckian was extreme in both his language and legal philosophy, but he voiced what was much in the editorial mind of the New South prior to 1910.

In Alabama W. D. Jelks's Eufaula *Times* became alarmed at the numerous account of crimes. It was worried for fear the public conscience had become so badly seared by strong stories that it no longer was capable of regarding murder and arson as capital crimes. It stated flatly that there was "no reason to hope" for proper punishment soon. "Under the present legal and judicial methods it is an impossibility."

Individual local judges were more often than not held in high esteem, but there was lack of confidence and respect in the court system as a whole. Lawyers commonly delayed trials; judges permitted them to do so; and usually by the time criminals were brought before a jury, the public had forgotten their crimes. The result was that if they were not let off entirely they received very light sentences.

The press had some direct influence on ending the wild orgy of postwar crime. It helped secure the eventual passage of fairly adequate laws and the reduction of frontier violence. However, the influence of the press is to be measured, as in so many other areas of its activity, less by its direct bearing on the specific social issues than by its successful fight against illiteracy and isolation. The papers worked to do away with the ill effects of civil war and reconstruction. Editors labored hard to stop crime.

In crusading against crime and the pistol, editors emptied their own desk drawers and hip pockets of deadly weapons and faced their angry patrons with nothing more lethal than a pair of fists. After 1920 the old contention stated years ago by the editor of the Macon (Mississippi) *Beacon* that it was criminal to make editorial hip pockets out of anything but a good grade of saddle leather lost its savor and was discarded along with the weekly advertisements which offered cheap pistols as premiums for soliciting subscriptions to papers and periodicals, or as prizes for selling balms and garden seeds.

Chapter 14

"The Day Goes by Like a Shadow on the Heart"

CLOSELY allied with the problems of race and law enforcement was that of lynching. A lynching made sensational news, and few Southern country editors could resist giving the full details of what happened. No one knew better than they, however, the conflicting forces mob violence released. They knew that the community involved would be bitterly criticized by both Southern and Northern exchanges. Columbus Heard of the Greensboro (Georgia) *Herald-Journal* said, "I feel sorry for the South that this blot is upon her. It affects us all over the world. It robs us of prosperity and the high moral and social position to which we are entitled. It ruins the worth of our investments. If it is not stopped then shut the school houses, burn the books, tear down the churches and admit to the world Anglo-Saxon civilization is a failure."

Some editors perhaps published details of lynchings in an effort to make them so horrible that public opinion would stamp out the practice. Others approved of lynchings as punishment for certain crimes, especially when it seemed to protect and further white supremacy. Patrons of country papers differed in their opinions. A fair portion of them were disturbed by the publication of such awful material, while others demanded every sordid detail. It is doubtful that an editor in a community wrought up by a lynching could take an entirely objective view of it. He ran the risk of bodily harm if he was too critical, especially if a sex crime against a female member of a good family had been punished. If he took an objective view of lynching he was liable to be confronted with that famous defeatist refrain of: "Why don't you write something good about the South?"

The country editor was always in a dilemma in respect to the whole subject. His community's moral reputation was at stake, but his readers always wanted sensational stories. There were enough lynchings and to spare. George P. Upton, associate editor of the Chicago *Tribune,* kept a newspaper record of them throughout the nation from 1885 to 1903. This was reprinted in a number of country newspapers. The Fayetteville (North Carolina) *Weekly Observer* quoted his tally of 3,337 unofficial executions in nineteen years. Every state except New Hampshire, Vermont, Rhode Island and Utah was represented. The South reported 2,585, or more than three-fourths of the total, the West 632, and the East and Midwest 120. Murder was the commonest reason given, with 1,099 cases, 654 cases followed rape, and the remainder were distributed among arson, rioting, plotting uprisings, maiming and robbery. Statistically it can be said that in a period of nineteen years there were more than 2,500 original lynching stories in the Southern country papers, with an incalculable number of exchange and subsidiary accounts.

On examining the Upton report, Bishop W. A. Candler of Atlanta said, "Lynching is due to race hatred and not to any horror over any particular crime, [and] unless it is checked it may involve anarchy; for men will go from lynching persons of color to lynching persons on account of religion or politics, or their business relations. The record already begins to show cases of this kind." The Georgia bishop was unquestionably right that lynching without check could develop into anarchy. Although he was perhaps too positive in stating categorically that race hatred rather than horror over any crime was the impelling force behind lynching, he is certainly right that racial feeling was a powerful factor in the majority of cases. Violence boiled up when white men were strongly moved by their fear of the Negro as a race. The powerful influence of this dread on the mental patterns of white Southerners has been brought out earlier in this book. But Bishop Candler may have been too ready to dismiss their horror over a particular crime as a motivating force in lynching. The subconscious fear was usually rationalized and formulated at the conscious level as a horror of black men molesting white women. And by this formulation, the subconscious fear was reinforced by a subconscious racial jealousy.

These two underlay many high sounding pronouncements. For instance, in March 1905 Governor James K. Vardaman circulated an appeal for law enforcement among the Mississippi country weeklies. He called on peace officers everywhere to check the "reign of lawlessness now in the state." He wrote, "The stealthy manner which characterizes the conduct of the perpetrators of this crime [rape] resembles the tiger when pursuing his prey. The presence of the fiend is never known until the terrible deed has been accomplished and the victim left bleeding and dying with seldom a trace of the identity of her [sic] destroyer. . . . Forty years of freedom and public education have not fulfilled the utopian dream of the Negro-philist of the North and the North-flavored vagarist of the South. It has not improved the Negro's morals, awakened within him an intelligent love of country or cultivated an up-lifting, passion-restraining self-respect. He is a barbarian still, with a thin veneering of civilization, and the education of forty years seems only to have increased his aspiration to arise in the world and stand on a dead level with the white man socially and otherwise manifests itself in beastly assaults upon white women."

No doubt much hatred arose from the fact that after 1865 the Negro was more or less associated with Northern carpetbaggers and politicians. They had become symbols of defeat in the war and of exploitation in the Reconstruction which followed. Their votes threatened the white man's regional solidarity. Intimidation of the Negro began in the late sixties and gained force in the next four decades. Fanning it were fear, hatred, sadism and a complex jealousy. But fear was much the strongest emotion driving a mob to the most horrible acts of cruelty.

There is no way of knowing how many times stories of extreme violence were published. Certainly lynchings were given wide coverage. They made sensational stories although the details were so revolting they would make humane readers want to throw the paper from them. Many editors did not spare their readers' sensibilities. Whatever their motives, they wrote full, detailed accounts. Turning through many volumes for the period from 1875 to 1920 is somewhat like walking through a chamber of horrors. Although both editors and readers had many attitudes toward lynching, on one point there seems to have been unanimity. The country papers apparently felt that it should be reported in full and in few instances does there seem to have been any effort to suppress or tone down even the most lurid details.

It is not necessary to cite more than a single account to show how realistic and precise this type of news-reporting was. Perhaps the

SAM HOLT BURNED AT THE STAKE BY ENRAGED PEOPLE.

MAKES CONFESSION OF HORRIBLE CRIME AND IS TORTURED TO DEATH IN THE PRESENCE OF 2,000 ONLOOKERS.

DOOMED VICTIM WAS MADE TO SUFFER UNDESCRIBABLE AGONIES.

His Ears Were Cut Off Before He Was Executed and After the Burning There Was a Scramble For the Charred Bones of the Victim, Which Were Carried Away as Souvenirs.

Sam Holt, the negro murderer of Alfred Cranford and the assailant of Cranford's wife, was burned at the stake one mile and a quarter from Newnan, Ga., Sunday afternoon at 2.30 o'clock.

Fully 2,000 people surrounded the small sapling to which he was fastened and watched the flames eat away his flesh, saw his body mutilated by knives and witnessed the contortions of his body in his extreme agony.

Two counties, Campbell and Coweta, directly interested in the crimes of the negro, and the entire state have waited with impatience for the moment when the negro should pay the penalty for his fiendish deeds.

Such suffering has seldom been witnessed, and through it all the negro uttered hardly a cry. During the contortions of the body, several blood vessels bursted.

The spot selected was an ideal one for such an affair and the stake was in full view of those who stood about and with unfeigning satisfaction saw the negro meet his death and saw him tortured before the flames killed him.

For sickening sights, harrowing details and bloodcurdling incidents, the burning of Holt is unsurpassed by any occurrence of a like kind ever heard of in the history of Georgia.

A few smouldering ashes scattered about the place, a blackened stake, are all that was left to tell the story. Not even the bones of the negro were left in peace, but were eagerly snatched by a crowd of people drawn from all directions, who almost fought over the burning body of the man, carving it with their knives and seeking souvenirs of the occurrence.

Self-confessed and almost defiant, without a plea for mercy and no expectation of it, Holt went to the stake with as much courage as any one could possibly have possessed on such an occasion, and the only murmur that issued from his lips was when angry knives plunged into his flesh and his life's blood sizzled in the fire before his eyes.

Then he cried, "Oh, my God! Oh, Jesus!"

Crowd Orderly But Determined.

The crowd that burned Holt made no mistake, as the man was identified by a dozen people. He admitted his guilt and told of the murder. He confessed that he had murdered Cranford and said the deed was done with the expectation of obtaining a reward of $20 from one Lige Strickland.

He confessed while being brought in by his captors, confessed when confronted by Mrs. McElroy, the heart-broken mother of Mrs. Cranford, and confessed when he was taken from the fire and asked to tell the truth about the crime. He told the details, always implicating Lige Strickland.

Although Holt was turned over to the sheriff and placed in the Newnan jail, his fate was sealed from the moment his captors put in an appearance with him.

The remonstrance of ex-Governor W. Y. Atkinson and Judge A. D. Freeman, two of the most prominent citizens of Coweta county, were of no avail.

The awful crime of the murderer and assailant was fresh in the minds of these people. The agony of the living victim of his criminality and the wails of a broken hearted mother were fresh in their ears. There was nothing that could have stopped them, there were few who desired to stop them.

J. B. and J. L. Jones, the captor of Sam Holt, won the admiration of the entire county when the news that the negro had been captured by them was received, and the fact that the reward money they will receive is to be given to the widow of Alfred Cranford has won for them still further praise and admiration.

One of the strangest features of the entire affair is the part played in the execution by a northern man. This man, whose name would not be divulged by those who knew him, announced that he was from the north, while he calmly saturated Holt's clothing with kerosene oil.

The intention and desire of those who had the negro in charge was to burn him at the home of Mrs. Cranford, and the people of Palmetto, when they learned of the capture, made elaborate preparations for the execution, but they were disappointed.

Mrs. Cranford was not permitted to see the negro, although she was in Newnan at the time, and it was suggested that he be carried before her. She is ill, and it has been feared her brain is deranged. It was thought the shock would be too great for her, and the crowd was satisfied with the positive identification by Mrs. Cranford's mother and a number of others.

No identification was necessary, but the crowd was cool and went about its work carefully and almost with a system.

Masks played no part in the lynching. There was no secrecy; no effort to prevent any one seeing who lighted the fire, who cut off the ears or who took the lead.

Story of the Capture.

Sam Holt, the murderer of Alfred Cranford, and the assailant of Mrs. Cranford, was captured at Marshallville, Ga., Saturday night at 9 o'clock by Messrs. J. B. and J. L. Jones. He had been in hiding at the home of his mother since the Friday after the crime.

When found his face was blackened with soot in an attempt at disguise. The story of the capture was told by Mr. J. B. Jones as follows:

I read of the terrible crime and took particular notice of the description of the murderer. A few days after a strange negro came to my plantation. He filled the description given to The Constitution, and my suspicions were at once aroused. The negro worked for me about two years ago, but under another name, and when he left he had been indicted by the grand jury for attempting to assault an old negro woman in Macon county.

My close observation of Holt seemed to have aroused his suspicions, and he left the place. It was several days before I could again locate him, and then I had to enlist the aid of another party. This person was intimate with Holt and agreed to deliver him into my hands last night. Holt was enticed to a certain place, and as he was passing through a dense grove of woods my brother and myself sprang upon him and secured him before he had time to offer any resistance.

LIGE STRICKLAND'S BODY FOUND HANGING FROM A TREE.

Lige Strickland, the negro who was implicated in the Cranford murder by Sam Holt, was lynched early Sunday night.

The body of Lige Strickland was found swinging to the limb of a tree about a mile from Palmetto early Monday morning. The ears and fingers were cut off and on the body was pinned a placard containing the following words:

"WE MUST PROTECT OUR SOUTHERN WOMEN."

Lige Strickland was arrested on the farm of Major Thomas, about seven miles from Palmetto, at 10 o'clock Sunday night, and carried off to the woods.

BILL ARP'S WEEKLY LETTER

BARTOW MAN TAKES A FEW RETROSPECTIVE GLANCES.

TALKS OF FRIENDS OF HIS YOUTH.

William Gets Letters From Some of Them In Which They Recall Scenes of the Long Ago.

How these old men do cling together. Almost every day brings a good kind letter from some venerable man who is lonesome or has a community of interest with me, and wishes to write, for he knows that I will listen. There are many more of them living than I thought, for old men grow silent as they near the end. They ponder and ruminate, but make no noise. Providence is kind in giving to most of them children and children's children to comfort them and to brighten up the passing hours. An old man must be forlorn, indeed, who has none of these. Charles Lamb, in his old and mellow days, wrote sadly when he said.

"Where are my playmates, the companions of my childhood in the joyful school days? All, all are gone—the old familiar faces gone before me to that unknown and silent shore." But Lamb was wifeless and childless and had a right to be sad. He should have adopted some bright little orphan child who would love him and call him father and cling to him in his declining years. Every old bachelor should.

I have just received a good long letter from an old and forgotten friend whom I knew in the long ago and supposed was dead. He is nearing his four score years, but writes the same old school master hand that his generation were taught to write. He is in good health and strong of mind and loves to commune with memories of the past—the halcyon days, as he calls them. I wonder how many college boys know that the pretty word halcyon comes from two Greek words that mean the sea and an egg.

When the elder duck lays her eggs on the cliffs by the sea, it is always warm and pleasant weather, and hence came the word halcyon—als, the sea, and oon, an egg. My friend's name is J. J. Richards and he is the survivor of the three brothers William C. and T. Addison Richards, who were our foremost literary men away back in the forties. They published "Georgia Illustrated" and the Orion Magazine, and many beautiful legends of the Cheorokee Indians. This brother published a war paper called The Soldiers' Friend, of which I have some copies issued in 1864, in Augusta, Ga., and are little gems, both in editorial and selected matter. He now lives not far from McPherson barracks, near Atlanta, and is the postmaster at Golden Gate, and still finds time and pleasure in writing poetry when the spirit moves him. He, too, has added some verses to "John Andersen, My Joe." These old men do not like the way that Burns left John, and his spouse sleeping at the foot of the hill, but want them to rise again and enjoy heaven.

Wallace Reed ought to go out to that Golden Gate and interview Mr. Richards and chronicle some of his memories, for he is about the only literary link between the present and the past. These pioneers should not be forgotten. Most all pioneers are. We eat the fruit of the orchards and vineyards and take no concern about who planted them. Not a dozen people in Rome, a city of 13,000 people, know who planted the trees that give such magnificent shade around the churches, or who first laid out and ornamented the beautiful Myrtle hill cemetery. Who knows of the long and patient toil of Mark A. Cooper in developing and building up the iron industry of Cherokee Georgia? What engineer sought and found the winding way for a railroad from Atlanta to Chattanooga nearly 60 years ago and planned all its curves and spanned the rivers and creeks with bridges?

Not long ago I asked a conductor on the Nashville & Chattanooga railroad to tell me who planned that magnificent work across the Cumberland mountains, and he could not tell me. Who founded old Franklin college, now the University of Georgia and who conceived and projected the establishment of the Wesleyan Fe-

[illegible]
Conrad Rhenanus, [illegible]

Now if this be Melanchthon['s genu]ine autograph these volumes [are of] great historic value, for no [greater] man has lived or died in all the [cen]turies—the man at whose feet [Luther] knelt in reverence, and of whom [Eras]mus exclaimed, "My God, how [pro]found is his learning, how ex[alted] his virtue." These two, Luth[er and] Melanchthon, sleep side by [side at] Wittenberg, and in 1860 the [King of] Prussia erected over his grave [a beau]tiful monument, a duplicate [of that] over Luther's. I do not know [what] evidence this veteran has that [Mel]anchthon ever owned these volumes, but I will know. It is [cer]tain, however, that they were publish[ed] in his day and he could have own[ed] them.

The Latin inscription reminds [me] of another that was sent to me [for] translation not long ago by a fr[iend] in Alabama. It is on the top of [a] massive gold-headed cane that is [an] heirloom in the family. There [is a] crown engraved upon the golden h[ead] and underneath are these w[ords] "Epis [illegible]," which are not [pure] Latin or Greek, but I suppose are [ab]breviations. At any rate they [pass] my comprehension. The cane [de]scended from a distinguished Epis[co]pal bishop of New York city. [The] more I try to solve such problems [the] more I am convinced that "a li[ttle] learning is a dangerous thing." W[ill] not some college boy tell me what [that] Latin means?—BILL ARP in Atl[anta] Constitution.

BRYAN AND BELMONT

Entertain Large Audience From the Platform at Buffalo, N. Y.

Fully 3,000 persons crowded M[usic] Hall at Buffalo, N. Y., Friday nigh[t to] listen to Colonel William J. Brya[n].

Col. Bryan appeared upon the st[age] accompanied by a large company [and] was enthusiastically received, the cr[owd] rising and cheering for some ti[me]. Among those on the platform [were] Frank L. Hapet, chairman of the d[em]ocratic general committee; Norman Mack, Supreme Court Justice Rob[ert] T. Titus and Oliver H. P. Belmont.

Justice Titus presided. He sp[oke] against territorial expansion and ur[ged] the democratic party to plant it[self] squarely in the opposition to [the] "heresy."

The chairman introduced Mr. [Bel]mont, who was received with he[arty] applause. He said in part:

"The democratic party today has [a] great responsibility toward the peo[ple]. It remains with it to decide whe[ther] existing conditions shall continue [or] not. The party has never been g[iven a] greater opportunity to vindicate [its] claims that it is the party that st[ands] for government by the people and [for] the people with equal rights to all [and] special privileges to none.

"The responsibility of the de[moc]ratic party is doubled from the [fact] that if it fails to oust the enem[y in] 1900 it will by so doing give it a [new] lease of the seal of the governm[ent] and allow it to intrench its positio[n in] the intricate system of patronage.

"I am a believer in democ[ratic] principles, and I believe the min[ority] should acquiesce in the decisio[n of] the majority, but I believe that th[e in]terests of every city, state or secti[on of] the country should be considere[d in] framing a national policy.

"The city of New York is democ[rat]ic, and I can say the state, though [we] were beaten in the last election, [is] also democratic, and its vote wi[ll be] essential in the election of 1900."

Justice Titus paid a high tribu[te to] Colonel Bryan, who was received [with] tremendous cheering.

Mr. Bryan said that he had [been] accused of not having wordly g[oods] sufficient to make him a safe cust[odian] of property, but that he was glad [that] the one who preceded him (Bel[mont]) had enough of wordly possession[s to] take him out of the ranks of th[e an]archists at least.

Mr. Bryan said he loved the d[emo]cratic party, but he loved the p[eople] better. He said that the republi[cans] now look to Alexander Hamilton[, while] in 1859 they celebrated the birt[hday] of Thomas Jefferson. He ass[erted] that the republican party had rev[ersed] its former policy of man above [the] dollar, but that now, he charg[ed, the] republican party places the [dollar] above humanity.

Keep abreast of these stirring [times] by subscribing for your home [paper]. The price is little, and you [cannot] afford to be without it.

most notorious case in the South was the burning of Sam Holt or Hose (the editors seem never to have known precisely which) in 1899 in Newnan, Georgia. Holt had murdered Alfred Cranford, a white farmer, ravished Mrs. Cranford and dipped their children in the blood of the father. He was a known criminal and sheriffs in Coweta and Campbell counties had conducted a "still-hunt" for him, but were unable to locate him.

After the Cranford murder and rape nearly all of Georgia was aroused, and a $1,250.00 reward was posted by the state, the Atlanta *Constitution* and the people of Georgia. Holt was captured by two farmers near Marshallville and brought to jail in Newnan. In Atlanta, Governor A. D. Chandler was well aware that he had to work fast to prevent a lynching and he pleaded with police authorities to guard their prisoner against a mob assault. Former Governor A. Y. Atkinson and Judge A. D. Freeman likewise urged that the courts be given an opportunity to hear the case. The evidence seemed clear, and there was every reason to believe that Holt would receive a severe penalty if the courts were allowed to function in an orderly way.

By Sunday afternoon 2,000 persons were assembled at the jail and mass tension developed to an explosive point. The Negro was removed from the jail and, after some debate among the leaders, taken before Mrs. Cranford's mother for identification. He was led to a sapling and securely strapped to it, and kerosene-soaked wood was piled high about him. Holt confessed his guilt, and in so doing involved Lige Strickland as an accomplice. As the crowd milled about the stake, one man was busier, so it was said, than the others. The editor of the Schley County *News* wrote, "One of the strangest features of the entire affair is the part played in the execution by a northern man. This man, whose name would not be divulged by those who know him, announced that he was from the North, while he calmly saturated Holt's clothing with kerosene oil." As the flames spread over the funeral pyre, Holt's body was slashed with knives, and the intense heat distorted his features. His eyes bulged out of their sockets, his veins ruptured and the blood sizzled in the fire, but the Negro remained stolid to the end. "Such suffering," said the *News,* "has seldom been witnessed, and through it all the Negro uttered hardly a cry. During the writhing of the body several blood vessels burst. The spot selected was an ideal one for such an affair and the stake was in full view of those who stood about with unfeigning satisfaction, [and] saw the Negro meet his death and saw him tortured before the flames killed him. For sickening sights, harrowing details and blood-curdling incidents, the burning of Sam Holt is unsurpassed by any occurrence of a like kind ever heard of in the history of Georgia. A few smouldering ashes scattered about the place, a blackened stake, are all that was left to tell the story, not even the bones of the Negro were left in peace, but were eagerly snatched by a crowd of people drawn from all directions, who almost fought over the burning body of the man, carving it with their knives and seeking souvenirs of the occurrence. Self-confessed and almost defiant without a plea for mercy and no expectation of it, Holt went to the stake with as much courage as any one could have possessed on such an occasion, and the only murmur that issued from his lips was when savage knives plunged into his flesh and his life's blood sizzled into the fire before his eyes. Then he cried, "Oh, My God, Oh, Jesus!"

In summarizing the Holt atrocity the Atlanta *Constitution* made an enlightening observation, which was reprinted by the country papers, commenting on the state of mind in the South at the turn of the century. The *Constitution* had contributed a $500 reward for the capture of the Negroes Sam Holt and Lige Strickland and explained its action by commenting upon the practice of lynching. "The *Constitution* makes this offer," said its editor, "fully convinced of the fact that we have reached a critical period—one in which the safety of the home must be measured against the chances for criminals to escape. The people of Georgia are orderly and conservative, the descendants of ancestors who have been trained in America for 150 years. They are a people intensely religious, homeloving and just. There is among them no foreign or lawless element. When, therefore, a lynching occurs among such a people, it has connected with it premeditation and purpose, and it follows that when such a people can be so moved behind it there is a motive so strong and overpowering that all bonds of conservatism have been broken. Georgia is an agricultural state. Her people are forced to the isolated life of the farm, and as the farmer goes about his daily labor, he must leave mother, wife or daughter in the lonely cabin to await his homecoming. Are they safe? The answer comes from the humble home in Campbell County, where an industrious citizen who bore his part toward family and state was brutally murdered by a Negro to whom he had given food and employment."

Of course the Holt case was a horrible extreme among lynching stories but there were many others almost as hideous in the weekly papers.

Lynching was a major question requiring a fundamental decision of the editor. If many editors had followed their first impulse they would probably have ignored the whole unhappy subject. But they were seldom in a position merely to stand aside. It was a subject loaded with dynamite, involving the conflicting loyalties of racial and social groups on one side and to law, order and human decency on the other. Local feeling was high and explosive. A brave man might oppose it. A weaker man usually found it expedient to conform to local belief and feeling. If he was sociable and easygoing he could do so sincerely and without violence to his principles; he was not essentially different from his neighbors.

Editors differed radically in their approach to the issue. A majority, probably large, disapproved of lynching and believed that the practice threatened the whole structure of their law and civilization. Others disapproved of lynching in general but approved it as punishment for rape, particularly when it involved a white woman and a colored man. The difficulty here was to draw the line and make it stick. A smaller group approved the summary justice of the lynch mob and encouraged it. They gave a variety of reasons. They criticized the weakness of the courts, the delays and legal chicaneries that interfered with punishment and spoke warmly of the quick, stern though occasionally inaccurate judgments of the lynching party. They complained of the jury system. They emphasized the bestial nature of the Negro and generalized the attitude that usually accompanied rape cases. Behind all their arguments it is usually possible to discern the drive for white supremacy and the fears and jealousies of racial feeling.

Some publishers had strong convictions and stuck to them through thick and thin. Others took different attitudes at different times and formed separate judgments for each case. Sometimes an editor seemed to approve the general practice of lynching but objected to unusual ferocity and cruelty. For instance in 1893 the editor of the Port Gibson (Mississippi) *Reveille* wrote, "We are glad to see that the burning of the man Smith with unparalleled cruelty by the people of Paris, Texas, calling forth some indignant protests in that state. At Laredo for instance, several hundred citizens assembled in mass meeting and passed resolutions condemning the burning, and Governor Hogg likewise has expressed himself in strong terms of censure. Guilty as the wretch was and definitely deserving death, nothing can justify the savage cruelty of his punishment. In truth, the infliction of such fiendish torture lowered the perpetration to a level of barbarism no higher than that of the brute on whom they wreaked their vengeance."

On the whole the attitude of the Port Gibson paper can be taken as unfavorable to lynching. When a community was strongly stirred by a crime there was no such moderation. Then a paper was likely to come out frankly in favor of the rope and pistol. Sometimes editorial attitudes must have helped to assemble a lynching party. These three paragraphs from the Choctaw (Mississippi) *Plaindealer* (1893) are indicative of irresponsible editorializing. "Kentucky had a necktie party this week. It was carried out in the good old Southern Style—a nigger standing on nothing and looking up a rope." "A Negro murdered a white man in Arkansas last week. There followed: a crowd—a rope—a limb—a dead nigger." And, "Lee Walle, a Negro, assaulted a white woman in Memphis one day this week, and the dusky Lee has since climbed the golden stairs by the rope route. It is an unwritten law in Mississippi and the South that rape means rope and this law will continue as unchangeable as the laws of the Medes and the Persians. As long as black brutes continue to lay hands on fair women of the South, just so long will mob law obtain."

Taylor Cook of Athens, Tennessee, ravished a twelve-year-old girl near Niglin, in Henderson County. The Negro's wife beat him away from the child, and was a witness against him. Cook escaped, and the editor of the Athens *Post* wrote, "Strong hopes are entertained that the wild beast who perpetrated the outrage will be caught and terribly punished. No ordinary death should be his for his crime is the blackest in the calendar, and his race should be taught the terrible examples that such crimes invariably end in horrible deaths. No one who reads the papers can fail to see that crime [sic] of this sort, perpetrated by ignorant Negroes, is on the increase, and a close student of events will not fail to trace the cause to the teachings of those who would make the Negro the equal of the white man."

Sidney Lewis of the Sparta (Georgia) *Ishmaelite* took the attitude that lynching was a safe question for Yankee editors to leave alone. He was indifferent to outside attitudes and did not care what other people thought. "The people of the North," he wrote, "are too much worried over the alleged defects of southern civilization to give the necessary attention to the spots and wrinkles in their own. The fellow who thanked God that he wasn't as other men was a fair type of Yankee editor."

A more analytical attitude toward the rightness of lynching was cogently pressed by the Waycross (Georgia) *Herald*. It was argued that if one white woman could be saved from bestial defilement then the national elections could be ignored. "Our women," said the editor, "must and will be protected as long as life lasts." Lynching had prevented rape and murder of untold thousands of Southern white women, and it was the only punishment sufficiently austere to prevent these crimes. Color made no difference to the Georgia editor, "white or black," they should be hanged to the nearest tree. "There will be no more of raping 15 year old girls in the neighborhood soon. The brute, be he white or black, who ravished and kills [sic] a child or women (most of them seem to be children) is in our opinion outside the pale of the law and is a hundred times worse than a mad dog or a wild animal let loose on a community, and should be dealt with as such." The gladiatorial air of public hangings was conducive to some unfortunate attitudes toward the criminal. "The Negro," said the *Herald*, "arrested for outrage, kept in jail, tried by jury and sentenced to be hung with all the honors of war and the law, becomes a hero and goes straight to heaven from the gallows, thus setting an example which some of those witnessing the scene will afterwards emulate. . . . Let it be understood that lynchings will stop when the ravishing of our women stops and not before. Almighty God this is the truth, if the United States never has another president."

In complete agreement with the attitude of the Waycross *Herald* was the Selma (Alabama) *Southern Argus*. A mixed jury in Mobile failed to agree upon a verdict against James Smith, a Negro charged with rape upon a white girl. "Of course not," said the *Argus*. "Such cases ought never to go to a jury." Many editors believed rightly that public opinion was highly in favor of lynching as a means of covering up the weaknesses of the laws. At Lexington, Tennessee, a Negro raped a young girl. He was hanged in the courthouse yard, and his body filled with bullets. "Terrible was his crime," wrote editor Wisdom of the *Whig and Tribune*, "and terribly did he expiate it. But who will say his fate was not a just one? While the laws of Tennessee make highway robbery a capital and rape only a penitentiary offense, such scenes as that of Friday night will be enacted. Public opinion, which is stronger than all law, sustains such proceedings and under the circumstances public opinion is not wrong." This editor believed lynching was a part of the unhappy race picture. "We do not think that white men will quit hanging black men," he wrote, "until black men quit outraging white women. The law ought to be sustained, but public sentiment is to a law what the ground under a house is to the superstructure. The public sentiment is not a part of the law, the ground is not a part of the house, but neither law nor house can stand on nothing."

A kindred sentiment was that expressed by a Charlotte, North Carolina, grand jury empaneled to investigate the death of Tom Jones who assaulted Mrs. Will Smith. The jail door was battered open and the Negro taken to the woods and hanged, and his clothes cut into souvenirs. The jury's findings, as reported by the Greensboro (Georgia) *Herald* said, "We the undersigned empanelled as a jury to enquire into the cause of the death of Tom Jones, find that he came to his death by gunshot wounds by party unknown to the jury, obviously by an outraged public acting in defense of their homes, wives, daughters and children. In view of the enormity of the crime committed by said Tom Jones, alias Frank Hill, we think they would have been recreant to their duty as good citizens had they acted otherwise."

Many papers pointed to the weakness of the law, the certain delay and the uncertain vigor of the courts and the incompetence of jurors. Some regarded the feebleness of the legally established courts as an excuse or even as a justification of lynching. Others believed that lynching further enfeebled the legal system and was therefore doubly bad for the community.

As early as 1878 Clarence Stephens of Crawfordville, Georgia, published in the McDuffie *Journal* a long editorial in which he reviewed the sad story of lynchings. He assured his readers that the stock reply that some guilty persons escaped the clutches of the law was no excuse to disregard the regularly constituted courts and their orderly trials. An analysis of local excuses for lynching was undertaken frequently. The common reasons were usually given in the following order: first, counties had poor and insecure jails in which it was considered unsafe to leave prisoners for fear of a jail break; and, second, the courts were too slow in handling cases involving capital crimes. The editor of the Greensboro (Georgia) *Herald* said he realized fully the dangers of mob law, but there was a demand for "*speedy and certain*" justice in rape cases. Courts should be called into immediate session in order to hear these cases. Finally, there was a feeling that lawyers were more anxious to earn fees than they were to see the ends of justice served, and that they produced one technicality after another to delay the trial of capital cases. Editors looked on delays as a cause for the gathering of mobs. There was a general fear that through technicalities and unreliable courts, rapists would be turned loose to continue breaking lives as they pleased. A. H. Aull, the sane editor of the Newberry (South Carolina) *Herald and News,* wrote that it was a rare thing for a Negro to be given a trial. Rape had been regarded as a crime demanding summary punishment. He did not voice his personal opinion, but he used this point to emphasize the importance of speedy regular court trials.

Once a case came into the courts, editors warned that evidence produced in the trial might actually lead to lynching. To begin with, nearly every prisoner accused of a major crime stood convicted in the court of public opinion before he reached the prisoner's docks in the criminal courts. Rumor was already accepted evidence, and there was grave danger that any facts brought out in the trial would only aggravate the possibility of a lynching. Cases were cited where mobs went into courtrooms and took prisoners away from the courts. At Springfield, Tennessee, four Negroes killed a white man named Laprade. The murder was a barbarous affair in which the victim was hit on the head with a rock, his teeth were knocked out, his testicles were cut off and the body was thrown into a sinkhole. The Negroes were brought into court, and the case was tried before a jury in a regular and orderly manner. Just as the judge finished his instructions to the jury, a mob of 200 men marched in, took the prisoners, rushed to the east veranda of the courthouse and there hanged them. There was no commotion, and as soon as the victims were dropped from the veranda, the leader commanded, "Disperse, my men, to your homes." They divided into three parties and rode away in three directions. Back in the courtroom the dejected judge dismissed court with the statement that he was tired of obtaining prisoners for mobs to hang. The editor of the Pulaski *Citizen* said that in ten years in Pulaski ten men had been lynched. Of these it was believed two were innocent and the other eight would have been convicted by the court.

Most editors were sorely troubled by the practice of lynching. In their anxiety to find a solution for it they failed to give sufficient weight to some significant points. Trials could be speedy only when sufficient evidence was readily obtainable to permit their immediate consideration. When cases depended on a maze of circumstantial evidence, and it was necessary to call in a large number of uncertain witnesses, delay was inevitable. Some of the aggravated cases were so confused by the very heat which they generated that either a cooling-off period was necessary to insure justice, or a change of venue was called for.

No doubt criminal lawyers needlessly complicated many cases which perhaps could have been adjusted at once. Often they introduced pleas of insanity and psychopathic irresponsibility. Although some of these claims were very likely valid, the average person, having no psychological training, believed they were made merely to delay and confuse the court. Men who became highly excited over most of the crimes which caused lynchings were seldom, if ever, capable of weighing evidence objectively. There was even danger that persons who were convicted and received prison terms would escape either through the bars of the prison or by political pardons granted by governors. The country papers touched on all these points but without assurance or conviction.

A correspondent signing himself "Bakersville Voice" in the Salisbury (North Carolina) *Watchman* said in 1884 that twenty-one men had been lynched in Yancey County and seventeen in Mitchell County since the Civil War, and that the same situation prevailed in many other places. "There is no lack of law to punish murderers," he wrote, "though greatly encumbered by decisions which complicated almost every case. Through the perversions of law and the unfaithfulness of juries and judges, the recklessness of lawyers, the guilty escaped. It would be better to go back to the Mosaic System, in respect to murder, in which there were few laws and simple, easily understood by all. Better justice is administered by savages, by the Indians, and Africans."

"Bakersville Voice" quoted statistics to those who complained that appeals to the higher courts resulted in a circumvention of justice. Since 1865, including fifteen cases in Phillips' *North Carolina Cases,* and one in volume 89, 1884, of the North Carolina *Reports,* there were 116 decisions involving capital crimes. Of these, new trials were granted in thirty-two cases and six were discharged because of technicalities. Thus out of 116 cases only six were discharged and these six for good and sufficient reasons. This made the popular demand for the speedy justice of the Mosaic Law a savage voice crying out in a wilderness of social chaos. This commentator did not doubt that the machinery of the court should be regeared, but certainly there was nothing wrong with the general administration of the principles of justice. Earlier, the editor of the Chatham (North Carolina) *Record* published a story of the lynching of a man named Church. He was accused of raping a Miss Thompson in Alexander County. In spite of the nature of the crime, the editor felt that this, the fourth local lynching in six months, was disgraceful and alarming. North Carolina, he said, had always been conservative, but now it was going mob-crazy. He maintained that juries and courts were still good enough protection for the law in North Carolina.

A vigorous point of view was that expressed in 1887 by the Winnsboro (South Carolina) *News and Herald.* Johnnie Goode was murdered near Yorkville by Negroes, and the murderers were lynched. The Winnsboro editor believed these lynchings were a gross miscarriage of justice. Only two views were possible: "(1), [the] act was flagitious, (2) a bold declaration that the law is irretrievably impotent in South Carolina." Lynching, he said, was an act of the "ungovernable rage of ignorance, an ignorance which can only appreciate the majesty of the law when it itself is placed in the dock." All the details of this murder were available and could easily have been made known in court. The murder was horrible, but the lynching which followed was a social travesty. Editor Raggsdale, in commenting on court proceedings against the lynchers, said that any effort to bring the lynchers to trial would be a fruitless expense. The fault, said the *News and Herald,* lay with the press. It had the responsibility for creating a more civilized attitude, but that in many instances South Carolina papers were instrumental in reducing the courts to a state of impotency. In the Yorkville case five human beings were lynched without trial, despite the fact that court was in session at the time.

Opponents of lynching argued—often with apparent justice—that it accomplished nothing good that the courts could not do as well. Colonel W. P. Walton in the upper South was direct in his views on lynching. In 1877 he vigorously denounced mob rule. "The infernal mob business," he wrote, "showed itself this week in Fayette

County. A negro hit a white man named John Denton, on the head with an ax, giving him probably a fatal wound. The negro was arrested and taken before a magistrate and held to await the result of Denton's wound. That night a mob took the negro from the officers of the law and hung him to a neighboring tree. Each man engaged in that cowardly work, is a murderer and the law should see that they do not go unpunished. There is no palliation for the deed. The negro had committed a horrible crime but he was in the hands of the law, and would certainly have gotten the full punishment for it. Mobs are always cowardly and as great breakers of the law as the criminals they propose to take into their hands to punish."

Public opinion was sometimes opposed to lynching, and this fact appeared in the weekly papers. It was difficult, however, to determine what part of the population of a county was involved in a lynching. Mobs varied in size. If the crimes which they punished were widely publicized, some of the participants were often drawn in from other communities, even from other counties. Whole communities can be arraigned historically for acquiescence but not for universal participation. Even passive acquiescence reflected a failure of the press, pulpit and community gatherings. There was some indication of a sense of responsibility in a resolution adopted in mass meeting by citizens of Dallas County, North Carolina, following the lynching of Erin McCully in the county jail. The resolution said: "That we feel it our duty as law abiding citizens, publicly to express our condemnation of this high-handed outrage! That we are shocked that such a brutal, barbarous act should be perpetrated in our midst, and that we hereby protest against and condemn all unlawful proceedings as a thrust at liberty."

Even where mobs were opposed, they were not easy to stop. Take as an example the Mississippi mob of 500 men who broke into the Carroll County jail. Bessie McCroy, her son Belfield and daughter Ida, who were being held for the murder of Mr. and Mrs. Talliferro, were seized by the mob, taken to the edge of the town of Carrollton and hanged and their bodies riddled with bullets. While the mob was at work the Honorable W. S. Hill and Judge W. F. Stephens stood on the jail steps with their arms around the leaders begging them to desist in favor of the courts. Soon after, Governor Andrew Longino arrived on the scene and delivered a long lecture in which he condemned lynching.

Some editors seemed to understand the reasons for many lynchings. There has always been an unhappy affinity between institutional and social failures in the South. Where educational standards were almost too low to be called standards there was corresponding ignorance of the law and social justice. Incomes were low, semifeudal local political systems failed to function, and there was competition between Negroes and whites. Poor public officials, poor institutions, malnutrition, disease and crime, and ineffective legislative and tax programs prevented a reasonable sanctioning of the agencies of the law. Because of this state of affairs large segments of the population of many Southern communities were incapable of comprehending the significance of the majesty of the law.

Peace officers were often products of inferior local political systems and refused to stand against the impact of the mob. Conscientious sheriffs realized how flimsy their jails were. Thousands of published grand jury presentments are almost universal proof of this fact. It was not too difficult for mobs to batter down flimsy jailhouse doors with sledge hammers and bolts of wood.

Sheriffs grew nervous at the first threat of a mob. To begin with, the office has always been a political plum with many opportunities for extra income. In the South it often went to a good politician rather than to an upright and courageous peace officer. As a consequence, sheriffs have not wanted to face maddened constituencies on so treacherous an issue as lynching and racial animosity. In a twinkling of an eye they could lose their entire political following. In most instances where a sheriff had foreknowledge of a mob he attempted to spirit his charges away to other communities and away from local emotional tensions. A representative case of this kind was that in which Sheriff J. W. Nichols of Spartanburg County scurried around over upper South Carolina with the Negro John Williams who had killed Mayor Henneman of Spartanburg. Governor Ben Tillman remanded the Negro to the Spartanburg jail, and instructed the sheriff that he was looking to him to be obedient and to see that state law was upheld. The Newberry *Herald and News* commended Governor Tillman for his stand, and said that the act of sheriffs running from jail to jail with prisoners looked bad for a law-abiding state. When mobs learned that sheriffs would stand their ground it was believed no further efforts would be made to smash jails. "If we pretend to have courts," wrote the editor, "they should condemn law violators."

Dealing with lynchers in the courts attracted much and varied editorial attention. When a jury in Abbeville, South Carolina, acquitted Bill Parkman and Wyatt Holmes for complicity in a lynching, the Winnsboro *News and Herald* said, "To what a pass have we come in the 19th century. A bold, brutal band of ignorant men, snatch a prisoner from the custody of the law, murder him without mercy, and rely upon the venality of that much vaunted institution, 'jury of their peers,' these were tried by a jury of their peers no doubt on this point."

This same courageous paper called for the trial and punishment of lynchers in the famous Culbreath case in Edgefield County. "It made no difference," said the editor, "if the Culbreath lynchers were some of the most responsible people in Edgefield." Equality before the court, he thought was the soul of the law, and there was no artificial question of respectability involved. "The lynching of Culbreath was a barbarous pagan act. They [the lynchers] forfeited all claims to respectability," and were entitled to no clemency. The "blood of [the] murdered Culbreath cries out for revenge from the barren sands of Edgefield."

More sobering than the above forthright editorials was the stern act of Governor Richardson of South Carolina. He pardoned three Negroes, William C. Williams, C. Williams and Harrison Heyward for lynching Manse Waldrop. Waldrop, a white man, had raped Lula Sherman, a thirteen-year-old Negro girl. A. H. Aull of the Newberry *Herald and News* thought the governor was right. "It was the concensus that lynching should prevail, and there had never been a conviction of lynchers for rape. This case was a dirty one. If the lynchers are allowed to go free in other incidents then these ignorant Negroes should not be made to suffer. They were following in the footsteps of their enlightened white neighbors." This case provoked the signing of the largest petition for pardon ever presented a South Carolina governor. In fact, there were fifty-two petitions, signed by 3,000 to 4,000 whites and Negroes, among whom were at least a dozen of the state's most distinguished citizens. Governor Richardson said he did not condone lynching, "but he could not discriminate against Negroes. These men had seen the law broken and lynchers go free countless times"; under similar conditions he said he would not show clemency to whites.

Rape in the context of racial jealousy tended to confuse issues and make a difficult problem even more difficult. Outspoken opponents of lynching recognized this cause alone as an excuse, perhaps a vindication. Z. W. Whitehead was against lynch law, yet in a half-column editorial he wrote of rape that "the absolutely certain commission of that nameless and revolting crime which crushes peace and joy forever out of a fair young life's consolation can ever deny [sic] starts the pulse of indignant manhood at fever heat, transforms the quiet citizen into the stern avenger, and sets the whole community in arms to rid the earth of the wretch who cumbers it—the fiend whose life is an offense against God and humanity."

If the line could have been neatly drawn between lynchings for rape and lynching for other crimes, people might have been clearer in their minds. But the justification for the one was constantly being extended to cover the other. In point of fact there were at least two lynchings resulting from murders to every one following a rape. And lynchings for murder were in many cases just as brutal as those punishing rape. Many editors recognized these facts but the knowledge did not lead to any solution of the problem.

Lynchers sought vengeance, not justice. The horror of the crime for which they exacted payment, not evidence of guilt, was uppermost in the minds of a mob. Rumor passed for fact, and innocent men were executed along with the guilty. They were denied orderly trial and conviction by public officials whose identity and responsibilities were known and clearly described by law. It was easy, in a moment of hysteria, to go from one category to another in the alleged crimes for which the extreme punishment was meted, until no margin was left between high crimes and personal spites which could not stand exposure in an organized court.

In 1881 the editor of the Marietta (Georgia) *Journal* wrote that he deplored lynch law. It was unacceptable under all circumstances. To lynch was to perform an act of madmen, and to prostitute justice in every respect. Counties where lynching occurred served notice that they had become victimized by an intense form of social neurosis from which they could not soon recover. Principles so precious as the due process of law and the sanctity of property were placed in jeopardy. The Georgia editor could not see any possible excuse for mob law, and he believed the time had come to discontinue its application.

Z. W. Whitehead of the Fayetteville *Weekly Observer* wrote that a resort to lynch law can never be justified, though it might be excused. To him murder, arson, burglarly and robbery were major crimes which deserved severe punishment. In explaining lynch law he said it had grown out of the defects of the post-Civil War jury system and the ineffectiveness of local courts. Pleas of insanity and for mercy had been granted without proper assessment of their reasonableness. But even though "redhanded" criminals had gone "unwhipt" by the courts there was still no justification for a mob taking the law into its hands.

After the lynching in 1889 of two men named Stock and Boone of Morganton, North Carolina, in which a mob of masked men held prayer services before dispatching their victims, Whitehead wrote, "If matters get any worse in some portions of North Carolina, it will be found about as well to confine the courts to the transaction of civil business and the trial of jail and penitentiary offenses, leaving the adjudication and settlement of capital cases to the people in mob assembled. As they have introduced the new features of religious services in conjunction with the hurriedly improvised gibbett, the malefactor will at least have the advantage—while he is hustled out of this world with more precipitation than is pleasant—of being introduced into the next world with all due ceremony."

Clearly the Southern country editor was in a state of quandary over lynching. It is not possible to make sharp distinctions for the entire period from 1865 to 1930, between editors who did and did not favor lynching, but it is clearly evident that a strong sense of the injustice of this terrible form of extralegal punishment was developing. Country papers over a period of years showed some sense of the changing attitudes toward lynching. Editors apparently acquired more social perspective, and they began to understand that violence was less chivalry than an aggressive reaction to deep-seated fears and uncertainties. They came to understand that a county had to struggle hard to heal the wound of a lynching. They gradually realized that the courts had to be protected, and more editors campaigned for the orderly procedure of the law.

They, like every other social group, were timid. When peace officers and coroners' juries said victims met death "at the hands of persons unknown," they refused to try publicly to identify mob participants, although such knowledge was often easily obtainable. It was in this connection that the press might have been more vigorous. Perhaps it was too much to ask individual editors to announce the names of lynching parties. There was, of course, constant danger of physical injury and libel suits, but the publication of names of even the leaders of mobs would have had a highly chastening influence. In all honesty, it was too much to ask the earlier Southern country editor to take a bold and highly unpopular stand in a field where sheriffs, coroners juries, grand juries, prosecuting attorneys, church leaders and courts were unwilling to crusade for the right.

The influence of the press in this area of opinion and culture is not to be measured in terms of open crusading against the specific crime of lynching. The weekly press's work for better schools, better roads, somewhat improved political conditions, better jails, better economic opportunities and improved state penitentiaries operated indirectly to reduce the psychological causes of lynching, as well as public approval of it. As community intellectual and economic conditions improved and the racial and social frictions and economic jealousies were lessened, hope grew that lynching might gradually die out.

Many editors, as has been said, were freehanded with space in publicizing lynchings, and there is no doubt that their highly colored, detailed stories were read with avidity. It is possible that the realism of these stories did something to plant in the saner Southern mind a germ of doubt that lynching was effective in punishing crimes. Statistics kept by Upton of the Chicago *Tribune* and by Tuskegee Institute showed an ultimate reduction of lynchings over a period of approximately seventy years. How much credit the country editors can claim for this is impossible to judge. At least, editors publishing the dramatic facts of an unbelievable number of lynchings refused to accept the philosophy that "the least said the better off the South would be."

Book Four

THE NEW SOUTH

Chapter 15

In the Wake of Time

THE country papers liked feature stories. A great portion of the material published in the weeklies was of feature interest, and of course certain subjects were given special attention. Editors who had served in the Confederate Army vividly recalled the famous Beecher family and welcomed an opportunity to attack it. Occasionally they commented acidly on the activities of Harriet Beecher Stowe but usually they dismissed her as a nosy old woman who was beneath the notice of a decent paper. But her authoritarian brother, Henry Ward, was given much space. Like many famous ministers of his day, he commented freely on contemporary politics, especially on Southern Reconstruction.

The Southern editors liked Henry Ward Beecher no better than he liked the South. They granted that the imperious Brooklyn divine spoke with great piety and spiritual authority, but he had supported Grant and had closed his eyes to "Boss" Tweed, Jay Cooke and other scoundrels. He had yielded to the dollar craze of the age. He was accused of overlooking the sinning of his congregation if it was done by the wealthy. Because of his nature and because of the affluent society in which he lived, Beecher at times assumed an air of omniscience. There was God and then there was Beecher. When he referred to conditions in the Southern states it sounded like Moses reporting on the recalcitrant Hebrew Children. Few Southern editors ever forgave him for his famous reference to the South as a land of "fourteen vagabond states." Below the Potomac, the benignant countenance of "St. Beecher," topped with its flowing name, was a symbol of gross hypocrisy. With all the Southerners' respect for ministers of God's word, they could not accept the Brooklyn preacher. They put him and Ben Butler in the same category—one was a thieving, fraudulent man of God and the other a thief of spoons and human rights.

In 1872 a faint rumor came from Brooklyn that Beecher had been intimate with at least one voluptuous member of his congregation. Here was an opportunity for Southern editors to heap damaging coals upon their region's pious critic. Few if any of them took the trouble to enquire into the source of the rumors. They were not acquainted with Victoria Woodhull, Mrs. Nathan B. Morse and all the other gossip-mongers. The editors neither knew about nor could understand much of Victoria Woodhull's indefinite theories of free love and stirpiculture. The only thing that mattered to them was that Henry Ward Beecher was charged with immorality.

Beecher, so it was said, had been having "criminal commerce" with the inviting Elizabeth Tilton, and from the Southern editors' point of view that was a delightful scandal to attack. During 1874 and 1875, at the high tide of bitterness against the exploitation of the South by Northern politicians and carpetbaggers, news columns of the country papers contained accounts of Beecher's scandal. In July 1874, a story appeared telling how Beecher refused to permit a charge of sensuality to be lodged against him by Victoria Woodhull. The papers reprinted a letter from Beecher to Theodore Tilton in which the writer begged forgiveness and humbled himself before God. He said, "I will not plead for myself, I even wish I were dead." Later Beecher claimed he did not know he was being blackmailed by Tilton. Editors scoffed at him. They alleged the famous preacher had paid Tilton the sums of $2,000 and $5,000, and he was forced to mortgage his home in order to raise the money. This gossip revealed Beecher to the weekly editors as an exceedingly lumpy and faulty piece of human clay. In fact, they believed him to be not only an adulterer but an infamous liar as well. "It may seem quite natural," wrote D. M. Wisdom of the Jackson (Tennessee) *Whig and Tribune,* "to the committee [of the governing board of Plymouth Church] that a man should pay $7,000, mortgaging his house to do so—to hide the awful secret of his innocence, and conceal from the world his [lack] of purity and virtue."

Only the most gullible could accept Beecher's feeble explanation of innocence. Timid and stupid men perhaps could be blackmailed without knowing it, but Beecher was neither. One journal said, "A very weak and timid man may submit to be blackmailed even when he is innocent, but this 'fine old platitudinarian' as Gath styles Brother Beecher, is not a weak and timid man, and no confession from him short of one announcing actual guilt could have a more damning effect on the public mind."

In the midst of the excitement of the Beecher-Tilton trial a reporter succeeded in getting an interview with Elizabeth Tilton. Actually the reporter wished to form a firsthand impression of her physically. His eloquent description got into the weekly exchanges and was widely published. The writer described a woman with a high degree of romantic and physical appeal. In strict dimensional terms she had "a most symmetrical head, intellect and poetry predominating; a wealth of silken hair; fair skin; soft, soulful eyes of richest hazel; a face of exquisite sweetness and tenderness, and ripe with culture and character; a mouth curved by the gods, and lips full, warm and suggesting robustness of modest passion; a chin indicating a gentle firmness and abundant will; a shapely neck and graceful shoulders, and finely developed bust—all harmony—all beauty, all vigor and tenderness of young life and fascination. The witching eyes seem to brighten when looked into; a very smile so sweet as to thrill me appeared upon the face when I involuntarily fixed my gaze upon it."

Stories were written of Mrs. Tilton's hard life. Theodore Tilton was pictured in them, fairly or unfairly, as a spineless liar and professional exploiter who had neglected his wife at least four months each year while touring the country to lecture on politics and religion. Elizabeth was portrayed as a beautiful and innocent woman who had been victimized by the two men in her life. One of them, it was said, had exploited her fair name, and the other had shamelessly ravished her body. Sam P. Ivins, of the Republican Athens (Tennessee) *Post,* wrote that he believed it fantastic to say that the cause of this famous adultery case "lay in the atmosphere of Plymouth Parish which distorts every impression that is wrought upon the eye, the heart or the brain of its unhappy victim."

No longer was Beecher to be feared in the Southern press. He immediately became "that old lecher Henry Ward Beecher." It said he had always been a political and religious demagogue. "He appears to have been a successful hypocrite, who interlarded his theological and political discourses with private sermons to the wives and women in the congregation, in which he argued to submit to his lecherous embraces was no moral wrong; that this gospel 'Thou shalt commit adultery,' took precedence over the commandment forbidding that crime." Editors held the male congregation of Plymouth Church up to public ridicule. They said that nobody but Beecher, and even he perhaps had lost count, knew how many husbands of that fold had been cuckolded by their shepherd. Not since the memorable fall of Lucifer himself "had man fallen so far."

The editors played games with this famous case. They said in pithy "observation" columns, "When she gets to tilting, beech-her." Two towns, Beecher, Illinois and Tilton, New Hampshire, were petitioning postal authorities for permission to change their names. Yet some Southerners found certain highly descriptive uses for the two names. An ox driver near Elberton, Georgia, called his team Beecher and Tilton, because "it is needless to say Beecher is a bull, while Tilton is the worst thief in the county."

Hardly had the ink dried on the last Beecher-Tilton tale, and the last moralist quit shaking his head, when the famous Garfield assassination story filled literally thousands of columns of print. Just as the Beecher story was printed and read because of its principal actor's attitude toward the South, so was the Garfield story. James A. Garfield, although a former officer of the Union Army and a Republican, had been liked by the Southern weekly papers. Because of his opposition to the Stalwarts he had succeeded in convincing the South of his genuine desire to restore national unity and harmony. Hayes had begun the task of reconciliation and Garfield had been committed to its completion. One of the most certain signs, in fact, that the South was back in the Union was its attitude toward Garfield.

In the summer of 1881 the country weeklies were in a quiet streak. They were carrying the usual columns of local news, editorial observations, reports of hangings, lynchings, shootings, cuttings, weddings and minor disasters, as well as some comment on the Yorktown Centennial. At Washington the new administration had settled down, and the last inauguration story had long since appeared. Although the weeklies praised Garfield warmly, they were already running editorials pleading for a Democratic victory at the next election. In the midst of this somewhat drowsy summer scene, on the morning of July 2 at twenty minutes to nine, two sharp pistol shots rang out in the ladies' waiting room in the Baltimore and Potomac railway station. One bullet struck President Garfield in the arm and the other plowed into his back between the kidney and the hip.

Garfield had entered the ladies' waiting room on a short cut to the train. He was accompanied by James G. Blaine and they were on their way to join the President's family at Francklyn Cottage in Elberon, New Jersey. Before Garfield and Blaine had appeared, attendants had seen the assailant walking restlessly through the station. Witnesses recalled later that the little man was impatient and hustled around as if laboring under great responsibility. He was short, frail, bewhiskered, no different in appearance from the army of cranks and self-seekers who daily kept vigil in the national capital. The man was about thirty years old, his whiskers were cropped squarely across at the point, his hair was close-cropped and his clothes were those of a man who had managed to live without working but who had not lived well enough to dress neatly. Somewhere in his coat he carried concealed a revolver which could be brought into immediate use. The young man appeared to be so commonplace a figure that George W. Adams, publisher of the Washington *Star,* mistook him a few moments after the shooting for a countryman who was attempting to quiet the panic-stricken crowd.

When the two shots were fired, and Garfield threw up his arms and sank to the floor, persons near at hand captured his attacker. No one knew who he was, and it was not until the captors brought the struggling prisoner to the jail that they learned his identity. There the turnkey recognized him as the man who, a few days before, had attempted to visit the jail, and who had introduced himself as Charles Guiteau, a Chicago attorney. Guiteau was famous for his letters to the papers, to prominent Republican politicians and to General Sherman in particular. He had also distinguished himself as the author of a pamphlet entitled *The Second Coming of Jesus Christ.* Immediately Guiteau's personal history was unfolded in news stories. He was known to be a family black sheep, a tramp, a lawyer by courtesy only, a former member of the Oneida Community and a Stalwart partisan. He had on one occasion or another aired his views on virtually every subject relating to national, social and political progress. He was known to be against Garfield's tolerant administrative course.

By his two ominous shots in the ladies' waiting room at the Baltimore and Potomac Station, Guiteau shot his way into the pages of history. His act came as a shock to Southern editors. Typesetters stood long hours before their cases and set up four and five columns detailing the national tragedy. Lewis M. Grist's Yorkville *Enquirer* was characteristic of the Southern press. It carried five full columns of the story in a single issue—two columns contained the details of the tragedy, and two described the South's reactions. Here was a heavy blow at the nation, and at the South in particular. A week after his paper publicized the Garfield tragedy, editor Grist became philosophical. Garfield's injury was a sad trial for the American people, but "God moves in mysterious ways his wonders to perform." In this train of reflection he was led to observe "that the hand of the assassin was raised against the President for an all-wise purpose, which would be consumated by more firmly than ever uniting the two sections that had been estranged by war, and which alienating, designing men, for base purposes, were endeavoring to perpetuate!"

It was said that Garfield, on the fatal morning of July 2, had expressed the belief that all was well with the nation, and that the South wanted harmony. In the face of tragedy, Southern country papers carried numerous editorials bemoaning the sad fate of the country, and proclaimed the region's gallantry, courage, love of constitutional rights and liberty. There was nothing like deep sorrow to bring an estranged people into a common union.

While editors gathered comments from over the South, and their printers "stuck" them into endless columns for their readers, harried surgeons probed the thick torso of the wounded Garfield for the bullet which had torn its way along his spinal column. These blundering searches caused the injured man the suffering of the damned. The suffocating heat of the humid Potomac flats was almost more than the patient and his doctors could endure. Prominent Republican politicians took their turn at fanning their stricken chief, but the task of creating a comforting breeze was too much for them. Professor Alexander Graham Bell rigged a crude electric fan to draw the air in from the outside, and to relieve the gasping politicians.

Week after week columns of news were distributed over the South giving a full bedside report of Garfield's condition. Prayer meetings were held to seek the President's recovery. Democrats thronged into dusty county courthouses to speak softly of Garfield, to sweat and to swear at Charles Guiteau. Eloquent local orators proclaimed Garfield the greatest friend of the South a Republican could ever be. They pictured his condition in the dolorous terms so popular at that time. Quickly speakers switched from the hushed tones of sadness to fierce harangues against the criminal Charles Guiteau. The President's assassin was regarded as an unbalanced anarchist, an infidel, a ne'er do-well, a criminal and a fool. Murmurs were heard that all he was good for was to stretch hemp and he should be put to work at it at once. But Guiteau was beyond the reach of the direct-action elements of these meetings. Fortunately most of them ended on a tenderer note in lament for Garfield. Down in Texas the people were angry with Governor Roberts for not setting aside a day for the celebration of the recovery of Garfield. Defiantly they got together in a mass meeting and prayed for the President and condemned their governor for his lack of patriotism.

From July to September the Garfield story filled newspaper columns. Weekly papers crammed into each issue a full summary of a week's development, and carried much rich human-interest material on the side. Even a reporter from the Philadelphia *Press* went to the trouble of interviewing Jefferson Davis on the news of Garfield's injury. Davis felt the tragedy was a serious blow at the South, for the stricken President seemed to have the capacity to make all sections kin.

On September 19, at 10:35 in the evening Garfield died. He had been moved by special train from the hot and crowded White House bedroom to Francklyn Cottage at Elberon where it was believed he would be more comfortable. Papers appeared next week with heavy funereal reversed-rule borders, and the stories enclosed with them were the epitome of grief. Church and courthouse bells tolled in mourning for the dead executive. Churches were filled with Democratic mourners who were gathered to revere the memory of a friend.

For almost a year after the assassination of Garfield the country papers contained long stories of the sensational happenings which occurred in the Washington courtroom where Guiteau was being tried. Every detail of that poorly managed trial, and the wild ravings of the demented prisoner were published. The weeklies carried these stories, and when Guiteau was at last convicted there were periodic descriptions of his prison life and of the preparations for his execution. Long before he was hanged the assassin had become a legendary character in the country papers. The story did not end with the hanging, but was continued to cover the ghastly disposition of Guiteau's body. The average editor felt forced against his inclination to publicize the fact that at last Guiteau's bleached bones were mixed with others of the Medical Museum's collection. Thus ended a great news story.

When Guiteau was gone, publishers had to look elsewhere for sensational feature material. From the Kentucky mountains came one of the most repulsive rape and murder stories in the criminal annals of the South. Three cousins named Craft, Ellis and Neal called on relatives in an isolated section of the hills. When they arrived they found the older people gone, but two female cousins were at home alone. The girls were ravished, murdered, their bodies sprayed with kerosene, and the house burned down on them in an effort to destroy all traces of the crime. At the funeral of the girls one of the culprits drove the hearse and another was a pallbearer. Evidence, however, indicated the guilt of the three cousins and soon they were under arrest. People became so infuriated that a mob undertook to snatch the prisoners away from the sheriff and hang them. Enraged neighbors commandeered a Chesapeake and Ohio train and backed it into the railway station at Ashland in an attempt to prevent the sheriff's taking his prisoners from Catlettsburg to the Mt. Sterling jail. When this occurred the officers fled the train and rushed aboard a waiting steamboat to escape down the Ohio River. Again the mob was alert and followed close behind in a ferry boat, carrying on a running gun fight with the officers. But they failed to get the prisoners away from the sheriff.

For a period of five years Southern country papers published accounts of the Craft trials, convictions and executions. Few horror stories ever attracted so much sustained attention. Despite the competition of continual lynching stories, the Kentucky murder feature remained a sensational and blood-curdling account of violence.

While the story of the brutal Kentuckians and their shocking murder was being publicized all over the South, other Kentucky mountaineers were making news copy. The numerous feuds which grew out of Civil War animosities and economic and political rivalries in the mountains resulted in open warfare among various local factions. The most famous of these were the Tolliver-Martin, Hatfield-McCoy, Hargis-Cockrill and French-Eversole wars. For a period of twenty years the periodic outbreaks of fighting filled almost as much space in the weekly papers as did the subject of education. Sometimes half pages of the weekly papers were devoted to accounts of these mountain vendettas.

When Judge Jim Hargis and Ed Callihan of Breathitt County, Kentucky, took law into their hands and were shooting their political enemies at will, one stirring story followed another. Especially was this true when J. B. Marcum, a prominent mountain lawyer, was killed by the feudists. The long series of trials which followed this incident made a highly readable feature and contributed much to the unhappy reputation of the Kentucky mountain counties. The names of Hargis, Callihan, Jett, and Marcum became about as well known in Georgia and Alabama as in Kentucky.

As a part of the same bloody Kentucky political and feudist pattern was the famous Goebel assassination in 1900. William Goebel, a defeated candidate for governor, was shot by an unknown rifleman while approaching a state office building in Frankfort. Goebel was said to have lived for four days after the shooting but was unable to name the killer. After his death, his memory was kept fresh by a long series of disputes and trials, during which William S. Taylor, Republican governor-elect fled the state, and the Democratic lieutenant-governor, J. C. W. Beckham, was installed as chief executive. For four years after this incident, Democratic papers delved into the tangled threads of trials and political disputes growing out of the murder. Sometimes full pages were given over to this unpleasant chapter of Southern political history.

Tragic stories had a great fascination for both editors and their subscribers. In fact, the stories that went all over the South were nearly all of a tragic nature, and often told of the deaths of prominent people. Perhaps no tragedy was more shocking than the shooting by Dr. T. B. McDow of Captain Francis W. Dawson, the Charleston editor. During the first years of the decade of the eighties Captain Dawson's name was much in the local news in connection with the intense agitation for Southern industrialization and attempts to attract immigrants. With Henry W. Grady, he was an original apostle of the New South. He had encouraged the industrial exposition in Charleston, and his *News and Courier* was one of the loudest press voices urging Northern industry to come South.

On the afternoon of March 3, 1889, the famous South Carolina editor put on his hat and overcoat and picked up his cane to make a call at the office of Dr. McDow. The two men apparently had never met, but the impetuous Captain Dawson was going to lecture the younger man about his improper relations with the Dawsons' Swiss domestic maid, Marion Durbeyon. Captain Dawson and his wife had brought this beautiful girl home with them from Europe. For several weeks before their meeting Captain Dawson had private detectives investigating Dr. McDow's activities, and when he was convinced they knew the truth he was determined to bring the affair to a close. Some of the country papers said the captain had threatened to publish the story in his paper.

Once inside the insolent doctor's office, Captain Dawson lost control of his hot temper and began caning McDow. The latter shot him fatally, and then spent two hours attempting to bury the body under an inside stairwell. Failing in this, he gave himself up to the police. Within two weeks the story had found its way into the weekly papers all across the South. Dawson's murderer was a brilliant young man from Kershaw County, valedictorian of his class in medical school. In his practice, however, the young physician had showed an indiscreet fondness for his female patients. In addition, he was interested in foreign languages, and when Miss Durbeyon appeared at his office he engaged her in a long conversation in French. From this first meeting their acquaintance became increasingly more intimate. It was said that McDow actually came to see her in the Dawson home when the editor and his wife were away.

When the Dawson murder trial began, the lawyers seemed to share Dr. McDow's passionate interest in the Swiss maid. They kept her on the witness stand for a long time, and a reporter described her as an unusually voluptuous young woman who fascinated the jury. In a two-column story in the Newberry (South Carolina) *Herald and News*, Marion Durbeyon was described as "a pretty girl of exquisite form and strikingly beautiful features; dark eyes, dark hair and olive complexion, with the faintest blush of roses on the cheeks; large lustrous eyes—she has a most captivating manner of making little moves and of shrugging her plump shoulders when answering questions. Attired in a close fitting clinging costume of black jersey which outlined a bust fit for a Venus, with a black chip bonnet, trimmed with jet black ribbon, this maid sat on the witness box for two hours!" She described her meetings with Dr. McDow, and said that he had begged her to run away to France with him, but she had put him off with the excuse that he was not "the only man living with a dissatisfied wife!"

The prosecution produced a copy of Jesse Ames Miller's amorous novel *Twixt Love and Law* which Miss Durbeyon had presented to Dr. McDow. It also exhibited from Dr. McDow's effects a *carte de visite* photograph of Miss Durbeyon on which was inscribed "Marie the Mountain Girl." In the process of the trial the girl was called upon to describe Dr. McDow's kisses to the crowded courtroom, and when she was finally allowed to leave the witness box, the reporter thought that the examination "was altogether one of the most remarkable ever held in a courtroom."

Dr. McDow pleaded self-defense and he was absolved of murder, but he spent the rest of his life an unhappy victim of his impulses. A few years after the Dawson murder, the McDow family went to spend the summer in the mountains of North Carolina, leaving the doctor at home. Within a short time a brother found him dead in bed. He had lain unattended for perhaps a day or two. There was some evidence that possibly he had died by his own hand.

The shooting of the popular ex-Confederate Captain Dawson had given the country editors an opportunity to review his adventurous career. He was born in London in 1840, and immediately after the firing on Fort Sumter he came to America to join the Southern Navy. On his way to New Orleans from Norfolk, at a time when the Confederate Navy was practically disappearing from the seas, the young Englishman joined the Confederate Army and fought in Longstreet's corps. In his military service he was in the battles of the Wilderness, Chickamauga, Mechanicsville, Fredericksburg, Five Forks, Gettysburg and many others. In fact, the scenes of his active service almost constitute a roll call of important battles in the East.

When the war was over, Captain Dawson became a member of the editorial staff of both the Richmond *Examiner* and the *Dispatch,* and within a year's time he followed B. R. Riordan to Charleston to work on papers in that city. Between 1873 and his death in 1889 he became one of the most outspoken proponents of improved methods of farming, anti-racism, and industrialization to bring the mills to the Southern cotton fields. Perhaps he was able to see possibilities of the region in a clearer perspective than were many of his troubled contemporaries.

A trial of much longer duration, and almost as fascinating, was the famous Myra Clark Gaines will case which first appeared in court in 1833. In 1868 the United States Supreme Court handed down a decision which awarded to Mrs. Gaines the fabulously valuable New

Orleans property involved. This litigation grew out of a secret marriage of Daniel Clark to a New Orleans woman in the early nineteenth century. It was contended that before Clark could make public his marriage and acknowledge Myra as his daughter, he died, and a scheming administrator denied the girl possession of her lawful property. Periodically the country papers published stories about the fate of this persistent woman who dragged her case from one court to another, and who bedeviled the tenants of her property in New Orleans. It became, in fact, a newspaper legend to be held in reserve and dragged out as filler copy when there was a news shortage. Far from settling this famous case, the Supreme Court decision only added a new angle to it. There followed considerable discussion of Mrs. Gaines's attempts to bring about settlements with her so-called tenants. It remained for Myra Clark Gaines death in 1885 to close finally what was perhaps the longest newsworthy litigation in American legal history.

Long drawn-out lawsuits had a way of attracting the attention of the press. New developments continually supplied material for follow-up stories. The famous "Mule Case" of Oxford, Mississippi, supplied filler for more than the normal lifetime of a Southern cotton mule. In fact it lasted so long that most editors forgot precisely when the first story of this famous lawsuit appeared in the country papers. It involved a mule trade in which all the standard representations were made but the mule proved defective. An attempt was made in court to rescind the bargain. Lawyers, principals and judges either postponed the case or involved it in so many exceptions and counterclaims that it soon lost its original identity as a simple damage suit and became famous for the breath-taking progression of its costs. It was given space in order to emphasize the amount of money which lawyers could collect from two stubborn men. When finally the plaintiff spent a small fortune and was bankrupted the suit was nol-prossed to the sorrow of the weekly press.

A subject that stayed alive as long as the Gaines case or the Oxford mule was that of the Mormon attempt to evangelize the South. From 1865 to 1900 news stories told of this sect's activities. Two elders were at work in Cherokee County, North Carolina, said the Chatham *Record,* until enraged citizens "began to tickle them and their converts with hickory twigs." Most of their converts were women who had disposed of their belongings and were preparing to go to Utah. Numerous feature stories told of the horrors of polygamy in the United States. Ready-print pages had contributed part of this publicity, and anti-Mormon books and pamphlets were distributed throughout the region. Perhaps the most telling blows were periodic letters from women who claimed they had been converted to Mormonism only to discover that they had practically sold their lives into prostitution.

Because of these stories the elders were regarded as more evil than the carpetbaggers. In Clay County, Alabama, said the Calhoun *Times* in 1882, two Mormon disciples had mysteriously disappeared. The *Times* had run a story in which a female convert described the outrages which she claimed she suffered because of polygamy. People became aroused against the Mormons, and a rumor was set afloat that the two elders had baptized fifty converts in the nude. On the following Monday they were ordered to leave the county, and they refused to do so. Nevertheless, they disappeared. The common belief was that they were murdered and their bodies secretly disposed of.

In that same year Lycurgus Barrett of the Hartford (Kentucky) *Herald* described an uprising in Butler County, Kentucky. Outraged church members in that section ran the Mormons away, and the editor bid them godspeed in a challenging editorial. "I suggest," he wrote, "to Mormon Bigelow and Company that they visit Huntsville and make some stronger efforts to Mormonize the people of that vicinity. Preach doctrines more openly. Urge them to forsake the teachings of their fathers, disobey the laws of the land. Tell them they are bastards, and their parents are living in fornication, and they must be re-baptized and re-married. Try to get men to have from two to twelve wives each, and women from a half to a twelth of a husband each." Barrett implied that if "Bigelow and Company" attempted to do this in western Kentucky they would soon be dispatched to a land where Mormonism would not much matter, and there would be no prospective converts anyway.

A more moderate view of the problem was presented by Columbus Heard of the Greensboro (Georgia) *Herald*. Mistakenly he believed this sect was gaining "an enormous" foothold in Georgia, and it should be checked without the use of violence. The Constitution of the United States presented a real difficulty, but there was hope that the order could be destroyed on the ground of licentiousness. The state legislature could declare that liberty had been abused, and that further proselyting struck at domestic peace and happiness. In the opinion of the editor the Mormon missionaries "sowed the seeds of hell in the happiest spot on earth, the home circle; and we trust the law will speedily strike at the root of the evil by providing severe punishment for the ring leaders and instigators of this species of licentiousness."

For thirty-five years the missionaries worked with the Southern people in isolated communities in an effort to convert them to Mormonism. During all this time stories of mob violence appeared in the papers. Gun battles were fought in meeting places, elders were subjected to inhuman indignities, and the whole question of freedom of religious worship became hopelessly involved with an irresponsible local vigilantism. The editor of the Albany (Georgia) *Herald* condemned the mob near that place which attacked three Mormon missionaries in the process of holding a peaceable religious meeting. He thought the penitentiary would be sorely cheated if members of the mob escaped conviction.

Taking the same attitude, the Covington (Georgia) *Star* said the elders had a right to worship God as they pleased, and that mob action in subduing a religious service was a grave offense against the guaranteed rights and privileges of the individual. "Intolerance of religious freedom," said the *Star,* "is one of the most dangerous encroachments on the rights of the people ever attempted."

In 1899 the Mormons themselves conceded that they would perhaps never gain a solid foothold in the South. They published a general report on their Southern activities. A band of 488 elders had walked 10,967 miles to visit 2,553 families, and they were refused the hospitality of 578 homes. At Barnesville, Georgia, 37 elders walked 985 miles, visited 304 families, were refused lodging and food 98 times, and held 49 meetings in which they succeeded in converting only two people.

Publication of the Mormon statistics of failure destroyed interest in the sect's Southern activities. By 1900 the editors were reasonably assured that the South's Protestantism was not being endangered by these invaders, and they looked elsewhere for bogy men to attack. The more important national incidents crowded out local prejudices as human-interest subjects. After 1895 events leading to the Spanish-American War took the country papers, for the first time, well beyond the pale of their communities. Highly colored accounts of this international conflict appeared in the ready-print pages and boiler-plate matter. Soon some of the weeklies took up the Hearstian and Pulitzer hue and cry and aroused their constituents. Cuban atrocity stories, following the line of the New York *World* and *Journal,* were given considerable notice. There was some short and rather scanty editorial comments on the foreign policies of the United States, but only occasional articles treated the diplomatic side of the war with more than casual concern and understanding.

When the war finally began, the country newspapers were somewhat confused. Events moved too fast for them to prepare for a discussion of international crisis. Unlike other American wars, this one lasted too short a time to be brought home to the people in the forms of hardship and privations. Southerners, however, were anxious to be off to Cuba to prove their loyalty to the Union, and there was a considerable amount of editorial pleading that the region be allowed to bear more than its share of the fighting. It was with great pride that the country publishers extolled the deeds of ex-Confederates such as Fitzhugh Lee and "Fighting Joe" Wheeler. The weeklies gave some accounts of the brief battles where Southern boys were engaged, but otherwise the actual campaigning passed with surprisingly little publicity on the "home-set" pages. Occasionally a troop train stopped in a country town, and soldiers whooping and carousing on the streets imparted some of their war excitement to the populace. But editors were reluctant to allow foreign material to break into the routine of purely local and political news.

Ready-print services supplied the bulk of the features on the actual campaigns of the war. Admiral George Dewey's rousing victory at Manila Bay was fully exploited in the patent pages. Pictures of the *Olympia,* of Manila Harbor, the Spanish fleet, and countless poses of Admiral and Mrs. Dewey appeared from week to week. So long as the naval hero was a potential candidate for the presidency this kind of publicity was kept alive. The papers told of a grateful people presenting him a house in appreciation for his gallant services in the Pacific, and later published the arguments over his widow's disposition of it.

Perhaps no single individual except Teddy Roosevelt received more publicity in the Southern press than Captain Richmond Pearson Hobson of Greensboro, Alabama. The weeklies took great satisfaction in publicizing his heroic exploit of June 3, 1898, when he attempted to sink the collier *Merrimac* across the narrow channel of Santiago Harbor. Returning home, shortly after this adventure, the handsome naval hero toured the country, dispensing kisses to simpering females and receiving a colossal amount of praise from the newspapers. Hobson, however, found that fame was about as fleeting as one of his famous kisses when he engaged in Alabama politics. Perhaps few congressional races in Southern history have received more publicity than the one in 1906 between Captain Hobson and John H. Bankhead.

While Hobson and Bankhead slugged it out in the political arena, Admirals Schley and Sampson delighted the public with their squabble over Schley's dilatory action at Cienfuegos, and the subsequent battle maneuver of the flagship *Brooklyn* on July 3 when Admiral Cervera's Spanish squadron steamed out of Santiago Harbor. This famous quarrel, in all of its picayunish detail, was exposed to public view, and provoked considerable caustic editorializing. Actually editors gave this noisy controversy more space than the vital issue of imperialism which dominated the political discussion of the immediate postwar years. Weekly papers scarcely gave their subscribers a glimmer of world events in which the United States was involved. Far Eastern diplomacy was meagerly presented, and the name of John Hay and his famous Open Door policy in China were practically unknown to country readers. Theodore Roosevelt's Big Stick Policy received more attention than other diplomatic policies because its author was personally such a highly controversial figure in the South.

When the Spanish-American War and its subsequent incidents were in the past, country papers returned to regional features. Recurring stories of cyclones which took heavy tolls of life and property had broad reader appeal. The awfulness and unpredictability of storms gave them a fierce attraction everywhere, and they received considerable space. Yearly from February to June the stock headline "The Storm King is Loose in the Land" appeared almost as frequently as those telling of local runaway scrapes. Many storms were local but others roared across the South from Virginia to Texas.

Nature was never more mysterious than when it swept the region with its furious tornadoes. Paths of the powerful twisters were strewed with wrecked homes, fallen timber and broken human and animal bodies. Whole families were destroyed in the twinkling of an eye.

At other times everybody except helpless children was killed. It was not unusual for a baby in a cradle to be carried away from a house that was being torn into kindling and deposited safely in a quiet corner. Miracles were common. Straws and timbers were driven through trees and into weather-boarding of houses. Household goods were strewed along the route of the storm in distant communities; chickens and haystacks were swept up in one county and hurled into another without serious injury. Habitually editors collected every strange and horrible fact of these catastrophes and gave unlimited space to their reports. For weeks at a time after unusually heavy storms long lists were published recording deaths and property damage.

The nineteenth century was generous in producing newsworthy events. The massive volume of feature stories which appeared in weekly papers constituted an informal and bulky outline of contemporary history. The process of national expansion competed with catastrophes and strong personalities for space. They made the kind of strong, colorful stories newsmen pray for. Both editor and reader enjoyed them and begged for more. Publishers did their best to satisfy their patrons, even slanting much of the news with their own vigorous personal observations. This reporting was the only contact which a majority of country paper subscribers had with the bigger world about them.

Chapter 16

Between the Plow Handles of Experience

THERE was one subject on which virtually every editor was progressive and completely free of guile. His politics might be dictated by strange and unorthodox local alliances. His ideas of race relations may have been waterlogged with prejudice. His respect for morality and religion may have been assumed for the edification of the paying subscribers. He may have written his social notes with his tongue deep in his cheek. But what he wrote about farming carried a deep stamp of sincerity and his attack on agricultural evils, especially the one-crop system, had the fervor of a crusade. Here he had a fundamental subject with a clear-cut issue and no mental reservations. Single-crop farming kept the whole economy of the region teetering on the brink of ruin. Simple self-preservation dictated diversified farming but convincing the farmers of the obvious fact was an uphill fight.

The editors realized their educational campaign required space and they gave it space. Sensational stories of crime, lynchings, hangings, circuses, politics, schools and churches made their brief appearances in featured positions. They were the diversification in the newspaper business. But week in and week out the staple was farming.

That the New South was predominantly agrarian was substantiated abundantly in every issue of a country paper published since 1865. The editors had two major approaches to agriculture. One was to run original and exchange stories on the proper method, the art, of doing things about the farm. The other was to attack the system in use.

For more than forty years the weekly paper served as a meager extension bulletin from which farmers could learn of elementary advances in agricultural methods. Perhaps of more fundamental importance were the frequent summaries of agricultural progress in the South and the nation. Three or four times each year many papers published general crop reports for the cotton and tobacco belts.

Weather conditions over the South were given as they affected production of cotton and tobacco, and estimates, of cotton especially, were published. Aside from formal reports, the activities of farmers were given in special news columns. Livestock trading on county and circuit court days was described; and often upper South papers ran columns of news about the activities of livestock traders who traveled through the cotton belt with droves of horses and mules. Fertilizer and compost recipes, such as the famous Furman formula, were given, and much editorial advice was offered farmers.

In the main, however, the tone of the country press toward agriculture was critical. The whole structure of Southern farming, according to the country papers, was based on a false premise, and it was the country weekly's responsibility to conduct a forthright publicity campaign to correct this basic error. The common method was to indict the system of staple or single-crop planting, and then to produce a steady fire of incriminating evidence against it. As prosecutors, editors played a quixotic role, thrusting their quills against impenetrable walls of ignorance, stubbornness and indifference. They were offering leadership to an opinionated, stubborn group which had no desire to be led.

No editor failed to realize that agriculture in the New South was the economic life line of the region. Ambitious young publishers unpacking type and putting old-fashioned hand presses in motion quickly discovered that their own success rested squarely on the prosperity of farmer subscribers. For over sixty years more intelligent editors kept the wasteful and ineffective system of Southern agriculture at the bar of public opinion while they worked to find a practical way to correct agrarian maladjustment.

Beginning with the decade of the eighties, editors were concerned with the question of impending agricultural panic. Why had the postwar South failed? This was the central question. They got almost as many answers as there were ways of putting the question. The Old South had been a region of staple crops dependent on slave or very cheap free labor. The close of the Civil War brought little important change in the fundamental concept of agrarian economy, except in the vital field of labor. Where the source had been the Negro slave, it became the free Negro. Where field hands had been paid in keep and kind, freedmen had to be paid in cash or shares of the crop. For the first twenty years after the war a stable supply of cheap labor was possibly the most sought-after commodity in the New South. An excellent summary of conditions, made by the Gibson (Alabama) *Enterprise* in 1884, somewhat expresses the whole situation during these years. Southerners, wrote the editor, are not willing to try things on a small scale. They want big cotton mills, big industrial plants. They are not willing to be one-horse farmers, but want at least a dozen plows dragging around. The result: poor mules, poor homes, poor food, poor Negroes, and poor everything else. The editor also believed that "if he [the farmer] had sold his mule stock down to one good mule, and took his family without depending too much on trifling Negro labor and worked his farm, he would have been independent and happy."

In December 1871 the Marion (Alabama) *Commonwealth* commenting upon a forced sale of cows, wagons and teams gloomily predicted this was the beginning of the end. "The farmers in great measure are responsible. They overpaid Negroes to induce them to live with them. Refuse to secure a living by planting corn and small grain, but crowd everything with cotton, cotton, more cotton. Famine, starvation, and hopeless bankruptcy will alone put an end to farmers' cotton mania—the cure seems near." A year before, the Selma (Alabama) *Southern Argus* reported observations made by Bishop G. T. Pierce on a trip into Georgia. He found the soil fertile, a fine wheat harvest in prospect, but the cotton mania had seized the people. Land which was wholly unsuited to the crop was being exhausted. Without an immediate change of policy, King Cotton's scepter would become an empty symbol. At no time would a short cotton crop pay expenses. Soon there would be no sign of pig, lamb, calf or chicken. The Bishop offered one of many postwar solutions to this dilemma. He advised growing root and grain crops, centralizing production of cotton, thus "keep cotton high, money plentiful and be independent of everybody but God."

Some editors who saw failure in cotton believed this was not the only cause of the South's economic problem. The majority of farmers had never made up the lost year, the fateful crop season at the end of the war. Failure to make a full crop then and the temptation of high-priced cotton for five years thereafter had headed the average farmer in the wrong direction. To regain the lost ground required sweating out a year without money or credit and reordering his whole economic life by producing the goods he needed at home.

The Boll Weevil

We are not alarmists, but the boll weevil is sure to come, and NOW is the time to prepare for his reception. How can this be done? By diversifying our crops. Raising corn, meat, molases, potatoes, horses, mules, and everything we need as far as possible. Buy as little as possible on a credit and make your money go as far as possible in buying what you are compelled to have. We propose to do our part and feel sure that we can and will help you in every way in our power by making specially close prices on everything we handle. Hope you will not hesitate to call on us to serve you in anyway in our power.

CONTROL BOLL WEEVIL

Insect Is at Mercy of Planter in the Fall.

Better Results in Work of Destruction Obtained at That Time Than Remedial Measures Applied at Other Seasons of Year.

(By R. W. HARNED.)

Years of experience and careful study have brought to light many facts in regard to the life and habits of the boll weevil. By taking advantage of some of these, much can be done to lessen the damage of this pest.

Read carefully all available bulletins or publications concerning this insect and verify the statements in these publications for yourself. Make observations as to which fields are most seriously damaged by the boll weevil, and try to determine the cause for any difference upon fields in the same neighborhood.

Test different varities of cotton under the same conditions so as to obtain the variety that does best on your farm under boll weevil conditions.

[illegible] destroyed the fewer weevils will survive to damage the crop next year.

Some very valuable experiments were made by the secretary of the Louisiana State Crop Pest commission two years ago show clearly the value of the early fall destruction of boll weevils.

He found that where the plants were destroyed before October 15, only three per cent. of the weevils survived the winter to infest the next year's crop. Where the cotton plants were destroyed between October 15 and October 27, about fifteen per cent. of the weevils survived the winter. Where the cotton plants were destroyed between November 1 and November 25, about twenty-two per cent. of the weevils survived. Where the cotton plants were destroyed between November 25 and December 7, 28 per cent. of the weevils lived through the winter, but where the destruction of the cotton plants was put off until the middle of December or later, over 43 per cent. of the boll weevils survived the winter and were ready to attack the next year's crop.

These figures are so convincing that it is incomprehensible that any farmer should continue to try to grow cotton without picking out his crop early and completely destroying the cotton

WINSTON'S CURIOSITY.

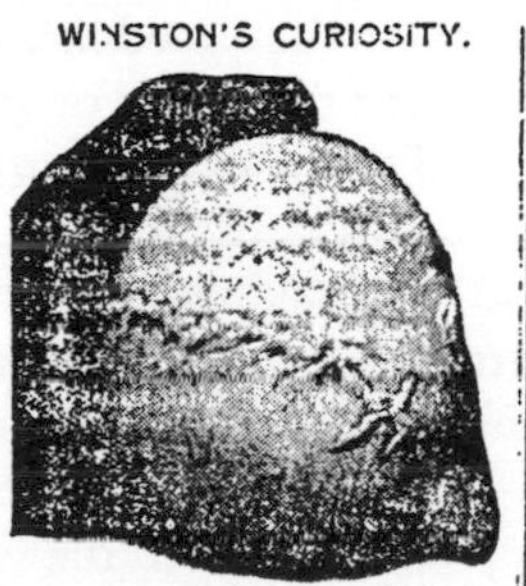

A Patched Egg.

The picture above is a fair representation of a hen egg produced in our county, which is quite a curiosity in that it represents perfectly an egg that had been broken while in the soft state, and then sewed up, afterwards forming a hard shell, and is in as strong and perfect condition otherwise as any other egg. The ridges which extend half around this shell are not as perfect in the picture as in the natural egg, which represents thread stitches as perfectly as if the egg had really been sewed up with needle and thread.

An Editorial and Part of an Article on the Boll Weevil; a Barnyard Curiosity

No one was more certain of the real foundation of the farmers' troubles than the newspaper editors. To them no piece of state legislation affected directly the lives of more people in the South than the lien laws (laws which permitted farmers to mortgage unplanted crops in order to secure supplies and capital to finance production) which state after state enacted immediately after the war to permit the mortgaging of unplanted crops. This legislation received continuous discussions in the press. Country editors who lived close to the farmers who were most affected by it realized that the lien law was a snare and a delusion. They deserve commendation for seeing, with amazing perspective, the insidious effects of this law even before Reconstruction had ended. Scarcely a line appeared in a weekly paper justifying its existence, and when the rumor went around that the next general assembly of a state would try to amend the law, editors let it be known that they favored outright repeal.

In 1875 the Greensboro (Georgia) *Herald,* published in an old farming area, said the lack of money following the war forced the legislators to resort to this means of creating a credit facility. It laid blame on the Freedmen's Bureau, in the belief that it advised Negroes to accept only cash or supplies for their labor. This editor was convinced the plan was a gross error. Negroes got too much of the crops. On farms in their hands, abuse of livestock and tools and crop failure and indebtedness were common. The Southern farmer was being carried to ruin. This paper advocated immediate and complete change of the whole capital structure of Southern farming.

Near Greensboro, the Oglethorpe *Echo,* using a slightly different approach, attacked the lien laws. The *Echo's* editor believed that cotton farmers should eventually be convinced it was folly to plant cotton year after year, going on as they did when they knew that each weary step took them hopelessly into debt. He believed his neighbors were greedy for destruction and determined to follow the ruinous phantom to its bitter end. There were causes for this state of affairs. The Southern lien laws might have been necessary for one brief period. The motives behind their passage might have been good, but the period of their utility was passed. By them, it was said, farmers were encouraged to indulgences and extravagances on what seemed easy credit. Actually they were forcing their necks deeper into the cotton noose and were carrying extreme burdens of interest. The only deliverance a farmer had from the curious jackals who lay in wait for him all the way from the door of his cotton house to Wall Street was to stay out of debt and live at home.

Two years before, the grand jury at Rome, Georgia, had presented a report that the "present lien laws are detrimental to the best interest of the planter, tenant and merchant." The legislature was requested either to repeal or to amend them materially. The grand jury claimed that the laws existed only as a safeguard to the debt collector, and that shylock creditors were their only defenders. In Mississippi the Woodville *Republican* called on its readers to oppose candidates for the legislature who were unwilling to repeal the lien laws. The only way to make labor free, said editor John Bryant, was to remove the opportunity for it to involve itself in debt twelve months in advance. After the South Carolina Senate failed to defeat the lien laws, the Choctaw (Alabama) *Herald* said that the senators should have been taken to task by the press. A forthright educational campaign in advance of the vote on the lien-law issue would have been better tactics.

Captain Put Darden, an ex-Confederate, was fighting in Mississippi for improved farm conditions. During the latter part of the century he was an active reformer. In the *Weekly* (Hazelhurst) *Copiahan* he said that a Yazoo farmer, an ex-Confederate soldier and a good civilian, had lost $500 worth of land because he gave a $100 lien on his crop. It was sold at public auction. The merchant holding the lien did not want the land but had to buy it in to save himself. "We do not feel any timidity in saying that the present lien law in this state is one of the greatest, if not the greatest barrier to the prosperity of our agricultural interest," said Captain Darden, "and we look to the next legislature to at least modify it, or abolish it altogether." The editor of the *Copiahan* favored this point of view and stated that he would continue to denounce the law "so long as it remains to disgrace our statute books."

In the heart of the Mississippi Delta cotton region, the Greenville *Review* was extremely critical of the lien law in the hard years of the early eighties. "The agricultural lien law," said the *Review,* "has caused more regrets, more extravagance, more losses, more woe and more wretchedness to the laborer and merchant and planter than all of the laws on all the statute books ever made in Mississippi. It created a false basis for credit. It gave us that credit at a time when our people were just fresh from the destructive war where they had been trained to destroy, not preserve. It encouraged what we had learned, extravagance. Extravagance begot debt, and debt failure—and failure misery and want. This curse should be wiped from our credit books—and the sooner the better."

Everywhere the story was the same. Countless editorials advised farmers to grow food and supplies at home. The Winnsboro (South Carolina) *News and Herald* said in 1886 that it "would be astounding to people to know just what the South pays for meat and grain." In Greenwood, South Carolina, "from January 1 to May 15, 1886, 57 carloads of bacon, 9,560 bushels of meal, 2,391 barrels of flour, 445 barrels of molasses [were purchased from the outside]—no wonder times are hard!" There was not a single item on the list which could not be grown much cheaper in South Carolina.

Disasters sometimes showed up the failure of Southern farming. A "flash" spring flood cut off the farming community around Dawkins on the Wateree River in South Carolina. Farmers were unable to secure supplies and were in a pitiable plight. "Think of farmers being in danger of starvation," wrote the editor of the *News and Herald,* "because railroad communications have been cut off! Farmers in want, not for the luxuries of life, but for bread and meat! In want of the very articles which they are presumed to produce and furnish to other citizens of the country. If these be the 'bone and sinew' of our southern country, God help it, for its sinews are made of jelly and its bones composed of chalk. Let us hope that in the experiences of this year we'll try to become independent of railroad connections, or disconnections with western corncribs."

This was the principal mode of attack upon agricultural evils for more than fifty years. Success lay in living at home and staying out of debt. It was not necessarily an easy formula. Making a living at home was so unusual that publicity was given those who succeeded in doing so. J. T. Collins of Buck Creek, Georgia, the Schley County *News* said, killed 8,500 pounds of pork, made 1,000 pounds of lard and produced corn, potatoes and other edible products, an almost unheard-of thing in that part of the cotton belt. The *Weekly Copiahan* in Mississippi boasted that A. G. Fortenberry went home with $100 cash in his pocket after settling his year's account. This was a unique experience for him. His formula of success was that preached everywhere by the country press—he grew an abundance of hog and hominy. At Marietta, Georgia, a newcomer to that area was successful in diversifying his crops. The *Journal* reported him as saying that "all my neighbors raised cotton and they are now buying corn and provisions. I made all grain, have sold a quantity and have plenty left and more to sell." This same paper said that H. G. Denton of Cobb County had produced 800 bushels of sweet potatoes, or 250 bushels per acre, from which he realized a dollar to a dollar and forty cents per bushel. "We are always glad to make a note of such thrift," wrote the editor.

Mississippi's cottonfields were snowy white in August and September but its jaded farmers faced hard winters on short store rations and had bad dreams of the same exhausting round of growing more cotton to produce more credit year after year. A successful farmer told the editor of the Choctaw (Ackerman) *Plaindealer* that he got his start away from cotton by growing hogs. Two shotes brought him $52.00 and he was able to make a cash beginning. Perhaps the entire situation was best expressed in an editorial of the Marietta (Georgia) *Journal:* "No man will ever succeed in the South raising cotton at 10 cents per pound and paying 12 cents per pound for his meat and $1.35 per bushel for corn. . . . No meat in your smokehouse, no corn in your crib, no hogs on the place, a planter will ever be in debt to his merchant. Should one bad year overtake him he is crippled financially for the next five years."

Sidney Lewis at Sparta boasted that J. G. Brown of Houston County had killed 23,000 pounds of pig meat, 10,000 pounds of which he sold in Macon. "This goes to show the old red hills of Georgia can do it. No parching winds, no floods, no withering blasts. Here is the ideal land for tiller and stockman."

The one-crop system was not the only villain preying on Southern agriculture and keeping it impoverished. Interest rates, in fact, the whole capital system, freight rates and extraregional bonuses for supplies all co-operated to keep farm books perpetually in the red. Most farmers felt that editors knew nothing about farming. They believed that men who did not participate in actual work in the field could never understand the complex problems of agricultural production. One reason the country press had so little effect on farming methods was its inability to make most of its readers distinguish between the actual physical process of production and the equally important economics of production. Only a small percentage of the local editorials dealt with the methods of farming. Most of this material appeared in farm hints prepared by ready-print and boiler-plate editors and was seldom usable by the ordinary Southern farmer because of his limited skill in handling even the simplest carpenter and blacksmith tools.

Interest rates and other cost factors fell outside the ordinary farmer's comprehension. A poorly educated man lacked the background to understand the fine points of even his own economic situation as it was related to the bigger field of regional and national business. Very likely the majority of Southern rural people never had a clearer idea of their economic condition than the hazy feeling that they were constantly "in a panic." Most country editors, however, had a more acute awareness of the true meaning of the New South's ruinously unbalanced system of production. In 1881 the Yorkville (South Carolina) *Enquirer* published a speech which A. P. Butler, Commissioner of Agriculture, had delivered before the state grange and the South Carolina Agricultural and Mechanical Society. Farmers in eighteen counties in South Carolina had signed 24,470 liens in 1879 for an average of $86.83 each, and 67,518 for an average of $109 in 1880. At $50 a bale of cotton produced, the cotton crop yielded $25,824,500, but it was necessary to pay out 17.70% of this as a carrying cost on liens, sometimes higher than 50%. Merchants, it was said, made 50% profit, and this took $2,000,000 more from the crop. If farmers had been able to borrow money at 6 per cent they could have saved at least $2,000,000 in clear profit to themselves, an amount which would have meant the difference between success and failure.

Sidney Lewis of the Sparta (Georgia) *Ishmaelite* was able to bring home to his readers a realistic view of their confused economy. Farmers of Hancock County were buying 16,000 bushels of corn a year, and were paying out $16,000 to Western farmers and railroads. Pertinently he asked his subscribers if they thought it would cost them $16,000 to grow that much corn? He warned that it was physically impossible for them to break even by practicing such slipshod business methods.

Staple foodstuffs were not the only supplies which cotton and tobacco farmers had to purchase. Commercial fertilizer dealers caught them in an anacondalike grasp. Guano was an annual necessity on worn lands of the older cotton belt if a level of production comparable to earlier days was to be maintained. The fertility of the soil exhausted by growing the same crop year after year had to be restored by artificial means. In Georgia alone the cash outlay (for privilege tax payments made by dealers) on this one item jumped from $41,000 in 1880 to over $70,000 in 1881. Practically all fertilizers and three-fourths of the provisions used by the farmers were purchased on credit, said the Marietta *Journal.* A failure to grow supplies and to save compost and manure was a source of high interest payments. It estimated that rates were from 25 to 100 per cent. "I urge no complaint against merchants who furnish the supplies"; wrote the *Journal* editor, "for as a rule, considering the advantage they have and the risks they take, they deal about as leniently with the farmers as the generality of masters would with their slaves."

Everywhere editors were certain that their farmer subscribers, operating on a credit basis, were in fact enslaving themselves to a greedy and heartless master, foreign capital. In 1896, after cotton and tobacco farmers generally had suffered practical bankruptcy from panic conditions of earlier years, the editor of the Brookhaven (Mississippi) *Citizen* wrote a soliloquy on the work of a mortgage. He warned his readers, "A mortgage makes a man rustle and keeps him poor. It is a strong incentive to action, and a wholesome reminder of the fleeting months and years. It is fully as symbolical in its meaning as the hour glass and the scythe that means death. A mortgage represents industry, because it is never idle, night or day, it is like a bosom friend, because the greater the adversity, the closer it sticks to a fellow. It is like a brave soldier, for it never hesitates at charges nor fears to close in on the enemy. It is like the sandhog [sic] of the thug—silent in application, but deadly in effect. It is like the grasp of a devil fish—the longer it holds the greater is its strength. It will exercise feeble energies and keen activities of a sluggish brain, but no matter how hard debtors work, the harder the mortgage works still."

This plaintive note of the Brookhaven editor almost sums up the editorial attitude toward Southern farming from 1865 to 1930. As the Greensboro *Herald* said in 1884, politics and cotton were wrecking the country. A better day would dawn if the South had less of each. Especially was the editor wrought up over the strangling influence of outside credit interests. Most notable of these was the New England Mortgage Company, known locally as the Association. It "has instituted proceedings in the court for the foreclosure of mortgages given by some people who have defaulted in the payment of interest on loans. This is the beginning of the end—a sad end to some."

Farming was the major Southern economic way of life. Many editors were schooled as youths by those jealous masters, the plow handles. They knew the hopes and disappointments which came to the farmer. They too had seen the grass grow, the rains and droughts leave havoc behind. They had taken great pride in a growing crop, in the ripe rich harvest of fields white with long flowing locks of good cotton. They had known the joys of spring, the delights of farm summers and the melancholy beauty of harvest months. They had followed a year's hard labor to the gin and the warehouse, and finally to the big leather-bound account book at the store. Most editors knew by experience how it felt to start home heavyhearted at the end of ginning seasons atop creaking cotton wagons. They knew the meaning of stooped shoulders and bowed heads. They had tried futilely to get ahead with cotton. Editors wrote about the difficulties of farming not as empty theorists but as practical men who had experienced them.

Southern editors shared with their better-informed readers the belief that agriculture was fundamental in the economic and social structure of civilization. Many of them felt real reverence for farming as a calling. It was not treated as an ordinary form of human employment, but as a God-sent mode of life. Farming was above the workaday activities of the wage earner, it was a close and sacred link with all of the mysteries of nature. A favorite topic for editorializing was the virtue of the farm boy and girl. Many editors professed to believe that boys and girls who lived in villages and small towns were inferior to those reared on farms. Fresh air, good food and solid work made the rural Southerner a sturdy individual who was equipped for a life of productive work anywhere. Country boys and girls, they believed, constituted a reservoir of human resources on which the nation was dependent for staffing its businesses and professions.

When agricultural panic in 1893 tended to drive young people away from farming the editor of the Charlotte (Tennessee) *Independent* said the country boy was the hope of the nation, and a sustaining foundation of prosperity. A strong body and a healthy mind gave him stamina to withstand temptation. To the editor the freedom of country life was a character builder. It escaped the too close associations in which all of human vices thrived; the activities of the farm were too numerous and exacting to allow the mind to concentrate on vices. Along with the Tennessee editor, other publishers were continually advising rural people to remain on the farm. Those who moved to the city would only have to return and begin farming again with less than they had when they left the country.

City daily papers were frequently accused, and rightly so, of making farm life appear drab and unattractive. Cartoonists and urban humorists needed someone to whom they could feel superior. They often made the farmer appear illiterate and grotesque and gave him an uncultivated drawl. Quick to take up the cudgel and to swing it at the heads of the city critics was the Schley County (Georgia) *News*. "In fact," said the *News*, "the average country-bred man or woman is more cultured, and presents a better appearance than the average town dwellers. It would surprise a good many city folks to learn how many of the fine-appearing people they see on the streets are farmers. They recognize as a farmer only the careless or impoverished individual with unshaven face, misfit clothes and [sic] who talks improperly."

Although criticizing the prevailing methods of farming, W. S. Glassener of the Americus (Georgia) *Times-Recorder* admonished the country boy to stay where he was. "Let the winds of spring blow dust in your eyes, boys; be proud of the name 'hayseeder,' and by brawn, show the world that energetic, substantial and true men are what make up a good community, and that you are out for just that purpose."

Nostalgia seized many an editor as he worked long hours at his desk and type cases. In moments when he was worried about meeting his monthly bills, his heart went back to the farm. He shared sentiments with twenty-one-year-old Thomas E. Watson of Thomson, Georgia, who published a poem in John E. White's McDuffie *Journal*.

"There's joy in the wide waving corn fields,
  Whose stalks, like a party of girls,
Entice the light fingers of zephyr
  To play with their gossamer curls,
And a low moan steals from their bosoms,
  As the wind floats lazily by,
Which is sweet as the echo of music at night,
  And soft as a tremulous sigh.

"There's joy in the far rolling forest,
Its vista, savannah and dell,
Where the rivulet sings of the flowers,
And primeval solitudes dwell.
There's joy in the emerald meadows—
In the low of the cattle at eve—
In the untainted air whose cheerfulness gives
To languor a blessed reprieve."

Editors were alert to the failures of Southern farming and at the same time sentimental about its joys. Their everlasting refrain of "raise at home the supplies needed at home" became a tiresome tune. Thoughtful farmers knew the editors were right but they were so deep in the rut of cotton or tobacco that they had lost the will and energy to change.

With all their discussions of farming, the country papers failed to deal realistically with the octopus of farm tenantry, one of the fundamental weaknesses of Southern agriculture. They frequently mentioned tenants, but the subject was usually lumped in with farmer owners, and both were spanked with the same editorial paddle. But there was almost complete silence on the whole economic structure of tenant farming. It seems to have been accepted as a matter of course. Perhaps the press longed for the day when its rural constituency would be a landowning one. Profound regret was expressed at the loss of land under the omnivorous system of farm credit which enslaved the owner and turned him out finally to waste his life in the yoke of share cropping or laboring for wages. There is, however, much evidence that throughout the postwar years editors led themselves to believe paradoxically that tenant farming was to a considerable extent a natural result of human shiftlessness or inability to do better. Certainly it was not until the depression of 1929 and the publication in 1938 of the National Emergency Council's report, The *Report on Economic Conditions of the South,* that the Southern country editors were jolted into anything like a realization of the full implication of tenantry to the region.

Occasionally brief articles appeared in the papers discussing the shadowy subject of peonage. Editors in Alabama, Florida, Arkansas and Georgia were angrily regretful that such a condition should prevail in the South. But no general editorial policy was ever directed at tenantry itself. Joe Patterson, a Negro of Goodwater, Alabama, borrowed a dollar on Saturday morning and promised to pay it back on Tuesday. When he was unable to get back at the appointed time he was arrested and carried before a justice of the peace who found him guilty of accepting money under false pretense. Since he was unable to employ a lawyer, the judge fined him $25.00 and sold him to a man named Hardy, who worked the Negro a year and then sold him for $40.00 to a man named Pace. The Negro, in an attempt to escape, cut a boat loose in a near-by river but was captured and given six months more in peonage by a justice of the peace. It was claimed by the Birmingham *Age-Herald* that peonage was widely practiced on the farms of the state. Peonage, said the editor of the Linden (Alabama) *Reporter,* belonged to South America, and the court owed it to the South to be stern with the corrupt practice by those scoundrels of local government, the justices of the peace, and the unprincipled farmers who were willing to purchase laborers from their courts as peons.

Near by in Prestwood, Alabama, a turpentine farmer and his justice-of-the-peace son conspired to oppress a poor white family into peonage. Again the daily papers were outspoken, and their articles were carried in the weekly journals. The Atlanta *Constitution* reporter said, "A fearful condition of affairs exists in a number of communities in the lower tier of southern counties in this state [Alabama]." At Birmingham the conservative *Age-Herald* was unwilling to publish the barbaric details of the mistreatment of an old white man and his sons who were made peons by a justice of the peace. A call was made on the state legislature to investigate the merits of this petty judicial office, and even to abolish it if corrections could not be made. All cases of peonage, it was said, arose in the justice courts, and it was best to wipe out the system altogether, rather than have unfit justices disgracing the state and the South.

A constant flow of material relating to Negro migration away from the older sections of the South to the newer cotton areas, or to the North and Northwest, was published in the country papers. Always there was an undertone of the failure of the Southern system of tenantry. Politics and the bitterness engendered by Reconstruction were at the bottom of much of this movement, but fundamentally the share-cropping system was a failure from its beginning. In 1870 the editor of the Selma (Alabama) *Southern Argus* regretted that local planters were finding it necessary to accept Negroes as tenants. "They are indolent, shiftless, improvident and destructive," said the *Argus*. Renting land would be at the cost of fences, land, houses and timber. Eventually southern Alabama would be converted into a wilderness of miserable old fields.

Progressively farm tenantry became more prevalent after 1870 and continued so until 1940. Despite the fact that the rural press chose for the most part to ignore it, tenantry was a vital part of the agricultural system which they so severely criticized. It was one of the main pillars of the whole cotton and tobacco system. When an editor criticized the farmer for his failure to "live at home" he was raising the whole issue of the social and economic structure of the human relationships on the farm. A significant number of families within the territory of every country paper were poorly housed in tenant cabins.

Sometimes descriptions of conditions in these homes were printed in papers. At Winnsboro, South Carolina, a tenant, Robert T. Toatly, started a veritable storm of protest in the Winnsboro *News and Herald*. He complained that the health and safety of a large portion of the people of the county were threatened by poor housing. His house, he said, could not be made livable, even if the landlord were willing to try to improve it. A landlord, J. G. Blair, took up the fight. He asked Toatly if it appeared to him that the tenant class, especially the Negro, was suffering so much from ill health that it was threatened with extermination. "What will our friend Mr. Toatly want next?" asked the landlord. "He will want us to furnish him with his whiskey to drink and cigars to smoke and other things too numerous to mention. It is as much as we can do to furnish 'Cuffy' with a little bacon and meal without building him a fine house and furnishing him all the necessaries of life. I'm glad that our friend Mr. Toatly is empowered with the money qualities and is willing to help keep 'Cuffy' comfortable."

Occasional outbursts against the failure of tenantry did not constitute an editorial policy on the part of the rural press. There was, however, a subject, which from 1865 to the present did involve the editorial writer in a broader economic problem. This was the wasteful use of land. From time to time editors drove about the country side in buggies to see firsthand what crops were being grown, and what changes were taking place. On the basis of these trips they wrote editorial travelogues designed to bring about an improvement of agricultural conditions and to give their readers a picture of the status of crops throughout the county. They often traveled beyond county boundaries and might even take in a considerable portion of a state or of the South itself. They often spoke of the abuse of lands and the wanton destruction of timber. Near Aiken, South Carolina, the editor of the *Journal and Review* saw timber being rapidly destroyed, and he pleaded for conservation. Trees were cut down and left to rot or were burned for no reason at all. Woods smoked continuously from February to June, set afire by ignorant people. Gullies caused by careless use of fire cut deep red gashes across land which should have been appreciating in fertility from natural accumulations of humus.

In Georgia, said the Oglethorpe *Echo,* there was scarcely a man owning a woodland who did not suffer serious loss every year. Tenants assumed they had a right to cut and slash timber as they pleased. They would cut a white-oak tree with enough timber in it to make fifty plow stocks, just to get a green stick. "Possum and coon" hunters, said the *Echo,* went forth nightly in the fall to lay waste the forest and farm with ax and match. The time had come for farmers to draw contracts with tenants that they should have certain specific quantities of wood for fuel, and no more; and night hunting should be stopped.

It was not difficult for editors to understand the many causes of soil erosion. They wrote frequent editorials on it. After 1,900 state agricultural experiment stations were developed to the point where they could begin community programs which would attempt to change the wasteful techniques of cultivation. New methods received wide attention in the papers, and resistance to these new ideas were greatly lessened by this publicity. Terracing was sensible even to an illiterate man, but to a man bound down by the weight of folk ways and methods it was change, and change involved new habits and new customs. This economic and mental development is eloquently documented in thousands of columns of news material aimed at bringing gradual changes on the farm.

Many editors rejoiced when agricultural and mechanical colleges and their associated experiment stations were founded, while others were either skeptical or bitterly opposed to them as just so much humbuggery. One discordant voice was raised in Mississippi by an editor who was quoted by the Macon *Beacon* as believing a $15,000 budget for entomological research at the Mississippi Experiment Station a flagrant waste of tax money. "O! we are great on bugology down in this part of the vineyard," he wrote, "and it is a demonstrable fact that there had never been found a bug in this latitude more expensive to the farmers and less use to the general public than the species that infest the experiment station at Starkville."

At the moment this reactionary Mississippian was writing so vigorously against "bugology" at Starkville, the boll weevil was winging its way across the Rio Grande. Before another decade the miserly $15,000 spent for scientific study was less than the loss on many individual cotton crops in the region. Like a cloud which loomed on the horizon and threatened a storm at the moment its corners were drawn into contact with the earth, the impending crisis of the boll weevil hung over the Southern cotton fields. Exchanges from Texas, Louisiana, Mississippi and across to South Carolina told of devastation. Editors published stories of destruction and gave advice on how to avert disaster in the uninfected areas. It was a pitiful thing, this spread of brown destruction which traveled on wing. Old one-crop methods were threatened, and helpless farmers were at last to be economically wrecked.

So frightening were accounts of the approach of the weevil that many a subscriber rushed to newspaper offices with harmless insects which he thought were boll weevils. Then one day a farmer came with a tiny brownish-gray bug trapped in an amber glass snuff bottle and the editor announced the weevil had arrived. "Mr. A. G. Hammill recently sent us a boll weevil from the northern portion of the county," wrote Will C. Hight of the Winston County (Mississippi) *Journal* in 1910. "Our people had as well make up their minds to accept these pests next year; they will be with us."

This was the beginning of the end of a system of agriculture, the end many editors had so long predicted. Southern farmers were faced with destruction. Too long they had worshiped at the throne of fabulous King Cotton, and in idolatry they had shrugged off editorials on diversification as the impractical space fillers of editors who needed something to write about.

Although editors had been unable in forty years to persuade farmers that they were pursuing the wrong track, the hard decade from 1900 to 1910 brought them to a realization of the fact. There was the boll weevil working its way across the cotton belt and leaving havoc in its path; the Texas fever tick came from the same direction. Finally came the disclosure of Dr. Charles Wardell Stiles, a persistent scientist, that he had discovered the presence of hookworm. Those were momentous years in which a distraught rural South took a drubbing from insects and parasites.

After July 1, 1906, the law required that cattle in certain broad-range areas of the South be dipped. Not since Reconstruction had a simple domestic act of Congress run into more wrathful resistance than did this sensible one. Perhaps no other measure could have revealed so clearly that much of the South was still frontier country. When the federal government undertook to step between the average piny-woods Southerner and his scrawny range cattle, it was invading one of the most sacred of regional personal rights. For the next ten years country papers divided their space between pointing out the necessity for dipping cattle and publishing stories of vats being blown up by ignorant vigilantes.

At the same time the campaign was being pushed against the fever tick, Dr. Charles W. Stiles, Thomas Nelson Page and John D. Rockefeller were trying to destroy the hookworm. Rural Southerners, it was said, were being sapped of their energy by these parasites. Like the tick, the new invader was easy to destroy, provided the ancient barrier of folk resistance could be pierced. The most effective means of winning over the people was to use the columns of the country papers.

In the early years of the present century, news of the "germ of laziness," the boll weevil and the Texas tick robbed weddings, local columns, obituaries and the Democratic primaries of space. Often country editors found themselves mouthpieces for Dr. Stiles, Dr. Seaman A. Knapp and an army of local experiment-station experts and "tick doctors" who sought to speak to the people.

Despite the publicity given it, the boll weevil swept on like a cyclone out of the Southwest. Cotton farmers failed in its path. Their ancient king weakened and dropped his scepter. Newspaper subscription lists showed the effect of agricultural failure. Everybody was in trouble just as the editors had so long predicted they would be because of a failure to diversify crops. Diversification was still a golden word to the editors. But by itself it was not a cure. If new crops were to be profitable, buyers with money had to be found.

Diversification without adequate markets was meaningless. No new agricultural tragedy or frantic babbling of broadening the agricultural base could make it less so. Farmers could not live in a moneyless world any better than editors and businessmen, nor could they depend entirely on home-grown products.

Newspaper publishers tried valiantly to create new markets for new products and to batter down the old habits of planting cotton and tobacco. Their perennial sermons hammered away. Still the weeklies could not measure their real accomplishments with much pride. They had kept alive the germ of better farming methods and dinned basically sound principles into the reader, but the situation required stronger remedies than the press could administer. Two world wars and two progressive periods in national politics were necessary to direct Southern agriculture toward the goal which country editors had always believed was the golden mean of the balanced agrarian way of life.

Chapter 17

Politics, Southern Style

IN ONE respect the country weekly and the city daily were just alike. Politics was the reason for the existence of both. Editors might often have their pet causes and their hearts might be on the farm, but their best arguments went into politics. This suited readers. The Southerner was just as political after 1865 as he was before the war. Politics made subscribers and they paid for papers. So did the candidates who paid announcement fees and bought quantities of campaign materials.

Editors made and followed broad professions of political faith. When papers were founded, or ownership changed, the new editors took the first opportunity to declare the political attitudes which would prevail. On national issues they usually did prevail. They were pretty well determined by the position taken by the major party to which the paper gave its allegiance. On local issues a paper's views were much less stable. In local politics each new alliance disturbed the balance of power. The country editor sensitive to even the smallest shifting might throw his weight in a new direction to meet each change. Intense factionalism kept an editor always on the alert. Because Southern weeklies operated predominantly within the Democratic Party, a certain uniformity was natural on a few national issues. As the scope of the issues diminished, so did the uniformity. Studying the point at which it disappeared gives a measure of the alleged solidarity of the South.

Before 1876 politics in the New South went through two troubled stages. Immediately after the war there was a period of watchful waiting to see what would happen to the states. Attention centered on Washington. Would the Secession States remain as they were, or would reorganization wipe away the Old South? What attitude would President Andrew Johnson take, and what would Congress do? In the first year after the cessation of hostilities much of the political news originated at the national capital. In the South there was a surprisingly dispassionate discussion of events. When the provisional governors took office, however, tension rose, and when Congress revealed the shape of future events the weekly editors expressed forthright resentment at the treatment of the South. At first there was bitter criticism of Johnson. This quickly changed to defense of him and there was considerable praise of his attitude. In 1868 the Abbeville (South Carolina) *Press* called the impeachment proceedings infamous, and this judgment prevailed elsewhere.

The native country press attacked the radical leadership in Washington and scalawags and carpetbaggers who were creating trouble at the state capitals and in local government. Thaddeus Stevens provoked strong invectives, and he was accused of almost every crime a man could commit. Charles Sumner, Edwin Stanton, General B. F. Butler, Ben Wade, General W. T. Sherman, General U. S. Grant and a score of other Union officials often drew fire. So long as papers remained reasonably free they pounded local exploiters with editorials which exposed them for the rascals editors knew them to be.

Some of the tirades against the radicals were coarsely vituperative while others were comical. An oft-repeated attack said that "[Charles] Sumner so hates anything white that he refuses white pocket handkerchiefs, never wears a white necktie, avoids white-washed rooms, never wears white kid gloves, dislikes snow, takes ipecac in preference to magnesia, writes on colored paper, has his boots blacked at every corner, defends yellow fever, mitigates black vomit, objects to the bleeding of calves because it makes the meat white, never rolls up the whites of his eyes—it is said he even dislikes the Whitehouse."

Of the many targets at which Southern editors cast their wit and venom none drew more fire than Benjamin Franklin "Spoons" Butler. Countless uncomplimentary stories were told of the escapades of this enemy of the South. An article was excerpted from the Fort Wayne (Indiana) *Sentinel* in 1872 in which it was said that Butler had spoken in behalf of Grant's candidacy at Kokomo. When he returned to his hotel he ordered whisky and sugar. A Negro waiter appeared with the liquor, sugar and a spoon. The "Beast" dismissed him, but the servant refused to budge. After three or four commands to leave the room the Negro was still there. General Butler lost his temper and shouted, "Get out, you damned nigger!" The

Negro replied, "Not so fast, Massa Butler! I can't go yet—I'se 'sponsible for dat 'ar spoon!"

When the intent of radical Reconstruction was clearly revealed, editorial resistance became vigorous. At this point country editors began to draw together the remnants of Southern political forces and to help mould them into a solid barrier to halt further radical intrusion. In 1874 the Jackson (Tennessee) *Whig and Tribune* expressed the sentiment against the Civil Rights Bill. "The Civil Rights Bill, notwithstanding the efforts of Butler, Hoar and Poland [sic] is dead," he wrote; "but the evils, the seeds of race bitterness and antagonism, its agitation has sowed, will rankle in the hearts of the insulted whites of the South, and the deluded Negroes, for years. However, it has doubtless accomplished one good, it has damned the Republican Party for all times to come."

The memory of man is short, and nobody knew this better than the country editor. For this reason D. M. Wisdom's statement damning the Republican Party was a strong one. Following this lead weekly editors cultivated the Southern memory and kept it green by periodic assaults on the radical party. Opposition to Republicanism was a rallying point around which opposition to specific policies naturally centered. The Republican invasion, lasting from 1865 to 1876, was enough to keep the press on guard for the next seventy years.

Hundreds of weekly stories reveal the details of dissolution and failure of the forces of Reconstruction. They bring out the means by which local and state governments were restored to native control, and Negro and Republican voters were relegated to the background. Stories crept into most of the papers about the activities of the Ku Klux Klan. Often these were published in the immediate areas where it operated. They took much the same tone they used in reporting local killings or other community disturbances. The press often reported the Klan's raids unemotionally, almost with detachment. Some papers criticized the order but generally they seem to have accepted the Klan as a questionable but righteous thrust against an intruder who had thrown the South into political and social chaos. When it appeared that a few papers would be curbed in their freedom of expression by the military governments, their neighbors quickly protested in their behalf. Temperate editors, when not provoked, seemed to recognize a potential danger in the Klan.

Along with the reports of the activities of the Ku Klux Klan were those of other resistance groups. Vigilante activities of rifle clubs were noted, including those of the famous South Carolina Club. The papers regarded these organizations as laudable efforts to rebuild local white political strength and to bring about some much needed community reforms. Activities in one state were given widespread coverage by the exchanges in other states, so that the whole South got a fairly accurate notion of what was happening.

By 1876 the local press was celebrating the completion of the early steps to the restoration of native-white rule built on the foundations of the deteriorated Reconstruction governments. The papers also went on speaking bitterly of eight years of "Grantism" and its abuses of the South. They attacked individuals in the central government at Washington and indicted all the radicals in the South. They made a vigorous effort to stamp indelibly on the minds of the people a sense of the failure of Reconstruction administration.

The most exciting news was provided when tensions broke out in riots. Almost every Southern community experienced some sort of commotion. The biggest outbreaks were at Cainhoy, Hamburg, Ellenton and Barnwell in South Carolina. In the lower South, the bloody "Kemper County War" in Mississippi attracted widespread attention. These conflicts between native whites, Negroes and carpetbaggers amounted to miniature civil wars. Stories of these upheavals were widely published and kept people in a constant state of uneasiness. The political resentments joined with the intensified racial frictions to make a highly explosive atmosphere.

The new state constitutions provoked an enormous amount of editorial bitterness. Generally the weeklies advised their readers passively to oppose the revised constitutions. As the Abbeville *Press* said in a full-page editorial in 1868, the process of Reconstruction had become a simple question of decency, honesty and civilized virtue. Constitutions which were not adopted by an honest vote of black and white were dangerous documents. It directed a vigorous attack against all the new constitutions, but aimed its most corrosive criticism against that of Georgia. The *Press* said the preamble should read, "We the niggers of Georgia, in order to destroy all permanent government, establish robbery, insure domestic disgrace and discord, and secure the curses of anarchy and despotism to all races and their posterity! Acknowledge the guidance of the radical party, the author of all bad government, do ordain and establish this constitution of Georgia." This attempt at constitutional revision was, in fact, said the South Carolina editor, exposing Georgia to wholesale theft.

The stories that stand out most clearly in all the complex mass of newspaper material relating to Reconstruction are those dealing with the frauds in the Grant administration. The Whisky and Belknap scandals and the Credit Mobilier were all given generous space, along with the incidents of Black Friday. There can be little doubt that two of the strongest factors in the Southern reaction against the Republican Party, aside from the issue of the Negro vote, were fraud and scandal. The country papers did a thorough job of arousing public opinion. Opposition to the radical party became a religious passion. Southern political attitudes were so shaped in this period that for most Southerners voting the Republican ticket would have been like committing an act of treason or falling from spiritual grace.

After 1870 the forces of radicalism rapidly spent themselves in many areas. The South was being restored to the Union. Everywhere in the region there was rejoicing that this was true. "The days of the Carpetbagger are at an end," prophetically wrote the editor of the North Georgia *Citizen*. "And we thank God that it is so, for the people of the South they have been as great a curse as any one of the plagues to the ancient Egyptians." The *Tri-Weekly Republican* of Americus, Georgia, said that the South after 1871 was more in the Union than out of it. This should be true, for enough time and money had been wasted on radical confusion, corruption, usurpation and misrepresentation.

Editors emphasized the fact that the South was loyal to ancient American principles and the democratic patterns of Washington, Jefferson, and Jackson. They contended that no group of states was more patriotic, but it felt open animosity to the forced state constitutions and the amendments of the United States Constitution. Likewise the Southern states did not try to hide their opposition to local and state governments run by usurpers. Since the end of the war, the weekly press had regarded native white political leadership as the only pattern the region would voluntarily accept. The editors wanted loyal Southerners in power.

Five months after the cessation of hostilities, the Camden (South Carolina) *Journal* quoted the New York *Herald* as saying that ex-rebels were being elected to office "for the simple reason; there are no other men whom the people will trust. They know, that with few exceptions, the so-called Union men of the South are slippery fellows, weak-kneed trimmers who were rebels when the rebellion was up, and Union men when it was down."

All this was to be emphasized by 1876. Although the country press had advocated Seymour in 1868 and supported Greeley in 1872, it did not get around to a full-scale assault against the ramparts of Republicanism until the Hayes-Tilden campaign. The pent-up emotions of ten years were released in this election. Long columns of newsprint defined the South's position, hailed the end of Reconstruction and condemned bitterly the thieves who denied Tilden his election. This campaign was to establish a Southern pattern in national politics for the succeeding decades. Every four years the whole region gave strong support to the Democratic cause.

Every paper kept two sets of stock illustrations which were used to announce the success or failure of the Democratic Party. Cannons booming away and flags flying at the head of lead stories meant the party was victorious. A gamecock crowing lustily symbolized the buoyant feeling of Democrats, but a droopy scrofulous half-picked rooster meant the party would have to wait four more years for victory.

With the end of "Grantism," an internal revolution occurred in the South. Carpetbaggers and scalawags either folded their tents and fled or became Democrats and took a back seat. The Negro was left an object of political confusion and scorn to await complete ostracism. Nowhere was the re-establishment of home rule more dramatic than in South Carolina. Democratic activities there were widely publicized, and the campaign of Hampton's Redshirts was hailed by the press as a political rebirth. Southern editorial pages were filled with viewpoints, speeches and news of the flamboyant Redshirt crusade. Final victory at the polls was greeted with ringing acclaim wherever a Democratic paper was printed.

In the presidential election of 1884 the country editors savored to the fullest their golden opportunity to turn a Republican on the hot spit of public opinion. From February to November they raked up all of the sins of the party and used them to oppose James G. Blaine. They attacked him for his shady dealings and fastened onto him the name of "Little Rock Robber." They devoted full pages to the publication of the "Mulligan Letters," and every Democratic weekly made capital of Blaine's other errors. In a sense the election of 1884 was for the Southern country editors the final act in breaking the back of radicalism. Once again they felt the South could become a decisive factor in a national election. Although Rutherford B. Hayes had pleased the editors with his conciliatory policies, and genuine understanding between Garfield and the South seemed likely, it was hard to forget that the moderate Hayes had "stole" his election. When he died in 1893, Lem Seawright of the Choctaw (Mississippi) *Plaindealer* wrote, "R. B. Hayes, the only man that ever stole the presidency is dead. Let us hope he has gone where stealing is not a legitimate business."

In the ex-Confederate states the restoration of native government was a great subject for news and editors. The names of Southern leaders such as Lamar, Gordon, Colquitt, Vance, Stephens, Brown, Hampton, Beaureguard and many others were mentioned with great editorial reverence. Almost immediately after native regimes were back in power, editors commended them for lowering the costs of government. In 1881 the Marietta (Georgia) *Journal* said that the state's native white legislature had reduced taxes and governmental costs by half. Georgia's credit was so much improved that interest rates were reduced from ten to four per cent, and floating debts were reduced enough so that even half taxes promised to create a surplus. Everywhere except in Virginia the story was similar. In Alabama the cry was to get rid of Republicans. After Cleveland's victory in 1884 the Choctaw (Mississippi) *Plaindealer* wanted to remove all postmasters; even if they were "good," they were still Republicans.

Public expense touched the South's fundamental economic problems. Every Southern editor knew that full recovery would be difficult because of existing maladjustments. Pleas for economy did not come merely from reactionaries. Everywhere editors turned they faced poverty and a lack of funds to support even the most necessary functions of government. Frugality became an inescapable Southern policy, and the first Southerners to realize it were the journalists. General income and tax returns did not meet the needs of society. Whatever else may be said about Southern politics after 1876 it must be remembered that many of the region's failures grew out of insufficient money to support an adequate functioning of government. Like the government, private individuals lacked capital to take advantage of opportunities. As a consequence, the income that went with political office looked exceptionally attractive, and after 1876 lists of candidates often grew to astounding lengths.

The papers were all for free-white home rule. Publishers backed the new native state officials and were prepared to support them through thick and thin against external attacks. In point of fact the editors cared less about the individual officials than they did for the returning strength of the Democratic Party. For this reason most weekly papers were bourbon in political viewpoint (that is, they took the most conservative attitude toward regional problems). This led to avid quotation from the public addresses of such men as L. Q. C. Lamar, John C. Breckinridge, Wade Hampton, Alfred Colquitt, John B. Gordon and the "old line" daily paper editors in the South-wide exchanges. Within a remarkably short time the weeklies' attitudes toward state and national politics congealed within rigid lines. Bourbonism was synonymous with white supremacy and native-white rule.

After 1880 the feeling grew up that factions in state and local politics would not endanger the Democratic Party's dominance. Rampant candidates without issues often sought office by abuse of their opponents, although they were exceedingly sensitive to criticism of themselves. Political letters, cards, arguments and campaign news appeared in the papers with the regularity of wedding announcements, obituaries and yarns about big snakes. Periodic elections were so staggered that no considerable segment of the country press was free for more than six months of some kind of campaign news. While candidates tussled among themselves, editors disputed over men and issues.

The only major rule involved in the game of local politics was that everybody had to be Democratic, otherwise office-seekers were free to use their own techniques. Name calling, accusation of lying and stealing and ridicule were accepted as standard practice in gaining votes. All was fair so long as no Republicans got mixed up in the races except in Kentucky, East Tennessee and a few recognized Republican areas of the other states. The columns of the papers were open to sensitive candidates who wished to clarify their positions in public letters and to brand their opponents as being unworthy prospects.

In every election scramble there were the perennial candidates who popped up each spring with the jonquils and wilted down by election time. Often editors grew weary of having to give publicity to these persistent office-seekers. W. P. Walton of the Stanford (Kentucky) *Interior Journal* wrote, "What the bed bug is to a tired and sleepy traveler, what the chicken cholera is to a poultry yard, what a boil is on the end of one's nose, what the summer complaint is to children, that is Mr. F. P. Bobbitt to our county politics—an annually recurring source of petty irritation, annoyance and worry. Let us be thankful therefore, that on next Monday the great Reformer will once more be disposed of for this year. Not long, however, about the time the next crop of caterpillars begin to drop from the trees down our necks, we may look for Mr. Bobbitt again, for by that time it will have again become the patriot's duty to do battle for the sacred rights of the poor man, and to strike with the lightning of righteous indignation the man who wears a clean shirt. . . ."

Post-Reconstruction Southern politics assumed a sporting aspect. Southerners loved oratory. As one editor said, the mere ringing of a courthouse bell would bring out at least two candidates for Congress and a whole flock of local officeseekers. On Saturday afternoon empty wagons standing under the shade of courthouse yard trees were more than ambitious local politicians could resist. At certain seasons candidates became as thick as peckerwoods in plum thickets, and their revenue-bearing cards not infrequently filled an entire page of a paper. There were so many of them, in fact, that it was necessary to devise plans for public meetings where everybody would have an opportunity to be heard. Barbecues were revived as political devices. Thousands of ravenous voters fed on free meats but were forced to listen to storms of bull-voiced orators in payment. On these occasions victory flags were hoisted atop unusually tall skinned poles to honor national tickets, and candidates spoke for themselves and the party. These barbecues assumed the air of carnivals where young people played ball, danced and courted, while the old folks listened to the speeches and argued politics by the hour. The Tilden campaign of 1876 was the occasion for a revival of barbecues everywhere in the South. Four years later Alexander H. Stephens rewarmed "the grand old principles" before an audience of well-fed Georgians at Elberton. Up in North Carolina, Zebulon Vance made the Democratic eagle scream before roaring audiences, and John C. Breckinridge, Luke P. and J. S. C. Blackburn added zest to Kentucky gatherings. Political meetings were again virtually social affairs, which received full attention in the country papers.

Barbecues were used to gather a crowd not only by candidates for office but also by promoters of the granger movement. By 1875 the activities of this organization had become news for Southern papers, and for the next fifteen years its doings filled much space in them. At first jubilant editors went out into the country to be lionized at numerous farmer picnics and barbecues. They sat long hours listening to discussions of the plight of agriculture and to clumsy farmer parliamentarians framing and adopting endless resolutions of protest.

After attending these grange assemblies, they often published editorials on farming as a way of life. In 1875 W. P. Walton of the *Interior Journal* attended such a meeting and came away to prepare a column describing his experience. The dinner was bountiful—old ham, turkey, chicken, Southern mutton, beef, roast pig, light bread, corn dodgers, delicious cakes, confectionaries, hot coffee and fresh fruit. The Colonel was impressed both with the bountiful dinner and also with the farmers' comely daughters. "We will show Kentucky girls," he wrote, "against the world—ancient, medieval and modern belles for beauty, vivacity, general intelligence and cleverness. They will carry captive any heart, not even excepting that of the most frigid Zeno himself. We must not particularize here, as on this occasion there were at least half a score or more of those whom the gods have endowed with wondrous fairness." Along with this gallant recognition of the beauty of Kentucky farm girls, the *Interior Journal's* editor wrote about the evident need for agrarian reforms and the signs that Kentucky farmers were about to become involved in politics.

Elsewhere Southern country editors shared Colonel Walton's experience and his apprehensions. That the granger movement was to be involved in politics was inevitable. No nonreligious assembly of Southerners could long remain untainted by politics. The Athens (Tennessee) *Post,* quoting another paper, said right from the start that a strange new agrarian style in politics and dress was about to appear. This new canvassing garb was purely agricultural in origin. "It consists of rye, oat, and wheat straw hats trimmed with cotton blooms. Shirts of homespun, with shuck collars ruffled with potato vines and bound with corn tassles; coats manufactured from corn and cotton staples, cut long capacious pockets, and fringed around the tail and collar with corn silks and clover blossoms. Pants made of pea vines, fastened with cymbling buttons and held up by onion top suspenders. These suits are so contrived that as the wearer moves along hay seed fall in gentle showers along his path."

Although country editors frequently attended farmer picnics and gave much space to what went on at them, they reserved judgment on the granger movement. Always there was danger that such an organization with tenuous connections outside the South might boom up into a third party. Farmers were admonished to stay out of politics. The editors also knew the grangers proposed to strike a blow at one of the conservative press's advertising patrons, the general merchant. The editors wrote much on this subject and cast ridicule at the cooperative efforts of impractical farmers to take business in hand. They had some reason to be apprehensive about the political future of the Grange. In the 1870's and 1880's William F. Felton and Emory Speer of Georgia highland Congressional districts capitalized on rural discontent and created real fear in the hearts of the state's bourbon leaders. This type of insurgency was a dangerous threat to the Democratic leadership. Quickly the editorial dogs snapped at the heels of these insurgents until they were safely off the political scene.

Other fundamental issues confronted the Democratic Party in addition to its opposition to Negroes and Republicans. While the South was caught in Reconstruction, the rest of the nation was undergoing an expansion of industry and economic interests. Monetary maladjustment was a national issue. The old question of the tariff was being fought out again by the two major parties. It made the Southern farmers shudder as it always did. Democratic candidates talked low tariffs, editors wrote at length on the subject, but little that the farmer could see was done to lower them. Many a cotton farmer had to find justification for his undying loyalty to the solid Democratic Party in high-sounding statements favoring a low tariff. He read in his local paper that the party's position was right, even if he did not always understand why. He also read about the furious, distant struggle over greenbacks, silver and gold, and he was for any type of free coinage which would lift him out of the abysmal depths of his indebtness.

National issues of a somewhat technical nature were ideal for the presidential election years, but for downright human interest the rowdy local political fights were more satisfying. Local politics shucked off high-sounding discussions of issues and got down to the earthy matter of personalities. Editors themselves found local elections more exciting to their rugged provincial natures. They could come quickly to the point and speak of the home boys with a wholesome frankness which made their profession both dangerous and challenging. Once it was safe to fight among themselves, Democratic editors could bare their teeth and meet their antagonists with genuine relish.

In 1876 Founting P. Bobbitt stumped central-eastern Kentucky for Congress. He told the people he was "clay in the hands of the potter." W. P. Walton agreed, but "the plastic hand of Nature, long since [had] molded *that clay* into a certain domestic utensil—yellow striped, of great occasional utility, but not mentionable in a strictly family paper." Unfortunately a Kentucky Congressional district sent a chunk of inferior clay to Washington in John D. White. The Toccoa (Georgia) *News* said there was one thing which both Democrats and Republicans could agree upon and that was "the stupendous, unutterable and monumental jackassery of John D. White of Kentucky."

The Breckinridge (Kentucky) *News* in 1870 opposed returning John S. Williams to the United States Senate. He lacked, it was said, dignity, intelligence and personal fitness. He had supported every party but the Republican and had always been a political hack. "The only bill," said the editor, "he ever introduced excited the risibility of the whole country, the silliness of which entitles it to rank with Gregory's famous idiotic bull against the comet. If there ever was a time when it was profitable to use a man of his caliber to stop a hole with in that exalted body, as farmers sometimes use a cob for jug stoppers, that time has gone by. Another era has dawned upon the country. . . . It is not an era for the exaltation of mediocrity, for the uplifting of such cheap humbug Ebenezers as John S. Williams. Because an ambitious frog swells with self-conceit until it imagines itself an ox. General Williams is the ambitious and conceited frog of Kentucky politics."

This outburst of the Kentucky weekly was part of the political pattern which prevailed in country journalism for several decades. County officials were continuously being lectured for their lack of intelligence, courage and integrity. Editors sat in judgment on the public servants and let "the chips fall where they may." Critical of all, the editors were often least charitable to state legislators. This was true despite the fact that no Southern general assembly was without a fair sprinkling of editor members. With these chances to observe from within the ineptitude of legislatures they could give their criticism cruel precision.

Legislators were sometimes indiscreet in their behavior, and country editors rebuked them for lapses from propriety. When Kentucky assemblies awaited the governor's message in a final session they engaged in childish play which invoked the wrath of the *Interior Journal.* "What a beautiful spectacle," wrote Colonel Walton, "the representatives of the people must have presented last Monday night! Shooting paper wads, laughing and yelling in their seats, while waiting a message from the chief executive." The spit-ballers had spent eighty days arguing over local bills which would affect fewer than one-twentieth of the people. Now was the time for the people to send better men to Frankfort instead of the "*non compos mentis* majority in her legislature."

In 1888 the Mississippi legislature adjourned without the president of the Senate and the speaker of the House affixing their signatures to a railroad assessment bill which would raise $30,000 of necessary funds. The governor was in a quandary as to what to do, said the Choctaw *Plaindealer.* He proposed calling the assembly into special session, but he was warned against such action by his close adviser, Colonel David Johnson. "Don't, please don't call the legislature back. I will pay my pro rata share rather than have them here again. Yes, I'll subscribe $10 to make up the deficit if that body never meets again. Besides if the governor were to call them back, the people would arise and hang him, and it would be a case of justifiable homicide."

These views are characteristic of most critical editorials. It was impossible, of course, to please the whole press, but when assemblies stumbled through entire sessions with neither program nor effective leadership, the whole press was displeased. Editorial comments were often unduly caustic, but even so they revealed the aimlessness of much Southern legislation. Sometimes disgusted editors referred to the state assemblies as "menageries of incompetents," and "assemblies of imbecility." The press quickly spotted legislation designed to benefit special interests.

When legislatures were not in session country editors focused their attention on the governors. As soon as the Republican threat had been safely removed they appraised the chief executives on a factional basis. When papers supported a governor in hard-fought intraparty campaigns they excused his failures and did his rationalizing for him. If on the other hand they had opposed his election, they were warmed up ready to fight by the time he took the oath of office. Criticism of a governor could be extremely bitter. On the eve of the Kentucky election in 1883, W. P. Walton thanked God that Luke P. Blackburn's term was near an end. His "Fraudulency," as he called him, would soon pass into oblivion, except in the foggy memory of cut-throats, murderers and blacklegs. Governor Blackburn, a hero of the yellow-fever epidemic in the late 1870's, incurred the wrath of much of the Kentucky country press. It was said that he went about the state holding receptions, attending parties, frolicking in boudoirs and parading behind brass bands. "It is difficult to stir them [the governor and the legislature]," wrote a critic. "Shocking tragedies at their very doors do not startle them to a realization of the evils of her own citizens, barring us against the current of immigration and commerce, and presenting us to the eyes of the world as a reckless, God-defying, reeking band of law-breakers and murderers." The Owensboro (Kentucky) *Record* refuted Governor Blackburn's claim that he lost 10,000 votes by being engaged in yellow-fever work at the time of his election. "This is only another evidence of the inordinate egotism of the old imbecile," said the *Record*. "His best friends never claimed that he had any other qualifications for the office than his yellow fever record."

This truculent criticism of Luke P. Blackburn is a sample of the vigorous denunciation of many Southern governors. They usually found it more difficult to draw praise from the papers. Occasionally, however, an incompetent governor could keep his shortcomings hidden because a friendly press overlooked his failures.

By the decade beginning in 1880 editors were publicizing accounts of another Southern political revolution. Conventions were called to revise the Reconstruction constitutions so as to place the states once more under home-drafted rules of government. The last vestiges of radicalism were wiped away, and the country press was jubilant over their disappearance. Encouraging the calling of constitutional conventions was a new experience for editors because they had been notoriously conservative about constitutional reform. For once they were willing to advocate changes in government without chanting the ancient objection that the times were out of joint for constitutional revision, or that men were no longer qualified to perform the task.

About the same time they began to take notice of the revolution in politics caused by growing dissatisfaction among the farmers. The rise of the Populist Party was one of the important events of country paper history. At first most country editors were so bourbon in outlook that they were willing to sacrifice the Southern farmer's best interest to insure Democratic solidarity. They had been trying hard to stop the failures of Southern agrarianism. They had worked to improve the position of the farmer. But the farmer was second to the Democratic Party.

Farmers themselves quickly detected the conservatism of the country editors and engaged them in arguments within their columns. Characteristic of these disputes was the one in 1887 between T. S. Brice and the editor of the Winnsboro (South Carolina) *News and Herald*. Brice accused the local editor of being devoid of both brains and beard, and the editor retorted that farmer Brice had vastly more beard than brains, and that he was the last man who should provoke a fight and use intelligence for a weapon.

Puerile arguments like this were only the beginning of a revolution in both Southern politics and weekly publishing. Within ten years a great number of bourbon editors changed over to acceptance of most of the Populistic principles, except those that might weaken Southern political solidarity in national elections. The same economic forces which revised farming as a way of life bore on publishing as a means of livelihood. When farmers suffered reverses it was but a short time before editors experienced the same fate. Fighting valiantly, editors undertook to stave off the revolution, but in the end they accepted its inevitabilities without realizing fully when they did it.

One of the first changes wrought in the 1890's was the country papers' acceptance of the new Southern political leadership. As the old brigadiers marched off the scene, vigorous new personalities took their places. Where once the golden voices of Lamar, Gordon, Colquitt, Vance and Hampton had been raised in eloquent speeches about the old order there were now the bombastic tirades and repartee of the common man's candidates. Among the first of this new generation of political leaders were Benjamin Ryan Tillman of South Carolina, Robert Love Taylor and Alfred Taylor of Tennessee. These men made splendid news copy, even though many papers fought them. For instance, the South Carolina press resisted Tillman, with some of the editors holding a strict bourbon line against him. However, his plea for Clemson College and a college for farm girls in South Carolina was widely publicized. His speeches were reported with regularity and much criticism. Tillman's blustering utterances provoked some of the most vigorous editorials in South Carolina press history.

In Tennessee the famous "War of the Roses," as the Taylor brothers called their gubernatorial campaign of 1886, was good news material. The press gave this unusual campaign full coverage, and Democratic editors were captivated by Bob Taylor's humor and fiddle tunes. Bob himself had been an editor. The year before, he had given up the coeditorship of the Johnson City *Comet* and its debts to become a pension agent at Knoxville. On deserting the editorial stool, Bob wrote, "Today I bid farewell to the *Comet,* and wipe my weeping eyes. I love my babies because they give me so much trouble. I have a tender feeling for the *Comet* because it has given me more trouble than forty babies. I have nursed the *Comet* and sung lullabies to it." If "Fiddling Bob" had trouble with his paper, he at least learned the useful lesson of getting a favorable press for his political activities.

In Georgia, Alabama, Mississippi and Texas names of new and ambitious political personages began to appear in the weekly news. Tom Watson, a rebel from bourbonism, early learned the art of securing publicity. From boyhood he attracted the attention of country editors. He had played baseball and his name appeared in the columns of the Thomson, Georgia, *McDuffie Journal* as a member of the local team. He had written verse and once prepared a soliloquy on the glories of country life. Occasionally he gave an editor a basket of peaches and got his name in the paper in exchange.

Although Tom Watson was active in Georgia politics in the 1880's, he kept on good terms with the press until he turned toward Populism. Then Sidney Lewis of the Sparta *Ishmaelite* led the Georgia press attack on this potential enemy of the Democratic Party. The old Sparta editor was of the opinion in 1892 that Watson "ought not to complain because of the moist condition of his political galligaskin. Had he put off jumping until the boat got to the third party landing he would have kept dry." Paradoxically Tom Watson was thought to be sincere in his political folly, and "a demagogue on purpose—

without equivocation or mental reservation." He was given credit, however, of being the best of the "Lease litter."

Perhaps Tom Watson received more publicity than any other Southern politician in the crucial transition period. Nearly every country paper opened fire on him. He was accused of being an insincere rascal, of favoring the Republican tariff, of speaking falsely about free trade, of being a socialist, of associating too closely with Mary Lease and, worst of all, of threatening the security of the Democratic Party. The St. Louis and Ocala Alliance platforms were lambasted. Old-line publishers, who had always claimed to be the farmer's friends, fought the Populists and their efforts to establish local journals to take their campaign to the people. So bitter against Populism were these bourbon editors that they opposed many obviously necessary reforms. Grover Cleveland was their political messiah. The McMinnville (Tennessee) *Southern Standard* said he was the greatest Democrat of all times. He had betrayed no trust and his financial policies were sound. This paper favored preventing Populists from voting in the Democratic convention, and so did the vast majority of the Southern papers.

Characteristic of this attitude was a note which appeared in the North Mississippi *Democrat* after the second election of Grover Cleveland. "It would be difficult," said the *Democrat*, "to exaggerate the influence of the country papers in Mississippi in achieving the overthrow of the enemies of the Democratic Party. The press almost solidly fought the heresies of the third party from the hour the war cry was shouted."

But by 1904 most papers had succumbed to the leadership of the so-called demagogues. Papers which had sneered at Populists in the early nineties were won over by Taylor, Tillman, Vardaman, Jeff Davis and their long line of successors. Only Tom Watson remained unforgiven and unaccepted as the twentieth century began. In 1904 the Selma (Alabama) *Canebrake Herald* accused the old Georgia warhorse of selling out to the Republicans. It said, "A snow ball has more chance of lasting in hell than the King Doodle has of getting elected president." With old time vigor the Canebrake editor aired his views on the Georgia renegade: "For a few paltry dollars he [Watson] is willing to crawl under the shirt of the sweet scented (?) African and shout to his fellow prophets: 'Come boys! It's not

WINSTON COUNTY JOURNAL.

VOLUME XIX. NUMBER 45. LOUISVILLE, MISSISSIPPI, FRIDAY MORNING, AUGUST 4, 1911. SUBSCRIPTION $1 PER YEAR

VARDAMAN WINS BY LARGE MAJORITY OVER OPPONENTS

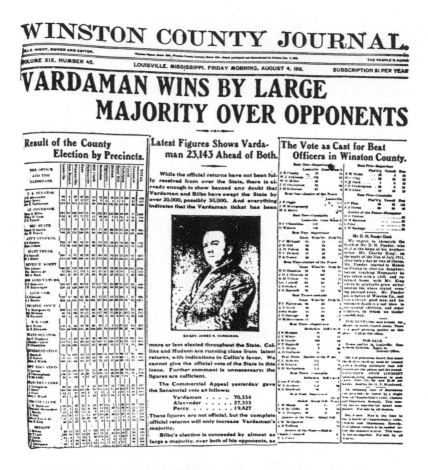

Result of the County Election by Precincts.

Latest Figures Shows Vardaman 23,143 Ahead of Both.

While the official returns have not been fully received from over the State, there is already enough to show beyond any doubt that Vardaman and Bilbo have swept the State by over 20,000, possibly 30,000. And everything indicates that the Vardaman ticket has been

EX-GOV. JAMES K. VARDAMAN.

more or less elected throughout the State. Collins and Hudson are running close from latest returns, with indications in Collin's favor. We cannot give the official vote of the State in this issue. Further comment is unnecessary; the figures are sufficient.

The Commercial Appeal yesterday gave the Senatorial vote as follows:

Vardaman	70,534
Alexander	27,553
Percy	19,827

These figures are not official, but the complete official returns will only increase Vardaman's majority.

Bilbo's election is conceded by almost as large a majority, over both of his opponents, as

The Vote as Cast for Beat Officers in Winston County.

Mr. D. H. Ponder Dead.

We regret to chronicle the death of Mr. D. H. Ponder, who died at the home of his brother-in-law Mr. Charlie King, on the night of the 31st of July 1911, after only a day or two of illness. Mr. Ponder started to Mobile on Friday to visit his daughter, but on reaching Noxapater he was taken with a chill, and returned home with Mr. King where he gradually grew sicker until on the above stated evening passed away. Mr. Ponder was a native of Winston Co., and was a clever, good man, and his untimely death is a sad blow to his several children, and other relatives, to whom we tender condolence.

WINSTON COUNTY JOURNAL.

VOLUME XIX. NUMBER 40. LOUISVILLE, MISSISSIPPI, FRIDAY MORNING, JUNE 30, 1911. SUBSCRIPTION $1 PER YEAR

Three Days of Political Speech Making----Bilbo Thursday, July 6th; Percy, Saturday, the 8; Vardaman Tuesday the 11th.

SEN. PERCY TO BE HERE ON JULY 8th.

Hon. Leroy Percy, present U.S. Senator and an aspirant for reelection, will be in Louisville Saturday July 8th, and address the people. Everybody invited to attend. The speaking will take place at the Fair Grounds.

Geo. R. Edwards.

The voters of the first district will soon have an opportunity to express their approval of the fidelity to official duty, which characterized State Treasurer George R. Edwards, when he refused to pay out $10,500 of the people's money illegally to the holders of the State bonds, by voting for him for Railroad Commissioner of this district. While Gov. Noel will doubtless ask the legislature to reimburse the rich money lenders who expected to pick this little sum up as lagniappe, he will not probably ask the legislature to reimburse Mr. Edwards for the considerable sum that

EX-GOV. VARDAMAN WILL SPEAK IN LOUISVILLE ON TUESDAY, JULY THE 11TH

Ex-Gov. Jas. K. Vardaman, candidate for U. S. Senator, will deliver an address to the people of Winston County in Louisville on Tuesday July 11th. Everybody invited to attend. This will be the only date Mr. Vardaman will be able to get to Winston before the election, owing to the many counties he has to visit. Ladies specially invited. Music by band.

S. S. Hudson.

Hon. S. S. Hudson ... for re-election as Attorney General of Mississippi, but the discharge of his office duties require so much of his time that it will be impossible for him to make a close personal canvass of the State. The office is highly a honorable one and in recent years, by reason of the great growth of the State and the investment here of large sums of money by corporations it has grown to an importance second only to the office of Governor. Mr. Hudson has filled the office very acceptably since his appointment, which came to him unsolicited, and

SEN. BILBO WILL SPEAK HERE JULY 6th

State Senator Theo. G. Bilbo, candidate for Leut. Governor, and the man who has created more comment, both favorable and unfavorable, than any man who ever lived in the State, will be here on Thursday, July 6th, next Thursday, at 1 o'clock p. m., and deliver his famous

TYPICAL POLITICAL HEADLINE

half so bad as it's cracked up to be. I don't smell anything, except the inviting aroma that is constantly arising from crisp new bank notes which the good, loyal, generous-hearted Republicans have stuffed into my pockets.' " In time, however, the "Sage of Hickory Hill" was to change these tirades of criticism against him to nods of approval. He became as dramatic in his anti-Negro editorials as was the editor of the *Canebrake Herald.*

After 1900 news of the raucous campaigns for every office in the gift of the people appeared in the papers with the same regularity as election day. In Mississippi, Vardaman, Bilbo, Charles H. Alexander, Leroy Percy and a score of other gubernatorial aspirants kept the waters of public opinion churned muddy. Most Mississippi papers outside of the bourbon delta supported Vardaman. As governor, Vardaman succeeded in having his acts widely publicized. His institutional and educational reforms were as popular as his bitter antiracial tirades were sensational. A country editor himself, the "Great White Chief" understood the manipulation of the weekly press. In his campaign for the United States Senate in 1911 his headquarters organization published a weekly summary of country editorials favoring his election. These excerpts were printed by a ready-print service and nearly every paper in the state used them.

There was nothing bourbon about Vardaman's newspaper support. News stories and editorials were composed in the same strong language he used in his speeches. A sample is an anti-Percy editorial in the Okalona *Messenger.* Somewhere Percy had referred to voters as "cattle" and the weekly press never let him forget this slip. "Leroy," said the *Messenger,* "is French for king. Hence Leroy Percy is king of the Percys. He may have thought when at Godbold's Wells he was a 'cattle king' but when the simple-minded, low-browed, rednecked hill billies get a whack at him next August there will be a demand for abdication which His Royal Highness will find it difficult to decline." This type of story was to set a pattern of political writing for most of the present century up to now. Each succeeding campaign has produced its own colorful editorial polemics.

Always the press had doubts about the honesty of elections. In the early campaign for white supremacy, editors had said that getting rid of Negro voters would tend to end the corrupt practice of buying and manipulating votes. In 1899 the Barnesville (Georgia) *Gazette* contended: "Everybody must be elected by a white primary. . . .

Scrambling for Negro votes degenerates the white man and debauches the Negro." The Greensboro (Georgia) *Herald* said its exchanges were unanimously for white primaries because corrupted Negro voters were the greatest evil of that generation. A year later the Sparta *Ishmaelite* pleaded for safeguards on Georgia elections because it was doubted that they expressed the will of the people. Across in South Carolina the Edgefield *Chronicle* in 1904 said, "The primaries are over, and without a doubt they were the dirtiest ever held in South Carolina. More dirty, malicious falsehoods were distributed to defeat men for office than ever before. We never want to see another primary election if they are to be conducted like recent ones. There must be a change, for good men will steadfastly refuse to submit to such an ordeal to serve their states."

Forty years later the Edgefield editor would have discovered little fundamental change in either editorial attitudes or primary election morals. With one exception, the South has almost always voted Democratic and fought its local political battles inside the prevailing framework of factionalism which bars no holds. Such an electoral system has produced the strong editorial meat so much relished by Southern readers. As threats to the Southern political alignment have perennially developed in Washington, country editorial sanctums have fired back with strong feeling. Repeatedly the Southern shibboleths have been dragged before Congress, and the weekly presses have rolled with burdens of fiery protests. Since 1865 special reporters and columnists have kept country paper readers informed about the happenings at Washington. Occasionally congressmen and special appointive officials in government bureaus have sent home weekly reports for publication, and ready-print services have summarized both Congressional news and national issues.

Editors and candidates crossed swords often enough to keep readers alert to political contests—and to help the papers expand circulation. Possibly the country paper has been the most powerful single influence on political opinion in the South. Circulation statistics do not give a true picture of the extent of its power. Many voters have always waited for editors "to come out" for candidates before they made up their minds. Even for voters who did not read, editorial attitudes were often decisive. Hearing by word of mouth that a local editor favored a candidate was reassuring to them, and without further ado they took him as their candidate too. On the other hand it was not unusual for editorial support to create opposition. Disagreement between editor and reader over politics often led to subscription cancellations, but editors long ago learned that they would gain enough new subscribers who agreed with their points of view to offset the few losses. Whatever their subscribers thought, the editors served as persistent guardians of Southern political traditions. They can take credit for the relative political solidity of the South, for their fairly accurate predictions of election results and for their own personal victories at the polls.

Chapter 18

That Man Teddy Roosevelt

ON FRIDAY afternoon September 6, 1901, the Ohio Pole, Leon Czolgosz, sneaked into the great reception hall in Buffalo and fired two bullets into the body of William McKinley. The President fell, as Garfield had twenty years before, mortally wounded at the hands of a mentally unbalanced anarchist. The dailies received the news by wire, and in their next issues the weeklies carried syndicated stories of what had happened at Buffalo. Only a few months before, the same columns that now told of McKinley's assassination had bitterly condemned his Republicanism. To a great majority of the editors the dead President's politics were anathema. But they could imagine worse still. One editor said, "From McKinley to Roosevelt would be a very far leap from bad to very far worse."

McKinley's policies had not been those of the South. It could be said of him that he had been a gallant President during a heroic struggle, and the South had regarded the Spanish-American War as a final act of reunion. Likewise the stricken President had been a loyal Methodist, and it raised him somewhat in the eyes of Southern readers to have their editors declare that he was a fine Christian gentleman, a thing which most of them had never considered a prime Republican attribute.

With rules turned upside down, the papers told the rural South in the first issues after September 14, 1901, that McKinley was dead. Special feature articles and full pages of ready-print gave news-hungry readers the morbid details of the President's shooting, suffering, death and burial. For the first time most Southerners got anything like an honest notion of McKinley and his background. Always before he had been presented as a Republican, or as a war President in articles glorifying the nation. So honest were many of the deathbed reports that a few editors became worried lest the press was overdoing the martyr angle and exaggerating the extent of the national grief. After all McKinley was a Republican, and Czolgosz had killed only the man and not his party.

Scarcely had the ink dried on the long funeral columns expressing the nation's grief, and the type been redistributed, before the papers were considering McKinley's colorful successor. It was true that the name Roosevelt was not altogether a newcomer to the columns of the weeklies. He had appeared there often as a member of the Civil Service Commission, and later as commander of the Rough Riders. He had first tasted the gall of a critical Southern press in the late eighties. Just after Benjamin Harrison succeeded Cleveland, the upstart Roosevelt appeared on the public scene looking for a fight. The Statesville (North Carolina) *Landmark* described him as looking like "a typical Roman Catholic priest, except that he has teeth like a cannibal." Nothing about the new member of the "Civil Service Humbug Commission" suited the Carolinian. Every time this little New York "Roman, just come in from his ranch out West" and full of ozone, opened his mouth he played the devil. He strutted around calling people liars, and the best that could be hoped for him was that he would find a choice fight.

Later as Undersecretary of the Navy and as an important officer of the Rough Riders, Roosevelt excited some admiration among Southerners. It was a fine thing for him that the Southern papers ran the famous picture of the new President taken in company with General Leonard Wood and "Fighting Joe" Wheeler. Editors of the ubiquitous "patent" pages were lavish with war stories of the Rough Riders, and their sprawling illustrations made the round stocky head of Roosevelt and his famous bucktoothed smiles almost as familiar as the portrait of Lydia E. Pinkham.

A full-page spread of Roosevelt and his activities appeared in the papers for the week of September 19. The Western Newspaper Union and other distributors of ready-print worked overtime assembling the story and pictures. Just as the mournful valedictory stories closed McKinley's career, the salutatory ones began Roosevelt's. He was portrayed as a soldier, a scholar and a vigorous citizen. But most important of all, for those isolated readers who laboriously read the news a word at a time while propped back against the post of a shady Southern veranda, or who leaned close to the narrow limits of light given out by a flickering oil lamp or a sputtering pine-knot fire, Roosevelt was portrayed as a fecund man of family. There was a full-face cut of the grim Teddy, one of his handsome wife and a family group in which the new President sat stiff among his progeny. Portrayed as a soldier, he appeared with close-cropped mustache and hair, dressed in army clothes, with his legs encased in wrinkled leggings.

Roosevelt was said to be a friendly man who had suddenly found an arduous burden thrown on his shoulders. Virtually standing over his predecessor's bier, and in the presence of McKinley lieutenants, he had solemnly declared that he would continue the administration's none-too-well-defined policies. To Northern Republicans this was reassuring, and at the same time to Southern Democrats the new President was half-Southern and proud of it. His mother was a Bulloch from Roswell, Georgia. One of her brothers had been an admiral in the Confederate Navy, and another had been the last to fire a gun aboard the *Alabama*. It was a matter of great pride to Roosevelt that his Spanish-American War regiment contained so many men whose fathers had fought in the Confederate Army. In those exciting moments of assuming the responsibilities of the presidency Roosevelt expressed the hope that he could visit Roswell and Atlanta in the fall and revive his ties with the South.

Roosevelt hardly had time to lower his arm after taking the oath of office before Southerners were descending upon him. On September 30, Senators Stephen B. Elkins of West Virginia and Jeter C. Prichard of North Carolina, and Congressmen Theodore F. Klutz of North Carolina, Henry R. Gibson of Tennessee and Leonidas F. Livingston of Georgia, and many others called on him to seek assurances that he would support the South.

Senator Prichard told the new President, "The South will support you most heartily. The Democratic newspapers are predicting good for you and of you, and the feeling of all the people for you, irrespective of party, is most kindly." Truly the first two weeks of the new administration were a love feast. Roosevelt scarcely had time to settle down to work between the time one Southern delegation left and another appeared.

He was quick to sense the childlike apprehension of these callers, and in an interview on September 21 he attempted to allay once and for all these sectional fears by dramatically declaring that he expected to be President of all the United States. "Before the words were spoken," said the Confederate editor of the Chatham (North Carolina) *Record,* "the people of the South felt kindly toward Roosevelt because of his tribute of respect published by him to General Lee and his army. No man can be unfriendly to the South who has eulogized the South's immortal idol, Robert E. Lee."

In South Carolina the editor of the Edgefield *Chronicle,* published in Pitchfork Ben Tillman's home town, congratulated Roosevelt on his good sense and taste. He said the President had acted every inch a man in the face of the crisis, and that so far he was above criticism. Earlier the *Chronicle* had said that it was a long leap from McKinley to Roosevelt, but often when "wild, reckless, sensational, egotistical fellows" feel the weight of responsibility they settle down.

There was a searching of Roosevelt's books to see if he had said anything objectionable. Editor Powell of the Tarborough (North Carolina) *Southerner* was pleased with what he found. Roosevelt had compared Lee with Marlborough and Wellington in his *Life of Thomas Hart Benton.* "That he said this in sincerity," declared the editor, "there can be no doubt, and the fact that he did say it when there could have been no selfish motive in it is creditable to him as a broad and liberal-minded man, even in these days of broad-minded liberality. It is a noble tribute to the Southern soldier and to the matchless leader, and it is also a tribute to Roosevelt himself." Since Roosevelt had a virtuous Southern mother, "there must be some good in him."

Sitting by his stoveside in the office of the Sparta (Georgia) *Ishmaelite,* Sidney Lewis stroked his long beard and concentrated his thoughts upon the new turn of national events. It mattered not that Roosevelt had praised Robert E. Lee or that he was sprung from the womb of a Roswell, Georgia, mother; he was a dangerous man. He was a strange threat to national well-being, whom the fiery old editor labeled "an anarchist of wealth," who suited Morgan, Schwab and the tyrannical trusts. At heart he believed Roosevelt worse than Hanna, that shortly he would either cause general revolution or complete enslavement of the masses.

Despite a few such isolated sour notes, the Southern Democratic press responded favorably to Roosevelt. Editors had just begun to settle back into their well-worn local routines when a blow fell which virtually upturned their rickety old California type cases and stalled their creaking presses.

Screaming headlines in the daily papers for October 19, 1901, pub-

"After You, My Dear Booker."

The above cut shows what actually took place in the White House in Washington. A few months after Mr. Roosevelt accidentally became President he invited Booker Washington, the negro educator, to a private lunch in the White House. Whether the members of the President's family were present was not stated, but it is known that the President wrote Washington a note inviting him to dine and that the latter accepted. This is the first time a President has ever invited a negro to a private lunch in the White House. Many Republicans have preached social equality, but few have practiced it. Some say that Mr. Roosevelt did this to show his contempt of the social customs of the Southern people. At Arlington he said Confederate soldiers were anarchists. In one of his books he said that our people were of a coarse strain of blood. He also declared his contempt of our small farmers and agricultural laborers by declaring that drunken cow boys were "better fellows and pleasanter companions." Read his book on Ranch Life and Hunting Trail if you don't believe this. White man, will you vote for him? Aye more, will you vote for any candidate who supports him?—Smithfield Herald.

ALABAMA PRESS VIEWS OF INDIANOLA INCIDENT

From the Alabamian.

THE trouble at Indianola, Miss., over the postoffice being held by a negro woman and the appointment of W. D. Crum, a negro, as surveyor of customs of Charleston, S. C., as well as the possible nomination of the negro Vick as postmaster of Wilson, N. C., brings the south squarely face to face with the President's alleged southern policy. The issue has not been [illegible] defined since [illegible] the case of Mrs. Cox, the postmaster of Indianola, it was alleged in a dispatch to the postal authorities at Washington that she tendered her resignation on account of intimidation and possible danger to herself, whereupon the President ordered the postoffice at that place closed. It is stated that the ill threats against the woman were purely on the ground of her being a negress. The appointment was made on the ground that she was duly qualified to fill the position and a democratic state senator went on her bond. It is on these grounds that the administration, so the President signifies, makes appointments in the United States, the applicant's color being no detriment. From the point of view the south takes, the President has a distinct southern policy and appointments are made on the ground that the applicant is a negro, and is made also to heap humiliation on the south. The issue is clearly defined. President Roosevelt is not the kind that backs down, and the south seems determined that the negro shall neither vote nor hold office. The President cannot go behind the state's constitution until declared unconstitutional, but he can make appointments. It is a good time for the conservative element to keep cool and assert itself. We make no headway by makes any official a fixture, and if the people want a change, where is the crime in asking the official to resign? That the citizens of Indianola had submitted without complaint to their office being filled for six years by a negro woman speaks well for the community as law-abiding citizens, and to have their office closed and they placed at a very great inconvenience just because they requested the resignation of the official is hardly in accord with the ideas of free government.

The postmaster herself says she was not threatened and there is no evidence that any lawless element was at work, but there is strong evidence that there is a national convention to be held next year and in several northern states the negro holds the balance of power and the President is very anxious to have delegates.

The attempt of the President to force negroes upon the southern people will not be submitted to without objection, and the President may as well learn this at the outset.

From the Talladega News-Reporter.

The President is nothing if not original. He has a head of his own and is using it regardless of his friends and advisers. He has not only appointed a negro in South Carolina against the wishes of his party, but has discontinued a Mississippi postoffice because the citizens objected to a negro postmistress, whose resignation was not accepted by the department. A postoffice inspector has been sent to Indianola, Miss., to investigate the trouble between citizens and the colored postmistress there, and, if possible, to locate the blame. It is alleged by men familiar with Indianola affairs that the town's people in general are not responsible

---

Just think of it, Mr. President, you are keeping your dear negroes from getting their mail. Shall these innocents suffer for the sins of others?

If Roosevelt has the right to close our postoffices just to spite us, we would like to know if we have any inviolate rights as citizens?

This Roosevelt trouble reminds us of what a desperately dangerous thing it is to elect a man vice-president who is unfit for president.

Roosevelt is awful loud in the enforcement of negro domination upon Mississippi, but he can't speak above a whisper when the national bullies fire upon the Monroe doctrine.

licized what Mark Sullivan declares was "the most talked-of luncheon ever eaten." The sensation-loving Roosevelt had invited Booker T. Washington to the White House for a meal. (B. F. Riley in his biography of Booker T. Washington says that President Roosevelt only shared a tray of food brought to his desk at lunch time and that it was purely accidental that the Negro educator was there at that time.) News of this incident broke over the South like a wild, overwhelming tidal wave. A veritable flood of curses thundered down on the presidential head from hundreds of papers.

It can be safely said that never before had a President of the United States exposed himself to so much heartless abuse and ridicule as Theodore Roosevelt. Editors ceased to respect the office of chief magistrate and poured out a tirade of bitter abuse. Editors who had just guilelessly heralded Roosevelt's rise to power lacked words to express their fury. They had been fooled by one of the shrewdest Republicans ever to discriminate against the South. A South Carolinian said he had always regarded Roosevelt as a bold, brave, eccentric man, but now he had made the unpardonable mistake of trying to break down the color line which God had placed between the Caucasian and the Negro. Following a long-established line of reasoning the editor was positive that the racial barrier would never be lowered by the American people. It was only a short step from fraternizing with the Negro at the dinner table to miscegenation, and whites would accept neither.

A calmer, more judicious view of the incident was that expressed in an interview in New York by Major W. W. Screws, editor of the Montgomery *Advertiser*. He felt that although having dinner with Booker T. Washington was not in itself too serious an incident, the excuse it gave for criticizing Washington was a colossal error. The Negro educator enjoyed the respect of the white South, and his work at Tuskegee would perhaps suffer from the whites' fear of social equality. In a similar interview Governor Charles Brantley Aycock of North Carolina expressed practically the same sentiment. The Southern people were anxious for the colored race to advance, but they did not want the prevailing social structure overturned. He saw in Roosevelt's act an excuse for the opponents of Negro education in the South to raise the social-equality issue.

The sentiment against the Negro in the decade which marked the turn of the century was intensely bitter. Hardly had the last crumb been brushed from the President's dining table before the rickety country presses were pouring forth stacks of newspapers to alarm their readers.

Beckoning his fellows into the fray, Will C. Hight of the Winston County (Mississippi) *Journal* shouted, "Let's all take a crack at him!" Throughout the South the brief little paragraphs of the country editors cut through the air like the piercing barks of feist dogs snipping at the heels of a bull. Behind the staccato yapping of the little fellows hot on the fresh scent of "the coon" was the thunderous baying of the rabid dailies. The fanatical editor of the Memphis *Scimitar* declared the President's act the most damnable outrage ever perpetrated upon the people of the United States. Roosevelt had gone out of his way to invite "a nigger to sit down at table with him—a nigger whose only claim to distinction is that by comparison with the balance of his race he has been considered somewhat superior."

The *Scimitar* editor knew only too well that political equality was one of the South's bitterest remembrances and he believed social equality was sure to follow. No white man's daughter would ever again be safe. In fact, this was not an incident, it was an epoch in history. Henceforth, said the editor, "any Nigger who happens to have a little more than the average amount of intelligence granted by the Creator of his race, and cash enough to pay the tailor and the barber, and the perfumer for scents enough to take away the nigger smell, has a perfect right to be received by the daughter of the white man among the guests in the parlor of his home."

This was heavy support for the little editors. If the big dailies could speak so freely, so could they—and with even more persistence. Summed up in the *Scimitar* editorial was the policy which rural editors followed for the next seven years.

An argument developed over whether any other Negroes had ever dined in the White House. Old files of newspapers were ransacked by the Republicans to see if they could uncover any such evidence—especially during a Democratic administration. A strong claim was made that Grover Cleveland had entertained Frederick Douglass at dinner, and that Mrs. Cleveland had "kissed a Negro wench." This, however, was regarded as a poor defense. Teddy Roosevelt had not only dined with the "saddle-colored nigger" Booker T. Washington, but he had also entertained at dinner in the White House the crews of the presidential yachts *Sylph* and *Mayflower*. Among the sailor guests who came to shake the stubby presidential hand and to dine at his table were six dusky-colored tars.

To the country editors Teddy was coming to seem as bad as James K. Vardaman said he was. A rumor was afloat that the President loved Negroes so much that he was considering appointing Booker T. to a cabinet position. Vardaman railed out, "Well, why does he not do it? He has the power to do it. So far as I am concerned, I should not care if he filled the White House so full of the copper-colored crop of contemptible concubinage that the effluvia arising from their rancid carcasses would asphyxiate a buzzard riding on the cow-catcher of a cyclone a hundred feet above the dome." It was bad enough to arouse the alliterative Vardaman, although his field of action was limited to the narrow confines of Mississippi and his hearers were converted already to his racial philosophy. But to arouse Bill Arp was to make certain that Roosevelt's social-equality gestures were to be given coverage throughout the South.

However disposed a Southern editor might have been to soft-pedal the unhappy incident at the White House, he could not very well eliminate the Arp pieces. They were securely entrenched in the ready-print pages and had to be accepted in full. Bill said that he agreed with Robert Toombs that the fanaticism of his Northern brethren about the Negro fatigued his imagination. Roosevelt had sent his children to school in Oyster Bay with Negroes, and as President he was following his natural inclinations. It was enough to say that both Georgia and the village of Roswell had been dishonored. Like the chameleon the White House was now guilty of changing colors instantancously. It could now take on the color of any guests who happened to sojourn beneath its roof. Along about Christmastime, said the sage of Bartow, it was going to assume a dark ivory shade when Miss Washington came down from Wellesley for a visit. During the vacation period there would be much entertaining and warm fraternizing. "Maybe Roosevelt's son will fall in love with her and marry her without having to elope." This business of racial fraternization in the White House, thought Bill Arp, was going diametrically against the laws of Nature. To labor was the Negro's lot, and higher education only unfitted him to fulfill his mission in life.

There can be little doubt that Roosevelt did both himself and Booker T. Washington a grave disservice by his impulsive foray against discrimination. Perhaps nothing could have served better to bring both Roosevelt and the bitter race issue more clearly to the surface than this affair. Both personalities were dramatic in themselves, and the moment was indeed an unpropitious one for any radical approach to the adjustments of social evils. In the columns of the Southern weekly press Booker T. Washington became a marked man. He attracted the attention of Southern editors wherever he went, not because he was successfully pioneering in the field of Negro education but, as one editor said, because he was "the saddle-colored coon" who had the audacity to eat a meal in the White House.

Booker T.'s eating habits became the public property of the country press generally. In 1903 he and a group of Negro teachers were on a circuitous journey from an educational conference in Knoxville, Tennessee, to North Carolina. Their train stopped at Hamlet, North Carolina, after having lost four hours en route. The Negro passengers were invited into the main dining room of a railway cafe, and the handful of white passengers were served in private dining rooms. During the progress of the meal the Hamlet Negroes gathered around the station to witness this strange arrangement of diners and to make remarks. While Booker T. and his party were being served in the so-called "white dining room" a second and unexpected train arrived from the south. Among the new arrivals were Senator A. O. Bacon and several prominent Atlanta people. They were shunted to the side dining rooms. When they discovered the reason they left the restaurant to parade up and down the tracks. Again Booker T. was in the columns of the local papers, and once more Roosevelt was before the court of public opinion. To the editors it was a matter of "President Roosevelt's quondam guest being given 'a dead head' meal, and the other Negroes paying at the regular desk, just as did the white folks as they passed out."

Wherever Booker T. Washington went he was certain to get his name in the papers. Certainly there was no way for him to please any appreciable number of Southern editors. When he was in the East, white people extended social courtesies to him which caused unfavorable publicity back home. On one occasion he was the guest of John Wanamaker and his daughter at luncheon in Saratoga, New York, and the rural Southern papers published an account of it. After a bitter outpouring, the editor of the Okalona (Mississippi) *Messenger* concluded, "What's the use of pummeling Booker? That is the glory of his existence, and he fattens on it, no matter how much harm may be done his race. Wanamaker is the silly party to the incident, and he don't know any better than to be worked by Booker."

Just as Booker T. Washington's social affairs were made public through the papers so were his speeches. Often there were answers to his accounts of the backwardness of Negro education in the South. Editors occasionally resented his saying that the South was dependent on the Negro as a source of labor since the war. It was argued that only half of the cotton was grown by blacks, that in sections of Texas the Negro was unknown, and that in no other business except agriculture was he of any importance. Sometimes editors were sensible and saw the real question at stake in spite of the acrid smoke of race hatred. In Alabama itself there were reasonable editors who believed the Tuskegee plan was a sound one. The Selma *Canebrake Herald* said that all Negroes should hear Booker T. Washington's message. Many worthless Negroes had mistaken freedom for liberty, and they had developed the idea that education was harmful to the race.

Unfortunately few editors agreed with the *Herald.* Instead many of them publicized the head of the Tuskegee school as a genuine menace to Southern society. In very few instances did they show any understanding of the work which was being done at the school. Often they assumed the attitude that it was another Yankee infiltration into the South. As an answer to Northern monetary gifts, it was said that Booker T. was the idol of the Northern rich man, that Northern money was at the Negro's disposal. But Booker was not acceptable to all Northerners; at one hotel a white chambermaid refused to make up his bed, and Southerners were sending enough money to enable her to retire from being a chambermaid. In Springfield, Massachusetts, Booker T. was denied lodging in a hotel, and the editors were elated. They wondered what "Terrible Teddy" thought of such impolite Yankees.

The snare of associating with Professor Washington even enmeshed Andrew Carnegie. When he gave Tuskegee $60,000, the editor of the Charlotte *Observer* thought it a fine gesture. He was ready to grant that Booker T. was doing more than any other man to adjust the ticklish race problem, until Bill Arp's column appeared. Bill looked upon the $60,000 to Tuskegee as so much "blood money" poured down a rathole and wasted. It was bad enough for Carnegie to give money to libraries, but for Negro education it was positively a sin in the sight of God. He believed Carnegie too small and conceited to handle his great wealth with any intelligence. He had gouged it out of the poor employees in his steel mills, and it rightfully belonged to these laborers.

Hardly had the last bitter flare-up of indignation about the Booker T. Washington luncheon died down before the President again aroused the dogs of white supremacy. Clearly Roosevelt had not only known of the bitter criticism which he had stirred up in the South by his policies but bitterly resented the attitude of the editors. The President was even more embittered by realization of the intense anti-Negro feeling which existed in the Mississippi Delta, where the proportion of Negroes to whites was large. In 1897 William McKinley had reappointed Effie Cox, a Negress, whom President Harrison had originally appointed postmistress at Indianola. Her husband, Wayne Cox, was a mail clerk on the Columbus and Greenville Railroad. Apparently there had been little resentment against the colored postmistress. She was held in high esteem by a large number of people, she performed her duties with entire satisfaction to the patrons of her office and racial friction was at a minimum until the Booker T. Washington incident occurred. In the fall of 1901, however, Effie Cox was threatened with violence by local rowdies, and she decided to resign as postmistress. She asked Postmaster General Henry Clay Payne to relieve her of her duties on January 1, 1902. Roosevelt and Payne, however, refused to do this and keep the office open. If Effie Cox were forced to resign because of local conditions then the post office would be closed. Instructions were issued for the closing of the office, and railway mail clerks were instructed to take all the Indianola mail to Greenville, twenty-five miles away. Because of this unhappy incident the patrons of the Indianola post office were without mail service, but they were not without friends and sympathizers. Everywhere in the South this incident was publicized.

Editors who were already in fine trim after the Booker T. Washington affair were glad to fight again for the white South. They reminded the President in positive terms that he was not merely inconveniencing the white patrons of the Indianola post office but he was injuring the office's Negro patrons. White patrons could either have their mail forwarded by special arrangement to nearby Heathman or employ a carrier to bring it from Greenville. Subscriptions were sent to help finance the Heathman office. Even one Union veteran sent $16.50, a month's pay in the army in 1865.

Congress called for an investigation. In the Senate Senator Ben Tillman of South Carolina used this incident as an excuse to deliver a blistering tirade against Roosevelt. He posed the embarrassing questions: "For whom does the post office exist? Is it for the postmaster or the people?" Roosevelt was asked to recognize the fact that the difficulty in Indianola was due to the acts of a few hoodlums, and that because of his impetuosity innocent people were made to suffer humiliation. It had always been a principle of Anglo-Saxon jurisprudence that it was better that a hundred guilty men escape than that one innocent man should suffer. If it were a matter of authority alone, then "it is not the dream of the wildest ass that roams the South with a white skin on, not to acknowledge that the federal authority is supreme in every corner of the country."

Before January 1903 had ended it was apparent that President Roosevelt had enough of the Indianola row, and Senator Crumpacker, often called "Stumpsucker," recommended that the post office at that place be reopened with a new postmaster in charge.

Before this was done Roosevelt touched off a third explosion by appointing Dr. William D. Crum collector of the Port of Charleston. Dr. Crum, a respectable Negro, enjoyed the esteem of the citizens of Charleston. He was nevertheless a Negro, and any attempt on the part of Roosevelt to put him in office was considered a slap at the white South. Actually, in the years following, the Crum appointment was not to be so much an affair of racial antagonism as it was a tug of war between the President and Senator Ben Tillman. Every time the United States Senate met, from 1903 to 1909, the Negro issue was raised, and the Crum appointment was discussed in that body. In the South the newspapers kept the issue alive. Editors not only fired their own bolts, but also published Ben Tillman's speeches.

Sidney Lewis summed up the attitude of a vast number of his fellow editors when he criticized the citizens of Charleston for overdoing their entertainment of Roosevelt at the Exposition in February 1902. Officials of the Exposition were accused of being Lazaruses snatching crumbs from the rich man's table. As for Roosevelt personally, Lewis said that he "has studiously avoided meriting the respect of the white people of the South. A pretender in war and a marplot in peace, he has never sought anything higher than the feathering of his own ambitious nest, whether commending the gallantry and patriotism of Confederates, in the South, or denouncing them as anarchists in the North. He is not the man to be honored in our section, or even to be looked to for the slightest consideration of justice and fair play." It was said that despite Roosevelt's display of good intentions and feelings at the Charleston Exposition he actually would not have exchanged a half-dozen Negro delegates to the next Republican convention for the respect and good will of every white man and woman in the South.

Roosevelt was to become the butt of an endless stream of stories. The editor of the Hattiesburg (Mississippi) *Progress* said the President was addicted to wearing patched pants, though for that matter some of the smartest men of the country, including editors, wore patched pants. Immediately a central Mississippi journal took exception, saying the editors "may wear patched pants, but won't appreciate being compared with Roosevelt." A more personal story grew out of an incident involving Roosevelt in Ohio. When the presidential car was on its way to the Louisiana Purchase Exposition in St. Louis, the train stopped in a small town for a few moments, and just as it moved out of the station a Buckeye Democrat threw on to the rear platform a young coon. Southern editors remarked that now the President could have a "coon" of his own at every meal. "However, it has not been announced that the President has dined with his 'coon.' Perhaps he prefers a more Book(er) ish one—his pet being unlettered and his 'race' being deprived of a vote."

Congressman James M. Griggs of Georgia was offered a fine bird dog by his friend Joe Beverly. Griggs knew of the dog's splendid reputation and was much pleased to accept him. When he asked what the dog's name was, Beverly said, "Teddy Roosevelt."

"What!" exclaimed Congressman Griggs. "That dog named Teddy? Joe, old man, I like you and I like the dog, but I don't want that animal if his name is Teddy."

"But," said Beverly, "you will like the dog immensely. He is a fine dog."

"Yes, I have seen him work in the field. But what in the name of common sense makes you call him Teddy?"

"Because," said Mr. Beverly, "he follows every Negro that passes the house or that beckons at him."

The same kind of heartless story was told of the President's hunting trip to the Mississippi Delta as the guest of the president of the Illinois Central Railroad. This trip was widely publicized by the daily press, and the weeklies had echoed the news for several weeks.

Luck was against Teddy, and, in the language of a Mississippi editor, he killed "nary a bear." Later, the papers reported, on the basis of an alleged White House leak, that he had actually seen a bear and was close enough to shoot it, but when he discovered that it was coon-colored he could not bring himself to shoot it.

These stories prepared the South for the campaign of 1904. When the Republican convention met, the average Southerner regarded Roosevelt as the epitome of Yankee evil, a tyrant who would force racial equality upon every white person south of the Potomac. Many editors declared him the greatest enemy the Negro ever had, and some even went so far as to say that by his social activities and official appointments he had encouraged the lynching of many Negroes who might otherwise have escaped the rope. Never was an idea more firmly planted in the Southern mind than that the Republican Party was out to destroy Southern traditions. All other issues of a partisan nature were subordinated to this disturbed point of view. It was of little importance to the Southern papers that Roosevelt had started a move to curb James J. Hill, E. H. Harriman and J. P. Morgan, or that Congress had passed the Elkins Act, or that Mark Hanna and his big-business friends were almost as much disturbed about Roosevelt as were the Southerners.

Editors kept up a doleful whining. Its general tone was that they might as well prepare for "a few more niggers to office up North, and a few more to Southern post offices." Preparing for the political orgy of 1904, Bill Arp examined the "Great Bear Hunter" phrenologically. Roosevelt, he declared, was both a fool and a knave. Actually he was not responsible because as a doctor said, "his occiput goes straight up from the medulla oblongata and meets the sinciput at right angles and leaves no room for moral attributes." A perpendicular back head, he added, indicated "a fighting, bear-killing, athletic and foolhardy man." He said on inspecting the sinciput or forehead, that the nose and cheek bones generally rested "on an enormous jawbone, or, as you might say, the jawbone of an ass." In Samson's day he would have rejoiced to be the Biblical giant's armor bearer. In short, said Arp, "the back of the cerebellum and medulla oblongata and occiput has made Teddy crazy about bears and Negroes and other black and woolly things."

As early as February 1904 an Alabama weekly regretted that Mark Hanna was ill and could not oppose the nomination of Roosevelt.

When Roosevelt was nominated, Southern editors leveled their heaviest editorial guns on him. "A nigger lover" was seeking reelection on the Republican ticket, and more than ever Southerners wished to see the Republican nominee defeated. Scores of editorial columns listed the sins of the "Terrible Teddy." Some called him a twentieth-century Falstaff bent on destroying the nation, while others looked on him as a radical Republican preparing again to seize the South for another siege of Reconstruction debauchery.

Perhaps no more effective charge could have been brought against Roosevelt in the South than the fraternization of the two races at Chicago. It was said that a young white girl and a grinning Negro boy, named Corbin, were placed on the front stage to wave flags. They were there ostensibly to symbolize the President's sense of racial equality. Whispers said the servant problem had grown worse because of Roosevelt. Negroes would not work so long as they were aided by the President and the United States Government. They would not work during the summer, said a southern Tennessean, and the taxpayer was getting tired of supporting them. Negroes were leaving the farms and moving to town because of Roosevelt, and once they had left the country they ceased to be decent.

Really nobody blamed Teddy for loving Negroes. People thought he owed them a debt of lasting gratitude. In the important charge up San Juan Hill a Negro regiment, it was said, had saved the Rough Riders. If the 9th Regiment had not been there Roosevelt's career would have ended immediately, and the Rough Riders would have been ingloriously mustered out of the army.

Not only had the Rough Riders been saved by Negroes of the 9th Regiment, but Teddy had acquitted himself badly. He had showed the yellow feather when he signed the Santiago "round robin" to the Secretary of War, in which all the officers, except "Fighting Joe" Wheeler, threatened to desert the field of battle because of yellow fever if they were not recalled. Roosevelt had proved in Cuba that he was "a brave man with his mouth, but, otherwise, a regular Falstaff."

At times the President must have doubted either that his literary career was a political asset or that Southern editors were willing to read his books with proper objectivity. His *Life of Thomas Hart Benton* and *The Winning of the West* were combed meticulously for political dynamite. He was accused by Senator Furnifold Simmons of North Carolina of proving on "page 10" of his *Ranch Life* that he loved rough people. He did not consider Southern small farmers as good as cowboys. Here, said the indignant Carolina Senator, Southerners were compared with cowboys, "the toughest, roughest element in American life, an outcast class, who hold law, society and God in equal contempt." Roosevelt had never written or spoken a sincere word about the South. Except for George Washington he had belittled every Southern president. In his *Life of Thomas Hart Benton* he had found fault with all of them.

Weekly from May to November 1904 editorial columns fairly sizzled with paragraphs against Roosevelt. Every sort of defamation was published. He was called a lunatic, a dictator, a "nigger lover," a fool, a knave, an imposter, a weak character and everything else that editors thought would not be too strong for their subscribers. But fight as they could, the Southern editors had to stand by and see the rest of the nation outvote the South. On the eve of the election Sidney Lewis said that four more years of Roosevelt would make reform through the ballot box an impossibility. He was determined to make life a burden for the Southern white man.

On November 8, 1904, a majority of the country's voters chose to leave the shadow of Roosevelt across the South. Again the man with the abnormal medulla oblongata and the misshapen sinciput which rested on the jawbone of an ass was in the White House. Sidney Lewis wailed loudly in the Sparta *Ishmaelite* that within four more years the country would become a monarchy. The old man said bitterly that his paper would have "supported a reputable Negro rather than Roosevelt a good Negro is better than a white renegade."

That these bitter little paragraphs sandwiched in between advertisements of consumption cures, now buried in the yellowing files of Southern country papers, embittered Roosevelt was more than once made evident to the public. When he lunched with Booker T. Washington it was said that Roosevelt sat back and grinned at the furor which he caused. In 1903 he was roaring mad because ruffians threatened Effie Cox at Indianola, but in 1905 his attitude was again conciliatory. He knew the art of stroking the Southern fur in the right direction. Speaking at a prearranged affair in February of that year he referred in generous terms to the gallantry of the Confederate soldiers who had followed Lee into battle. Each side, he said, had fought bravely and with sincerity of conviction. The Chatham *Rec-*

ord was "pleased to note that the scales have fallen from the eyes of the President, and that he no longer compared Confederate soldiers with anarchists."

After his inauguration on March 4 most of the papers were resigned to four more years of Roosevelt and turned their attention elsewhere. But there were always the determined beagles of the Southern journalistic pack who, once getting the scent of a Republican, kept up a loud trail barking even though the quarry had left the field. It was said that Teddy was in a big hurry to take the oath of office and get back to the White House, but the dispatches from Washington failed to say whether or not he wished to get back to lunch with Booker T.

One further story drifted down to the local papers, and then the Southern rural editors were practically through feuding with the President. A dispatch appeared saying that a proposal of marriage to Alice Roosevelt from a soldier held in the Governor's Island Prison caused some excitement. By special order he was removed from that place to another which was believed more secure. The editor of the Okalona (Mississippi) *Messenger* observed that it was hard to see "why he wants to break into that family. He must be crazy."

Again in office, Roosevelt apparently made some earnest efforts to woo the South in the manner of the first days of his administration. He not only talked piously about the boys in gray, but also showed an interest in the cotton trade. After an extended trip through the South, where he was given cordial receptions in Kentucky, Tennessee, Texas, Georgia and North Carolina, he came away feeling more kindly toward the region. Along the route he talked of the bravery of Southern soldiers, and old Confederates hobbled out by the hundreds to raise the rebel yell wherever his train stopped. In Mississippi, editors actually pretended to be embarrassed because no town in the state had invited Roosevelt to speak. Even if he was a Republican he was President of all the United States. Fortunately for Roosevelt at least, his journey was truly a love feast, and he disappointed some of the Southern editors mightily by not making some sensational appointments of Negroes to office. Frankly, both Roosevelt and the South had matured somewhat, and the *rapprochement* was fruitful of some good to both sides.

Next to his speaking favorably of the valor of Confederate soldiers, the cotton trade offered Teddy Roosevelt the most direct approach to Southern affections. Beginning in April 1905, the President talked of plans to extend it to all parts of the world. He assured Southern Senators and Congressmen that he hoped to develop a market for twenty to thirty million bales. Editors jubilantly gave this news to their readers. One so far forgot the past as to say, "If the President succeeds in carrying out his plans, he will prove himself to be the best friend the South ever had."

There was strong evidence that the Cotton Growers and Southern Cotton Association, meeting in Birmingham, felt that Teddy was a stanch friend. On his visit to that city in October 1905 he was received with a great show of esteem. A lock of cotton was attached to the lapel of his coat with a costly diamond pin given in appreciation of his Atlanta speech during which he had talked of reaching the rich Oriental market. It was pleasant to hear him say that with proper care for cotton culture the South would be greatly enriched. Interest in cotton and its returns tended to alleviate the old race hatreds which had made the name of Roosevelt anathema.

With profound understanding of his section, one editor observed, "A long step forward has been made when the cotton farmers of the South meet to do honor to a Republican President."

Chapter 19

And Still the Presses Roll

AFTER the Theodore Roosevelt-Booker T. Washington storm had ceased blowing, Southern editors settled down to face the more realistic aspects of the twentieth century. In many respects the South was a changing land. Boll weevils threatened ruin for the one-crop system, and diversification, for which editors pleaded so long, was being forced by Nature. In many sections industrialization was making considerable headway. Likewise the public-school movement was showing real progress, especially after the vigorous campaigning of the first decade, 1900-1910. Editors crusaded not merely for schools where there were none, but also for improvement of existing schools by consolidation. Before consolidation was accomplished the subject of compulsory attendance was receiving much attention in the press.

Certainly no twentieth century improvement was more far-reaching than that effected by the organization of state highway departments and the building of good roads. Hard surfaced highways were constructed not only from courthouse to courthouse, but to all sections of the South. Newspapers were forceful in helping to bring about this modernization, but perhaps no more so than the new machine appearing in their advertising columns. The automobile was a revolutionary instrument in the South. After 1915 it became common enough to be no longer a mechanical curiosity.

The automobile soon crowded the standard cuts advertising wagons and carriages off the pages of the country papers. The sedan claimed space formerly given the surrey, the runabout supplanted the phaeton and the truck replaced the wagon. Gasoline station advertisements retired the famous blacksmith cuts to dusty cases to lie untouched, and garages crowded into livery stables.

Southerners traveled faster, spent more money and perhaps sinned more than ever before. Old editors were brought up with a start.

They were shocked by the reckless manner in which the younger generation was headed for hell. Mobility now became a new target for editorial attack. Even lackadaisical jokesmiths who ground out witless fillers that passed for humor had to accept the changing times. They produced endless "horseless carriage" stories which were about as wearisome as repairing clincher-rim tires beside muddy country roads. Ancient arguments against immoral circuses and dancing seemed tepid in this modern day. Sin had become more mobile than ever and the automobile was a bigger threat to life on the small-town streets than holes in sidewalks, runaway horses, and stray livestock had been at their worst. Careless drivers of preceding decades, who had left children to hold their horses or dashed off on errands leaving unhitched teams, now committed manslaughter with greater efficiency at the wheels of automobiles. They were quicker with the throttle than the brake pedal, and great was their execution.

Where leisurely merchants, editors and villagers once whiled away lazy hours playing checkers in the shade of trees on the streets they were now crowded into buildings, or they were dashing around in too big a hurry for so placid a pastime. For ages dirt roads and streets provoked varying degrees of editorial wrath and admonition, but the automobile stirred village dust beds and quagmires with such thoroughness that crusades for paving succeeded.

By 1910 every railroad of consequence was built. The last gloating editor with note pad in hand had gone to the depot to greet the arrival of the first train. Long ago he had raced back to his office to tell his readers of the world-shaking events which had occurred in their midst. Already long rate wars had been fought, state legislators had established railway commissions and the press sometimes thought railroads had ceased to serve the local community's best interests.

After the turn of the century lumber companies expanded their operations in the heavily forested hardwood and pine belts. Virgin Southern timber stands were being systematically destroyed, and local population patterns were rudely altered by internal migration. Occasionally an influx of non-Southern immigrants destroyed the old provincialism. Sleepy cotton and tobacco towns suddenly came alive as rowdy lumbering centers. The slow pace of agricultural towns, synchronized with the seasonal changes of their surrounding countryside, gave place to perpetual cash "settling-up" pay days. Towns assumed the raw, boisterous manners of the happy-go-lucky lumberman, and many communities came more to resemble the boom mining towns of the West than cotton villages of the South. Cash was handed out with a more lavish hand than ever before in Southern history. With free money came the evils of boom times. Gambling, drinking and loose women led to fighting and murdering. A new strain was placed on the antiquated system of law enforcement. Even the traditional evils of gunplay and lynching took on the more gaudy aspects of frontier industrialism.

But the most pronounced change of all took place along the Southern main street after 1915. The old-time general merchant, who had been reluctant to advertise in the country paper and who supposed that everybody knew what he had in stock, waked up to find stifling modern competition. Merchants who had supplied an agricultural trade on prevailing credit terms never bothered too much about advertising either their stock or prices. Goods were offered customers somewhat on the basis of their individual reputations as credit risks. Merchandise was secretly marked, and seldom if ever were prices publicized. Immediately after the First World War the chain stores came on the scene with their brightly painted fronts and catchy advertisements telling of both their goods and their prices. In the neighborhood of Memphis the ubiquitous Clarence Saunders increased store advertising considerably with his new merchandising ventures, the Jitney Jungle and the Piggly Wiggly chain stores.

Imaginative businessmen appreciate the value of advertising, and they saw to it that every issue of the local paper carried itemized or display advertisements of their goods. This modernization forced the old general merchant either to close his doors or to adopt better business methods. Where once W. L. Douglas advertised both his Clevelandesque face and his cheap shoes with such consistency, there were now many local columns telling of the shoes and clothes kept in stock by local merchants. Milliners began to display their seasonal wares to the trading public. Hardware merchants ceased using ghostly illustrations of coffins to let the public know they were in business and made known the more alluring fact that they were in the general hardware business. Even the conservative apothecary's shop crept out from behind its dingy front and ornate vials of colored water to become a bright-windowed drugstore. Soda fountains became community loafing centers, and even editors were not averse to drinking

Atlanta's famous carbonated beverage while picking up publishable community gossip or planning druggists' advertisements which included everything from Doan's Kidney Pills to banana splits.

But nowhere in the twentieth-century South was change more pronounced than in the country print shop itself. Outmoded Franklin and Washington presses were thrown on junk piles or moved aside for drawing proofs. Installed in their places were country Campbells, Babcock, American Type Founders, and Cincinnati drum or cylinder presses. Some of these were bought as early as the 1870's and 1880's and were turned by faithful Negro handymen, water wheels or steam engines. In time gasoline engines supplanted these, and later electric motors replaced the noisy and smoky gas engines. Some modern shops, with considerable circulation and job business, installed the more efficient modern presses which feed paper stock from a continuous roll, print and cut it, and deposit assembled and folded papers ready to be labeled and mailed.

The muscular Negroes who once ground out weekly editions of papers by hand now grew soft feeding the new power presses and running errands. The most revolutionary machine in the country plant was Mergenthaler's mechanical type setter. This innovation came into general use in the South in the decade from 1910 to 1920. It required skill, but a trained operator could set a large amount of type in a day's time, and it made a big difference in the weekly paper's general appearance. Tramp printers, who were most always welcomed in country shops, were now either given temporary jobs making up forms or running the presses. More often they were handed small sums of money to enable them to move along to the next job. Battered cases of hand type were either sold to collectors and scrap metal dealers or were reserved for setting special advertisements and job orders.

Publishers had to give more attention to advertising for the new machines and the skilled personnel to run them called for a greater capital outlay. The machines themselves cost far more than hand-set equipment in both initial outlay and upkeep. This new age of mechanization and of merchandising was having a double effect upon the country paper. Publishers received more money than ever before in the history of Southern publishing, and papers grew from two pages of "home-set" matter to six, eight and sometimes twelve pages. The job shop became an important adjunct to the publishing business, and editors ceased bartering subscriptions for cordwood and country products. Delinquent subscribers were still loose in the land, but they were promptly dropped to make places for new patronage. Public schools taught more people to read, and rural free delivery greatly facilitated distribution of papers. Never before did publishing a weekly paper hold such bright business prospects.

But even in the face of so much improvement there is serious doubt that twentieth-century editors have generally maintained the strict editorial standards of their nineteenth-century forebears. Perhaps most earlier editors had a professional feeling for their calling which sprang from experience and a sense of great responsibility. Editing a paper was a proud profession which demanded both ideas and courage. Superior journalism, measured by this older standard, contained elements of rugged frontier individualism well tinctured with a contemporary rough-and-tumble rowdyism where courage was necessary.

So long as more capable editors had leisure time in which to read and give serious thought to local, state and national affairs their editorial pages reflected a genuine intellectual penetration. Such men as James Cranston Williams, who for thirty years edited the famous old Greensboro (Georgia) *Herald-Journal,* William C. Hight, for fifty years editor of the Winston County (Mississippi) *Journal,* Dan and A. A. Bowmar of the Woodford (Kentucky) *Sun,* Sidney Lewis of the Sparta (Georgia) *Ishmaelite,* Benny C. Knapp of the Fayette (Mississippi) *Chronicle,* W. P. and Ed Walton of the Stanford (Kentucky) *Interior Journal,* and Lewis Grist of the Yorkville (South Carolina) *Enquirer* were editors of courageous opinion. They freely criticized both social and political leaders in their states when they believed they worked against public welfare. Right or wrong, editors of this type were unshakable in their individualism. With scores of others, they refused to let a rising tide of twentieth-century commercialism sweep them from the course of valid journalism in the public interest. This, however, was not true in many instances where newspapers were published as adjuncts to commercial shops. Many pages were prostituted to advertising, and even the sacred editorial column space was for sale for advertising purposes if it could be made to bear revenue. News columns suffered in quality. Often local news reports were cast aside. Every issue showed the lack of that pride in the general tone of the paper which made so many country journals and their editors important to Southern communities.

Many present-day editorial shortcomings are due to papers' falling into poor hands. Editors often grew old without training successors. Sometimes they were forced to sell their papers to less capable publishers in order to secure money to support them in their retirement. Sons have assumed editorships with varying degrees of success. Often editors died unexpectedly and left widows and inexperienced children to struggle on with only the assistance of faithful printers. Sometimes newspapers were either given or sold to employees, who knew how to print a weekly but who knew little about editing one. Within the last thirty years chain publishing has entered the field of country journalism with its impersonal and cold canned news and editorials. Occasionally business interests and politicians have bought country papers to control public sounding boards for their particular points of view and to prevent damaging publicity against them. On occasions investors have bought papers in the same manner as they might acquire real estate and have operated them as private property rather than as informed public organs of healthy local opinion.

Currently there is internal evidence that many editorial pages have been sacrified to commercialism. Some local editors perhaps lack either the ability or the courage to take unpopular stands on public problems. So long as no editorials appear in a paper, subscribers do not expect editors to discuss community problems. So long as a paper is free to ignore controversial issues neither patron nor advertiser can ask embarrassing questions. Doubtless another reason for weakness on the editorial page is that many editors spend so much time bending over the composing table arranging advertising matter that they cannot sit in their jumbled offices, feet on table, reading widely in books, daily papers and weekly exchanges to formulate colorful opinions about contemporary situations.

State press associations have existed since 1870. At first these organizations were primarily concerned with bringing editors together for three or four days of inspirational speaking and socializing. Sometimes the earlier press meetings consisted of excursions to historic spots or to the perennial expositions. Editors remembered to aid their substitutes and wrote letters home reviewing their travels, and when they returned they described the press meetings as larks in which little serious business was transacted.

The early associations held to a minimum the rules by which this individualistic profession lived. After 1890, however, more attention was given to advertising policies and rules of ethics. The practice of accepting paper, ink, proof presses and other supplies from medicine companies and advertising agents as payment for advertising was condemned. Something approaching classified subscription and advertising rates were adopted. A movement was begun to buy only news matter from ready-print services. In time a responsible system of accounting was instituted whereby the truth of circulation could be determined, and most papers based their advertising rates on guaranteed circulation figures.

Free space was not given away with so lavish a hand, and obituaries, memorial notices, cards of thanks and other personal matters were charged for at modest advertising rates. News was seldom so scarce in the eventful twentieth century that editors needed such gratuitous material to fill their pages. In fact the bigger problem was that of selecting the best of the available material to publish. Despite its plentifulness, news in the more modern period was more difficult to collect and possibly required more imagination to prepare it for publication.

With the passage of time modern weekly newspaper personnel underwent some pronounced changes. Where the old editors were men of limited formal training, though often graduates of the school of hard knocks, younger editors have come from high school and college classrooms. Many of them have even received formal training in the science of journalism. Their approach to their readers, of necessity, has differed from the more direct method of an earlier day. Some younger editors have been willing to fly in the face of modern times and adopt the more informal earlier patterns of country journalism by making their papers reflect a purely rural condition of society. Others have looked cityward to the practices of metropolitan editors and have tried desperately to make vapid city papers out of country weeklies.

Occasionally publishers have become too sophisticated to continue using many of the old interest-catching features which were so much a part of the earlier papers' contents. Their sophistication has not become so thick, however, that it cannot be pierced with a genuine snake story, an account of a fight or many of the other sensations which have made capital features for three quarters of a century. But the frontier flavor is missing which gave so much zest to news before the era of good roads. Editors no longer request people to come South to help exploit wide stretches of land, and no longer do the activities of Southern people reflect the rawness of a country filling up with people. Most of the editors still want industry to move South, but possibly it is wanted primarily to help develop both capital income and an urban society.

Increasingly the daily paper has influenced the weekly existence. Since 1900, the local weeklies have reflected the steady encroachment of the city paper on their territories. As feature services expanded their coverage they began to supply more and more special material to country papers which took weeklies beyond their immediate communities. Sporadic reports written by Congressmen on affairs in Washington were supplanted by more objective materials.

In recent years more news syndicates have successfully invaded the rural market. Daily columnists boil their materials down to comprise a weekly summary of national affairs. Professional gossipers, popular psychologists, advisers to the lovelorn, and arbiters of etiquette have all discovered this rather profitable outlet for their wares. Cartoonists like the late Memphis artist, J. P. Alley, have sold their drawings to a widely dispersed market. Alley's richly native Hambone was at one time the South's leading philosophical figure. From Kentucky, George Bingham's "Dog Hill Paragraphs" poked fun at the crossroads reporters and their neighborhoods in an inoffensive vein of humor. Bingham, himself a country journalist, portrayed the country reporter in a whimsical manner which contained a generous amount of truth. In some instances state officials like Walker Wood of Mississippi have supplied local papers with weekly columns filled with news from state capitals, or with original or exchange bits gathered from entire states. Local town gossip columnists have come to compete with crossroads scribes for space. They gossip in the manner of the famous syndicate writers. Sometimes they have turned counties upside down by spilling the social beans, but most of the time they have gathered popular local folk stories and given them wider coverage in print.

Earlier editors felt that world and national news coverage lay within the province of the metropolitan press, and they refrained from printing it. They conceived their task to be that of garnering materials of interest from their own localities, and they remained steadfastly in this field. On the other hand the daily made an effort to stay out of the weekly's field by giving a broader and more impersonal coverage to its stories and editorials. On the surface, at least, most of the slanted material carried by the dailies appeared in their editorial or special columns.

Daily papers became serious competitors once decent roads were built and rural free delivery routes were established. When this situation developed there had to be a more clearly defined division of fields of interest between the two types of papers for the weekly to survive.

Though the city journal enlarged its patronage, the fact remained that large segments of the Southern population still had access to news only through the weekly paper. It was effective for publicizing local legal matters, giving the common man the satisfaction of seeing accounts of his social affairs in print and of supplying the county with a bulletin of events and public affairs. There was no way for a daily to compete in this field, and for this reason the two types of paper learned to exist together with fair success.

Although the country paper was not primarily concerned with the larger field of current news coverage, events of the twentieth century forced it to revise its general perspective. On April 14, 1912, the luxury liner *Titanic* collided with an iceburg in the North Atlantic and went down, taking with it 1,600 of its 2,300 passengers. This was a story specially adapted for the ready-print and boiler-plate services. It had splendid news elements: catastrophe, human suffering, bravery, supreme sacrifice and a thrilling rescue. For several weeks the country papers pieced out the details of this tragedy. Editorial columns sympathized with the bereaved families and praised individual acts of bravery, but they could not refrain from some criticism for those who were pleasure-bent. To many editors it appeared sinful for so many people to be idle and drifting around in the Atlantic Ocean with what appeared to be no worth-while motive or reason.

The sinking of the *Titanic* was only a prelude to greater disasters immediately ahead. Occasionally there appeared in country papers some hint of disturbed world conditions. There were brief stories of international incidents which seemed to be leading to a showdown among the larger powers. However, the common man, reading no other paper than the one published at his county seat, had little understanding of the nation's foreign policy. He lived in an almost perfect state of isolation, and events leading to the outbreak of the

World War in 1914 were as far removed from him as the Russo-Japanese War had been. Before 1914 local editors had been unwilling to reach so far afield for news. Between 1914 and 1918 the interest of the local paper in foreign affairs increased. Where traditionally most editors had been completely absorbed with local politics, havoc of the boll weevil and country correspondence, they now became concerned with European affairs. As the United States moved closer to war, news columns showed an awareness that the world of communications was suddenly growing smaller.

In 1916 the Presidential campaign brought the war much closer home. The subject of politics and the struggle abroad were so intertwined that local editors were forced to treat both as primary news. During his first four years in office Woodrow Wilson became something more than standard-bearer for the Democratic Party; he was an apostle of peace, and this suddenly became a subject of much editorial commendation. Later when the United States declared war against Germany, and the draft began taking boys into training camps, columns were crowded with accounts of their activities.

Once the American Army was in France, many Southern communities were stirred out of the ruts of provincialism for the first time in their history, and they eagerly read the international news. Two aspects of war held public interest: the gory propaganda atrocity stories of the Huns and the ominous lists of casualties. Still the country paper, despite increasing competition from the dailies, was important in purveying information to small-town and rural subscribers, and likewise in crystallizing their opinion.

Each week during the war an increasing number of copies of local papers were sent to the training camps and, in many instances, overseas. Columns were opened generously to soldiers' letters to the editor describing their army and battlefield experiences. Special Washington and New York columnists contributed analytical materials. In his book *Over the Top,* the Englishman Arthur Guy Empey offered the home folks an intimate and, as was soon proved, wholly fabulous view of the war. This account of battlefield experience was published in many installments. Additional weekly illustrated features described incidents on the sea, in the air and on the battlefield. Considerable "canned" copy describing new arms and tactics was distributed by the War and Navy Departments. Airplanes, tanks, machine guns and heavy artillery pieces were introduced for the first time to country paper readers. For Southerners the First World War soon became far more realistic than were the concepts of fighting gathered from the romantic stories of the Civil War as told by their fathers and grandfathers. In this war, heroes were not made overnight and allowed to return home to bask in short-lived glory like the volunteers who fought in Cuba.

When the war was over in 1918 the Southern country press returned somewhat to its old local news routine. Within twelve years two presidential elections stirred editorial interest to fever heat. The election of 1928 came at a time when the South was in a state of social and political unrest. International uncertainties were reflected in sectional confusion, a manifestation of which was the irresponsible Ku Klux Klan which bore no direct kinship to the original order of the Reconstruction years. Few editors were willing to strike at it; perhaps some of them were Klan members. In Georgia, where the order was most active, James Cranston Williams of the Greensboro *Herald-Journal* courageously fought the organization although only two other weekly editors showed enough independence to support him. Sometimes such social upheavals were overlooked because public opinion of a strong nativistic tinge was too powerful to be attacked by timid editors.

In other ways the "Jazz Age" was revealed in the country press. H. L. Mencken's *American Mercury* made some editors self-conscious while it spurred others to greater efforts to be peculiarly sectional in both editorial style and attitudes. These bucolic Southerners were quoted frequently by metropolitan dailies. Perhaps the most robust of those so honored was William Benjamin Franklin Townsend, of the four-page hand-set Dahlonega (Georgia) *Nugget*. From the "Peaks of Lumpkin" he issued an individualistic journal which was a curiosity everywhere, including his own county. He not only published "all the news fit to print" but unlike the New York *Times,* used a whole lot that should have been ignored. In a sensuous Rabelaisian vein, this mountain editor made bold and, not infrequently, nauseous comments on life in his country town. Libel suits were apparently as natural an accompaniment of publishing his paper as getting ink on his hands. Setting his material by hand and without benefit of script, he printed some of the most fantastic material in the history of American journalism.

In the presidential campaign of 1928, as editor Townsend would have said, the country publishers were "hemmed up in a tight corner." They were Democratic, Protestant and dry. To support Alfred E. Smith was to advocate a principle which most of them opposed; not to support him was to forsake the Democratic Party. The religious issue, though not too openly discussed, was likewise a deterrent factor. For those who wavered, one term of the Hoover administration was enough. Long before 1932 they were back in the Democratic fold pleading for a Democratic victory as vigorously as they had supported Grover Cleveland. Once in office, Franklin D. Roosevelt disturbed the editorial mind as much as did his cousin Teddy. For twelve years the New Deal caused many an editorial heart to falter. Editors enthusiastically approved the earlier measures of the Roosevelt administration, and reams of white space were devoted to the publication of information about its myriad agencies, copy which arrived in the form of matrices to be used in country casting boxes.

News of agricultural legislation and administration alone was almost sufficient to fill every issue of the papers. For the various phases of the New Deal's agricultural program to function smoothly in the South the country paper was a necessity. It served both as a device for conditioning public opinion and as a necessary bulletin board. The Agricultural Adjustment Administration and the numerous other farm agencies changed editorial policies toward publication of farm news. With the first application of the acreage-control principles of the AAA, editors became about as badly befuddled as were the mules used to turn under growing cotton. Henry Wallace quickly became a sinner who wasted the earth's substances in the cotton and tobacco patches, to say nothing of his famous bloodletting at the pigpens.

In this same manner the local paper served the FERA, PWA and WPA. The WPA was among the first of the New Deal agencies to stir editorial wrath. Never in the history of country journalism were editors willing to tolerate trifling, and quickly the WPA appeared to them to be nothing more than organized laziness. Every editor knew a large number of people who for one reason or another were shiftless, and when they appeared on the rolls of relief agencies the editors were unwilling to look beyond questionable personalities to the broader principles of public assistance.

So indignant did many editors become that between elections they were willing to substitute for Roosevelt almost any candidate the

Republican Party would nominate. During the campaigns, however, they appeared apprehensive lest he be defeated. Within a week after each of his last three elections they regretted having to tolerate him for four more years. His famous National Emergency Council's *Report* in 1936, in which the South was branded as the nation's "number one economic problem," set editors off in a tirade of anger. They considered the document a malicious slur at the South. When the President was not touching off journalistic fireworks, Mrs. Roosevelt, Henry Wallace, Harold Ickes and Frances Perkins were stirring the press. Especially was this true when Secretary Perkins made her famous remark about the South's need for shoes.

On February 12, 1948, the Port Gibson (Mississippi) *Reveille* summed up an appreciable segment of editorial opinion by saying, "Thinking people of the South are sick and tired of the New Deal. They do not want a packed Supreme Court. They are tired of the Communists which [sic] have held such sway in Washington these past eighteen years. They are tired of encroachment upon state's rights. They are fed up on government domination of private business. And they feel that the time has come to stop wasting tax money upon ne'er-do-wells and people who never had enough energy or ambition to make a living for themselves and their families."

The weekly attack on the New Deal was interrupted in 1940 by the exigencies of a second world war. By 1939 another international conflict was beginning. Again editors had to emphasize foreign events by steering their subscribers' attention to the world scene. From 1941 until 1945 news columns overflowed with stories of war activities.

The biggest difference between newspaper publication during the two world war periods was the fact that by 1940 most papers had improved equipment and were able to convert their papers into more effective organs of opinion. Where weekly publishers of the first war were limited by lack of mechanical facilities, their modern successors had up-to-date typesetting and printing equipment and with casting boxes they could utilize an astounding amount of illustrative material. The army mail service permitted much more direct communication from soldiers and the papers ran much more material about service personnel. Some papers ran special correspondence columns in which soldiers' letters were published. In addition attempts were made to gather as much news as possible about the personal activities of home boys and girls in the armed service.

Certainly in the recent decades of the twentieth century it was realized that the country newspaper was vital to community life. No accurate device, however, has been discovered to gauge its precise influence. Many methods for mechanically measuring papers and analyzing their various types of materials have been used, but there is no actual way of knowing specifically what effect they have on their readers. Strong editorial personalities have unquestionably shaped opinion. There are innumerable examples where the course of community growth has been directed by vigorous editorial crusading. Without it few Southern communities could so readily have cleaned up their streets, driven the hogs back to their pens, fenced the cows out of the cemeteries, closed public wells, installed waterworks, attracted factories and built roads.

Perhaps the most tangible evidence of the country papers' influence is to be found in the fact that since 1865 a fairly well-defined Southern tradition has prevailed throughout the region. This has resulted largely from an intense cultivation of the sectional idea by the weekly press. Throughout the South attitudes and customs have been standardized or unified. The culture of any state differs from that of the whole region in degree only, and not in its essential characteristics. Widely dispersed exchanges have nurtured this element of sectional kinship and common interest. White men in the Carolinas have never been allowed to forget their kinship with those of the Lower South. So far as local publishers have exerted an influence they have helped keep colloquial figures of speech, folk beliefs and superstitions, religious and political patterns, economic development and public attitudes within a roughly defined framework of Southern tradition. In this area of opinion there was a pronounced cutting across regional lines of economic interest. Without defining the Southern heritage, many editors have whipped their constituencies into a unified pattern of thought by frantic and sometimes quixotic appeals for a defense of their section's way of life. Wherever a threat to the Southern tradition was feared, the weekly paper was usually the medium by which many people first heard of it.

Since 1865 the country press has withstood at least four jarring revolutions in which it was driven out of its intensely conservative provincialism. These were Reconstruction, the Populist campaign and two world wars. But each time it has returned to its customary local pattern. Few or no editorial radicals have been left-wing liberals; rather they have been embittered conservatives who have battled the forces of liberal political and social reform. Between 1886 and 1893 Southern publishers advocated the execution of the Chicago Haymarket prisoners. They were vehemently opposed to third partyism, Populism and every other kindred movement. Many individual editors acquired great reputations because they were unrestrained in opposing enemies of Southern orthodoxy. In their abuse of politicians and the failings of Southern government they practically never suggested any remedy more drastic than the election of a new set of public officials. With rare exception, the country paper's opposition was that of an "out" shouting loudly against the sins of those in office.

In matters of both religion and temperance, the weekly press was a bulwark of reaction. No institutions have received more special concessions from the country paper than the churches. Almost without exception the Southern publisher has followed the thin line between toleration and open controversy with religious groups. He has realized fully the extremely delicate balance which had to be maintained in reporting denominational activities. He has had to use care in publishing news about individual ministers so as not to rouse the jealousy of their fellows. He has had to use the same sort of tact, of course, in dealing with other professions in which competition is keen.

Traditionally the country press has opposed liquor. It is evident, however, that many editors have written dry and drunk wet. The campaign leading to the adoption of the Eighteenth Amendment in 1918 climaxed a long period of temperance agitation. The editors opposed liquor, it appears, not because of its immediate evils but because they believed drinking begets crime. Repeatedly editorials and news stories cited liquor as the basic cause of local disturbances. During prohibition years news of crime was as plentiful as ever. There were stories of raids on illicit stills, of bootlegging and of moral degeneration. The fact that prohibition enforcement was a failure was too clear for even the most ardent dry publisher to ignore. As late as 1948, however, the contention of wet and dry forces in state legislatures still flavors the news and stimulates considerable editorializing.

Following the Second World War country papers again returned to emphasizing local news, although retaining the handouts of the governmental agencies and special business interest. Many contemporary papers show a willingness on the part of their publishers to accept generous amounts of "canned" copy provided by publicity seekers of all sorts and motives. Much of this material is vital. For instance, conservation agencies are able to reach a large audience with their prepared editorials on keeping the South "green." At the same time, however, private interests, sometimes irresponsible private interests, are able to do the same thing. There still remain subscribers who lack sufficient intellectual discrimination to distinguish between editor-written and ready-prepared editorials. Perhaps the saving grace of much of the "slanted" material is that it is dry and unimaginative. A majority of editors send it to the trash pile unused and what is printed may not be much read. A grave danger faces many country papers in their surrender of space to the canned releases of special interests. Some less responsible editors have already allowed the policies of their papers to be kicked about at will by publicity seekers who come bearing seductive gifts of ready-prepared editorials.

On one point many editors agree—the Democratic Party has never properly acknowledged Southern fidelity. The following letter to the Port Gibson (Mississippi) *Reveille,* February 26, 1948, expresses their feeling: "Southern Democrats have reminded us of a Little Red Riding Hood, as she trustingly hastened through the woods to carry her grandmother a basket of tasty food. In her childish, trusting manner, Red Riding Hood had no dream that a wolf would be in her granny's bed—deceiving her in order that he may gobble her up. Trustingly, for generations Southern Democrats have hastened to carry their 'baskets' to the Democratic Party. Now, to their utter dismay, they find the leadership has drastically veered from the path we have been accustomed to travel. We are proud that Mississippi's Governor Wright is the leader of the 'wood cutters' who have come to the aid of 'Little Red Riding Hood.' "

The election year, 1948, offers many perplexities to the Southern editors. In some respects President Harry Truman, in advocating the passage of the Civil Rights bills, has invoked much of the wrath poured out against Theodore Roosevelt and Booker T. Washington. "What a whale of a difference," wrote M. A. Richardson of the Sunflower (Mississippi) *Tocsin.* "Those sneak punches at the solar plexus of Southern traditions by Democratic national leaders are nothing new, but with both Houses GOP, Chairmanships are few and WPA money nil, our local leaders have risen in righteous wrath, issuing dire retaliatory threats. Materialization of the latter is hard to contemplate, but we admire effort and congratulate the instigators."

President Truman's ten-point program, however, did not destroy the country editor's sense of humor. There were other issues to be discussed. Casting around him the editor of the Butler (Georgia) *Herald* has found that another political breakdown has occurred. "Jack Tarver," he wrote, "is quoted as saying that down at Albany, Georgia, the City Commission has repealed a municipal ordinance against 'ogling,' or close scrutiny of the female sex, on the ground that it is no longer any use.' 'Was it ever,' he asks. Ogling began when Eve picked a fig leaf and came forth in the first new look. Ogling will continue as long as the male of the species has vision and the female has a make-up kit!"

For the Southern editors times have indeed changed in the last eighty years. In 1869, the editor of the Greensboro *Herald* cringed at the thought that Georgia girls would ride in a horse show. His young successor Carey Williams has come a long way in his attitude toward women. In the modern South, Carey says, "The old time girl that said, 'You'll have to ask father,' now chirps, 'Step on the gas, dear, dad's gaining ground on us!' "

BIBLIOGRAPHY

(A) Newspapers

Abbeville Medium, Abbeville, South Carolina, 1876-1900
Abbeville Messenger, Abbeville, South Carolina, 1884-1885
Abbeville Press and Banner, Abbeville, South Carolina, 1869-1948
Aberdeen Examiner, Aberdeen, Mississippi, 1878-1915
Ackerman Record, Ackerman, Mississippi, 1900-1901
Allardt Gazette, Allardt, Tennessee, 1891-1892
Advertiser, Laurens, South Carolina, 1889
Alexander City Outlook, Alexander City, Alabama, 1901-1905
American Union, West Bowerville, Georgia, 1885-1886
Americus Semi-Weekly Courier, Americus, Georgia, 1870
Americus Tri-Weekly Republican, Americus, Georgia, 1870-1871
Americus Weekly Sumter Republican, Americus, Georgia, 1870-1871
Athens Post, Athens, Tennessee, 1874
Bardstown Gazette, Bardstown, Kentucky, 1908
Bardstown Observer, Bardstown, Kentucky, 1900
Bardstown Record, Bardstown, Kentucky, 1879-1902
Barnwell Sentinel, St. Matthews, South Carolina, 1866-1868, 1930
Bennettsville Journal, Bennettsville, South Carolina, 1869
Bingtown Bugle, Jasper, Alabama, 1901
Bolivar Bulletin, Bolivar, Tennessee, 1867
Butler Courier, Butler, Alabama, 1882
Calhoun Times, Calhoun, Georgia, 1873-1889
Camden Weekly Journal, Camden, South Carolina, 1865-1866
Camp Hill News, Camp Hill, Alabama, 1907-1910
Canebrake Herald, Selma, Alabama, 1888-1920
Carbon Hill Weekly, Carbon Hill, Alabama, 1908
Carolina Review, Lancaster, South Carolina, 1878-1879
Carolina Watchman, Salisbury, North Carolina, 1860-1890
Cartersville American, Cartersville, Georgia, 1895
Cartersville Courant, Cartersville, Georgia, 1885
Central Record, Lancaster, Kentucky, 1888-1948
Chatham Record, Pittsboro, North Carolina, 1878-1915
Cherokee Georgian, Rome, Georgia, 1866
Chester Reporter, Chester, South Carolina, 1869-1887
Choctaw Herald, Butler, Alabama, 1885-1898

Choctaw Plaindealer, Ackerman, Mississippi, 1887-1940
Clarendon Press, Manning, South Carolina, 1868-1878
Clarksville Tobacco Leaf, Clarksville, Tennessee, 1875-1876
Clinton Weekly, Clinton, South Carolina, 1889
Critic, Dickson, Tennessee, 1893
Dadeville Spot Cash, Dadeville, Alabama, 1898-1915
Dallas Herald, Dallas, Georgia, 1892-1896
Dayton Gazette, Dayton, Tennessee, 1885
Dayton Weekly Leader, Dayton, Tennessee, 1887
Dickson County Independent, Charlotte, Tennessee, 1893
Dickson County Press, Charlotte, Tennessee, 1882-1892
Dickson County Press, Charlotte, Tennessee, 1899
Double Springs New Era, Double Springs, Alabama, 1900-1906
East Tennesseean, Kingston, Tennessee, 1869-1872
Edgefield Advertiser, Edgefield, South Carolina, 1869-1879, 1936
Edgefield Chronicle, Edgefield, South Carolina, 1900-1908
Elberton Gazette, Elberton, Georgia, 1872-1873
Elberton Gazette (News and New South), Elberton, Georgia, 1872-1882
Enterprise, Dresden, Tennessee, 1883
Eufaula Times and News, Eufaula, Alabama, 1880-1915
Examiner, Gallatin, Tennessee, 1872
Fairfield News and Herald, Winnsboro, South Carolina, 1876-1948
Farmville Chronicle, Farmville, Virginia, 1905
Fayette Chronicle, Fayette, Mississippi, 1880-1948
Fayetteville Eagle, Fayetteville, North Carolina, 1868-1873
Fayetteville Observer, Fayetteville, North Carolina, 1883-1890
Forest Weekly Register, Forest, Mississippi, 1868-1880
Franklin County Register, Carnesville, Georgia, 1878
Gibson Enterprise and *(Enterprise-Recorder),* Gibson, Tennessee, 1884-1892
Georgetown Times, Georgetown, Kentucky, 1865-1948
Green River Republican, Morgantown, Kentucky, 1888-1940
Greensboro Herald (Herald-Journal), Greensboro, Georgia, 1869-1947
Haleyville Enterprise, Haleyville, Alabama, 1903
Hamilton Journal, Hamilton, Georgia, 1872-1892
Hamilton Visitor, Hamilton, Georgia, 1873-1875
Herald and Georgian, Sandersville, Georgia, 1874
Hickman Pioneer, Centreville, Mississippi, 1878-1880
Hillsborough Gazette, Hillsborough, North Carolina, 1874
Horry News, Conway, South Carolina, 1869
Hortonsville Sentinel, Hortonsville, Tennessee, 1871
Houston Appeal, Pineapple, Alabama, 1884-1885

Houston County News, Erin, Tennessee, 1887-1888
Huntingdon Courier, Huntingdon, Tennessee, 1870
Huntsville Advocate, Huntsville, Alabama, 1879-1882
Independent, Huntsville, Alabama, 1879-1882
Indianola Enterprise, Indianola, Mississippi, 1900-1906
Jackson County News, Gainesboro, Tennessee, 1873
Jackson Hustler, Jackson, Kentucky, 1891
Jackson Sun, Jackson, Tennessee, 1876-1878
Jefferson Buzzsaw, Fayette, Mississippi, 1899
Jessamine Journal, Nicholasville, Kentucky, 1872-1948
Jimplicute, Springplace, Georgia, 1880-1899
Johnson City Enterprise, Johnson City, Tennessee, 1883
Journal-Review, Aiken, South Carolina, 1880-1915
Kentucky Standard, Bardstown, Kentucky, 1900-1948
Keowee Courier, Wallhalla, South Carolina, 1881-1900
Laurel Chronicle, Laurel, Mississippi, 1900-1912
Lebanon Register, Lebanon, Tennessee, 1890
Leitchfield Courier, Leitchfield, Kentucky, 1908-1909
Leitchfield Gazette, Leitchfield, Kentucky, 1900-1925
Lenoir Topic, Lenoir, North Carolina, 1875-1915
Linden Times, Linden, Tennessee, 1880
Linden Times, Linden, Alabama, 1879-1904
Livingston Journal, Livingston, Alabama, 1865-1893
Macon Beacon, Macon, Mississippi, 1875, 1881-1940
Marengo Democrat, Demopolis, Alabama, 1901-1904
Marengo News-Democrat, Demopolis, Alabama, 1873-1897
Marengo News-Journal, Demopolis, Alabama, 1873-1879
Marietta Journal, Marietta, Georgia, 1881-1883
Marion Standard, Marion, Alabama, 1880-1887
Marshall Gazette, Lewisburg, Tennessee, 1871
Maryville Republican, Maryville, Tennessee, 1861
Maury Courier, Mount Pleasant, Tennessee, 1894
McCormick Messenger, McCormick, South Carolina, 1930
McDuffie Weekly Journal, Thomson, Georgia, 1877-1882
McMinnville New Era, McMinnville, Tennessee, 1869-1900
Middlesborough News, Middlesboro, Kentucky, 1902
Mississippi Bulletin, Louisville, Mississippi, 1871
Mississippi Sun, Macon, Mississippi, 1876-1892
Negro Leader, Uniontown, Alabama, 1909-1915
Nelson Enterprise, Bardstown, Kentucky, 1909-1910
Nelson News, Bardstown, Kentucky, 1915-1917
New Era, Double Springs, Alabama, 1900-1906

Herald and News, Newberry, South Carolina, 1889-1936
News-Democrat, Russellville, Kentucky, 1906-1946
News and Herald, Winnsboro, South Carolina, 1865-1948
North Georgia News, Blairsville, Georgia, 1944-1947
North Georgia Times, Springplace, Georgia, 1885-1891
North Mississippi Herald, Water Valley, Mississippi, 1900-1940
Oconee Enterprise, Watkinsville, Georgia, 1891
Oglethorpe Echo, Lexington, Georgia, 1875-1906
Okalona Messenger, Okalona, Mississippi, 1902-1940
Okalona Sun, Okalona, Mississippi, 1902-1910
Old North State, Henderson, North Carolina, 1869-1870
Orange County Observer, Hillsboro, North Carolina, 1880-1915
Our Southern Home, Livingston, Alabama, 1895-1948
Patton Pointer, Patton Junction, Alabama, 1900
Paulding New Era, Dallas, Georgia, 1883-1898
Pee Dee Advocate, Bennettsville, South Carolina, 1895-1915
Progress, Union, South Carolina, 1900-1925
Pulaski Citizen, Pulaski, Tennessee, 1866-1938
Reporter, Ashland City, Tennessee, 1883-1884
Review Appeal, Franklin, Tennessee, 1892
Sandersville Courier, Sandersville, Georgia, 1878-1879
Sandersville Herald, Sandersville, Georgia, 1877-1879
Shelby Guide, Columbiana, Alabama, 1872
Southern Argus, Selma, Alabama, 1869-1879
Southern Argus-Times, Selma, Alabama, 1882-1886
Sparta Ishmaelite, Sparta, Georgia, 1878-1948
Square Deal, Haleyville, Alabama, 1906
Stanford Interior Journal, Stanford, Kentucky, 1870-1947
State Gazette, Dyersburg, Tennessee, 1866
Stuart Breeze, Dover, Tennessee, 1887-1888
Summit Courier, Summit, South Carolina, 1877-1888
Sun, Fayetteville, Tennessee, 1891
Talladega Courier, Talladega, Alabama, 1908
Tallapoosa News, Tallapoosa, Alabama, 1914
Tallapoosa New Era, Tallapoosa, Alabama, 1899
Tarboro Southerner, Tarboro, North Carolina, 1866-1902
Tennesseean, Gallatin, Tennessee, 1873, 1893
Thousandsticks, Hyden, Kentucky, 1901-1948
Times-Argus, Selma, Alabama, 1885
Toccoa News, Toccoa, Georgia, 1882-1883
Tri-Weekly Courier, Rome, Georgia, 1873-1876
Tri-Weekly Republican, Americus, Georgia, 1871

Troy Messenger, Troy, Alabama, 1882
True Southern, Sumter, South Carolina, 1879
Tuskaloosa Gazette, Tuskaloosa, Alabama, 1878-1902
Union Progress, Union, South Carolina, 1922
Union Times, Union, Georgia, 1873
Warren County Times and New Era, McMinnville, Tennessee, 1903-1929
Warrenton Clipper, Warrenton, Georgia, 1879-1883
Washington News, Choctaw, Alabama, 1891
Waverly Journal, Waverly, Tennessee, 1877
Weekly Copiahan, Hazlehurst, Mississippi, 1876-1885
Weekly Enterprise, Enterprise, Alabama, 1897-1904
Weekly Sumter Republican, Sumter, South Carolina, 1873
West Tennesseean, Huntingdon, Tennessee, 1868-1869
Whig and Tribune, Jackson, Tennessee, 1873-1874
Wilcox Banner, Camden, Alabama, 1909
Wilcox New Era, Camden, Alabama, 1899
Wilcox Progress, Camden, Alabama, 1898
Winston County Journal, Louisville, Mississippi, 1891-1948
Winston County Index, Louisville, Mississippi, 1878
Winston Signal, Louisville, Mississippi, 1881-1891
Woodville Republican, Woodville, Mississippi, 1880-1948
York Enterprise, York, South Carolina, 1887-1892
Yorkville Enquirer, Yorkville, South Carolina, 1860-1922

(B) Newspaper Guides, Directories and Handbooks

Alden, Edwin and Brothers, *American Newspaper Catalogue,* Cincinnati, 1883

Ayers, N. W. and Son, *American Newspaper Annual and Directory,* 1869-1948, Philadelphia

Advertisers' Handbook, Comprising a Complete List of all Newspapers and Periodicals, and Magazines Published in the United States and British Possessions, 1870-1877, New York

Cappon, Lester J., *Virginia Newspapers 1821-1935, A Bibliography with Historical Introduction and Notes,* New York, 1936

Gregory, Winifred, *American Newspapers 1821-1936, A Union List of Files Available in the United States and Canada*

Hubbard, H. P., *Newspaper and Bank Directory of the World,* 2 vol., New Haven, Connecticut, 1882

Kindead, Ludie J. and T. D. Clark, *Checklist of Kentucky Newspapers Contained in Kentucky Libraries*

Louisiana Newspapers 1805-1940. A Union List of Louisiana Newspaper Files Available in Offices of Publishers, Libraries, and Private Collections in Louisiana, Baton Rouge, 1941

Mississippi Newspapers 1805-1940. A Preliminary Checklist of Mississippi Newspaper Files Available in the Mississippi Department of Archives and History, Jackson, 1942

Pettengill, S. M., and Company, *The Newspaper Directory and Handbook,* 1869-1877, New York

Rowell, George P., *American Newspaper Directory,* 1868-1947, New York

Westcott, Mary and Allene Ramage, *United States Newspapers and Weeklies before 1900.* 5 vols., Durham, 1932-1937

(C) General Works

Adams, Samuel Hopkins, *The Great American Fraud,* New York, 1907

Atwood, Millard Van Marter, *The Country Newspaper,* Chicago, 1923

Baker, Ray Stannard, *Following the Color Line; An Account of Negro Citizenship in the American Democracy,* New York, 1908

Balch, William Ralston, *The Life of James A. Garfield, Late President of the United States,* Philadelphia, 1881

Bing, Phil Carleton, *The Country Weekly, A Manuel for the Rural Journalist and for Students of the Country Field,* New York, 1920

Bolles, Joshua K., *Father Was An Editor,* New York, 1940

Brooks, Robert Preston, *The Agrarian Revolution in Georgia, 1865-1912,* Madison, Wisconsin, 1914

Cash, W. J., *The Mind of the South,* New York, 1941

Couch, W. T. (ed.), *Culture in the South,* Chapel Hill, 1934

Coulter, E. M., *The South During Reconstruction 1865-1877,* Baton Rouge, 1947

Chadbourn, James Harmon, *Lynching and the Law,* Chapel Hill, 1933

Cutler, James Elbert, *Lynch Law and Investigation into the History of Lynching in the United States,* New York, 1905

Daniels, Josephus, *Tarheel Editor,* Chapel Hill, 1939

Dean, A. F. (ed.), *Observations from a Peak in Lumpkin or the Writings of W. B. Townsend Editor of the Dalonega Nugget,* Oglethorpe, Georgia, 1936

Dictionary of American Biography, 20 vols., New York, 1928-1944

Fackler, S. A., *The Ups and Downs of a Country Editor, Mostly Downs,* n. p., n. d.

Fellows, Dexter W. and Andrew W. Freeman, *This Way to the Big Show, the Life of Dexter Fellows,* New York, 1936

Felton, Mrs. William H., *My Memoirs of Georgia Politics,* Atlanta, 1911

Hammond, M. B., *The Cotton Industry,* Ithaca, N. Y., 1897

Hayes, H. G. and C. J., *A Complete History of the Life and Trial of Charles Julius Guiteau, Assassin of President Garfield,* Philadelphia, 1882

Hendrick, Burton J., *The Life and Letters of Walter H. Page,* Garden City, New York, 1925

Henry, R. H., *Editors I have Known Since the Civil War,* Jackson, Mississippi, 1922

Hough, Henry Butte, *Country Editor,* New York, 1940

Jennings, John J., *Theatrical and Circus Life; or, Secrets of the Stage, Green Room and Saw Dust Arena,* St. Louis, 1882

Knight, Edgar W., *Public Education in the South,* Boston, 1922

Malone, Dumas, *Edwin A. Alderman, A Biography,* New York, 1940

Marshall, Charles F., *The True History of the Brooklyn Scandal,* Philadelphia, 1873

Marshall, Logan (ed.), *Sinking of the Titanic and Great Sea Disasters,* n.p., 1912

McElroy, R. M., *Jefferson Davis; the Unreal and the Real,* 2 vol., New York, 1937

Meacham, Charles Mayfield, *A History of Christian County, Kentucky, from ox cart to airplane,* Nashville, 1930

Money, H. D., *The Indianola, Miss., Postoffice Incident to the Race Question,* Washington, 1905

Moore, Albert Burton, *History of Alabama,* University, Alabama, 1935

Mutzenberg, Charles, *Kentucky's Famous Feuds and Tragedies,* New York, 1917

Myrdal, Gunnar, *An American Dilemma, The Negro Problem and Modern Democracy,* 1944

Nichols, I. A., *Forty Years of Rural Journalism in Iowa,* Fort Dodge, Iowa, 1938

Nixon, Raymond B., *Henry W. Grady, Spokesman of the New South,* New York, 1943

Otken, Charles H., *The Ills of the South,* New York, 1894

Proceedings of the First Annual Session of the Southern Immigration Association of America, Nashville, 1884

Raper, Arthur F., *Tenants of the Almighty,* New York, 1943

Raper, Arthur F., *The Tragedy of Lynching,* Chapel Hill, 1933

Riley, Benjamin Franklin, *The Life and Times of Booker T. Washington,* New York, 1916

Robison, Daniel M., *Bob Taylor and the Agrarian Revolt in Tennessee,* 1935

Safley, James Clifford, *The Country Newspaper and Its Operation,* New York, 1930

Shay, Frank, *Judge Lynch, His First Hundred Years,* New York, 1938
Simpkins, Francis B., *Pitchfork Ben Tillman, South Carolinian,* Baton Rouge, 1944
Skaggs, William H., *The Southern Oligarchy, An Appeal in Behalf of the Silent Masses of Our Country Against the Despotic Rule of the Few,* New York, 1924
Vance, Rupert B., *Human Geography of the South,* Chapel Hill, 1932
Washington, Booker T., *Up From Slavery, An Autobiography,* New York, 1902
Watson, Elmo Scott, *A History of Newspaper Syndicates in the United States, 1865-1935,* Chicago, 1936
Willey, Malcom MacDonald, *The Country Newspaper, A Study of Socialization and Newspaper Content,* Chapel Hill, 1926
White, Walter, *Rope and Faggot, A Biography of Judge Lynch,* New York, 1929
Woodward, Vann, *Tom Watson An Agrarian Rebel,* New York, 1938

(D) Scrapbooks

Cox, Effie, Personal scrapbook, Indianola Post Office Dispute, in possession of Mrs. Ethel Cox Howard, Indianola, Mississippi.

INDEX

INDEX